Best of Both Worlds

THE STORY OF ELSDON BEST AND TUTAKANGAHAU

JEFFREY PAPAROA HOLMAN

PENGUIN BOOKS

PENGUIN BOOKS
Published by the Penguin Group
Penguin Group (NZ), 67 Apollo Drive, Rosedale,
North Shore 0632, New Zealand (a division of Pearson New Zealand Ltd)
Penguin Group (USA) Inc., 375 Hudson Street,
New York, New York 10014, USA
Penguin Group (Canada), 90 Eglinton Avenue East, Suite 700, Toronto,
Ontario, M4P 2Y3, Canada (a division of Pearson Penguin Canada Inc.)
Penguin Books Ltd, 80 Strand, London, WC2R 0RL, England
Penguin Ireland, 25 St Stephen's Green,
Dublin 2, Ireland (a division of Penguin Books Ltd)
Penguin Group (Australia), 250 Camberwell Road, Camberwell,
Victoria 3124, Australia (a division of Pearson Australia Group Pty Ltd)
Penguin Books India Pvt Ltd, 11, Community Centre,
Panchsheel Park, New Delhi – 110 017, India
Penguin Books (South Africa) (Pty) Ltd, 24 Sturdee Avenue,
Rosebank, Johannesburg 2196, South Africa

Penguin Books Ltd, Registered Offices: 80 Strand, London, WC2R 0RL, England

First published by Penguin Group (NZ), 2010

1 3 5 7 9 10 8 6 4 2

All line art and motifs by Tracey Tawhiao
Designed and typeset by Pindar (NZ)
Printed in Australia by McPherson's Printing Group

ISBN 9780143008422

A catalogue record for this book is available
from the National Library of New Zealand.

www.penguin.co.nz

The assistance of Creative New Zealand towards the production of this book is
gratefully acknowledged by the Publisher.

PENGUIN BOOKS

Best of Both Worlds

Jeffrey Paparoa Holman was born in London in 1947 and immigrated to New Zealand in 1950, living out his early years mostly on the South Island's West Coast. His colourful career path has taken him to sawmills, shearing gangs, social work, bookselling and, since 1997, a return to mid-life study at the University of Canterbury, graduating with a PhD in Māori Studies in 2007.

His interest in te reo Māori and Māori Studies in general, along with a postgraduate honours degree in English, led him to his thesis topic, the writings of Elsdon Best on Māori spirituality.

Holman is an award-winning poet, with two recent titles from Steele Roberts: *As Big as a Father* (2002) and *The late great Blackball Bridge sonnets* (2004). His poetry and reviews have appeared in the *New Zealand Listener*, *Landfall* and the *Press*. He lives in Christchurch, where he works as a freelance writer and creative writing tutor, and is currently working on a new book of poetry.

Contents

	Introduction	9
ONE	'White Noise': The History of Ideas and the Urewera	13
TWO	The End of Tradition and the Fleets of Print	19
THREE	Te Ao Hurihuri: The World of Change for Tūhoe	26
FOUR	White Tohunga: Best on the Frontier, 1856–1874	37
FIVE	Te Riri me te Ture: War and the Law, 1864–1893	49
SIX	Best Matures: From Parihaka to the Polynesian Society, 1874–1892	79
SEVEN	'Ki tā te Kāwanatanga te mutunga – The Government will have its way in the end'	104
EIGHT	Into the Mist: In Search of the 'Mythopoetic Maori'	125
NINE	'A territory for the Maori people and the indigenous birds': Tūhoe and the Rohe Pōtae, 1896–1909	162
TEN	'Wiped off the slate of life': The Last of the 'Mohios'	187
ELEVEN	The Māori according to Best: 'Ka tō he rā, ka ura he rā!'	219
TWELVE	'Kia Marama – let there be light!': The Half-life of Te Peehi in Our Midst	254
	Conclusion	280
	Acknowledgements – Ngā Mihimihi	291
	Bibliography	297
	Endnotes	310
	Index	332

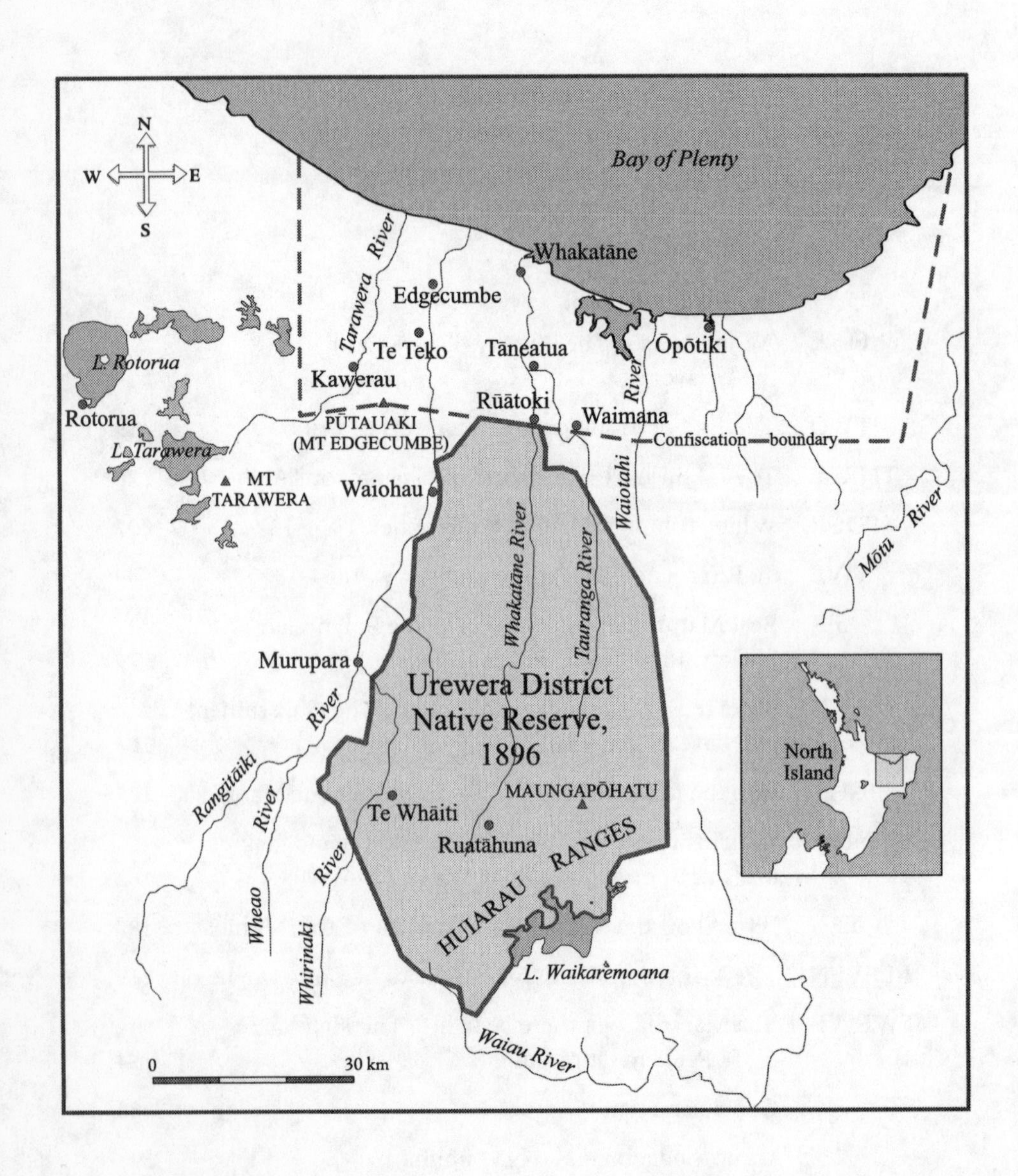

N
W
E
S
Bay of Plenty
Whakatāne
Edgecumbe
Tarawera River
Te Teko
Tāneatua
Ōpōtiki
L. Rotorua
Kawerau
Rotorua
Rūātoki
Waimana
PŪTAUAKI
(MT EDGECUMBE)
Confiscation boundary
L. Tarawera
MT
TARAWERA
Waiohau
Waiotahi River
Mōtū River
Whakatāne River
Tauranga River
Murupara
Urewera District
Native Reserve,
1896
North
Island
Rangitāiki River
MAUNGAPŌHATU
Te Whāiti
Ruatāhuna
RANGES
HUIARAU
Wheao River
Whirinaki River
L. Waikaremoana
Waiau River
0
30 km

Dedication

Ki te hunga mate: he mamae aroha ki a Cherry Heremahoe (Here) Hauwaho-Wilson (1944–2008), Ngāi Tūhoe, Ngāti Awa, Ngāti Porou. E Te Here, haere ki te poho o tō taumata okiokinga, te Runga Rawa, Ihu Karaiti. Moe mai, moe mai rā!

Ki te hunga ora: ki āku kaiārahi rangahau, he mihi kau ana ki a Lyndsay Head, he pūkenga tūturu, rāua ko taku hoa rangatira, Jeanette King, te putiputi kāneihana e!

Ki ētahi atu kaiāwhina.

'Me etahi atu tangata nana i ropine i nga taonga i koroutia e Nehe ma, a nana hoki i whakatuwhera i te putea whakanakonako ki te tangata rawaho.'

Elsdon Best: this was his mihi to all his other informants, Tūhoe ruānuku, who were not named with Tutakangahau and the five other principal informants.

Tuhoe (1925)

And to the others who have gathered the treasures desired from of Old, those who have opened up to this outsider the finely ornamented basket.

(This author's translation.)

Road Inspectors' camp at Te Whāiti, 1896. Best stands on the far left, next to Tutakangahau – this is the only known image of them together.
Elsdon Best Collection, Alexander Turnbull Library, Wellington, NZ, F-4607-1/2

Introduction

> Even as a written manuscript, the book served as a model for both the machine & bureaucracy. That is, it encouraged a habit of thought that divided experience into specialized units & organized these serially & causally. Translated into gears & levers, the book became machine. Translated into people, it became army, chain of command, assembly line, etc.
>
> By organizing society in the format of the book, the ancients organized specialists into elaborate social machines capable of building pyramids or *colonizing conquered lands*'.
>
> . . .
>
> We use media to destroy cultures, but first we use media to create a false record of what we are about to destroy.
>
> EDMUND CARPENTER (1974)[1]

In June 1896, Tutakangahau, a Tūhoe chief of the Tamakaimoana hapū from Maungapōhatu deep in the Urewera, wrote a letter to the

Premier Richard Seddon, mentioning among other things his agreement to a request by one Elsdon Best, government quartermaster on the Te Whāiti–Wairoa road project, to act as his guide on a trip to Lake Waikaremoana. While his son, Tukua-i-te-rangi, had been dispatched to Wellington to present a number of his father's concerns to the House, the old man would remain behind: 'kua noho au i runga i te whakahau mo matau ko Pehi ma kia haere ki Waikaremoana – I am remaining in response to Best's request to take him and others to Waikaremoana'.[2]

This letter forms possibly the earliest piece of evidence at the beginning of a relationship that was to last almost until the old man's death in 1907 – a friendship in which huge amounts of information regarding Tūhoe and Māori lore and customs were passed on to Best. In his unofficial role as ethnographer, he recorded this material assiduously, in a quest for what he would call 'the kura huna', the hidden knowledge of pre-contact Māori society. The significance of Best's work has long been recognised – and questioned – but aside from the old chief's descendants and those Tūhoe knowledgeable about their recent history, Tutakangahau is virtually a forgotten man. It was through him and many other Māori informants that Best gathered the material for the books that were to make him famous – and it is to such men, through the study of Tutakangahau's life and relationship with Best and other significant figures, that this attempt to balance the books now turns.

Anyone who sets out to understand Māori–Pākehā relationships on the basis of historical evidence is immediately confronted with a rush of what might be called 'white noise': the voices of Pākehā writers talking about Māori.[3] From Cook and Banks in the earliest ethnographic accounts, right through to Smith, Tregear and Best in the era under consideration, the vast majority of the written sources *in English* are from explorers, traders, missionaries, government officials, and finally, the amateur ethnographers of what became the Polynesian Society in 1892. The reader has to be constantly aware that their view of Māori in this literature is filtered through numerous European lenses; that to get at the earliest Māori voices in the mid-century Māori newspapers requires knowledge of the language and the historical context of the occasion of writing. Much of this material remains untranslated and thus unavailable to the monolingual 'dominant culture' – a hangover from a century of

Mangapohatu
Hune 29 /96
kia te hetana pirimia o te kawanatanga
te nara koe te matua o te pani o
te rawa kore kia ora koe ma te
atua koe e tiaki heoi te mihi aroha
e whaka atu kia koe ana ka tuku
atu e au taku tamaiti a tukua

Letter from Tutakangahau to the Premier Richard Seddon, 29 June 1896.
J1 1896/1082, Archives New Zealand/Te Rua Mahara o te Kāwanatanga, Head Office, Wellington

atua koe e tiaki heoi te mihi aroha
he whaka atu kia koe ana ka tuku
a atu e au taku tamaiti a tukua
te rangi ki te mau atu i aku take
ki te whare mau e whakamana mai
e kokiri ki te whare e hoa kia aroha
koe ki taku tamaiti kua nohoau
i runga i te whaka hau mo ma tau
ko pehi ma kia haere ki wai kare
moana kai te haere rawa kore atu
ia ka ore ona oranga heoi enaku
pu ko nga take tenei aku ka tuhi

Text of the letter to Seddon referring to Best as 'Pehi', as above.
J1 1896/1082, Archives New Zealand/Te Rua Mahara o te Kāwanatanga, Head Office, Wellington

neglect when the Māori language was devalued, and almost lost to its owners. Even where oral history is available today – predominantly in tribal areas with older native speakers of te reo – that knowledge too has been mediated by literary sources, Pākehā and Māori, so that the hope of any 'pure' transmission of pre-contact culture is forlorn.[4] The truth is that contemporary Māori culture is on the move, much as it was in Best's day, through any and every available media outlet.

On the other hand, the convenient myth that Māori society is somehow *constitutionally* oral, and that access to its metaphysical dimensions can only be had through Māori oral tradition, will not serve. The early Māori embrace of a mission-taught literacy – both attuned to and at times resisting the missionary aim of evangelical and cultural conversion – changed Māori society radically from the 1830s onwards. Tutakangahau was a product of this encounter with the print literacy that was in itself a shaping force in Western modernity. Once Māori began reading and then writing, and increasingly, writing in both Māori and English for and about themselves, their orality was joined to a literate modernity, as writing became part of their evolving culture. This evolution can be observed in Māori letters to each other, to government officials and newspapers in the second half of the nineteenth century, where the opening salutation would contain the forms of mihi given in whaikōrero, as the writers made the transition from the art of oratory, to addressing another person on the page.[5]

Just as Māori combined speaking with writing, so their writing, and that which was written about them, crept into their orality, their histories – every personal and communal form that recorded their accounts of what mattered. Māori and Pākehā histories have become irretrievably intertwined, and it is this relationship that Elsdon Best and Tutakangahau embodied in their time. Theirs was a compact both oral and literary, the fruit of processes at work since Māori and Pākehā had first communicated face to face in their attempts to gain access to what the other possessed – whether land or firearms, the saving of souls, or the power to read and write. It is in the writing of the ethnographic account of Māori culture that the story of the relationship between these two men takes shape.

CHAPTER ONE

'White Noise': The History of Ideas and the Urewera

Before we come to look more closely at the lives of Tutakangahau and Elsdon Best, it is important give some historical framework to the times they shared. The beginning of Best's fieldwork comes in the last decade of the Victorian era, alongside the emerging discipline of anthropology, the inevitable conflict of the great nineteenth-century colonial empires, and the slow reversal of declining Māori fortunes. These two men were different products of this changing order, and provide a fascinating insight into the intrusion of late nineteenth-century modernity into traditional and frontier societies.

Best was a bookworm run wild who had fled an early career in the civil service for work as a bushman and a sawmiller. His lifelong fascination with Māori culture was acquired in his growing years, the late 1850s around Tawa, in freshly settled smallholdings not far from the Porirua pā. Self-taught, he became a model for early twentieth-century fieldworking anthropologists: fluent and literate in Māori, Best was more than willing to live amongst those he sought to study. Hardly that mythical creature, the objective observer – in the Urewera, he was variously road quartermaster, Commission secretary, and health officer – nevertheless he collected, refined, edited and published huge quantities of the material he gathered while living amongst Tūhoe. He was a man with a mission: as a result of his labours, his major writings – still in print – are a seminal and ongoing influence on our views of traditional Māori society.

Tutakangahau, a man thirty years Best's senior, was also literate and bicultural, involved as was the Pākehā in what became known as 'salvage anthropology' – the recording of threatened traditional life-ways in the midst of massive cultural changes, and the pressure to adapt or perish. With a long history of military and political engagement as a hereditary Tūhoe chief, he was also a religious thinker, and a follower of Te Kooti. He had been present at the arrival of the missionary Colenso at his home marae in 1844, had fought alongside Te Kooti in the late 1860s, and joined with other Tūhoe leaders through the 1870s and the 1880s in efforts to preserve tribal lands and chiefly authority throughout a

Māori hinaki (eel trap) *c.* 1921.
Photographer: James McDonald (1865–1935), Wanganui River Expedition Album, Alexander Turnbull Library, Wellington, NZ, PA1-q-257-72-2

period of deepening Māori disillusionment after the mid-century land wars. He was a moderniser anxious to preserve the old ways in print (which helps to explain his attraction to Best), while adapting Māori spirituality to a Christian world-view. In this vibrant and changing world, evangelical orthodoxy might be found mixing biblical genealogy with Tūhoe whakapapa.[1]

To a man like Elsdon Best, present-day niceties such as intellectual property – when applied to Māori – would have made little sense, as would the charge of intellectual colonisation. In the Urewera forests in 1895, Best certainly saw himself as that man on a mission, dispatched by the Surveyor-General S. Percy Smith to recover and record vanishing knowledge – 'kura huna', the hidden treasure – before the last of its venerable retainers left for the final journey beyond Te Reinga to the spirit world. Such anxieties had been present amongst European observers since Cook first wrote his ethnographic sketches; and by the 1890s, Pākehā were not alone in this concern that Te Ao Mārama (the world of light, modernity) was sweeping before it all traces of Te Ao o Neherā (tradition, the old world). Older Māori such as Tutakangahau saw their past vanishing with the collapse of chiefly power involving mana, tapu, utu, and muru (power and prestige, sacredness, revenge, plunder and reciprocity). Also falling back into the shadows was the spirit world where tohunga mediated between Tane's children and a malevolent universe of atua in need of constant propitiation. Men like Best were rare indeed in a frontier society on the cusp of great change; for Tutakangahau to find a willing partner in his own preservationist project was a coup – as was the co-operation of this Tūhoe ruānuku (wise man) for Elsdon Best.

In this world, where ancient Māori systems of orally transmitted knowledge were fatally undermined by Christian literacy, the structures of transmission were fragmenting. Mission education of children, the growth of the money economy, accelerating post-war land losses and sales had brought irreversible changes to the world into which the old Tūhoe leader was born in the early 1830s. European technological expertise was eroding the authority of the Māori tohunga (experts) in both the material and spiritual realms. Knowledge of English was increasingly advocated by Māori parents and political leaders; younger Tūhoe men who once would have sat at the feet of teachers in whare takiura (houses of learning)[2] to hear and absorb traditional chants were now leaving their tribal areas to earn money in nearby Hawke's Bay as shearers and shed-hands. By 1914, Māori shearers comprised one in four members of the New Zealand Shearers' Union: technological globalisation, then as now, was part of a worldwide financial network that enmeshed local cultures, changing lives and traditions as it spread across the globe.[3]

Technological changes – whether of the book or the gun – are in themselves a product of intellectual revolutions over time and produce cultural changes in response, radicalising everyday life. Māori were facing the ongoing shock of the new in the nineteenth century – as indeed in their own different ways were those displaced European immigrants who swamped them, pushed and pulled by these same forces to settle new lands, unleashed in the wake of the industrial revolutions transforming the worlds they had left behind. In this time of rapid change, Tutakangahau was persuaded to share what he knew with Best both from an awareness of what was being lost, but also from a sense of equality with a man he had come to accept was as powerful and as intelligent as he was himself.

It is helpful in some respects to see these two men in their time as mediators in an often fraught bicultural situation requiring engagement and diplomacy from both parties. As we shall see, the roading of the Urewera was controversial, but the opportunity it afforded Best and Tutakangahau to share their skills and knowledge was unique and timely. Whether it was anthropology conducted under ideal or equal conditions is a question that must be addressed, but the alternative raises another query: if Best had refrained from his collecting and his informants had withheld what they knew, what would remain from that era today? It was Māori engagement with a literate modernity that made such anthropology possible, and Māori co-operation that made it happen. Men like Tutakangahau were not victims of Elsdon Best. The chief was an inheritor of the Faustian gamble Māori had taken in signing the Treaty of Waitangi in 1840: whether to engage with the Pākehā world or to retreat?[4] Just as the Treaty signatories expected to retain their mana and the control of lands, forests and fisheries, so too did Tutakangahau and

Tūhoe thirty years on look to manage the entrance of roads and schools into their territories and to avoid the damaging land losses overtaking other iwi. If the government and its servants could no longer be resisted, they needed at least to be met and managed, with the best results that existing Tūhoe power could hope to achieve.

The Best–Tutakangahau relationship is also to some degree modelled on earlier Māori behaviours, when missionaries were sought eagerly by rangatira as mōkai (pets, servants), to bring trade and status to their villages and areas of influence. Just as those arrangements were part of a search for equality and a statement of power and status, so too did this meeting of minds evolve into a friendship where mutual benefit and advantage were pursued, and gained. Sadly for the Tūhoe leader, his fellow chiefs and their peoples, the balance of power had shifted so far from those pre-Treaty days that all that remained for a traditional leader was the moral authority to invite treatment by Best as an intellectual equal. That Tutakangahau was as much a *new man* as the traditional elder

Waka kereru (pigeon trap), Ruatāhuna, 1899.
Photographer: Elsdon Best, Elsdon Best Collection, Alexander Turnbull Library, Wellington, NZ, PAColl-4249-06

Best was seeking, is part of the rich irony that a Māori Christian literacy delivered to the Pākehā seeker, bent on securing the last remaining ancient knowledge.

What he found was a mixture of both. Here was man born at the setting of one sun and the rise of another, who had lived in his youth as a Tūhoe warrior and grew to embrace Te Kooti's syncretic Old Testament fighting religion, that began in resentment and angelic epiphanies, ending in visions of peace for all under One Law.[5] Within this richly ambiguous interplay of beliefs, ideas and seismic social changes, we can see woven the tukutuku strands that joined the lives of Elsdon Best and Tutakangahau of Maungapōhatu: ka tō he rā, ka ura he rā (a sun rises, a sun sets)! This is a Māori–Pākehā story where you cannot truly have one side without the other, as it remains to this day.

CHAPTER TWO

The End of Tradition and the Fleets of Print

When academics use antiseptic terms like 'contact' to describe the earliest meetings of Māori and Europeans in the New Zealand setting, it is hardly surprising that such a neutral word bleaches the colour and drama from what must have been world-shattering events acted out in a paradisal yet everyday reality. The climbing sun; the burning beach; the fishing party; the sudden, white sail: there are times when only poetry can re-enact such moments. Academic language seems to place a further veil between ourselves and the humans who stood on shore and ship. As most of those who use such clinical terms have until recently been Pākehā descendants of the explorers and settlers, the view is predominantly *from the ship*, from Europe. The challenge now facing New Zealand historical writing on the past two hundred years is how to get closer to the people involved, especially those Māori who left some kind of record – without rewriting these accounts to suit the shifting crosscurrents of contemporary ethnic politics, here and elsewhere. How do we revisit the written records of the nineteenth century, without turning the Māori and Pākehā writers of those times into literary ghosts, unwilling servants of the latest school of historical revisionism?

The answer lies in part with the imagination: the informed and passionate imaginative process that good biography demands. Every intelligent reader knows from the experience of living life that all literary art edits reality, refining and selecting from a mass of material the substance of a believable narrative. To tell the 'true' story of a life, real or fictional, would involve following somebody around day in, day out, from birth to death – impossible, intrusive, and exhausting. Both biography and historical writing – which this book aspires to combine – require a sifting of evidence and the application of editorial judgement in the process, all of which is energised by this imaginative conceit: that a mere book is able to tell such a story, to invoke an excited sense of those meetings between Māori and Pākehā. Imagination can also remind us that these relationships go on into this very moment of reading and writing, shaping and colouring our everyday lives in a world once exotic, but now seemingly as worn and well-known as a taken-for-granted elderly relation asleep in the corner. The truth remains that history is now, our ancestors' deeds live on in us: if we fail to converse with the past and its makers, it is we, and not the dead, who are buried.

Anyone who has read a selection of New Zealand historical writing in the past three decades will be well aware that the nineteenth century was an era of imperial expansion, when Europeans sailed forth to annex and colonise those remnants of the New World not yet taken up by their rivals; to convert peoples and their cultures into agents of various economic and military arrangements; to bring the benefits of civilisation to the assumed unenlightened in the process of such capture. In the Pacific in general and New Zealand in particular, such military and colonial enterprises had been preceded by explorers, traders and missionaries, which led in time to either outright conquest or some kind of client status and the inevitable inclusion in the imperial webs of Britain, France, Holland, and later, the United States. Conquest and settlement gave rise to colonial societies, with links from the New World to the Old that persist to this day. From such meetings and collisions arose all the blessings and curses these

European and indigenous Pacific cultures would share, as they began to form completely new inter-racial and ethnic identities.

The inevitable mixing of peoples gave rise to new, syncretic cultural formations, in language, trading, religion, and war – and almost from the earliest moments of meeting, both 'sides' were expressing some anxieties as to what losses might occur amongst the gains. Recordings of what either party saw or believed, both by casual observers and more experienced commentators, began a process of recording that we designate ethnography – the description of differing groups of peoples by others. Dignified nowadays in dictionaries as 'the scientific study and description of different human societies',[1] these early accounts are often very unscientific. The Greeks regarded illiterate outsiders to their city-states as barbarians, and that category managed to survive as a descriptive term into the first serious works of late nineteenth-century anthropology – the kind of tomes that would later inform Elsdon Best's cultural theory.[2] Perhaps the earliest ethnographer we have is the great Greek historian, the globe-trotting and insatiably curious Herodotus, who liked nothing better than going amongst a strange new tribe or people and writing down carefully all the wonderful differences he saw.[3]

Herodotus is something of a model for later practitioners, such as the eighteenth-century French navigator Bougainville in his ethnographic explorations of the Pacific.[4] Whether or not James Cook had ever heard of the ancient Greek historian, the Yorkshireman's assiduous practice in the records that survive in his journals gives us one of our earliest New Zealand ethnographies.[5] For all that he has been rewritten lately as a harbinger of doom for Māori, the scientifically-minded naval captain left behind for tangata whenua as well as Pākehā an early ethnography – a picture in words – of Māori society in the late eighteenth century.[6] From the moment Cook entered into his journal on Sunday, 8 October 1769 that there were 'in the Bay several Canoes, People upon the shore and some houses in the Country', Māori of the area Cook named 'Poverty Bay' were *written* into English literature. They took on a literary existence, beyond the enclosed world of their traditional society.[7]

In their first week as English literary subjects, however, they were not at all passive, nor did they treat the crew of the white-sailed waka as gods, as some have contended.[8] Had they indeed perceived Cook and his men to be divine, they would have fled in the opposite direction and behaved in a contrary manner to that with which they challenged the strangers. In traditional Māori society, a sure form of danger was from those who came unannounced on the sea – but atua with supernatural powers were not to be trifled with. In the following week, Cook met repeated Māori challenges by way of haka ('as we supposed the war dance') and shaken rākau (spears he called 'darts') with musket and cannon shot (Monday, 9 October 1769): death was for Māori the first fruit of this encounter. Their curiosity and assertiveness did not end with these early reversals; even the three prisoners taken by Cook on the 10th were bold enough to ask to stay on board, telling the English through Tupaia his Tahitian interpreter that, if put ashore, their enemies 'would kill and eat them'.

With the exchange of gifts, trade began. The two significant tropes of earliest contact, violence and commerce, set in train a path to colonial conquest and the inevitable inclusion of Māori in the emerging global network of industrial modernity. 'George Island Cloth &c [given] in exchange for their paddles', wrote Cook (Friday, 12 October 1769). Not only were the English confronting a new people and their customs, and beginning immediately to write an ethnography of Māori – the tangata whenua of the area Cook touched first were also describing to each other how unusual these strangers were. Tupaia is recorded as relating to Cook that those Māori on board the *Endeavour* had tried to entice others more reluctant to join them, by 'telling them we did not eat men, from which it should seem that these people have such a Custom among them'. The ethnographic encounter, in its different forms and relations of power and dependence, was, from the very first meeting, a two-way process.[9] No matter how disempowered Māori might later seem in the era of Best's writing and collecting, they were constantly attempting to engage – when they did choose to do so – as equals of Pākehā.

Following on from Cook's three voyages, the ongoing creation of what we now understand as the ethnographic Pacific continued in earnest, with the arrival in New Zealand of successive waves of traders, missionaries, and, eventually, the settlers who would colonise and, most often, conquer the 'new' sea lands. In their written records – those that Best was to become very familiar with and later contest – missionary writers and, in due course, home-grown scholars such as Sir George Grey and John White began to set down, both in Māori and English, poetry, myth, beliefs, traditions and more recent histories. Theories

Elsdon Best, *c.* 1895, at the time he went to the Urewera, aged 39.
Alexander Turnbull Library, Wellington, NZ, PAColl-8066-09-28

derived from the French Enlightenment mingled with biblically-based anthropologies predicated on the essential unity of humanity, as created by one God from one blood. Comparative mythologists such as F. Max Müller would publish alongside the early evolutionists, while theoretical anthropologists such as Edward Tylor – the founding father of the discipline in the late nineteenth century – would introduce the doctrine of 'lower races' as primitive 'survivals' from an earlier stage of human development. In the span of Tutakangahau's life – and Best's – Māori as 'Other' were subjected to a veritable cornucopia of intellectual fashions, some of which they adopted and others they simply ignored.[10]

Whether seen by an early missionary writer such as John Nicholas as both 'fresh from Nature's hand' (citing the 'wayward philosopher of Geneva,*' – '*Rousseau'),[11] or later by the Rev. Samuel Marsden and others as one of the lost tribes of Israel,[12] Māori had their own views of who they were, and who they might become in their post-Treaty alliance with the Queen and her kāwanatanga (government). This will become increasingly clear in following the unfolding story of Tutakangahau as he grew to adulthood in the 1840s, and in his late-life encounter with Best – one of a new breed of frontier intellectuals who succeeded Grey and White. Best, Percy Smith and Edward Tregear were part of an emerging group of Māoriphiles: Pākehā settlers (the older two born in England), and Best, a native New Zealander. Each had in their own particular way a fascination with Māori; and as government servants in a socially progressive era for Pākehā, they used their positions and influence in 1892 to support the foundation of New Zealand's first serious attempt at organised anthropological study and its recording – the Polynesian Society.

Best at that point was not a civil servant like Smith or Tregear, having formerly pursued a career as a sawmiller, a bush worker and a general roustabout on farms. He had continually fed his obsession with Māori history and customs by learning the language he first heard (and almost certainly learned to speak) amongst his childhood Māori friends, from the Takapūwāhia pā of Ngāti Toa at Porirua, close to his parents' farm at Tawa. All the while, he continued to buy and devour weighty ethnographic works in a lifelong habit of autodidacticism, born in his teenage years. The core concern of salvage anthropologists such as Best and Smith was the anxiety mentioned earlier concerning rapid cultural losses. The aim of such men was to record vanishing knowledge from the thinning ranks of Māori elders before it died with them, as their experience and language base was increasingly penetrated by European thought processes and Christian theology in the form of mission-based literacy, along with the teaching of English to succeeding generations of Māori children in the Native Schools.

It was this imperative that drove Best all his life, and led him to his fateful meeting with the man who shares this particular story: Tutakangahau of Maungapōhatu, the Tamakaimoana elder of Tūhoe, with whom Best would develop a unique relationship over his fifteen-year sojourn amongst this hardy and combative Urewera iwi. As the story of their century unfolds, it will be necessary to return to some of the ideas and influences alluded to here: to set them in the context of their differing experiences in a complex arena of war, theology, land alienation, and the changing methods of cultural transmission occurring amongst Māori with the arrival of a transformative literary culture. Best and Tutakangahau are powerful and fascinating exemplars in the co-creation of a new national literature – their relationship inhabits the texts that survive this richly written era, down to the present day.

CHAPTER THREE

Te Ao Hurihuri: The World of Change for Tūhoe

The Tūhoe world into which Tutakangahau was born around 1830 was still for the most part tradition-bound.[1] While it is true that there are accounts of a Waikato prophet Te Toroa carrying to Ruatāhuna in the early 1820s some kind of message about a god called Wheawheau, inspired by a reaction to the new Christian deity, there is also evidence that Tūhoe did not embrace his teaching. It was not until the late 1830s that the written gospel portions of the printer Colenso began to find their way into the Urewera from Ōpōtiki and the East Coast.[2] By travelling with Te Toroa to Wairoa, where he was killed by Kahungunu in utu against Waikato, along with some of their own, Tūhoe were soon entangled in traditional warfare patterns – rather than responding in any radical way to an unorthodox religious message brought to them outside of their reigning spiritual norms. Local atua (spirits, deified ancestors, gods with a small 'g') were what counted in everyday life, and it is almost

Portrait of the Tamakaimoana chief, Tutakangahau, wearing a kākahu, and holding a ceremonial toki (adze).
Polynesian Society Collection, Alexander Turnbull Library, Wellington, NZ, PAColl-7273-04

certain that Te Toroa carried his message by word of mouth, not with the writing that would later so transform Tūhoe attitudes to the new atua of the book.

Yet this early stirring reminds us that the God of the Book was indeed in the land before Tutakangahau saw the light of day – and that the porosity of such a traditional society, with its small and scattered population, was nevertheless as sensitive to movements elsewhere in the motu (land) as is a spider to a trembling in its web. Traditional societies at this time – such as the Māori world entered by the missionaries – were held together with closed systems that are by now completely unfamiliar in the post-Enlightenment West, existing as it does today in a post-modern openness that revolves on the principle of *denying* closure to any system. The traditional world of Tutakangahau's early childhood was very much a closed universe, still able to explain everything in its own terms. This could only continue for as long as its people lived inside such a bubble, an enveloping and patterned culture in which 'nothing [was] spiritually meaningless'.[3] With twenty muskets in Tūhoe hands at Ruatāhuna by 1830, that universe had reached a point of no return.[4]

Tradition was a way of being and doing that provided a recognisable group identity, and was also the way the *past* operated in the *present* of that group's culture – thus, a lived tradition (then) was kept alive (now), in beliefs and behaviours that were supported by the tribal institutions. Tamakaimoana, the hapū of his father Tapui, lived at Toreatai near Maungapōhatu – one of the most inaccessible parts of the Urewera, overshadowed by huge mountain bluffs, north of the great inland lake Waikaremoana for whose prevailing wind Tutakangahau was named.[5] His genealogical origins or whakapapa are entwined in the major elements of Tūhoe tradition, tracing descent from Ngā Pōtiki, one of three major groups (the other two being Te Tini o Toi and Te Hapū Oneone) who reportedly inhabited these lands from before the arrival of the *Mātaatua* canoe, with whom the earlier inhabitants are said to have intermarried: 'One of the offspring of this first mixing . . . was Tuhoe Potiki, and it is from him that the Tuhoe believe they are all descended.'[6]

Tutakangahau's whakapapa connect him deeply with many strands of Tūhoe ancestry and inter-hapū relationships, and other iwi – including Ngāti Awa, Whakatōhea and Ngāti Kahungunu – in myth, tradition and history. He is related also to Toi-kai-rakau, an early inhabitant of the Urewera, as Best quotes in *Tuhoe*: '*Na Toi raua ko Potiki te whenua, na Tuhoe te mana te rangatiratanga* (The land is from Toi and Potiki, the prestige and the rank from Tuhoe)'.[7] In his relationship to Ngā Pōtiki he could claim supernatural descent from Te Maunga (the mountain) and Hine pūkohurangi (the mist maiden) – from which derives the pepeha (saying), 'Ko Maungapōhatu te Maunga, ko Tutakangahau te tangata – Maungapōhatu is the mountain, Tutakangahau is the man'.[8]

Such whakapapa and their accompanying kōrero (stories) – without which such lists would have been empty of significance – were the vehicle by which the growing Tutakangahau would have received his religious or cultural instruction. In these remembered kōrero were contained the rules and values useful in daily living, creating order in a society that lived by their repeated inner sanctions – without the need for a system of Western law. All this was perfectly viable, as long as there was no external challenge to the thought world that maintained such order, meaning and purpose. According to Best – who would have been told this by the old man – Tutakangahau was 'in the forties of the 19th century [. . .] taught much of *the old Maori ritual* by his father, Tapui'.[9] There were special houses or whare, teaching 'all matters pertaining to national or tribal history, religion, genealogies &c . . . known as the *whare maire*, *whare puri*, or *whare takiura*'. As a growing youth, he would have been instructed in the whare mata (house of woodcraft) on the intertwined arts of survival and the transmission of sacred knowledge, taught the arts of fishing and fowling, and the strict tapu to be maintained in the preparation of the necessary implements.[10]

It was material from this thought world that Best sought to gain from his ruānuku, hoping to access an untrammelled store of pre-contact tradition. Tutakangahau was certainly able to provide wide-ranging accounts of the everyday activities he experienced in his childhood, youth and maturity, before the penetration of mission, and the money economy, broke the web of tradition. As has been foreshadowed, the enclosed world of his birth was about to disappear, long before salvage anthropologists such as Best came knocking. In such activities as hunting, food gathering, and in early adolescence, his first experiences of warfare, Tutakangahau was living on the cusp of the traditional Tūhoe world and the modern. With the teachings of his father and other tohunga in his initiations into the whare takiura, he was still immersed in the pre-Pākehā world.

Best would later record the chief's early experiences of European influences: in a paper published in 1908, discussing Tūhoe food-gathering practices, he refers to a story the old man told him about the disappearance of the native rat, the kiore Māori. 'I saw the native rat die out in my youth. We called the introduced European rat the pou-o-hawaiki.' Tutakangahau recalled a particular expedition to gather tītī: 'when I was a lad I went with a party to the summit of the main range at Maunga-pohatu, in order to obtain mutton-birds'. They were disappointed: 'on our arrival there we found that a new species of rat had appeared, and eaten all the young birds'.[11] Best notes the approximate year of the old man's birth (1830) to give a close date for the rat's arrival in the deeper reaches of the Urewera (the birds and not the rats had been there the year before). This is a clear illustration of the hunter-gatherer lifestyle employed by Tūhoe before European influences encroached on their remotest settlements. The new rat's colonising habits and the disappearance of its indigenous relative was something of a prophetic occurrence for what awaited the people of Tamakaimoana and the rest of Tūhoe in the years ahead.

Between 1839 and 1844, with the arrival of written Scripture portions amongst Tūhoe, closely followed by their Church Missionary Society printer, William Colenso, this enclosed world was changing rapidly. The first Anglican missionary, John Wilson, had reached Ōpōtiki in December of 1839 and opened a mission station there. His teachers and evangelists were soon penetrating the Urewera, and in November 1840 William Williams travelled from Poverty Bay to Waikaremoana, where he found three Tūhoe at Onepoto 'with very considerable knowledge' and 'books from Rotorua'. Not only did he find the seed of the Word, but at Ruatāhuna three days later (29 November), many who were absent from his service were 'away at Wakatane planting corn to sell to Europeans'.[12] Inland Tūhoe were already engaged in the coastal trading that supplied Auckland and other Pākehā centres of commerce, becoming increasingly literate, as Colenso discovered in his two journeys through the Urewera, the second of which led him to Tutakangahau's village.

Colenso reported on his meeting with the young man's father in his account of a visit to Toreatai in 1844, with Tapui welcoming him onto the marae with an oration interspersed with scriptural texts and allusions. Colenso formally replied to this kind reception, absent villagers were summoned from work on the surrounding plantations, and a service was held. Till a late hour that night, he sat at the door of his tent and answered the shrewd questions with which he was plied. In his diary he noted: 'This is a very nice party of natives.' School was held next morning, and it was found that '*9 could read*'.[13]

This account – which Best was aware of – should have signalled to the ethnographer that if his informant's father was able to recite Scripture portions and include them *naturally* – that is, in a traditional manner –

Bluffs above Maungapōhatu, 2008.
Author photograph

within his customary form of welcome, the whaikōrero, then tradition was already punctured by an external force.

Already present in this tiny, isolated hamlet was the European thought world of print, which would provide for Tutakangahau and for all Māori in the future a revolutionary means of stepping outside of themselves and their closed system, to evaluate their lives from another point of view. Literacy, by the very fact of its virtual location both in and beyond the mind, guarantees that no system can remain closed for long. In the information age that now exists, where cyber-literacy is in its turn revolutionising time, space and cultural authority, this image should not prove too hard to grasp. As was that of Tutakangahau in the 1840s, our world is now being turned on its head faster than any one individual can hope to comprehend.

An earlier revolution had also affected this world: Pākehā food sources and agricultural implements. Tūhoe had not only begun to learn the arts of reading and writing: for this inland iwi, with its harsh environment and scarce resources, the arrival in the 1820s of the potato and the pig, along with iron tools, was a major and life-changing benefit.[14] Tūhoe were used to doing it hard in a harsh environment where berries, birds and fish were the main sources of nourishment. They were extremely resilient as a result, but their numbers were few, and their kāinga often mobile, shifting to follow the food – especially in the most marginal areas, such as Maungapōhatu. Best would comment in the 1890s on their legendary stamina, including the ability to run up hills and cover long distances in record time.

One look at the photograph in *Tuhoe* of Paitini Wi Tapeka of Ruatāhuna, another of his informants, and a veteran of Ōrakau, is enough to illustrate the kind of physique that such an environment and lifestyle could produce. A mature man, most likely in his fifties or early sixties when the photograph was taken, his trim well-muscled frame is without a trace of surplus fat.[15] The hardiness inherited from Tutakangahau's early Spartan lifestyle no doubt contributed to his longevity (he was in his mid

Paitini Wi Tapeka of Ruatāhuna.
Facing page 566 in Elsdon Best's Tuhoe: The Children of the Mist *(1925)*

to late seventies when he died in 1907). It is also more than likely that a reliable access to food crops such as the potato and maize, along with the protein available from the European pig breeds, enhanced his prospects of living a more generous span – as long as he managed to avoid early death in the endemic inter-tribal wars.

It has been recounted recently by Pou Temera that Tutakangahau did in fact as a small child take part in the consumption of human flesh; this took place after a battle at Te Kauna (between Maungapōhatu and Waimana) around 1834, when his hapū emerged victorious and brought home parts of their defeated enemies in the traditional practice of cannibalism at that time.[16] This was not done out of hunger, but was commonly practised after a battle as much to enhance the victor's mana as to sate the appetite. War was an inevitable feature of Tutakangahau's early life: again, it is Best who records at length the labyrinthine battles of Tūhoe with traditional foes, feuds which were a part of his childhood world and which as a young man he was trained to take part in – and duly did so.

Shortly after his birth ('from the early age of five days' according to Best), Tutakangahau would have been dedicated 'to the two great services of Māori economy – War and Labour'.[17] Taken by the priest to the wai tapu (sacred waters), he would have undergone the tū-ora ceremony, a rite performed to endow him with 'hau-ora (vitality), with physical and mental vigour'. An invocation – translated here but according to Best, like many ancient karakia, virtually untranslatable – would have been chanted to 'instil the qualities of bravery and dexterity into the child'. '*Korikori tama ki tūa / Ka riri ki tūa / Mau huata ki tūa / Kia niwha tama ki tūa / Mau patu tama ki tūa / Mau taiaha tama ki tūa – Lissome be the boy, through the tūa / Quick to anger, through the tūa / To wield the spear, through the tūa / Let the boy be fierce, through the tūa / To bear the weapons, through the tūa / To carry the halbert, through the tūa . . .*'.[18]

Through this baptism (tūa), the infant was inducted by a form of words (foreshortened here) into the world of the fighting man he was destined to become: someone quick to anger and to avenge insults, adept at wielding the club and the spear against any enemy. While this information could well have come from Paitini or Hamiora Pio (Ngāti Awa), two other of Best's most prolific and learned informants, there is a distinct probability that it was Tutakangahau who described this initiation to Best. These

HE KO KUTI, AN ANCIENT WEAPON OF WAR.

'He Ko Koti' (as corrected by Best from 'Ko Kuti'), from Best's copy of Richard Taylor's *Te Ika a Maui* (1870).
By kind permission of Warwick Jordan

were rites he had undergone and no doubt had seen performed over his own sons (one of whom, Akuhata, did indeed later fall in battle, fighting with his father for Te Kooti, at Ngā Tapa on 6 January 1869).[19] War in its bloody season was a fixed part of that traditional world into which Best's favoured ruānuku entered as a tiny babe in arms.

As a major informant for Best's gathering of the historical details to produce *Tuhoe*, Tutakangahau's accounts of ancient battles and his own memories of the changing culture of war go hand in hand with the ethnographer's desire to bring Tūhoe into history. This was done by means of calculating the generations in the whakapapa he was given, working backwards on the basis of twenty-five years per ancestor named. In describing Tūhoe's long-running feud with Ngāti Awa, for example, Best cites Tutakangahau's assistance. He admits the earliest dates for the beginning of that conflict are 'merely approximate' based on 'genealogies alone' – but once the nineteenth century is reached, 'from the year 1818 we are enabled to give dates with much greater exactitude'.[20]

Tutakangahau's ability to give precise information (as in the death of the chief Taurua) is predicated on his being taught this history so it would be remembered – as a record of 'payments' for losses incurred, which were 'equalised by the killing' of more of the enemy – in this case, Ngāti Awa.[21] It was into this feud, amongst others, this world of utu, that he was initiated – a culture of revenge made more terrifying and ultimately unsustainable by the arrival of firearms in Māori hands. Armed Ngā Puhi raids early in the century made it inevitable that other Māori such as Tūhoe would also obtain guns. The old man gave Best graphic details of their arrival in his village around 1836, when his father Tapuihina was engaged in another round of bloodshed against Ngāti Awa at Te Kaunga: 'I remember our fighting men returning to Maunga-pohatu from Matai-puku. When they approached the village they fired their guns to warn the people of their approach. We children were frightened and ran home to the village, to Torea-a-Tai.'[22]

By his twentieth year, no longer afraid of the new weapons, he was ready to fight Ngāti Maru with fellow Tūhoe warriors in the confrontation that took place near Whirinaki: 'he was about 12 years of age when Colenso made his first visit to Ruatahuna on January 1, but he was bearing arms at Te Takatanga'.[23] In the event, the Rev. Preece brokered a peace deal between the injured parties, but whether or not Tutakangahau had fought before this time, or shortly thereafter, he was certainly an active combatant in the Hauhau and Te Kooti era of the late 1860s and early 1870s. While much general knowledge may be posited about his early life, however, little is actually *known*, save for the meetings with Colenso and other missionaries – and these because Best wrote down the old man's recollections of his boyhood memories. Best's 'adopted son', his grandnephew and biographer Elsdon Craig, has written of Tutakangahau as 'a learned man . . . taught to read and write by the missionaries when he was a child', a man who 'knew the old native names of every tree, shrub, plant, or fern in Tuhoeland'. His fund of folkloric knowledge 'was immense', Craig writes, conversant as the old man was 'with the modes of thought of the ancient Maori'.[24]

His assertion that it was the missionaries that actually did the teaching is unsourced, but would certainly have come from Best; already we have seen that Colenso discovered a form of Tūhoe mission school operating in Tutakangahau's village, with nine readers, one of whom was assuredly the future chief. The Catholic priest Fr. Reine was also active in the Ruatāhuna–Maungapōhatu area in the early 1840s, where 'he seems to have taught the natives to read and write'.[25] What is obvious from Tutakangahau's discussions with Best is the impact of literacy on the dubious Tūhoe listeners to the gospel: at first, they doubted the 'use of written language', but after 'many tests', where messages were written and carried away, to be read at a distance 'by unseen persons', they saw that 'this writing was effective'. The 'god of the white man [was] more powerful than the Maori gods', and so they 'embraced Christianity'.[26]

Best wrote in his Notebook 11 (1912) that 'most of the older men of Tuhoe have learned to write from each other. In doing so, they do not utilise the true phonetic alphabet but use a syllabic form or syllabary.'[27] However he learned and by whoever he was taught, Tutakangahau became literate early in his life, and it is to literacy we owe his personal legacy in the historical record, in the form of letters to government officials from the 1870s onwards, and also those he wrote later to the various Māori-language newspapers. Whatever else he learned in his childhood and adolescence – and it was the traditional matters here that drew Best to him – by becoming literate and embracing a written faith, the faith of the book, Tutakangahau began by placing as much faith in the revolutionary new medium as in the message.

In the words of Marshall McLuhan, he had entered 'the Gutenberg Galaxy', a universe of printed media that is not simply an invention, but a *powerful re-inventor of people*. Tutakangahau, as subject, underwent in that process a change of consciousness, one that would make him not so much an 'old-time Māori', but a very new kind of Māori leader. This revolution of consciousness and subjectivity made him available to share what he knew with Best by the exact virtue of having entered so young into this galaxy of the printed word, in the form of the Christian message.[28] In the mid-century wars about to unfold, in the often misunderstood and pilloried manifestations of an indigenous Māori Christianity, this man bestrode the old and the new worlds, an ambivalent child to both historical parents.

CHAPTER FOUR

White Tohunga: Best on the Frontier, 1856–1874

Anyone standing at the mouth of the Waiapu River in March 1923, observing a group of local Māori setting manuka-lined weirs as fish traps, might have noticed an elderly Pākehā in shirtsleeves, his trousers rolled up schoolboy-style, joining with a mature Māori man in retrieving a pūrangi net from the flowing rapids, and emptying a nice catch of kahawai into a sack on the bank.[1] This scene – Elsdon Best and Te Rangi Hiroa enjoying life in the midst of a Dominion Museum expedition to obtain ethnographic material from Ngāti Porou – completes a circle begun in Best's childhood. As the son of pioneer farmers in the valley known as Tawa Flat, between Wellington and Porirua, he lived through the birth of the bicultural nation he was to chronicle so exhaustively as an adult. Much of his time he spent running wild, exploring the bush, working hard and playing with local Ngāti Toa children from the nearby Takapūwāhia pā at Porirua.[2] At the age of sixty-six and nearing the end

Frame enlargement of Elsdon Best and Te Rangi Hiroa/Sir Peter Buck from 'He Pito Whakaatu i te noho a te Māori i Te Tai Rāwhiti/Scenes of Māori Life on the East Coast' (1923).
Stills Collection, New Zealand Film Archive/Ngā Kaitiaki O Ngā Taonga Whitiāhua

of a long and arduous life involving hard physical work and countless hours of study, Best had returned to the one thing that as a child he loved more than his books: catching fish in the wide open spaces with one of his many Māori friends.

Elsdon Best was born on a bush farm at Tawa Flat on 30 June 1856, the son of English immigrants Hannah and William Best, on a Crown Grant of 108 acres, number 48, adjacent to a military road that joined Wellington and Porirua. The road was a reminder of the still-recent tensions of the previous decade, when Te Rauparaha and his nephew Te Rangihaeata had challenged the dubious purchases made by the Wakefields in advance of the signing of the Treaty of Waitangi. After Grey's capture of Te Rauparaha, and the retreat of Te Rangihaeata to the Manawatu in 1847, the Governor lifted martial law southwards of a line between Wanganui and Castlepoint – and Wellington was secure.[3] The colony would remain in a disturbed state in the decade approaching the boy's birth; he grew up in a country where tensions between Māori and Pākehā still simmered.

By the time he was five, a war had flared in Taranaki, pitting both peoples against one another and overshadowing the next ten years of his life. His father was enrolled in the Wellington Militia in 1860, along with all other males between 16 and 55 years of age. Best was later to capture something of the atmosphere of the times, writing that the 'Porirua district was not disturbed by the wars of the sixties, though the Ngati-Toa folk naturally sympathized with their countrymen, and expressed their intention of occupying the farms of Tawa Flat when the Europeans were expelled from the island'.[4] He was eight impressionable years old when General Cameron and his forces crossed the Mangatawhiri Stream on 17 July 1863, breaching the northern border of the Kingitanga; ten when the Pai Mārire prophet Te Ua Haumene died in 1866, as his followers fought both Māori and Pākehā in savage engagements, which would continue through the rise and decline of the next millennial leader, Te Kooti Rikirangi, until the last shots were fired in 1872.

Best moved from childhood to adulthood through an actual and proverbial state of 'wars and rumours of wars', listening to settler talk of how to bring Māori into line and solve the 'land problem'.[5] He lived in an unstable political environment in the nascent colony, surrounded by hills of native bush on valley land only recently cleared and made pasture. Elizabeth Greer, a settler who arrived in Tawa Flat in 1851 immediately prior to Best's birth, has described as recently as 1938 an area 'all heavy bush then, but very pretty and full of tree ferns'.[6] Wheat – generally sown as the first crop – was broadcast in amongst the burnt black shapes of newly felled native trees, on ground prepared by spade, grubber and the biblical sweat of the brow.

These were Bible-reading folk, and Best along with the rest of the children had to listen to his father at Sunday family prayers read from 'the massive family bible' – fermenting his adult antipathy to revealed religion along the way.[7] After the day of rest, the hard round of labouring, sawmilling and carting absorbed the adult energies, spent in establishing an English agrarian culture in the midst of what had so recently been the preserve of Polynesian hunter-gatherers whose penchant for the fray continued to discomfort settler visions of a better Britain in the southern seas. These were the unconscious forces in the child Best's imagination: the tough pioneer society and its fragile existence, shaping the frontier intellectual he would gradually become, in a storied locality where Māori and Pākehā had coexisted since the arrival of whalers on Kapiti in 1829.

The young Best made his own connections to the Māori world around him and made his own sense of it. Although his immediate family and community in Tawa Flat were European settlers, the world of local Māori was not far away, around Porirua Harbour to the north, at Takapūwāhia pā, Paremata (a trading centre), and Titahi Bay, a further destination for him and his family on Sunday-after-Scripture walks.[8] Craig asserts that 'his earliest playmates were Maori from whom he obtained . . . [his] first few words of the language. Above all he grew up among their kaumatua, [and] learnt their point of view.'[9] At Tinipia near Paremata, he saw a world of confident Māori traders gathering to sell 'wheat, maize, potatoes and pigs' near the trader London's store and accommodation house, complete with its 'bush licence' to sell liquor – the name 'Tinipia' apparently a transliteration of the ginger beer dispensed by their Pākehā host.[10]

Here in the bustle of frontier commerce, surrounded by Māori speakers and almost certainly a number of Pākehā who had also learned the language, he encountered the everyday bilingualism that existed in rural areas until at least the end of the century – a state of affairs mothered for Pākehā and Māori by commercial and political necessity. As settler Susan Wall had written to her sisters in England in 1842: 'I have got so I can talk the native language pretty well so I can be able to under stand them and make a bargain at all times.' It was a race to see who could be shrewdest: 'I have a good deal of trade with them at times. I get blankits and different articles of clotheing and bartur with them for pigs . . . but they are getting every day more knowing.'[11] Trade – as always – was a great school, with ready pupils and teachers.

Along with his relationships with Māori children, this situation presented the growing Best with a social norm: it was *natural* to be bilingual. It was necessary not only for the adults, but also for him to communicate with his Māori mates, most of whom would have had little English at that time, before the enforced learning they experienced later in the Native School system. This education took place both in children's play and his involvement in the ordinary life and work of the tangata whenua (locals) – such as catching tuna (eels). Craig tells a delightful story of the seven-year-old boy declaring to his long-suffering mother and an astonished aunt that rather than become the bush scout he had wanted to be – that is, a fighting man – he had a new ambition: 'I want to be a Maori tohunga.' To allay his aunt's horror, he then explained further he would 'be able to get those eels to go into [his] hinaki trap. That's what tohungas do.'[12]

Whatever image the adults around him had of tohunga (experts, wizards, priests) – most likely somewhere between a witch doctor or a shaman – Best had learned something true from his own observations and listening amongst Māori who, for the most part, still lived traditionally on their mahinga kai (food-gathering areas). He would have seen the intricate eel traps under construction, and then being set in the rivers; observing those men who both made them and later uttered rapid karakia (incantations) over special stones or snags nearby, he would have seen and heard enough to know that a tohunga had both material expertise and spiritual power.

Clyde Adkin and Māori eel trap, hinaki herehere, Hokio Stream near Lake Horowhenua outlet, Levin, 1925. *Photographer: Leslie Adkin, Museum of New Zealand Te Papa Tongarewa, B.021666*

The chanted prayers he would have heard were uttered over mauri (a material talisman, sometimes a favoured rock or a snag) to bring the desired result: in this case, to attract a good catch. He went on to add that he'd been told by Māori at Porirua that he would make a good tohunga – prophetic indeed, as Craig recounts the story. While there is little more surviving evidence of what passed between him and his Māori contacts at that time of his life, there is enough to convince us of an unusual interest that blossomed later into full-blown self-taught scholarship. This he would base on accurate fieldwork, and a linguistic ability out of the ordinary that proved well above average (he later learned Spanish for a projected trip to South America in 1883). The seed, his curiosity, is already evident here.

As for a more formal education, there was no school at Tawa Flat, so 'his father wrote the alphabet on his bedroom wall' before Best was five, and he learned to read and write in the best tradition of home schooling: parents as teachers, with the family bookshelf as the library.[13] The Best children (Walter, Isabel, Frederic, Edith, Madeleine, Elsdon and Katherine) were all encouraged to take up hobbies, from woodworking to landscape painting, instilling unusual powers of concentration in each of them.[14] The young Best was a naturalist by instinct and a keen axeman – something that would stand by him over many adult years as a bushman and sawmiller.

Living close to luxuriant native bush and Māori communities, free from the constraints of regular schooling but given access to teaching at home, adult books and conversation, hardened to physical work from an early age: Best, with hindsight, looks to be a man training for what he would later become – a Pākehā tohunga in matters Māori. The Tawa Flat idyll was not to last. In the year Best turned ten, his father – never the ideal farming type, who pined often for his native Northumbria – decided he had ridden the eleven miles to Wellington for his civil service job in the capital once too often, and the farm was sold. In 1866 this wild colonial boy was forced to move from Tawa to Tinakori Road. The first phase of his development – and his preparation – was over.

The end of this golden weather for the ten-year-old began a new stage of his education: confinement in a grammar school on Wellington Terrace for five and a half interminable years of formal schooling. Passing

Elsdon Best aged about 16, *c.* 1872.
Photographer unidentified, Alexander Turnbull Library, Wellington, NZ, PAColl-8066-01-44-1

the difficult Junior Civil Service exam, at his father's behest, he took a civil service job in the office of the Registrar-General, Dr Bennett, a family friend.[15] He lasted just one year. In 1874, defiant and rebellious, he fled the top-hatted, striped-trousered misery of the office boy for his brother-in-law's Poverty Bay cattle farm. From that day on, Best the autodidact taught himself what he needed to know, setting in train a pattern of defying authority and a lifelong thirst for learning – both of which are central to the psychology of the self-taught individual.[16] As will become apparent, his quest to know and understand more about who Māori were and where they came from took a more serious direction from this critical point.

Just as the mature Best would enter the Urewera in 1895 with a head full of ideas derived from an exhaustive and idiosyncratic reading of ethnographic writings, and the latest in overseas anthropological thinking – so the young man who had arrived on the East Coast twenty years beforehand was under the influence of an earlier literature on these subjects, undermining the biblical anthropology of human origins and diffusion he had heard in his father's Sunday Bible readings. Whereas Tutakangahau – who by that point had been involved in a shooting war with Pākehā as a follower of Te Kooti – had come to his intellectual maturity shaped by the opposing forces of tradition and Christian literacy, Best's mind maps were forged by the very opposite: emergent evolutionary theory and a scientific model of the universe. If any two individuals embody the history and conflict of powerful ideas as they played out on the New Zealand colonial frontier, it is difficult to find a pair more seemingly opposed than Best and Tutakangahau.

It is this mutual embodiment of nineteenth-century thought that makes their relationship such a fascinating and vital area of concern: the things that both drew them together and kept them apart. It is important here to recognise that none of what followed for Tutakangahau and Best – and for us who inherit their times right down to the present day – came out of a simple settler land hunger or an armed Māori nationalism. As Keith Sinclair has elsewhere observed, 'ideas were as destructive as bullets'.[17] It was ideas that had the most profound effects in changing Māori society in the nineteenth century, not all of which were destructive per se. It can be argued equally that literacy – the idea and act of writing – had in the end a powerful and positive effect for Māori.

There are at least two recorded sources to aid us in tracing the lineage of the adolescent Elsdon's formative reading – apart from his biographer's general observation that the boy had access to his father's bookshelf. Craig notes that not only did he write – and later destroy – a book of his own observations of the natural world at the age of twelve, he gives fascinating details of two important books read by Best in his teenage years.[18] Before he had left the hated schoolyard, he had saved his pocket money to buy a book Craig notes as '*The World's Deluge*', which was almost certainly a translation of the French author Louis Figuier's *La Terre Avant le Deluge* (*The Earth Before the Deluge*), published in France in 1863. It became immensely popular, and in 1865 was reissued and translated into English, in Best's eleventh year. Profusely illustrated with borrowings from a 'respected academic text book', Figuier's popularisation of science was based largely on the writings of others, and his own version of the 'two flood' theory, where the flood of Noah was seen as a local event – thus neatly evading the growing tensions in archaeology and biology between a tentative evolutionism and revealed religion.[19]

Full of sombre black-and-white drawings by Édouard Riou, progressive images of the prehistoric earth passing through phases of 'deep time', it is a cause of wonder as to what the young naturalist made of his seventeen shillings and sixpence worth. At conversion rates to the New Zealand dollar, that comes to approximately ninety-two dollars in today's money. This quite remarkable purchase was, by all accounts, eagerly devoured.[20] Figuier was a creationist when it came to humanity, and a monogenist or believer in a common human ancestor, attributing racial variation to climate. Humans, he thought, differed from animal nature by virtue of their powers of abstract thought.[21] While this was still close to creationism and assumed an intelligent designer, the next book Best is recorded as absorbing at this impressionable age has been famously described as a 'Victorian sensation' in its capacity to destabilise the established tenets of creationism: Robert Chambers' *Vestiges of the Natural History of Creation* (1844).[22]

Chambers was a Scottish journalist, bookseller, publisher and ardent naturalist: his explanation of the fossil record in early Victorian palaeontology – in its naturalistic account of human and species origin – constituted both a threat to the creationism of revealed religion and a goad to scientific students of comparative anatomy and embryology.[23] Attacked by believers for the challenge his writings made to the special status of humanity, and derided by scientists for his poor methods, Chambers died in 1871, still maintaining his anonymity, which was only broken in the twelfth edition of 1884. The reception of Chambers' work reputedly delayed the publication of Darwin's *On the Origin of Species* (1859): Darwin had learned from the other writer's experience not to get too far ahead of the facts, and to avoid attacking accepted opinion head-on. The hostile reception to Chambers had in some respects 'acted as a lightning conductor' and spared him 'some of the thunderbolts' that had fallen earlier on the *Vestiges*.[24]

There is little doubt the teenage Best was quite unaware of the turbulent background to his prized purchase. That he had come into the possession of a work by Darwin's herald, which he would have read cover to cover and absorbed, is a pointer to his intellectual roots, and also to his later fiercely articulated anticlericalism. Overlaying his family Sunday-school teachings was a new foundation; the tension between the two would surface again in late life when Best, the social scientist, became a propagator of a pre-Christian Māori monotheism, against his earlier better judgement. As a bright and opinionated secondary school pupil, he certainly had no wider framework in which to place and evaluate the controversies that became part of the intellectual life of the growing colony: clerics like Richard Taylor who read Darwin, versus atheists and agnostics such as Edward Tregear, who were fully conversant with the Scriptures they came to discount or deride.

What makes Chambers' work so important in understanding the development of Best's early thinking is the way in which so many of his later ideas can be found in embryo in the *Vestiges*.[25] Chambers' book has been described as an early 'well-publicised attempt at an evolutionary theory' whereby 'Man had come into being' by a chance process; it also contained a significant chapter on anthropology.[26] Naturalistic explanations of human origins were seen by Bible-believing Victorians as a threat to the special created status of humanity. Best, either in his youth or early adulthood, had accepted a line of reasoning that led him into the evolutionary camp.

Major themes in Chamber's anthropological thinking would emerge later in much of the adult Best. Chambers had a hierarchical view of our development, from savage to civilised, on a commonplace model of human progress. His view of human origins had a single common ancestor, with an Indian birthplace suggested for humankind: the lines of human migration converged and were concentrated 'about the region of Hindostan'.[27] He had read the philology of the leading Orientalist Sanskrit scholars such as Franz Bopp (1791–1867), and made comparative word lists part of his evidence for human commonality and diffusion throughout the globe. This was a field and a form of scholarship that would become important to Best and his colleagues in the Polynesian

Society later in the century, especially in the work of F. Max Müller.

Less fortunately, Chambers' middle-class views of the development of civilisation were inherently racist: leisure, art and property rights were seen as crucial in a world-view which placed Caucasians on the upper rungs of the ladder of 'Progress'. His evolutionary thinking explained racial difference on the basis of perfectibility, or '*development*' – the childhood of humanity reached its adult manifestation where the 'marked features of the true Caucasian . . . become perfectly developed'. Other races were somehow practising to become what Chambers already was: 'The Mongolian is an arrested infant newly born.'[28] These views he elaborated into a rationale for colonial expropriation of conquered indigenes. Inferior races were to be supplanted by their evolutionary betters: 'Look at the progress even now making over barbaric parts of the earth by the best examples of the Caucasian type.' Not only did these colonists 'fill up the waste places', they also managed to 'supersede the imperfect nations already existing'.[29]

While Chambers allowed that certain outstanding individuals might arise in the midst of a barbarian society and so elevate their fellows, on the whole he was a diffusionist in matters of cultural change – i.e. he held that civilisation was exported from the highly developed Caucasian world to uplift the benighted Other in the dark night of their savagery. Even though humanity was at root unified, certain higher types had first uplifted their own people, who had then 'become in turn *foci* for the diffusion of light over the adjacent regions of barbarism', fuelled by an 'aggressive ambition' that had led to 'the civilisation of many countries'.[30]

It was often the missionaries who later became a target of Best's hostility to such cultural imperialism, so insensitive they were said to be about the nature and value of the native cultures they seemed determined to uproot in their zeal to spread the gospel. It is hard not to read Chambers – on the basis of his anthropology – as the same kind of zealot, and to wonder what effect these ideas had on the teenage Best. Certainly, for all his enlightened attitudes towards the intrinsic interest and profound value of what he came to see as an essentially Māori world-view, his later imperative to record it for posterity was *as a result* of the application of a degraded and opportunistic view of human evolution.

Attitudes such as those propagated by Chambers underlay the genocidal behaviour by Pākehā that Māori leaders in the 1860s such as Renata Kawepo came to see as a harbinger of their eventual extinction by force of arms.[31] It was more than the missionary thinking that Sinclair has bemoaned that was to prove destructive to traditional Māori society, and more importantly, Māori autonomy, within the new polity of the rule of law. It was ideas like these – commonplace by the time Best left Wellington and went to find his way in the world – that justified the displacement of Māori, and their banishment to a predicted extinction in the deep rural hinterlands, away from a regular pricking of what remained of the settler conscience. It is this war of ideas – and of bullets – the struggle for survival and supremacy, that shapes what followed in the later lives of Best and Tutakangahau.

CHAPTER FIVE

Te Riri me te Ture: War and the Law, 1864–1893

Tutakangahau and Elsdon Best emerged from very different backgrounds, embodying the ideological battleground they were to experience during the decades 1860 to 1880, as each in his time took up arms to defend what he saw as their rightful inheritance. Not only did they both in very separate times and places, ways and means face each other's peoples with deadly force; over the same period, they continued to read about, think about, and write about their situation and the Māori–Pākehā relationship. This chapter and the next lay a foundation towards an understanding of their eventual meeting in the 1890s, and the relationship of war, religion and ethnography on the colonial frontier – a relationship that gave birth to our first distinctive national literature. Māori history as related by Māori to various Pākehā scribes, and refashioned by those writers, may not be a politically acceptable formula to white liberals or brown nationalists – but that is the bequest. Through the writings of Māori themselves *in Māori*, during this period, in newspapers and letters particularly, the kōrero (conversation) is further enriched and complicated.

This period of Tutakangahau's life is defined by war and religion: not war in the sense of constant conflict, but as in 'the fires of war burning the island', setting alight the previous two decades of relative peace.[1] A terrible instability grew out of the Waitara troubles from 1860 onward, creating home-grown Māori religious responses. Many were deeply disillusioned with the government's application of a system of law they saw as derived from God's law; adding insult to that injury was the perceived alignment of Pākehā missionaries with the illegitimate exercise of that authority. From his early beginnings as both a traditional Tūhoe leader by virtue of his chiefly birth and as a new type of authority figure, a Christian catechist who remained scripturally literate thereafter, Tutakangahau exemplifies the indivisibility of war and religion, the secular and the sacred, in Māori thought and practice.

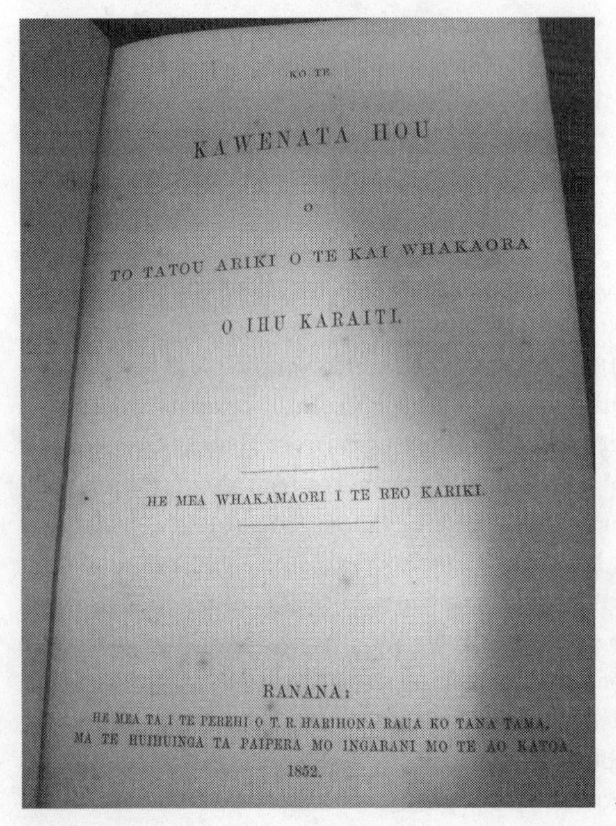
KO TE

KAWENATA HOU

O

TO TATOU ARIKI O TE KAI WHAKAORA

O IHU KARAITI.

HE MEA WHAKAMAORI I TE REO KARIKI.

RANANA:

HE MEA TA I TE PEREHI O T. R. HARIHONA RAUA KO TANA TAMA,
MA TE HUIHUINGA TA PAIPERA MO INGARANI MO TE AO KATOA.

1852.

Māori New Testament, 1852 (5th edition), revised by Robert Maunsell and William Williams, where the 'wh' was used for the first time.
Author photograph

He was a follower of, or was engaged with, all of the three major millennial movements that arose amongst Māori from 1860 until the first decade of the new century and his death: Te Ua's Pai Mārire / Hauhau, Te Kooti's Hauhau / Ringatū, and Rua Kenana's Iharaira (Israelites). As settler land hunger led inevitably to armed conflict, while at the same time the complete Old Testament in Māori was published in the late 1850s,[2] the seeds were sown for a new Māori identification with the Jews, as God's chosen yet persecuted people. The growth of indigenous millennial religions followed from these events, as Māori came to understand and use the Scriptures in their own ways, hammering out forms of what we now might recognise as liberation theologies.

Within twenty years of Colenso's arrival in Toreatai, disillusionment with the missionaries and the settler government was evident amongst Tūhoe. In 1862, C. Hunter Brown, the resident agent at Wairoa, journeyed through their territory on a mission to sound out the chiefs on Governor Grey's proposed rūnanga (council) scheme – but also to assess their numbers and military strength. Mohi, a chief from Maungapōhatu, travelled to meet him, and while he was conciliatory, Brown noted a widespread distrust of the missionaries and the government: 'Yours is a land-taking and man-destroying Church . . . You have deserted the faith, and set up the Queen as your God!'[3] This is a classic statement of Māori views at the time, echoing as it does the charge that Renata Tamakihikurangi (Kawepo) had delivered against the Hawke's Bay settlers and the Superintendent Fitzgerald in 1860, over Waitara: that the government was placing itself above a law it was bound to uphold, the law of God.[4]

Brown wrote of a state of disillusionment: 'the present political disposition of the Urewera may be summed up as intense suspicion and distrust of the Pakeha', and the dread of some kind of trap behind Grey's proposed new system.

> Sad confusion exists in the minds of some of the most thinking men in this valley [near Tuapuku] between the "ture" as they call the Gospel or

law of God, and the "ture" as they also call the law of men. They appear greatly to fear lest by the second we should be meaning to undermine the first. It is a pity that in general conversation they should use "ture" for either almost indiscriminately.[5]

Brown seems to be hinting that Māori had not yet developed a sophisticated sense of the way in which the Christian religion had to operate in a fallen world, and how the effects of that Fall still could lay claim to ministers both of church and state.

If they seemed theologically naive, however, he saw clearly that their distrust of the government was founded in the sharp political awareness of thinking men. While there is no record of Tutakangahau's thoughts and feelings at this crucial juncture – before he went to war against the settler government – he certainly was part of that climate of feeling; and when the Hauhau phenomenon reached Tūhoe, he was not slow to take up arms in defence of his territory. Before this occurred, though, there is a record of his people's response to another Pākehā conflict with Māori – recorded by Best – in the Waikato battles of Rangiaohia, Haerini, and in particular, the party of fifty Tūhoe warriors who took part in the defence of Ōrakau in April 1864.[6]

Joining a war against government forces was Tūhoe's first direct engagement with the Pākehā military, undertaken only after fierce debate. Best's account of the fighting rests mainly on the evidence of one of his other major informants, Paitini Wi Tapeka of Ruatāhuna.[7] Tutakangahau – who did not go – added to the account with his description of a hui (meeting) held at Oputao to discuss the war: 'All Tuhoe met [but] the Rua-toki and Wai-mana clans decided not to go. Those of Rua-tahuna, Te Whaiti and Wai-kare Moana decided to send a contingent.' This was agreed by the majority, who declared: 'Let Mātātua be sheltered. The fire [of war] is burning the island.'[8] The use of this proverb – 'Kia tauwharautia a Mātātua' – appeared in a new historical context for Tūhoe. Traditionally, Māori hapū defended their adjacent territories, or raided others within range, but here, a newer sense of global threat was apparent. The debate Paitini described and Best recorded was split two ways: defend Tūhoe land by fighting afar, or stay on the land and wait for war to come.

Mātaatua – the ancestral canoe, the vessel of Tūhoe identity, a metaphor for its people – was under threat. 'The island is in anguish', the leading chief Piripu Te Heuheu proclaimed – the whole country was in turmoil because of Grey's invasion of the Waikato and his war with the Kingites – and Tūhoe should stand with Waikato and Maniapoto, as Māori with Māori.[9] That was one way to protect the canoe; the other was proposed by Te Ahoaho: 'Leave it secure from harm, in the shed' – a strategy of holding one's line and attacking only when attacked. Te Whenuanui agreed and 'the bulk of the tribe agreed to remain at home and guard the tribal lands' (he later changed his mind, fearing the taunts of Te Heuheu, and went to fight).[10] This debate and the radical change that underlay it was a sign of further changes in Tutakangahau's world and the situation for Māori in general: this was not a war to defend tribal lands against a threat, but a conflict that signified the dangerous potential of Pākehā power to defeat, displace, and eliminate Māori altogether.

In the event, Paitini and the other Tūhoe fighters who stood with Rewi Maniapoto at Ōrakau fought with legendary courage, suffering 60 per cent casualties in a three-day battle, outnumbered four to one (his father died alongside him). His detailed account as presented by Best is a graphic tale of a valiant but doomed hand-to-hand combat: around sixty Tūhoe volunteers with their flintlock muskets, urged on by tohunga promising them immunity from the Pākehā bullets. In the end, there was a desperate escape through swamps, pursued by British bayonets, and an epic march home to their kāinga for the wounded and exhausted survivors.

They were met – as was Paitini at Ruatāhuna – by lines of reproachful women singing a whakatea, a jeering taunt song, at their defeat: 'I hoki mai koe, E Te Whenua-nui! ki te aha? Tē mate atu ai i te unuhanga o te puhi o Mātātua – Why did you come back, O Te Whenua-nui? Better to have died when the pride of Mātātua fell!'[11] This battle and its outcome was to prove prophetic for Tūhoe's dealings with the government forces thereafter – and although Tutakangahau did not go, he would soon be engaged in the next phase of what Tūhoe saw as the Pākehā war against Māori. A year later, in April 1865, the Hauhau movement would announce its arrival amongst them in dramatic fashion, and for the next five years of his life he would be swept up in a new form of religious guerrilla warfare.

Before tracing Tutakangahau's involvement with the controversial and often travestied doctrine of Pai Mārire and its emergence into Pākehā consciousness as the Hauhau rebellion, some background to the founder and the religion's emergence is necessary.[12] Te Ua's religious convictions were born in Taranaki during the 1860s, founded on a 'belief in national deliverance and ill feeling against the missionaries'. These cornerstones of his teaching included 'the right to defend territorial boundaries' – something that was an obvious position for Tūhoe to take. After his angelic visitations and the rapid creation of a new church structure, Te Ua began in January 1863 to record his gospels, 'Ua Rongo Pai', in which he set out 'the organization and ethical teaching of the Hauhau church'.

Far more than the fanatical warrior cult it was to be characterised as in Pākehā historical writings, Te Ua's teaching began as a Māori indigenisation of Christianity, taking the Pākehā religion into Māori control: 'Te Ua considered his teaching to be Christianity purified of error.' He was guided by pai mārire (absolute or transcendent goodness) – the name by which the faith was first known. This reflected the ecstatic nature of the movement in experience, where the nature of God was revealed as his followers performed acts directed by His Spirit, the Hau (breath, wind). This holy wind carried the messages or niu (news) to his growing band of faithful followers – who would later include Tutakangahau. The absolute belief in which its members held the teachings certainly produced behaviours that were fanatic: Hauhau soldiers standing up in gunfire and praying as the bullets whistled by.

What developed from this was a syncretic Māori Pentecostalism – an affective spiritual phenomenon that may be viewed as an outbreak of religious revivalism, little different in essence from other charismatic movements in the last two centuries. His followers spoke in tongues, in perfect accordance with New Testament promises to those who received the gift of the Hau (Spirit); they also 'prophesied as they circled the niu, or mast'. As promised in the Acts of the Apostles, they dreamed dreams and saw visions, forming a community of new believers, as had the first Christians in the early days and years of the Christian era.[13] Te Ua's goal of creating a righteous society was to founder in the context of war, attracting official attention after 6 April 1864, when heads were taken from government soldiers killed in an ambush at Ahuahu, Taranaki – gruesome trophies of which Te Ua became the guardian.

Te Ua proved unable to restrain his followers – in the case of Tūhoe, this was to prove pivotal – after the death of the Anglican missionary Völkner, ritually killed by two of the prophet's messengers, Patara Raukatauri and Kereopa Te Rau, at Ōpōtiki in March 1865. En route to speak to Ngāti Porou, they had disobeyed Te Ua, inciting action against missionaries as they travelled; by this one act, they enraged Pākehā opinion, providing the government with a useful martyr figure. This event was to bring pro-government Ngāti Porou into the fighting, and in no small way gave rise in time to another troublesome martyrdom: the 1866 arrest and exile of Te Kooti. Te Ua's example of separating Māori Christianity from 'dependence on the theology and ritual of the missionary church' passed on to this next millennial prophet, one not so reluctant to get blood on his hands, and who would be quickly included amongst the Hauhau rebels by the settlers and the government.

It is within this religious and martial synthesis of old and new that we can begin to understand Tutakangahau's marriage of tradition and modernity, in the transitional years through which he lived. These niu (new) nineteenth-century biblical traditions suppressed 'the spirituality of the Māori past', while at the same time permitting an outbreak of the former warrior traditions in the rightful defence of land. Settler imagery of Hauhau rebel fanaticism as the regression to a savage mentality served their own purposes, notwithstanding some of the extreme acts of cruelty and carnage that ensued, the corollary of virtually any war one could name. Distanced now from smoke of war and battle, it is possible to see Te Ua and Pai Mārire/Hauhau as 'the root of a tradition of biblical prophecy which has been drawn on by all subsequent Maori religious leaders' – a tradition which framed Tutakangahau's adult life and shaped the late-century Tūhoe world Best was to enter.

According to Best, Hauhau emissaries Patara and Kereopa introduced Te Ua's teachings to Tūhoe in April 1865: they met 'Tuhoe, Ngati-Manawa and Ngati-Whare people at Taua-roa, near Galatea', to explain the new religion and obtain converts.[14] In a section of *Tuhoe* pointedly titled 'The Hauhau Craze', Best gives a jaundiced but fascinating account of the new religion's entrance into Tutakangahau's world. While the chief is not mentioned at this point, he is clearly identified three years later in November 1868 as a Hauhau fighter alongside Te Kooti at Te Karetu. Tūhoe, according to Best's informants, 'accepted the new cult readily'; he does not pause to ask why, content to record the more sensational aspects of its arrival (the display of Captain Lloyd's head and its ritual humiliation) and his opinions on the mental state of those who took part in proceedings 'of a most revolting nature'.[15] Best the sceptic, however, is balanced by his ethnographic instincts and there is rare material here from his informant Paitini about early Pai Mārire practice amongst Tūhoe.

Paitini notes that these meetings of Hauhau were often held 'during the war, especially just before a fight or raiding expedition'. Best fails to make the connection that this new 'craze', in its application in time of war, was also an extension of tradition. He was well aware when this account was written, around 1905 to 1907, of Tūhoe war gods, and the matakite phenomenon, where a tohunga possessed of foresight would invoke a medium to predict the course of upcoming battles, and in his divinations seek signs to be watched for and obeyed.[16] He does, however, note that the ceremonies conducted around the niu poles seem to have replaced 'the *wai taua* rite of former times' – that is, the ritual cleansing of warriors before battle, to bring them under 'the extremely strict *tapu* of Tu, the supreme god of war'.[17]

He also discusses the Hauhau flags, Riki and Rura: Paitini's account of a niu ritual, including a display of the flags and the chanting of karakia (incantations) is graphic and helps to reveal the syncretic nature of the Hauhau/Pai Mārire culture. Flags flying on their poles were borrowed symbols of Pākehā military and governmental power, combined with modified pre-battle rituals from an older world of Māori warfare. The karakia themselves – dismissed by Best as 'gibberish . . . meaningless rubbish, containing many English words' – were in fact prayers that combined Māori and English lexical elements.[18] These were a form of liturgy, parts of an order of service devised by Te Ua Haumene, 'composed of lists of English words written in Maori form and divided into regular verses. These lessons were understood as evidence of Te Ua's gift of tongues.' They also included the names of foreign peoples, perhaps part of the prophet's recorded sense of solidarity with colonised groups who bore grievances against their mutual English oppressors.[19]

The religion and the warfare that combined in what became known as Hauhau – whose followers were written down in the Pākehā historical record as rebels and savage backsliders – was a creature born of its time, and for its time, to restore to Māori the power to act in the new order. Its attraction for Tutakangahau – for he assuredly was a follower, both before and during the Te Kooti manifestation of Hauhauism which eventually evolved into Ringatū – can only be surmised in the dearth of specific testimony by the man or his peers. Nevertheless, the same factors that would rally Tūhoe to Te Kooti's banner were at work at this point: the power to act, the right to utu (revenge), the revelation that God was with Māori and would fight with them as surely he would with Pākehā. That the faith of Tūhoe Hauhau was dipped in blood does not make it any the less a faith, where the new God and the old atua were serially invoked to bring deliverance to Māori, as Jehovah was known to have done for the Jews, so clearly seen in the Old Testament freshly translated and near at hand. 'Almost every hamlet had its niu', Paitini told Best. 'The Hauhau flags were suspended from the *niu* staff.' There were few places Tutakangahau could have gone where he would not have seen this, and been drawn in as a warrior, a chief, and a co-religionist.[20]

The presence of the Hauhau missionary Kereopa amongst Tūhoe had more than religious significance: in the eyes of the settler government, who had designs on the best of Tūhoe lands, the Urewera tribes were sheltering the murderer of a priest. In aligning themselves with the Pai Mārire faith, they had become rebels against the Queen and her officers. After the Rev. Völkner's murder in March 1865, Kereopa and other Hauhau evangelists had continued their mission on the East Coast and made converts, in the process making firm enemies amongst many Ngāti Porou and Kahungunu, who were to remain loyal to the Crown in the fighting which ensued.

Large numbers of Māori in the Gisborne area became converts and it was here in November 1865 that the siege of Hauhau forces in the pā at Waerenga-a-Hika took place. Government forces, comprised of Māori and settlers, inflicted a heavy defeat on the 'rebels'; included in those who fought there were Tūhoe Hauhau, some of whom were sent to the Chatham Islands with the other captives. They would soon be joined by another prisoner – Te Kooti Rikirangi – with whose fate Tūhoe and

Tutakangahau became deeply intertwined. Arrested at Waerenga-a-Hika under suspicion of Hauhau sympathies, then released, Te Kooti was taken again in the following year and exiled to the Chathams. From there, his spiritual rebirth would give rise to the next phase of Māori millennialism, as the leaderless Pai Mārire gradually lost power and influence in the aftermath of successive military defeats, and the death of Te Ua Haumene in 1866.

By January of that year, government forces were engaging Hauhau on the southern side of Lake Waikaremoana: the war was coming ever closer to Tutakangahau's traditional stronghold of Maungapōhatu. Assisting the government in prosecuting these actions was a Ngāti Porou officer, Ropata Wahawaha, who would later be a major figure in chasing Te Kooti out of his Urewera hideouts and bringing Tūhoe to the point of surrender.[21] Also in the pursuit were men of Ngāti Kahungunu led by Kopu Parapara and Ihaka Whanga, opposing some hundreds of the Pai Mārire persuasion,

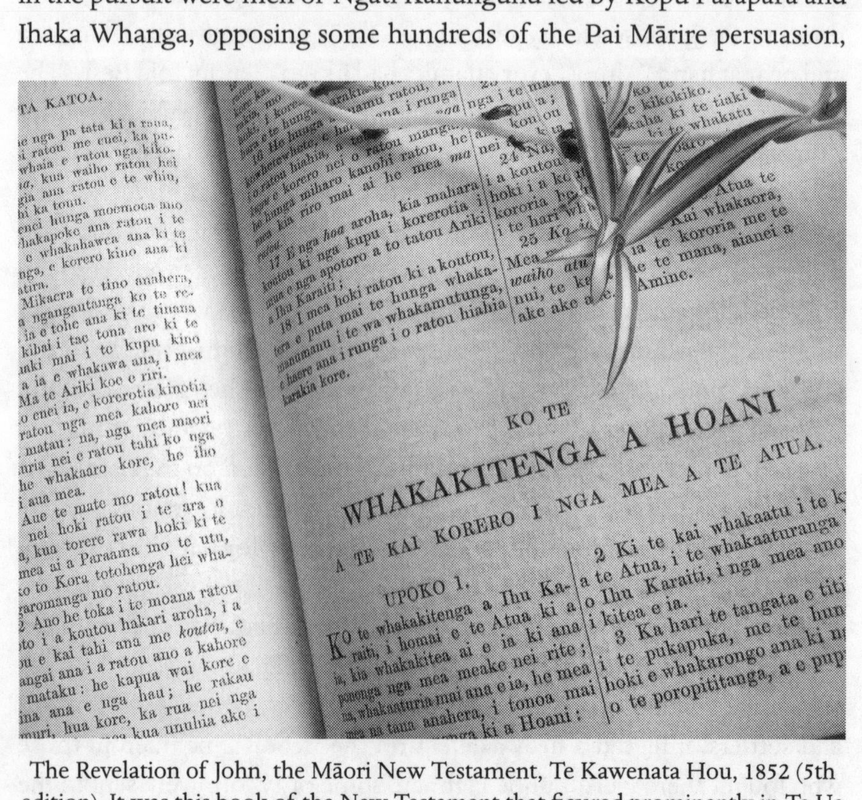

The Revelation of John, the Māori New Testament, Te Kawenata Hou, 1852 (5th edition). It was this book of the New Testament that figured prominently in Te Ua Haumene's millennialist teaching, 'Ua Rongo Pai'.
Author photograph

whose numbers included others from Kahungunu in Te Kooti's camp, Ngāti Ruapani (traditional Tūhoe enemies), Rongowhakaata and Tūhoe themselves. James Cowan's account of the battle – from which these details are drawn – makes clear the Māori-on-Māori nature of much of the fighting that ensued over the next six years, until the last shots were fired on 14 February 1872.

While settler governments wrestled with the financial cost of the wars, the cost to Māori in terms of lives and land lost was disastrous: Te Kooti was for years characterised in Pākehā histories as the murderer of innocent settlers. Yet he killed far more Māori than Pākehā, and the hatred and resentment that the wars buried deep in Māori memory was not for the government alone, but for fresh wounds they had inflicted on one another. The twenty-year period between the signing of the Treaty in 1840 and the Waitara conflict had promised much: a time when many Māori had begun to internalise the new rule of law, to act as British citizens, and to change their own social and economic structures to take advantage of Te Ao Mārama (the new world). The pressures of Pākehā immigration, however, and the subsequent need and greed for land and its profits, took the best of what was Māori whenua. With land loss – its power as a possession, and a sign of mana in sale or gift – the corporate real estate deal underlying the Treaty became more visible.[22]

Confiscation – or raupatu – was the second fire on the land to come upon Tūhoe in that January of 1866. On the 17th of the month, the government declared lands amounting to almost half a million acres to be confiscated under the provisions of the New Zealand Settlements Act of 1863, as punishment for Tūhoe involvement in the battle of Ōrakau, the deaths of Völkner and Fulloon, and their part in the growing Hauhau rebellion. This amounted to 'all the low-lying and relatively fertile lands on the northern edges of the Urewera'.[23] The threat of further actions had hung over Tūhoe and neighbouring iwi since martial law had been declared by the government 'for the districts of Ōpōtiki and Whakatāne on 4 September 1865', and troops landed at Ōpōtiki four days later. The expedition was ostensibly to 'arrest the murderers of Völkner and Fulloon' – but it was also allied with a threat that if they were not given up, the lands of the tribes who concealed them would be confiscated as compensation, and to allow peacekeeping operations to be maintained.[24]

It took some time for Tūhoe to realise that land had in fact been seized, and that they were to be punished for supposedly harbouring Kereopa in defiance of government requests to hand him over (he was actually ejected by them from their territory later, as too hot to handle). In searching for the wanted man and others, government troops had taken to ransacking and plundering northern Tūhoe villages, even when leaders like Rakuraku co-operated with them. Fear of the government soldiers and the intentions of their masters grew amongst the villagers. The arbitrary and illegal confiscation of their best coastal and river lands, to be given over to Pākehā soldiers and settlers, was soon seen for what it was: the declaration of an undeclared war, and so 'local acts of resistance then spread as a *consequence* of confiscation'.[25]

When traditional enemies such as Ngāti Pukeko to the east were given Tūhoe lands for their loyalty to the Queen, and Wairoa loyalists looked to be securing land to the south at Waikaremoana, the peoples of the Urewera began to close ranks, to resist the surveys and any further encroachment on the aukati (confiscation line) to the north. This is the background to Tutakangahau's emergence as a significant local leader and a resistance fighter, alongside the escaped Te Kooti after his arrival back on the mainland on 9 July 1868. There was little choice for the few available Tūhoe warriors but to defend their lands and attempt also through legal means to challenge the taking of their papakāinga (ancestral dwelling places).

The story of Te Kooti Rikirangi (Te Turuki), the elusive guerrilla fighter and prophet figure, is by now well known: his controversial arrest and banishment to the Chatham Islands with other Hauhau fighters, his religio-mystical experiences, and in July 1868 his escape and return to the mainland on the captured *Rifleman*. These were followed by his subsequent legendary exploits whereby Pākehā painted him as a murderous rebel, symbolising the so-called savagery of a pre-contact Māori psyche, while Māori themselves called him anything ranging from poropiti (prophet) to hoariri (enemy), depending on their own complex relationships in the new dispensation with its incoming tide of land-hungry settlers. Te Kooti became a kind of lightning rod, interpreted as friend or foe, prophet or madman depending upon where one stood in the new colonial order. Māori opinion at the time – including that of Tūhoe – was complex, and is not reducible to a simple 'for or against'. Those Tūhoe who made a covenant with him and sheltered him in the Urewera would later see him take their relatives captive, as an insurance policy against betrayal; other Māori who pursued him alongside Pākehā troops were sometimes recorded as firing warning shots to let him know they were near, ensuring his escape.[26]

It is against these ambiguities that his meanings for Tūhoe in general and Tutakangahau in particular must be assessed. Why would they join forces with, and follow, a man of no rank who was not of them, belonging as he did to Rongowhakaata? What would a man like Tutakangahau – a traditional chief – see in Te Kooti? In the old order, they were potential enemies; in the new, it was different – anything was possible in such an unstable climate of war, betrayal and fear. Both were fighting men, caught up in the religious ferment of the times; Tutakangahau had fought with Hauhau, taking part in their pre-battle rituals. There is little doubt he would have experienced the common fervour produced in ceremonies circling the niu poles under the flags and banners of war. Christianised to some degree by Colenso's Bible tracts and missionary work, self-taught in the wider context of the Bible's meanings, a man who had already fought his people's enemies – he was a perfect match for the times that produced him. The power of literacy, where slaves taught to read could become teachers, had given commoners status outside of the traditional order. Pan-Māori thinking and action was already at work amongst Tūhoe, as seen in the debates on joining the war in the Waikato. Tutakangahau would naturally defend his territory, his people and his status, alongside the Hauhau fighters.

News of Te Kooti's early victories against the settlers and their Māori allies would have encouraged Tūhoe Hauhau in the belief that the government could be resisted. As awareness of his matakite (visions) grew, his status both as a seer and a leader who acts and takes utu (revenge) increased his attraction to the disaffected – all within the framework of an Old Testament prophet-king figure, as realised in Te Kooti's deployment of the Scriptures in his charismatic and ruthless leadership. This man was a timely blend of the old and the new: Māori enough to embody elements of the traditional past, modern enough to qualify as an armed emissary of the God of the Book.

Te Kooti was a traditional warrior, a priest and modern leader rolled into one, accessing the newly traditional forms of biblical Christianity and making them indigenous. The settler government had broken a civil compact based on a higher law (Te Ture, the law of God): the Old Testament Scriptures, replete with angelic visitations, prophets and warriors who brought deliverance to an embattled Israel, supplied Te Kooti with a template for revenge and restitution. He would prove to be a seer who drew blood: not the reincarnation of a pre-European war chief, but a millennial warrior-prophet born of the stresses of the times that were shaping and changing hereditary leaders such as Tutakangahau.

Despite Te Kooti's early successes against the settler forces, Tūhoe did not give him shelter immediately, nor assist him in his stated aim of reaching Taupō. His initial victories over settler and Māori alike were short-lived. It was only after the serious military reversals at Te Kāretu late in 1868 and at Ngā Tapa in January 1869 that his letters to the Tūhoe leaders at Ruatāhuna and Te Whāiti began to have some effect, and his calls for support and shelter began to find some favour. At the same time, we find the first accounts of Tutakangahau's enlistment in the Hauhau/ Te Kooti phase of the struggle, when he tells Best of the loss of his son Akuhata at Te Kāretu and his own dramatic and narrow escape from the pā. In both of these battles, Tūhoe and the Hauhau ranks in general suffered severe losses in what proved to be major defeats for Te Kooti.[27]

By a touch of historical irony, Renata Kawepo (who had upbraided Superintendent Fitzgerald of Hawke's Bay for supporting the government war in Taranaki) was one of the Kahungunu 'friendlies' trying to kill Tutakangahau: both men saw themselves as defending their land and interests, one by fighting against the government, another with it.[28] Also amongst the Tūhoe killed in these skirmishes was Kenana, Tutakangahau's relative and the father of the as yet unborn Rua Kenana, the future inheritor of Te Kooti's mantle and later repository of Best's bilious contempt. They were amongst the thirty persons from Maungapōhatu who had already aligned themselves with Te Kooti in defence of their southern flank below Waikaremoana.[29]

These were bloodstained times and Tutakangahau was in the thick of them. His escape from Te Kāretu and his survival in the fall of Ngā Tapa certainly involved many close shaves; had he been captured by Ropata Wahawaha's Ngāti Porou fighters, summary execution would have been his fate. Women fought alongside their men – referring to the earlier massacre of many settler families, Best records that Tutakangahau's wife had actually taken part in 'the bloody work' of Te Kooti's raid on Mohaka in April. He describes her thus: 'Kura-wha, wife of Tutakangahau, a woman of great size and amazing muscular strength, whose fame as a wrestler still lives. She shouldered a rifle and took part in the fighting like a savage Amazon.'[30] Allowing for Best's hyperbole, this indicates something of the desperate nature of the times. At a major hui in Ruatāhuna in January 1869, Tūhoe debated on whether or not to give active support to Te Kooti by allowing him to take the fateful step of leaving Puketapu and move across the aukati (no trespass) line. Any offer of sanctuary would draw all of the Urewera into a showdown with the government – but such was their anger at the land confiscations that in February senior leaders invited him to come to a hui at Maungapōhatu, which led in the following weeks to a military alliance with the prophet.[31]

At Tāwhana in March 1869, Tūhoe and Te Kooti entered into a binding covenant, which according to Akuhata Te Kaha 'was to rest on the chiefs of Tuhoe', amongst whom were senior leaders such as Te Whenuanui, Paerau – and Tutakangahau.[32] According to this informant, 'these people gave their mana to be under the guidance of Te Kooti' – a powerful event – and like a latter-day Moses, Te Kooti is reputed to have cited Scripture: 'I take you as my people, and I will be your God; you will know that I am Jehovah. You are the people of the covenant.'[33] This solemn – and deadly – occasion is one of the first indications of Tutakangahau's seniority and the beginning of a bonded relationship to the prophet, which was to continue up until Te Kooti's death at Te Wainui in April 1893.

In spite of what Tūhoe might have hoped – that this fraught alliance to recover their confiscated lands under God's direction might now prosper – it served rather to bring down a more intense government campaign on the heads of their people, and would lead before the year's end to Te Kooti being escorted out of the Urewera. It soon became obvious that the covenant – with a wanted man, and not necessarily with God – was not going to regain the land. Instead, a government invasion in May, and a scorched earth policy in the months following, threatened the destruction of Tūhoe. When the prophet left, making for Taupō in June of that year, one of the chiefs who went with him was Tutakangahau; in February of the following year he was amongst a group who made representations to Te Arawa to let Te Kooti pass through their land.[34]

Te Kooti was forced to flee back into the Urewera, and in February 1870 military invasions of Tūhoe territory began on two fronts: Wahawaha heading for Maungapōhatu, and in March, Te Keepa pushing into the Waimana Valley. Divisions began to grow amongst Tūhoe about the wisdom of sheltering Te Kooti, as the government pursued a policy of forcing them out of the mountains into coastal reserves, such as Putere, where surrendered 'rebels' were displaced.[35] In spite of increasing pressure, Ngāti Huri (Tamakaimoana) of Maungapōhatu remained staunch: Tutakangahau was remaining true to the covenant he had made with the fugitive leader.

With Arawa forces under Mair attacking from the east from Fort Galatea in April, it was obvious that resistance would soon be overcome. Gradually, groups from various Tūhoe hapū began to surrender, beginning with Ngāti Whare in May. War-weariness, starvation and disease forced the leaders to sue for peace: Paerau surrendered in October 1870, and in December he and Te Whenuanui met with Ormond, the government agent at Napier, to discuss peace terms. According to Best, Tutakangahau and others of Tūhoe were with them 'on a peace mission', which would lead in time to the occupation and pacification of the Tamakaimoana chief's territory by Ropata Wahawaha's Ngāti Porou fighters.[36]

In February 1871, Captain Porter confronted Te Patutoro at Tāwhana, and after ferocious haka, in the whaikōrero (oratory) that took place, he noted that the Tūhoe chiefs – even while surrendering – did not see Te Kooti as a criminal: 'The killing of women and children was an ancient custom of their people' – and nor was Te Kooti a criminal for killing Pākehā, but rather a patriot. It was 'the duty of every Maori to fight the foreigner, to withhold the island that was slipping into their hands'.[37] As Ropata chased the fleeting shadow of Te Kooti from Toreatai itself, Tutakangahau's home, the drama of the chief's dilemma stood plain in Te Patutoro's words. Defending his territory was his culture, yet so was an emerging Māori Christianity, somewhere between what was Hauhau and an evolving Ringatū karakia (service).

Te Kooti's religion centred on the Psalms of David, the warrior-king who delivered Israel from her enemies; like David, the Rongowhakaata prophet had human failings – notably in the cult leader's habit of taking his followers' wives, and impregnating them (according to the testimony of a witness, this was Te Kooti's claimed obedience to divine rather than carnal imperatives).[38] His followers were often reputed to be in fear of him, and the account from which this is taken makes plain the power he exerted on potential defaulters: judgement would come upon those who faltered, from the hand of the Atua himself (God).

The prophet's visionary persona marks him out as a charismatic leader who could attract and organise a faithful following: above all, he was a *Māori* spiritual leader at a time when Pākehā authorities (including the clergy) were seen by Tūhoe and other disenfranchised Māori as mortal enemies who sought their demise. His creation of a Māori-friendly liturgical practice – 'Te Kooti's karakia' – combined the power of the Psalms of David with a Māori preference for the oral performance of spiritually significant material, along with a prodigious ability to recite vast amounts of Old Testament prayer and praise from memory. He appeared prophetically at a moment of deep disillusionment and anger: Captain Porter's diary at this time gives a graphic account of how Tūhoe felt.

There is little doubt that what was witnessed by Porter would have applied to Tutakangahau, who may well have been present on February 19th at Maungapōhatu, when the diarist records several chiefs as expressing 'perpetual hatred of the Pakeha'.[39] The entry details their response to Major Wahawaha who they welcomed 'for [his] own sake' while distrusting intensely the government he served. They pointed out that he might be deceived, not knowing what was 'hidden in the heart' of his masters. They were willing to accept peace terms – 'the *rongo pai*' – but would not be moved to the coast like other Tūhoe hapū: 'we will remain in our kaingas, lest, when all the wild cows are collected by the tame ones, you the Kawana should turn and destroy all, tame and wild' (i.e. the surrendered, along with those still resisting). They protested that Te Kooti was no longer amongst them, and said if he was found, Ropata and his forces should 'spare [him] as you spare us. We are cautious of the action of the Government.' Wahawaha replied that he would not be serving the government 'if [he] thought there was an after intention' (i.e. a hidden agenda).[40]

In spite of this deep distrust, Tūhoe were thus forced into dealing with the government, who in the following two years adopted a policy of pacifying the Urewera. In Tutakangahau's backyard, this took the form of building military outposts, strategic hamlets similar to the policy employed later (from 1961 to 1964) by United States forces in Vietnam. The ultimate betrayal for Tamakaimoana and Tutakangahau was when Major Wahawaha occupied Maungapōhatu and Ruatāhuna in October and November 1871, turning both into government outposts: a traditional sign of conquest, and an insult they would never have agreed to. He named the Maungapōhatu redoubt Kohitau ('gather the years', a reference to the lengthy pursuit of Te Kooti), while Ruatāhuna became Kohimarama ('gather the months', his closing in on the quarry).[41] Never mind that it was a Māori who had stamped his authority on them: the shame and the anger would have centred on the flag that now flew over Maungapōhatu – the settlers' Union Jack.

Ropata persuaded four hundred suspicious Tūhoe to come together and meet him at Ruatāhuna, to repair the damage done to the relationship between them and Ngāti Porou. All the leading chiefs were there including Tutakangahau, hearing men like Te Puehu (a former bitter foe of the settlers) declare he would have nothing more to do with 'Te Kooti, Kereopa or other evil men'. James Cowan states in this account that the two sides 'established friendly relations, which were never broken'; Best's account is not so sanguine, claiming that Tūhoe were only co-operating with the hunt for the fugitives 'in order to get rid of the hated Ngati-Porou'.[42] The man who would later become Best's informant was learning the harsh price of military defeat: the necessary arts of compromise and negotiation, which would become an essential part of his armoury in dealing with the government and its agents in the following decades.

Such compromises began to appear in November 1871, when agreements were made in a compact between the Urewera chiefs and the government: they would have their local authority restored if they co-operated in the capture of Te Kooti, or at least helped drive him from their boundaries. Te Purewa, Tutakangahau's senior at Maungapōhatu, had written on this matter to Ormond in Napier, and he had replied: 'This word of yours is accepted & it is to you the Govt. will look in future for the regulation of affairs at Maungapohatu. What is meant is that goodwill shall exist between your people & the Govt. & that Kooti and other evilly disposed people shall be given up.'[43]

Ormond had also proposed to the chief (Te) Makarini (on November 20th) that a road be constructed from Wairoa via Waikaremoana to Ruatāhuna, opening the way for a mail service, with the contract to go to his people. This long-term strategy of roads and mail runs providing employment was designed to open up the Urewera to land purchase, while avoiding the costly and damaging policy of internal policing by such as Ropata Wahawaha. Many Tūhoe resisted the ploy right up until and after Best's arrival as road quartermaster in 1895, but the Trojan horse policy would succeed.[44] Orderlies who carried the mail were attached to the respective chiefs, providing some regular income; Tutakangahau was involved as late as 1906, organising the Ruatāhuna–Te Whāiti contract until it was taken off him for his support of the prophet Rua Kenana.[45]

After the capture of Kereopa in November 1871, the noose tightened around Te Kooti, as Tūhoe ambivalence towards him was exploited: the various chiefs felt differently, some wanting him gone and others retaining loyalty. The overriding tension for them lay in the fact that, however undesirable his presence had become, he was still viewed as a patriot in the matter of the defence of land. Te Kooti's 'whai i te motu – flight across the land' ended for Tūhoe on 15 May 1872, when he crossed into the King Country territory of Rewi Maniapoto, by which time the major chiefs of Tūhoe had been manoeuvred into a working relationship with the government.

For many Tūhoe, his influence did not cease in his absence, as what became the Ringatū faith developed around him in exile amongst Maniapoto, where he was eventually given a pardon in 1883 in the second stage of his self-mythologising career: the pardoned prophet.[46] His elusiveness had conferred a charisma the government could not extinguish, and his doctrines and practices were carried back in amongst Tūhoe, some of whom, including Tutakangahau, did not desert him. They had been betrayed by church and state, and were among the visitors who streamed into his base at Te Kuiti, some for healing prayer, and others to learn of his newly forged faith. This spread widely, helped by Te Kooti's letter-writing activities, to communities from Tarawera to Te Whāiti.

There was fertile ground already broken in Tūhoe experience for the propagation of the Ringatū faith: Hauhau/Pai Mārire had shown them the possibility of a missionary-free Māori Christian derivative, and there was no problematic theological divide between the passing of one and the rise of the other. Culturally, this was Māori in charge of their spiritual literacy, and even some missionaries were quick to observe that settler land hunger, war, and government betrayal of the hopes of the 1850s had left the door open to the millennial prophets. Tutakangahau's involvement in what became known as Te Kooti's karakia was to shape his life in the years of negotiation ahead, after guns were again laid down and diplomacy became the only viable weapon for Tūhoe leaders.

Contemporary accounts make plain the religious and civil milieu in which the mature Tutakangahau now found himself. Hetaraka Te Wakaunua (no friend of Te Kooti) had noted the prophet's influence amongst Ngāti Huri a year after he had left the Urewera. Writing of the Maungapōhatu hapū to Ormond and Russell in December 1873, he stated, 'Kia mohio korua kaore he tangata o konei e whakahaere ana i nga ture a te Kawanatanga, kore rawa atu kia kotahi – You both should be aware nobody hereabouts is keeping to the laws of the Government, not a single one'.[47] This assessment does not imply anarchy, but rather that Tutakangahau's hapū were running their own affairs, including their choice of religious practice.

Missionaries such as Thomas Grace were clear-eyed about the spread of an indigenous Christianity, controlled by Māori, for Māori, based in Old Testament metaphors of a chosen people, persecuted by remote authority, exiled tribes, warrior-kings and prophets – all tending to exclude the suffering, redemptive Christ. Visiting Ōpōtiki in 1877, Grace observed that 'Colonisation, war, Confiscation . . . have followed each other in quick succession', noting that the expectations of the Treaty of Waitangi were dashed, and missionaries such as himself were seen as complicit in a global scheme to divest Māori of their lands.[48] He saw that they had assumed 'the entire management of their own spiritual affairs', looking upon such as him 'with distrust and suspicion'. Rather than reverting to 'Heathenism' as the missionary societies might fear, they were instead forging their own form of biblical faith.

This is crucial to grasp: those today who blame the missionaries for their attempts to destroy and displace Māori culture and belief, replacing it with supposedly civilised values, need to reassess the agency Māori had to choose their own past, present and future models. Te Kooti's blend of traditional and contemporary influences was not a retreat to the past, but an attempt to engage with the present, and create new cultural forms. Maungapōhatu was singled out by Bishop Leonard Williams in the same year as an active centre of 'Te Kooti's form of worship', placing Tutakangahau at the centre of the new faith amongst Tūhoe. On a diocesan expedition through the Urewera, he pointed out the sway of Te Kooti's influence, where 'the notion . . . that the missionaries had acted a deceitful part towards them' had taken a firm hold.[49] In spite of the hostility he chronicles, he received manaakitanga at Tāwhana, 'a genuine old-fashioned Maori hospitality', noting the zeal and promptness with which his hosts practised the Old Testament prayers that comprised the bulk of Te Kooti's karakia.

There is little doubt of Tutakangahau's involvement in such worship: as a former fighting companion of the exiled prophet, he would accompany him on his return visits to the Urewera. Distinctions between religion and the temporal realm were not applicable to Māori society at that time; the prophet's influence can be seen in the appearance of his syncretic religion in the newly formed organs of Tūhoe civil society, such as Te Whitu Tekau. This council of elders began to develop from the 1870s onwards, in order to administer Tūhoe affairs and organise their responses to the government. An early example of local self-government, Te Whitu Tekau – The Seventy, a biblical reference to Moses and his elders – was established in 1872, and will be discussed shortly. Te Kooti's influence amongst Tūhoe was noted at a meeting of the council in March 1874 by Herbert Brabant, the resident magistrate at Ōpōtiki, where the prophet's karakia were used to open the gathering. In a report to the Native Minister, he remarks that 'at the Uriwera meeting at Ruatahuna, one of the Ngatihuri, named Paumata, conducted service, morning and evening, according to what is called "Te Kooti's *karakia*". It consisted, as far as I heard, of chanting portions of the Psalms of David and saying prayers, some of which I recognised as extracted from the English Prayer Book.'[50]

Ngāti Huri were Tamakaimoana, Tutakangahau's people – making this the best evidence we have of him involved in the practice of what became Ringatū, and in what Pākehā at the time construed as the practice of Māori religion in the civil domain (which is why Brabant thought the matter worthy of comment to the Minister of Native Affairs). Te Kooti was banished and neutered militarily, but his influence was still pervasive – and troubling. Brabant notes in the same report that this meeting of the Urewera peoples was part of 'the only political movement of any importance' in the past year, aiming to persuade neighbouring tribes ('especially Whakatohea') to join them in 'demanding the return of the confiscated lands', and to become part of a 'land league, by which the Urewera were to be the guardians of the "*papa tipu*" [hereditary land] of all the tribes who joined them'. The object was to 'prevent road-making, selling and leasing of land, &c.', which they called a '"Union of Mataatua", a league of tribes who are supposed to have come to New Zealand in that traditional canoe'.[51] This short report lays out the shaping forces of Tutakangahau's later life: Māori religion, the return of confiscated lands, and mana motuhake (local autonomy) for Tūhoe and their relatives.

Tutakangahau would remain entangled in the prophet's life and concerns, and he in theirs, until his death in 1893. He appeared with the pardoned Te Kooti for a meeting with the Native Minister Ballance at Kihikihi in February 1885, to discuss a land grant at Ōrakau. Te Kooti had tried unsuccessfully to get back amongst his own Rongowhakaata people at Tūranga, and now looked for other land to settle on. Land already granted at Ōrakau to Te Rangihiroa of Tarawera was flood prone, and Te Kooti protested: 'Am I an eel, that I should have been placed by Mr Bryce in the water to reside?'[52] He was supported in this by 'Tu Takangahau of Uriwera' who 'seconded the request of the previous speaker, that some day land might be given them, instead of the swamp at Orakau'.

Ballance responded to the Tūhoe leader's words, saying Tutakangahau had quoted him to the effect that 'the Government have no wish to interfere with Maori religion'. The Minister had meant what he said, that 'the Government would protect you in the exercise of your religion' – this response in the light of Tutakangahau's comments about Te Kooti and his people travelling to the East Coast, the object of which was 'affection, and the making of the people one, and religion'. Te Kooti then replied that the road he intended to travel was that laid down by Bryce, Ballance's predecessor as Native Minister: 'your word to me, and affection, and the making of one, and Christianity'. What this apparently amiable exchange reveals is Tutakangahau's intimate involvement with Te Kooti's mission to return to the East Coast amongst his sworn enemies, and his advocacy of religious and civil freedoms for the former 'rebels', that the architect of Ringatū and his principal supporters might have the opportunity to practise and promulgate their faith.

Tutakangahau appears here as both a religious and civil leader: in defending Te Kooti's rights, he was also defending his own and Tūhoe's, symbolised in 1888 with the opening of Te Whai-a-te-motu meeting house for the prophet at Ruatāhuna, and his reopening and consecration of the wharenui in February 1891.[53] 'The pursuit across the land', the name given to the wharenui, spoke of Te Kooti's running battle with the government forces. His presence there – both in the name of the meeting

A mist-shrouded Te Whai-a-te-motu meeting house, Ruatāhuna, as it is today.
Author photograph

house and in person when he came – was a reminder of the need to hold on to that land and not to sell cheaply, which he warned them against. Many other meeting houses for the Ringatū faith were built for the prophet, but he was never to return to Tūranga and his people, dying on land he had finally been granted at Te Karaka near Te Wainui in the Bay of Plenty on 17 April 1893.

There is no record of Tutakangahau's reaction to the loss of his leader and co-religionist; a mere two years later he would meet Elsdon Best and a new phase of his life would begin. Whatever needs the relationship with the prophet had met may have been carried over, in some form or another, into the relationship with this Pākehā power broker. What did he learn from his experience as a follower and supporter of Te Kooti? Certainly, there was the realisation by the early 1870s that the settler government could no longer be resisted by force of arms; as Te Kooti was to prophesy, it was only by an appeal to the law, te ture, that they might find a moral weapon in their efforts to regain the raupatu (confiscated lands).

In the process of negotiations with Pākehā authorities, Tutakangahau absorbed the need to make relationships with their power – something that also enhanced his own standing – and marked him as open to the benefits of the modern world. As a member of Te Whitu Tekau, the Tūhoe arm of self-government from the 1870s onwards, the Tamakaimoana chief would aim at obtaining the more desirable fruits of Te Ao Mārama (literacy, schools, roads, mail runs, etc.), while maintaining as much control as possible over their own affairs. He must have known in his heart that some land loss was inevitable, even as he joined in the struggle to regain what had been taken illegally and prevent the encroachment of the Native Land Court and uncontrolled sale.

Attempts to chronicle the life of a nineteenth-century Māori leader such as Tutakangahau solely from Māori sources must face the fact that, until the early 1870s, there is very little to go on, and even then, only a few letters in Māori remaining in government and local archives, where the man himself speaks. Nevertheless, from 8 June 1872 onwards, until his death in 1907, there are a number of documents and recorded statements, where he appears in command of a new form of cultural literacy: the letter. Such letters were hardly personal disclosures – they are principally letters to government agents and ministers, to do with land and local autonomy – but they are still the voice of the writer, showing what he was thinking on certain vital issues, providing material open to analysis. As a local leader and a founding member of Te Whitu Tekau, Tutakangahau speaks from the historical record. This body was one of many semi-permanent committees or elected councils which were established at both hapū and tribal level: they were primarily concerned with the basic problem of settling land claims after the wars and preventing further alienation of tribal land by individual members.[54]

Tūhoe met to discuss these issues at Ruatāhuna in June 1872, and as a result, Tutakangahau wrote to Ormond, the government resident at Napier, to inform him of what had occurred. The address he gives on his letter is significant: 'Kohimarama, Ruatahuna', a reference to the outpost established there by Ngāti Porou troops under Wahawaha. Locating himself at the government redoubt, Tutakangahau is sending something of a loyalist signal: these names were hated by local Tūhoe hapū.[55] He writes that 'the Urewera boundaries are joined into one on the 7th June' and gives a list of four major points, amounting to a declaration of autonomy. A council of seventy – Te Whitu Tekau – would conduct their own affairs to the benefit of the tribe and to clarify the law;[56] they would control crime within their boundaries; no land would be sold in their jurisdiction, either to 'Natives or Europeans'; and he made clear their objection to the Native Land Court and surveying activities. Discussions were to be ongoing, but the chief wanted Ormond to ensure the letter would be published in the government gazette. For this he enclosed one pound in payment and requested that the gazette be sent to him, so he could see the news about Tūhoe's desire for mana motuhake (autonomy) was made public, and he also could read of the government's doings.

This is a clear sign of his literacy, and political acumen: by that time, Māori leaders such as Tutakangahau were either literate or left behind. A chief could not afford to eschew writing, and taking an active part in the new culture of the written word enabled both local and national politics to be carried on at a distance, as well as traditionally, kanohi ki te kanohi (face to face). This personal communication – while signalling community concerns – also enabled another facet of human behaviour to emerge: the ability to speak privately with power, and negotiate on one's own behalf, as well as for the group. Literacy – in the form of the letter – would enable Tutakangahau to present the case for Tūhoe in general, but also to distinguish where Ngāti Huri stood on matters where they differed with other hapū – as in their attitude to the vexed question of allowing roads within the Rohe Pōtae (Tūhoe lands). While he stood with others such as Makarini on the return of confiscated lands at Rūātoki and elsewhere (whose letter of September 1872 on this matter was simply filed, Makarini's request in December, rebutted),[57] he was more open than some other Tūhoe leaders on the matter of allowing road making within their boundaries.

In December of that year, along with Hetaraka of Maungapōhatu, Tutakangahau wrote to Ormond and McLean: Ngāti Huri had no objection to roads, but all the other leaders should agree. 'Kai te pai noa atu matou mo nga rori, ara kia rite nga rangatira katoa ki te whakaae kapai hoki kai te kaha ahau ki te korero ki nga rangatira kia rite nga rangatira hoki ki te whakaetia ko nga wahi pai ano na e tata ana ano ki te whakaae.' He was trying to get them to agree to the road and some were close to giving assent.[58] Here are clear early signs of his role as kaitakawaenga (mediator), a self-appointed go-between, which Best was later able to capitalise on. From the 1870s onwards, Tutakangahau was deeply engaged with Pākehā.

This is obvious in another letter sent at the same time to Captain Preece of the Armed Constabulary, who in November 1871 had attempted to push a road through from Fort Galatea, but had been stopped by Paerau's men near Ahikereru.[59] Tutakangahau writes that his people are agreeable to roading, as in his remarks to Ormond and McLean, and asks for paper and envelopes to be sent, along with a reminder to inform Paerau of the papers (panui, government newspapers) Preece is sending to him personally, by an official messenger (aorere, orderly). Clearly he sees himself as a partner in the roading project, despite his earlier letter outlining Tūhoe desires to keep control of their rohe.[60] In the years ahead, the Tamakaimoana chief would increasingly position himself as a Tūhoe insider, but inside also the government's plans.

Preece's road making had historical precedent in the work of Roman imperialism, and the military rule which enforced the Pax Romana. The 'Pax Pākehā' would also be kept with roads having both military and civil purposes. This was to prove a chink in Tūhoe armour and enable breaches to be made in their solidarity: they understood as did the government that roads meant military entrenchment, but also the arrival of a share in the material prosperity and the improved communications other iwi could now access. The interests of one hapū with another might not always coincide: a new solidarity had been forced upon Tūhoe by the threat of settler power, but old rivalries and territorial disputes would not disappear completely. A situation would develop over the next twenty years where an increasing tension between land loss through lease and sale conflicted with baulked desires to have the confiscated lands returned. Tūhoe resistance to road making, as part of a wider resistance to external governance and subjection to outside control, was gradually undermined by the attractions of wage labour, improved communications, trade and schooling.

Donald McLean's Native Councils Bill had initially encouraged Tutakangahau, as he followed the parliamentary debates in the gazette copies he had paid for, but any likely support of the Rohe Pōtae was lost when hostility from the Pākehā parliamentarians saw the bill withdrawn.[61] Tūhoe continued to claim their confiscated land and the government as consistently repulsed them. A major hui was held at Ruatāhuna on 23 to 24 March 1874, with raupatu land the agenda: McLean the Native Minister, Locke and Preece were invited, but only Brabant the Ōpōtiki resident magistrate arrived. Tutakangahau and Paerau argued for the 1866 confiscation line to be moved back (seawards): 'let it be agreed that it shall be moved', but Brabant told the hui that the land confiscations were not negotiable.

Concern was also expressed over government leasing practices, aimed at breaking down Tūhoe unity in a form of 'conquest by purchase' (leases often included a lien to buy). The paramount chief Kereru put the Tūhoe case bluntly: 'I adhere to my boundary. I and the *ture* will be strong enough to move the line. I shall carry it to Auckland, to Wellington, even to the other side of the water. I shall be right because *the law is on my side*. The Government stole the land . . . The Government said they took the land for our fault: we never committed any fault.'[62] The sense of injustice and the appeal to the law is obvious here, but the omens for Tūhoe were not good.

On 30 March, at a meeting there with Ferris, Locke and the journalist Price immediately following, with upwards of 700 in attendance, Locke told the assembled chiefs it would be impossible to keep the Urewera tribal boundaries intact. Leases with Ngāti Whare and Ngāti Manawa were already in place on their western borders – Pākehā incursions were well under way and irreversible. He completed the impasse by saying there was no need for 'the council of Seventy, or Maori Committee', which had no legal standing. If there were any disputes, they should be taken to the Native Land Court.[63] The recourse to law by a Māori minority – and the way it favoured the settler majority – was to haunt the remainder of Tutakangahau's political career.

His position as a moderate and power broker is clear in the early strife over leases, from 1874 onwards. Land leased to Swindley by Rakuraku and Wepiha Apanui at Raungaehe and Te Waimana in August of that year led to 'such a furore from Te Whitu Tekau' that the owners returned his money.[64] Yet Tutakangahau wrote to Brabant a month later saying his people would accept the lease, promising to call a hui at Ruatāhuna to argue for leases 'within the Rohe Pōtae, and to obtain schools within their borders, and a road'.[65] This willingness to compromise shows a man standing on the line between past and future: desirous to avoid being swallowed by settler power, yet anxious to avert being left behind in the wake of modernity's transformation of the old Māori world.

This meant a gamble, based on his awareness of the benefits and the risks of engagement; it was also true that the authority to lease lands and approve roading were acts of mana that demonstrated his status, and could bring benefits to his hapū. Maintaining the support and approval of his people and fellow leaders, as well as gaining favour and approval from the settler government, was a creative tension within which he had to exist. Hoping to lease land and yet retain control of settler incursions was an act of faith, and one that went against the evidence of Pākehā dealings with other tribes outside of Tūhoe boundaries – in reality, there was little choice. He must have felt that, sooner or later, the government would have its way; the choice he faced was how much involvement he and other Tūhoe should have in trying to manage and influence what shape this would take.

Men like Tutakangahau and other Māori leaders of his era, faced with engagement or retreat, were confronted with the bitter choices that ensued from military weakness. It was this experience of active engagement that made him so accessible to Best in his mission to record 'ancient lore', as opposed to any imagined dynamic of conservative withdrawal by such older Māori, assumed by Percy Smith and others in the Polynesian Society during the 1890s. Tutakangahau was a moderniser who had early lived traditionally – not an 'old-time Māori'. There *were* no old-time Māori by the 1870s, let alone 1895, when Best arrived in the Urewera. The Tamakaimoana chief was able to pass on what he knew of the old world because of his place in the new dispensation, attached as he was by this time to Pākehā power and culture.

It was here that the role of literacy counted most: letter writing, having his views disseminated in Māori and Pākehā publications, reading newspapers and parliamentary debates on land and law. Te Ao Mārama – the new world of modernity – had become his living culture. Culture is always 'now', organic, in the moment, continuous with 'then', but like any living process, unable to return to a former time, as if a river could flow backwards. Because he too lived in such a present, was literate and forward-looking, and not the backward-gazing sage of Pākehā romanticism, his psychology fixed by oral modes of transmission, alongside Best Tutakangahau would co-author a new literature of the Māori world.

In the years leading up to Best's arrival and their meeting, he was always active politically: he was present in 1891 when the Governor, Lord Onslow, met with Tūhoe leaders at Rūātoki, invited to hear men like Rakuraku remind his distinguished guest that government laws were not permitted in the Rohe Pōtae. The chief was harking back to the oral compact forged with McLean at Whakatāne twenty years earlier, on 15 April 1872.[66] Tutakangahau had been present there too, at the forefront of political activity after the failure of military action to forestall the settler government's incursions into Tūhoe territory. In those two decades before Best would meet and talk with him, he had become an established political mediator and a religious figure involved in both major indigenous Māori Christian movements, Pai Mārire and Ringatū. He was well versed in the

Paipera Tapu (Holy Bible) held by an ancestor figure, Rongopai, Ringatū meeting house porch, Waituhi.
Author photograph, courtesy of Albert Horsfall

politics of land loss, and the voicing of long-standing grievances to the deaf ears of the settler government.

Even before the establishment of Te Whitu Tekau in 1872, his role had changed from that of a hereditary fighting chief established by mana and enmeshed in tapu to that of a literate local politician, changed by the times, increasingly involved in a system which at root aimed to transfer land from Māori to settler. His later years of involvement with Best and the ethnographer's project of recovery and preservation were also the period of his final political role – as a commissioner in the Urewera Native District Reserve, where he would experience ultimate disillusionment with Pākehā power in the last decade of his life.

CHAPTER SIX

Best Matures: From Parihaka to the Polynesian Society, 1874–1892

When Best arrived in Poverty Bay in 1874 to work on the farm of his sister Isabel and her husband, Robert Macdougall, he was a mere seventeen years old. Freed from the hated confines of Wellington offices and respectable attire, he found himself living on newly settled land along the Turanganui River, amongst Māori and settlers for whom the conflicts involving Te Kooti and the government forces were recent, and still raw in the memory.[1] A mere ninety kilometres from his brother-in-law's farm, the Tūhoe chiefs would meet that same year in March at Ruatāhuna in an early vain attempt of Te Whitu Tekau to bring the government to the table over land confiscation. The lives of Best and Tutakangahau were slowly beginning to converge, but it would be twenty more years before this callow Pākehā youth, absorbed in his 'hobby' of amateur Māori studies, would meet the Tūhoe elder who was to prove so vital in the professional development of Best's ethnographic instincts. By day, the teenage adventurer earned his keep as a roustabout on Macdougall's cattle farm, honing and developing his skills as a bushman, as more land was cleared and brought into pasture. In the evenings and during any spare time he was granted, or could snatch, Best pursued his hobby of folklore studies amongst his books, with local Māori, in the relics of wars old and new.

Sequestered in his hut, where he jealously guarded his privacy, Best revived his career as an autodidactic amateur ethnologist: he mixed with Māori and began to learn again the language he had picked up as a child around Tawa Flat. He explored the sites of older inter-tribal wars, and at times, desecrated the evidence of more recent battles (he later admitted using 'the great puriri pillars from the famous Waerenga-a-hika pa for strainer posts').[2] With his sister as company to maintain the family bond, and his favourite pastimes close to hand, Best was able to recreate a semblance of the childhood world he had enjoyed around Grasslees Farm at Tawa.

By 1877, twenty and toughened by three years as a farm labourer, he struck out on his own and became a bush contractor – just in time for a severe recession to shrink contracts and throw many such ventures into idleness. Never one to rest, he dodged the prospect of unemployment by volunteering for the newly formed Armed Constabulary force – a cross between the police and the military – to go to Taranaki to deal with increasing Māori resistance on contested land, particularly the Waimate plains, which Ngāti Ruanui claimed had never been sold. With Number Six and later Number Two companies at Pungarehu, he pursued his interests in exploring the area, polishing his language with Māori members of the constabulary and local hapū – and making contact with two resident Pākehā authorities on matters Māori, Stephenson Percy Smith and Edward Tregear.

Meeting this pair of influential Māoriphiles was to change the direction of Best's life: recognising his flair for the language and a shared fascination with Māori history and origins, they began to supply him with books written by their forerunners, missionary collectors such as the Rev. Richard Taylor, whose *Te Ika a Maui, or New Zealand and its inhabitants* they pressed upon him. His sister Edith had married Captain Walter Gudgeon, another with an interest in Māori history, who also happened to be an officer

Shawl Party, 1879: Armed Constabulary, Taranaki.
Photographer unknown, Museum of New Zealand Te Papa Tongarewa, B.002029

in the Armed Constabulary. In his company, Best took part in the now infamous raid on Parihaka in November 1881. Te Whiti-o-Rongomai and Tohu Kakahi, the leaders of the community, had earlier been followers of Te Ua Haumene, going on to develop their own brand of Pai Mārire, in a very early form of passive resistance to the settler government's policies on land acquisition.

Part of the job of an Armed Constable was road making; ploughing and fencing the new roads was the Parihaka community's response. Conflict was inevitable: the Parihaka expeditionary force assembled, the pā was sacked, the leaders imprisoned and the community forcibly dispersed in the weeks that followed, to home kāinga such as Wanganui and Waitara – leaving a small rump of locals on the fringes of the ruined town. 'On the 22 November when the last batch of prisoners was marched away over 2,200 had passed through Bryce's hands. Only twenty had left voluntarily, some 1600 were scattered across hundreds of miles of pakeha-dominated territory and 600 were allowed to remain.'[3]

Pictured around 1880 in his Taranaki bush-fighter's kit, Best looks every inch the aggressive, determined colonial enforcer: attired in long boots, tartan bush kilt and Māori shoulder cloak, he gazes back at the camera a

Elsdon Best, in bush fighter's kilt and fighting cloak: Armed Constabulary, Taranaki, *c.* 1880.
Alexander Turnbull Library, Wellington, NZ, PAColl-8066-01-49-1

fit and lean adventurer of twenty-six. One hundred and thirty years later, in an era long since educated by Dick Scott's radical 1954 exposé *The Parihaka Story* (republished as *Ask That Mountain*, in 1975), many are now aware of the flagrant abuses of power and the racist underpinnings of attitudes prevailing in Best's day. It seems difficult to reconcile how a man who seemed so dedicated to understanding the Māori world, and as time went by, committing his life to preserving accounts of their culture and history in the pre-contact era, could so willingly take part in destroying their hold on the present.

It is the tension inherent in this apparent contradiction that drives the narration of a life like Best's: what kind of person would be so dedicated to preserving the past history of Māori at the expense of their living descendants – what is it that makes him so human, flawed and interesting? Much is explained by the intellectual climate of the times, the conflict of ideas and beliefs taking place in this colonial setting, beginning with Best's heated objections to the Rev. Richard Taylor's anthropological thinking in the book mentioned earlier, *Te Ika a Maui* (1870). This is the site of what George Stocking has called 'the central intellectual problem' of the 1860s: anthropology.[4] Why did Best react so violently to the missionary's account of Māori culture?

The intellectual and anthropological controversies that came to a head shortly after Best was born, shaping his adult thinking, date in the main from the publication of Darwin's *Origin of Species* (1859) and the appearance in 1871 of *The Descent of Man*. The publication of 'the *Origin* in 1859 focused a whole range of developing knowledge in the biological and historical sciences on the question of the origin and the antiquity of mankind and human civilisation'.[5] This focus on origins, the biological descent of humankind and their cultural ascent (or otherwise), was the global framework out of which New Zealand debates on Māori origins and culture arose and developed.

It was intellectual challenges such as these that animated the research lives of Smith, Tregear and Best – these frontier savants who saw themselves as pioneers in the 'noble science of anthropology'[6] as it grew in power and prestige, explaining human origins, and putting paid to religious 'superstitions'. As committed colonial ethnographers, these men were determined to carve a place for New Zealand thinkers in the developing 'science of savages'.[7] They saw themselves taking primitive societies seriously as an object of scholarly discourse (in this case, Māori) – unlike the missionaries, who seemed intent on stamping out immoral behaviour whatever its meaning in the cultures they evangelised, with no intention of understanding what they wanted to destroy and replace.

This caricature of the various behaviours and attitudes of missionaries over time was very much the position Best was to take after 1879, when he obtained, devoured and rabidly annotated his own copy of *Te Ika a Maui*, Taylor's missionary ethnography of Māori. He set out on a personal crusade to set the missionaries straight – hardly surprising, given the climate of the times. Revealed religions – those monotheisms whose God was seen and understood both in nature and in sacred texts

– were increasingly pressured by the conclusions that could be drawn from Darwin's theories. God was not needed to start the universe and create biological life, nor was humanity in some special category of creation. Human progress became linked to the existence of racial cultural superiority and the diffusion or spread of ideas and techniques; in the case of polygenist arguments, there were said to exist 'aboriginally distinct and permanently unequal' human racial species.[8]

The Archbishop of Dublin could argue in 1857 that peoples found in savagery had degenerated from a higher culture originally conferred by divine intervention (and were examples of the biblical Fall). Other writers such as the increasingly influential Edward Tylor saw our common human ancestors progressing from savagery to the existing level of Western Victorian culture in a continuous process that may have seen some local reversals, but was in fact always tending upwards.[9] His *Primitive Culture* (1871) refuted Whately's degenerationalist argument, particularly in denying the need for any external supernatural intervention, explaining the evolution of religious beliefs as governed by the same order of laws that maintained in the natural world.[10] It was out of this milieu that Best's anti-Christian polemic would develop, framing his view not only

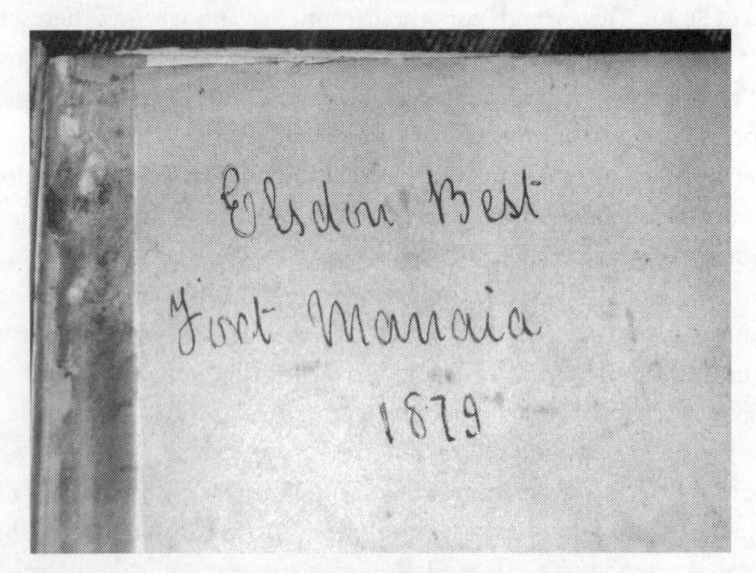

Elsdon Best's signature in his personal copy of the Rev. Richard Taylor's *Te Ika a Maui, or New Zealand and its inhabitants* (2nd edition, 1870).
Author photograph, by kind permission of Warwick Jordan

of revealed religion, but also the process by which Māori in particular came to develop their spirituality through an intimate relationship with the natural world and a dependence on remaining in balance with its unseen, malevolent forces.

On the front endpaper of Best's personal copy of *Te Ika a Maui* he had written in his backward-leaning copperplate hand, 'Elsdon Best Fort Manaia 1879' – fixing the time and the place he had acquired this historic work of missionary ethnography. This was only the beginning of the young Armed Constable's annotations: fresh from 'baiting hostiles' at his base in the military outpost he notes as his residence, at night and in his spare moments he engaged in another war. In this conflict, he used a sharp pencil to attack the Rev. Taylor's assumptions on human origins, based in a biblical anthropology that derived all humanity from Adam and Eve. Best's marginalia are heated and passionate: mocking Taylor's assertion on page 66 of the work (that vestiges of 'puerile myths' common in other religious traditions could not 'invalidate the scriptural account of man's creation'), the ethnographer in embryo snorts, 'And this man Taylor an M.A.!'[11]

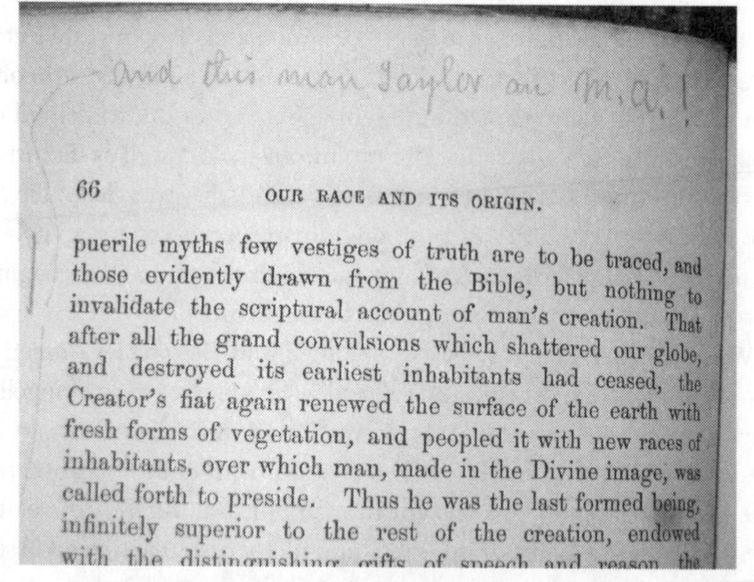

And this man Taylor an M.A.!

66 OUR RACE AND ITS ORIGIN.

puerile myths few vestiges of truth are to be traced, and those evidently drawn from the Bible, but nothing to invalidate the scriptural account of man's creation. That after all the grand convulsions which shattered our globe, and destroyed its earliest inhabitants had ceased, the Creator's fiat again renewed the surface of the earth with fresh forms of vegetation, and peopled it with new races of inhabitants, over which man, made in the Divine image, was called forth to preside. Thus he was the last formed being, infinitely superior to the rest of the creation, endowed with the distinguishing gifts of speech and reason, the

Best's annotation on page 66 of his copy of Taylor's *Te Ika a Maui*: 'And this man Taylor an M.A!'
Author photograph, by kind permission of Warwick Jordan

The man was indeed a Master of Arts: Richard Taylor (1805–1873) was an Anglican missionary who had been present at the signing of the Treaty in 1840 and by 1843 had begun a long career as an evangelist and peacemaker in the Wanganui area. He was often unpopular with the settlers for championing Māori points of view; culturally, his views were assimilationist: Māori would benefit from contact with – and inclusion in – a Christian civilisation. He was, like Colenso, an assiduous collector and ethnographer with wide interests in botany and geology, who kept up with developments in the battle of ideas described above. Along with his evangelical calling, Taylor was a gifted artist and something of a gentleman scholar; he was present in Māori society at a time of great change, a witness to – and recorder of – the powerful artefacts of the tapu world, so radically destabilised by modernity and Christian literacy.[12]

His main contribution to New Zealand ethnography, *Te Ika a Maui, or New Zealand and its inhabitants*, was first published in 1855, the same year that Sir George Grey's *Polynesian Mythology* appeared – the year before Best's birth. The book came four years before Darwin's *Origins*, without the chapter 'Our Race and its Origins' seen in the 1870 edition which Best possessed. This new chapter was clearly a response to the debate that had unfolded since the 1855 edition and Darwin's intellectual time bomb of 1859. Taylor had certainly read the naturalist's theories and other 'speculations of the present age', and set out to defend the creationist position and refute the evolutionists.[13] As well as discussing Darwin on 'Species . . . natural selection . . . [and] the struggle for life', he also mentions Crawfurd's theories on human species variety, a vital cog in the developing racial views of human differentiation and the imagined European superiority over savage and barbarian peoples.[14]

While Taylor had his own views about cultural hierarchies – based on human dispersal after the biblical Fall and Noah's Flood – as an evangelical Christian, he was avowedly monogenist and a degradationalist, in the school of Bishop Whately. Humans came from common ancestors (the biblical parents) and present human cultural differences related to a fall from grace into immorality and idol worship, followed by the various restorations made to humanity's divine image through God's intervention in his engagement with the Jews (Shem's descendants), Japheth (the father of Europeans) and Ham (Africa's ancestor). Taylor argued against humanity's original state of savagery – which contradicts the biblical account – noting that many sections of the 'human family have fallen from civilisation into barbarism . . . Maori is an example, he has retrograded'.[15]

Best annotates these claims with exclamation and question marks: 'Can this man be serious? What does he mean?' Among the milder forms of textual comment, 'Rot! Bosh! Rubbish! Not reliable!' pepper the margins, as the reader of Best's copy senses a barely contained contempt and rage that makes for fascinating viewing. As Taylor goes on to argue for the origins of all peoples in Chaldea, and Polynesians specifically, in Assyria, Best simply scribbles over the offending passages. When Māori (descended from Ham) are said to have enslaved '[New Zealand's] first sable colonists [Moriori]', for Taylor they have simply acted like Shem and Japheth's descendants (like the Europeans who had enslaved Africans). Best scrawls all this out, unable to follow the missionary's argument – which is based on the operation of Noah's curse on Ham in the Book of Genesis, after his son had revealed the nakedness of his drunken father to his two brothers.[16]

Evangelical anthropology derives from the scattering of Noah's sons into the wider world; Taylor was looking for origins and parallels in the Pacific, to locate his Māori brethren in the divine plan of salvation being worked out all around him. Best's anticlericalism would not allow him to see where the missionary was coming from; it is ironic that he would later espouse the pre-Māori presence of a Melanesian people, and agree with Taylor's rationalisation of European colonisation, pointing to the enslavement by Māori of Moriori and other Melanesian arrivals: those first 'sable colonists'.[17] Best would also become a supporter of the Chaldean origins of Māori, as the Aryan Māori of Edward Tregear and the Semitic Māori of the missionaries jostled for a place in the ongoing debate on Polynesian origins.

Taylor had divine history on his side in his mission to New Zealand: he was the agent of God's plan for human redemption, part of an evangelical awakening that had swept England and America in the late eighteenth and early nineteenth century, giving fresh impetus to worldwide evangelism. The growth of European colonial expansion consequent upon fresh explorations of Africa and the Pacific opened a door for the missionaries, as had the Mediterranean Pax Romana for the evangelists of the Early Church. The light Taylor was bringing to the Māori as descendants of Ham was as an English son of Japheth, 'in the office of the world's teacher, the great dispenser of God's will'.[18] If anything was guaranteed to enrage Best, it was a world-view such as this – he attacked it with relish and not a little bile. This latter claim is scrawled out in its entirety. Taylor's examination of Māori religious imagery, where he attempts to relate the death of Maui to the fall of Adam and Eve, while discussing the propitiatory sacrifice of Christ in comparison to Māori expiatory practices, has Best throwing up his hands in despair: 'Alas! The trail of the missionary is over it all.'[19]

There is some light relief to be had as the tyro ethnographer combs the older man's work for sins of omission and commission. When Taylor sums up his views on the origins of Māori religion, he lets slip an anachronism: whether Māori beliefs came from the West or the East, via the 'Suez or Panama' – there were arguments both ways. Best swoops: 'It came by Panama on the old "Nevada".' His jibe at Taylor's error reveals a side that appears in his later journalism, and keeps things from getting too serious even in his 'magnum opus', *Tuhoe: The Children of the Mist* (1925). The hard-bitten wisecracker is never far from the surface with Best, along with liberal doses of sarcasm for fools he refuses to suffer, gladly or otherwise. The value of this commentary on Taylor is in what it tells us about Best's position at the beginning of his amateur ethnographic training. To him, the biblical accounts of creation and human dispersal were merely 'Western myths and superstitions' – so why would Taylor want to introduce them into the discussion of Māori society?[20] By telling the reader what he does *not* accept, Best implies what he does. This is confirmed as his career develops in the 1890s, after he has worked in America, read far more widely in the available anthropological literature, and begun to contribute to it.

From his earlier reading of Chambers, Best was exposed to a racialised view of human progress, where an Indian birthplace of a single human ancestor group had led eventually to the arrival of a superior Caucasian type that now headed the evolutionary ladder of progress. Chambers' diffusionism (where the European race enlightened the 'childhood' of the savages next door) was a commonplace for Best in the 1880s. At that point he did not accept the three-wave theory of New Zealand's colonisation (Melanesian–Māori–European), but would be found arguing for this in later life. Māori displacement of Moriori, for instance, has remained to this day a seductive rationalisation of why Pākehā arriving on the next boat after Māori were justified in doing the same to tangata whenua.[21] He does not appear yet to have read one of his important later influences, the founder of Victorian anthropology Edward Tylor, whose major works, *Primitive Culture* (1871) and *Anthropology* (1881), became defining influences in the next decade and a half, along with F. Max Müller, whose *Anthropological Religion* (1892) was one of the more powerful shapers of his thinking. Best's view of himself as ethnographer-in-embryo, someone fascinated by human culture – and in this case, Māori customs and history – and an extreme anticlerical observer at that, was firmly set by the time he left Taranaki and two years later, in 1883, set off for America.

Taylor's attempts to find elements of kinship between Māori and Europeans were not so very different from a route Best would later travel, in arguing for the pre-Pākehā worship of a god named Io, the 'Maori Supreme Being'. At the time he was annotating Taylor, such a linking of European beliefs to those of Māori was a weakness that for Best disqualified missionaries from practising ethnography. Best appears to have genuinely wished to study Māori as they were (and had been), and to have valued what they had to tell him; nevertheless, he would inevitably bring a distorting lens to the work. There is an irony in his rejection of missionary thinking, in that he did not practise ethnography on the missionaries as well, to attempt to understand their relationship with and value for Māori in the present. To enter a rationalist modernity, he distanced himself from any thought of special revelation and the biblical anthropology of humanity.

At that same historical moment, Māori were managing their entrance into the modern world through the door Best was exiting: Christian literacy and biblical anthropology. He missed the significance of contemporary Māori experience in his search for an essentialised 'Maori mind' – a supposed mysterious and primeval psychology existing prior to European contact, persisting right through to his own day, untouched by half a century of Pākehā influence. This irony is further sharpened as it becomes obvious that his maturing view of himself as a social scientist was belied by an emerging transcendentalist religious temperament – finding his spirituality in Nature itself. The passion and commitment of this autodidact – so necessary at a time when there was no university training available – had a major weakness: an inability to step outside his own viewpoint and subject his evolving ideas to the scrutiny of others wiser and better read. The way he was quickly lionised by the older Māoriphiles, Smith and Tregear, and his own sense of inferiority, the class-based chip on his shoulder seen in the sneer at Taylor's MA degree, were to prove handicaps in his later career. His next adventure – a journey to the United States and his sojourn there (1883–1886) – would furnish him with fresh perspectives, and not a little hardship and danger.[22]

Returning to Poverty Bay in 1883, after discharge from the Armed Constabulary, Best endured a wet winter that brought with it the deaths of two of his sisters: Edith, Gudgeon's wife (of tuberculosis); then his favourite, Katherine, who had caught the disease nursing Edith, nine months later.[23] These personal tragedies were compounded when his brother-in-law Macdougall decided to sell up and leave New Zealand for a cattle-ranching adventure in Argentina – taking Isabel with him.

The twenty-seven-year-old Best, his only intimate female relationships gone, answered the depression induced by these losses by hatching a plan to follow his sister to Argentina. He set to work learning Spanish to help him on his arrival there. According to Craig, he mastered the language 'by mother-wit and with the help of a few simple books'. As unlikely as this sounds, Best did indeed acquire a facility with Spanish, at least in the written form: while out of the country, he read works of ethnography by Spanish writers, particularly those concerned with their colonial presence in the Philippines. Best's first published article in the newly founded *Journal of the Polynesian Society* in 1892 would be entitled 'The Races of the Philippines'.[24]

After arriving in San Francisco late in 1883, trying and failing in Hawai'i en route to impress the local women selling souvenirs with his knowledge of Māori, in the midst of high local unemployment he found work in the tough logging camps of northern California. He also worked as a ranch hand, and later in sawmills, where he deliberately absorbed as much as he could of American expertise in their mill machinery and techniques, to take home to New Zealand. His long-term plan was to cross the border into Mexico and make his way south to find Isabel and her husband in Argentina.

After some close shaves in Texas with locals who objected to his criticisms of their attitudes to 'their Negro neighbours' (he had to flee a lynch party in one encounter), and contracting yellow fever, he spent six months recuperating at the great World Fair in New Orleans in 1885. This huge event, the centennial of the cotton trade in the South, was also known as The World's Industrial and Cotton Centennial Exposition. Backed with a massive loan of one million dollars from the United States government – sited on 245 acres, with the Main Building alone occupying 33 of those – this city-size hymn to Progress must have had quite an effect on Best, a backwoodsman who up until that point had been living the life of that mythic American pioneer, the legendary Johnny Appleseed.

Like many of the other expositions that mushroomed over the modernising West in its colonies and upstart republics from the mid-nineteenth century onwards, the New Orleans extravaganza was a celebration of mercantile confidence. The power to run this temporary metropolis was switched on in Washington by the President himself: the Government Building, the Horticultural Hall, the Art Building and the Mexican Building all whirred into independent steam-generated electrical life, with endless lighted displays of engineering, manufactured goods and cultural artefacts. For the restless Best to remain in one place from November 1884 to March 1885, there must have been an almost inexhaustible supply of education and entertainment on hand.

Quite what the bush-happy farm boy from Tawa Flat took away from this experience of American civilisation's display of self-confidence, we do not know. Leaving this artificial world-within-a-world, that could be entered by railway, steamboat or ocean-going ship, he too might well have been reinforced with the same sense of technological and cultural superiority such massive exhibitions were designed to celebrate. As the Mayor of New Orleans had trumpeted on the grand opening day: 'This exposition marks a new epoch in the history of this country, and we may say in the history of the world . . . that [nations] may learn they have only one interest – the progress of the human race.'[25] What the African slaves whose sweat and misery had provided the riches thus celebrated – and the displaced Indian tribes on whose land the exhibition stood – might have replied to this belief in progress is not recorded in this *New York Times* report. Soon after leaving and travelling back west at the start of his journey home, Best was to see first-hand the results of American internal colonialism on the native peoples whose territories he passed through.

Fleeing the local taxman by the time-honoured expedient of hopping a freight train, Best returned westward towards San Francisco; after first attempting to cross the Mexican border south of El Paso, he was forced to go back to New Orleans by United States Army troops, in the midst of a war with Apache tribesmen. His observations of some of the Native American settlements he passed through were not positive: 'the degraded savages of the American West' interested him principally for links he thought he saw between American Indian and Māori cultural practices, such as the facial tattooing of women. Returning west again, any hopes of reaching Isabel via Mexico dashed, he passed through Pueblo territory and reached Reno in time to hear of the devastating Tarawera eruption in June 1886. After working his passage home on the *Mariposa*, this 'brake tourist' of the American West now found himself in Auckland virtually penniless, and looking to start again.

From his experiences as roustabout and observer of late nineteenth-century life in the United States, Best brought back with him a leather Texan cowboy outfit, a growing certainty that primitive peoples were doomed by the march of civilisation, and the confirmation of his Parihaka experience: that troublesome 'hostiles' with messianic tendencies were best dealt with by a dose of 'lead poisoning'.[26] These twin aspects of his character – compassion towards the bearers of a doomed traditional way of life, yet hostility for those native peoples who adapted Christian elements in new forms of resistance – seemed set at this point. This is the Best who would come to revere Tutakangahau as one of the last authentic old-time Māori – and yet despise Rua Kenana, his kin and inheritor, who by adapting to change had lost an imagined authentic Māori essence.

Over the next five years, Best and his brother Walter set up a sawmilling operation west of the Tararua ranges between Waikanae and Ōtaki, using the latest American carriage mill that Best had bought from suppliers in

Timber workers sawing logs in the bush, early 1900s.
Photographer unknown, Alexander Turnbull Library, Wellington, NZ, PAColl-8066-05-01-2

America – but the venture was to founder and the mill closed, with the machinery sold off. He had not wasted his spare time, still pursuing his old 'hobby': at night in the bush, he kept up with the latest texts in his studies of the emerging 'science of anthropology'. He was determined to chronicle the disappearance of the old Māori world, recording their vanishing cultural riches. Best's interest in Māori at this time was fundamentally historical: to record their contribution to the human story, while acknowledging their inevitable demise – explaining their extinction on the theoretical basis of European cultural superiority.

He returned to Wellington in 1891, his family dispersed, to find employment as an assistant in a general store. Unhappy as his social situation was, his room at 53 Thorndon Quay was close to the Colonial Museum, where he met Edward Tregear once more, and was introduced to other Māoriphiles such as T. G. Hammond and the Rev. W. L. Williams. With Percy Smith, these men were forming a plan to set up in the following year an organisation that would transform his life and fortunes: the

Polynesian Society. On 8 January 1892 'the first ethnological society in the Southern Hemisphere' was set up with Elsdon Best as a founding member. The 'official' career of New Zealand's first professional fieldworking anthropologist began quietly in the Colonial Museum; from that point on, his peripatetic and eccentric life as a sawmiller and bushman who carried weighty and important books in his swag began to change. As Sorrenson has observed, Best was 'the one man of the group of Polynesian Society enthusiasts who most nearly bridged the gap between amateur and professional . . . [and who would go on to devote] . . . a long stretch of his life to fieldwork'.[27]

For all his lack of formal higher education, and his own low estimation of his abilities, Smith and Tregear saw in Best their greatest hope of retrieving from older Māori the treasures of a dying culture – what he would come to call the 'kura huna' (hidden knowledge). He was intelligent, and battle-hardened by life in the bush; he was fluent in Māori, adding to his learning as he went; he was literate and well educated in both a general sense and in being abreast of the latest in the anthropological publications reaching New Zealand from overseas. Most of all – like them – he was a convinced salvage anthropologist, believing in a time-limited mission available to this committed group of Māoriphiles. Theirs was a window of opportunity, given to record what was left of such esoteric Māori knowledge, before its last authentic holders made their final spiritual leap beyond Reinga. At that same moment, a number of Māori movers and shakers – who would later join forces with Best and Smith in the preservationist project (with a vision of a future for Māori, not their demise) – were also forming into a loose coalition that would attempt to change the status quo for their people.

The Young Māori Party were graduates of Te Aute College in Hawke's Bay, a group of like-minded professionals, academics and politicians including Apirana Ngata, Maui Pomare, James Carroll and Peter Buck. They would advocate a Māori renaissance that began by embracing Pākehā educational and medical advances and continued with a revival of traditional practices in dance, arts and crafts, especially in carving and the reinvention of the communal meeting house on a larger scale. All this adaptation (with its assimilationist outcomes), and recuperation of whatever could be retained as essentially Māori, had the opposite aim from where Best, Smith and the founders of the Polynesian Society began their mission. The two forces would work together in many areas, however, not least in Ngata's support of the final publication of Best's major work, *Tuhoe*, in 1925.

Above all, the birth of the Polynesian Society heralded the arrival of Best as a writer: he had already contributed to local newspapers, with tales of his American adventures and speculations on Polynesian pre-history – media outlets he would continue to use over the next twenty years to supplement his income. In 1892, with his first published article in Volume I of the *Journal of the Polynesian Society*, Best, the scholar of matters Māori anthropological, made his entry into the field of academic writing – albeit he never had been, and never would sit, inside a university.[28] As a Council Member of a 'Society formed to promote the study of the Anthropology, Ethnology, Philology, History and Antiquities of the Polynesian races', he was expected to be a major contributor to the 'publication of an official

Elsdon Best (on left), and Tom Wyatt, members of 'The Old Shebang Club', Cuba Street, Wellington, 1883. The future founders of the Polynesian Society dress up for the work ahead. *Photographer: William Williams, E. R. Williams Collection, Alexander Turnbull Library, Wellington, NZ, G-104197-1/2*

journal' and to support the allied aims of collecting relevant 'books, manuscripts, photographs, relics and other illustrations'.[29]

The subject of his first contribution – 'The Races of the Philippines' – was the direct result of his American adventure, the learning of Spanish, and his pursuit of ethnographic studies and ideas beyond the confines of the field in New Zealand. The article appeared at a critical time in the theorising of Māori studies, where the implied disappearance of a pure Māori gene pool held sway. It was widely accepted that Māori would die out through disease and demoralisation, or be 'bred out' through intermarriage and assimilation. Many of Best's later notions of primitivism and human social evolution are found in this piece – ethnography was a tool he used in making sense of the world, and the relationship of Māori and Pākehā, in finding a language and a framework to discuss their impact on each other. Unpalatable as many of his conclusions and prejudices may seem to the twenty-first-century reader, Best was a man of his times, articulating both the commonplaces of the street corner and the essentials of what was then regarded as an informed theoretical debate on the subject of human origins and progress.

Unimpeded by his lack of tertiary study, Best wrote fluently and confidently at a descriptive level. His analysis of Philippines history and culture relies heavily on the haphazard accumulation of quotes from a variety of authorities, from Crawfurd to Tylor. He identifies two racial groups in the Philippines: the indigenous Aitea and the later arrivals, the Tagalo-Bisaya, both eventually conquered and subjugated by the Spanish, from whose historical and ethnographic accounts he takes his raw material. These 'primitive people', he writes, 'are an interesting study on account of their long isolation in a remote group and it will also be interesting to compare them with the southern branches of the race'. They were interesting in themselves, but also for what he thought they could tell the members of the Polynesian Society about 'Polynesian ethnology' – specifically, anything to do with Māori.

His opening discussion is a précis of the themes that preoccupied most late nineteenth-century Western anthropologists in their schemes of environmental or natural determinism: did nature or culture make the man? Issues of race and race identity, aboriginality and migration, diffusionism and the spread of civilisation, the nature of the primitive, and the equation of civilisation with culture on a comparative ladder of values run through this first serious attempt to make public his views. Underlying his analysis is the notion that if immutable – and inscrutable – laws of 'Nature' could explain cultural difference and value, then the colonial world order could be explained by rational scientific methods. Reason, of course, was that higher faculty predominant in civilised minds that had evolved the power of abstract thought denied to the savage, and only partially present in barbarian societies. There is an echo here of the later displacement theories that were used to justify the European presence in New Zealand: for the Aitea, could be read Maruiwi / Moriori; for the Tagalo-Bisaya, Māori; and for the Spanish, the English colonists of this country.

Best's main concern was to explain the historic situation of the Philippines in terms of the anthropological thinking he had acquired in the previous ten years – all his influences appear, and are given a substantial airing. The racial typologies and migration patterns he discusses go hand in hand with notions of the displacement of inferior cultures by those more advanced. Best had absorbed Tylor's embrace of the comparative method, which implied the psychic unity of humanity, and our progressive advancement in ascending 'culture stages'. This led to an equation of culture with civilisation, and a form of anthropology that was more prescriptive than descriptive. The 'office of ethnography' Tylor opined, was to 'expose the remains of crude old culture which have passed into harmful superstition, and to mark these out for destruction'.[30] These views were inherently moralistic, and dangerous to those classified as savage or barbaric (as were the Aitea and the Tagalo-Bisaya). Colonial situations such as the Philippines – and New Zealand – were believed to contain contemporary pockets of active primitivism. Tylor called these 'primitive survivals', a view that Best adopted in speaking of the Aitea (and later, Tūhoe) as living examples of an earlier stage of development: 'the original state of humanity, the very childhood of the human race'.[31]

The Aitea – and the Tagalo-Bisaya – presented the ethnographer with a golden opportunity to visit one's own human psyche in an earlier stage of cultural evolution, and to witness how progress had overtaken the weaker intellect, devoid of the civilised refinement of abstract reasoning. The essential primitive is defined in this reading: certain features of their savage state rendered them impermeable to change from within or without, so they were frozen in a cultural stasis. The Aitea was 'a savage in the primeval forest and a savage he will remain', unable to 'advance towards a higher state'.

Best addresses here three major defining factors in his view of the primitive mind: the influence of diffusionism, the development of abstract thought, and the psychological determinism that he saw as inevitable in such superabundant natural conditions as existed in the tropics. All of these are vital in the way he would go on to view and analyse Māori history, psychology and religion. Some peoples are doomed to irredeemable savagery: they do not have the ability to raise themselves to a civilised level of culture by either their own efforts or adapting to changing cultural forms imported from outside their territory. This is an inherently racial view of culture and within it can be heard the approaching footfalls of genocide – by malign extermination or benign neglect, the inevitable would occur.

How providence supplies the spark of abstract thought in those races fortunate enough to advance in the arts of civilisation, Best does not tell the reader, nor why some peoples are open to receive the diffusionist waves of new knowledge and others not. The Tagalo-Bisaya he regarded as a more hopeful case who could be placed on a higher rung of evolution than the doomed Aitea, who while 'a particularly interesting race', held on to the 'customs of a remote past . . . in the face of their approaching destiny'. The Tagalo-Bisaya, on the other hand, had made significant intellectual progress, especially in moral and religious matters: they were 'beginning to renounce the old Nature worship . . . [for] a more or less confused idea of a superior religion, of which the central figure was a Supreme Maker'. They were absorbing the doomed Aitea, warped and debased by a nature worship born out of the psychological terrors of the tropical forest.

This was due to the supposed environmental determination of human psychology: primitive peoples in this view were victims of a 'vague feeling of awe . . . of utter helplessness . . . intense loneliness and littleness', oppressed in gloomy forests peopled with malignant spirits, whose 'dark depths' they feared to enter. Not having visited the Aitea or the Tagalo-Bisaya, and relying for his information on Spanish accounts,

Best's description of a religion of terror is of a psychological – not an actual – wilderness. He would soon begin to rectify this lack of substance with fifteen long years spent in the Urewera – but here, for the first time, are the foundations of his psychology of religion. Religions begin in primitive superstition, awaiting the arrival of reason, literacy and scientific explanations of natural phenomena to supersede the need for such beliefs, ranging from animism to monotheism.

Best concludes by addressing the place of religious ideas and systems, as part of a hierarchy of cultural development: humans produce gods or a God according to their level of intellectual progress, and their ability to move beyond mythic archetypes to abstract thought. Those willing to study peoples such as the Aitea and Tagalo-Bisaya will observe 'the struggling intellect of primitive man' moving into 'the dawn of intellectual day'. The key issue regarding cultural survival and change – here, and for his work with Māori later – is what occurs when people classed as savage and barbarian contact those envisaged in this model as civilised.

Best argues that the Philippines example proves that 'rude savages' such as the Aitea are unable to adapt, incapable of new ways of thinking, whereas the more advanced Tagalo-Bisaya had travelled further 'on the highway that leads from barbarism to a higher culture'. The latter, more open to assimilation, were 'enabled to receive the teaching of the Iberian invaders'. The comparison of these two different responses – as he understood them – would shape his attitude to Māori engagement with Pākehā in the years ahead. His experiences amongst Tūhoe would change his thinking – to a large degree, through personal contacts and the friendships he made with the more important informants such as Tutakangahau and Paitini. This hierarchic, ahistorical view of human social development however, would remain as a distorting mirror, even as he found himself in the midst of men he would view as his equals, and betters.

Best's first foray into what was a form of academic publication would link him into international 'webs of influence'; he became part of a colonial intellectual marketplace which Ballantyne has described as an 'imperial system of circulation, recovering the transmission of ideas, information and identities across the empire'.[32] Colonial ethnographers like Best were now being read by the great men they so admired,

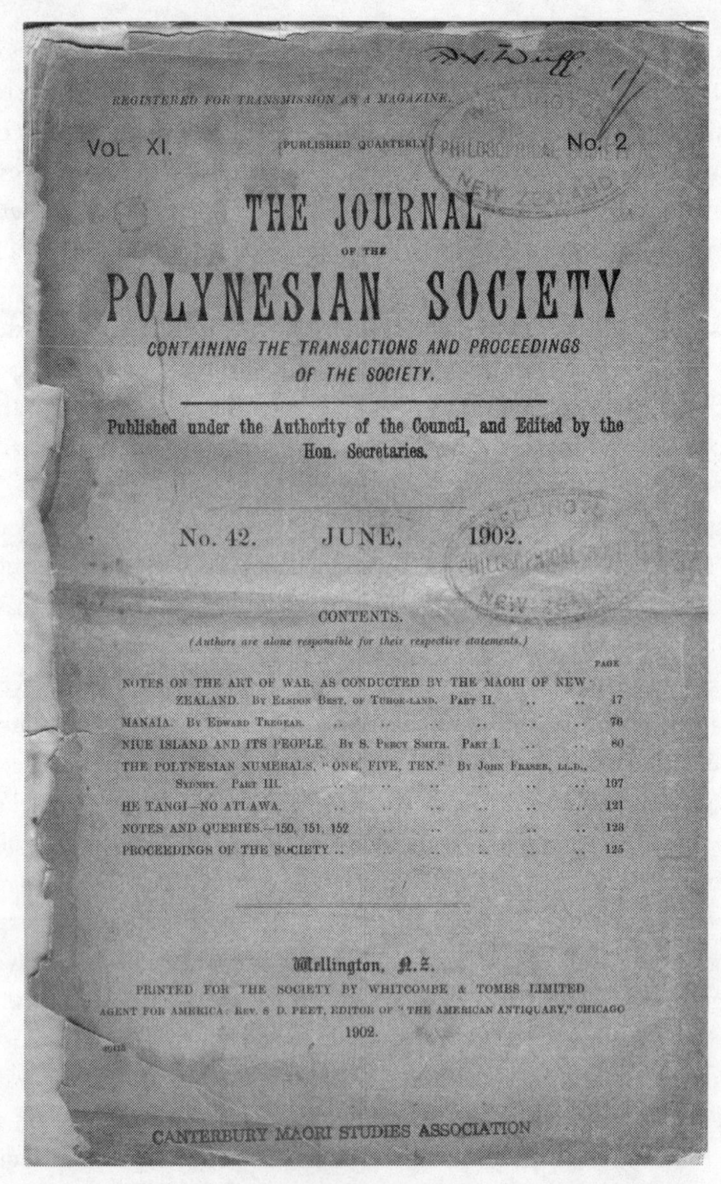

REGISTERED FOR TRANSMISSION AS A MAGAZINE.

VOL. XI. [PUBLISHED QUARTERLY] No. 2

THE JOURNAL

OF THE

POLYNESIAN SOCIETY

CONTAINING THE TRANSACTIONS AND PROCEEDINGS OF THE SOCIETY.

Published under the Authority of the Council, and Edited by the Hon. Secretaries.

No. 42. JUNE, 1902.

CONTENTS.

(Authors are alone responsible for their respective statements.)

	PAGE
NOTES ON THE ART OF WAR, AS CONDUCTED BY THE MAORI OF NEW ZEALAND. By Elsdon Best, of Tuhoe-land. Part II.	17
MANAIA. By Edward Tregear.	78
NIUE ISLAND AND ITS PEOPLE. By S. Percy Smith. Part I.	80
THE POLYNESIAN NUMERALS, "ONE, FIVE, TEN." By John Fraser, LL.D., Sydney. Part III.	107
HE TANGI—NO ATI-AWA.	121
NOTES AND QUERIES.—150, 151, 152	123
PROCEEDINGS OF THE SOCIETY	125

Wellington, N.Z.

PRINTED FOR THE SOCIETY BY WHITCOMBE & TOMBS LIMITED

AGENT FOR AMERICA: REV. S. D. PEET, EDITOR OF "THE AMERICAN ANTIQUARY," CHICAGO

1902.

An early copy of the *Journal of the Polynesian Society* (June 1902, Vol. XI, No. 2), containing Part II of Best's article on Māori warfare.
Author photograph

the European and American 'authorities' such as Edward Tylor, who substituted as professors and guides in an early form of distance learning for these New Zealand frontier scholars who had little or no access to a university education. A key to this Orientalist web and a major influence on Best's thinking into the 1890s was the German linguist and scholar of comparative religion Friedrich Max Müller (1823–1900).

Described as something of 'an academic cult figure', this Professor of Comparative Linguistics at Oxford University achieved a level of fame akin to that enjoyed today by Noam Chomsky, or Joshua Fishman.[33] While he is not specifically mentioned in the Philippines article, Best would certainly have been aware at that time of this famous scholar's work in the fields of philology and comparative religion. Müller had written the preface to the Rev. William Wyatt Gill's 1876 volume *Myths and Songs from the South Pacific* (Gill was a missionary based in the Cook Islands, who Müller had encouraged to publish). Edward Tregear's studies in comparative religion were deeply influenced by Müller's work, and the German's theories of the Aryan origin of humanity and the spread of languages from India are prominent in an article by this close associate of Best, published in 1885: 'The Maori in Asia'.[34]

When Tregear argued there that 'the Maori has crystallized his speech in that mode which the primitive Aryans used, perhaps 4,000, perhaps 6,000 years ago', and followed this assertion with a long list of words comparing those of the Sanskrit with Māori, he was acting as a faithful student of the master, Müller. This was also a technique Best and others in the field would employ, without the training in philology (linguistics) that might have enabled them to think critically about its shortcomings. Müller's prime contributions to Best's ideas about primitivism and abstract thought centred on the Oxford scholar's scheme of human progress, based on language, in the unfolding of a universal history. Amongst the phases of human linguistic development, Müller identified a '*Mythological* or *Mythopoeic* Age', an illogical hiatus in the otherwise 'regular progress of the human intellect'.[35] In this period, when the Aryan language existed before 'national separation', there was no abstract thought, the word was the thing itself, the referent; and properly understood, each word would reveal its mythological root: 'the creation of every word was originally a poem, employing a bold metaphor or bright conception'.

For Müller, the great majority of mankind – those not acquainted with Western science – still thought in this primitive way. These children of the mythopoeic age, whose intellectual apparatus did not include the power of abstract thought, were living survivals of a former stage of human progress (as they were for Tylor). Mythology itself was 'only a dialect, an ancient form of language', concerned in the main with nature, and explaining humanity's place in the grand scheme of cosmic events. This myth-making stage was prior to civilised life, and the processes of abstract thought that made such life possible. This analysis provided a convenient framework for Best to differentiate the essential nature of the primitive from the modern – it was not long before his own standard conception, 'the mythopoetic Maori', would appear in the writing he was to undertake on their origins, religion and psychology.

The later Best is steeped in Müller's thinking, citing him liberally in both the general studies such as *The Maori: Pt 1* (1924) and the longer monographs, especially *Maori Religion and Mythology*, Pt 2 (1924, 1982). In the former he acknowledges the great man's preface to Gill's *Myths and Songs from the South Pacific*, while in the latter, Müller's 1892 study, *Anthropological Religion*, is listed amongst the 'Authorities Quoted', and references to Māori and their mythopoetic nature pepper the text (Tylor is cited to similar effect here).[36] A list of Best's personal books noted by Craig in 1964 mentioned a copy of Müller's *Anthropological Religion*, one of the Gifford Lecture Series published in 1892 – complete with annotations by Te Peehi himself.

What a treasure that might have proved for the nation – bearing in mind the revelations of Best's psyche in Taylor's *Te Ika a Maui* – but sadly, his biographer sold the book at auction in 1969, realising a meagre four dollars on the day. This denied the National Library the opportunity to acquire another unique resource (they also failed to buy at auction Best's annotated *Te Ika* in 2003, reasoning the copies held in the Turnbull were sufficient).[37] From the auctioneer's notes on those books sold, we discover Best had initialled Müller's tome 'E.B. 1895' – which dates his purchase of it in the same year he entered the Urewera and made the acquaintance of Tutakangahau.

The contents of this volume – especially Best's use of Müller's expertise in classical Greek in his attempts to define important spiritual terms such as mauri and hau – will receive some attention in the following chapters. The point of this intensive survey of Best's intellectual pedigree up until his fateful journey north to the Urewera and his Tūhoe years is that no ethnographer of his day could have encountered Māori with any kind of objectivity, any more than Māori might have seen him with neutral eyes. The moment Best first spoke with Tutakangahau, his presence was changing the older man's circumstances, and what Best saw. If the Pākehā had a mission of cultural salvage, so too did the Tamakaimoana chief – not the least part of which was to find a way to pass on what he knew to posterity.

Between the two of them, they embodied differing but communicable views of the worlds they shared: Māori Christian literacy, and a desire for both autonomy and inclusion in the colonial polity, met with nascent Pākehā social science and the global reach of Western power and wealth. Within their parallel projects or kaupapa, these two formed an alliance, which became over time a mutually satisfying friendship. While Tutakangahau's journey to maturity had begun in tradition and an oral universe, transformed by the power of the biblical Word, Best was the child of its opposite: an evolutionist's rationalism grown out of a scientific model of the universe. The intellectual armoury derived from the younger man's confident and self-satisfied milieu came face to face with the tarnished millennial hopes of a battle-hardened Tūhoe elder whose lifetime of reading had begun with the ngahere (bush) and continued with the Scriptures.

CHAPTER SEVEN

'Ki tā te Kāwanatanga te mutunga – The Government will have its way in the end'[1]

> Herodotus lived at the junction of two epochs: although the era of written history was beginning, the oral history still predominated.
>
> RYSZARD KAPUSCKINSKI (2007)[2]

The era of written history for all Māori, including Tūhoe, was well under way in the years immediately prior to Best's arrival in the Urewera in 1895. While oral records of both the distant and recent past were still powerful, a new form of literary consciousness had been transforming their world and was about to be laid over the Urewera: the surveyor's map. Ever since Cook had touched these shores with his phenomenal ability to chart the uncharted, and map the unmapped – and later, the Treaty of Waitangi had laid out an assumption of the sovereign power to purchase the new lands thus presented – Māori found themselves facing not just the new technology of the book and the gun, but the intellectual universe out of which had emerged the theodolite.

Such techniques of measurement, in an age of growing military and mercantile confidence, gave the European powers the ability to map the natural world for political and economic ends – to demarcate territory at home and abroad, backed at all times by the advancing technology of modern war. Mapping the world as part of a process of exploration was a precursor to annexation; mapping New Zealand's marine borders proved to be a prelude to an eventual process of internal mapmaking and surveying. The Māori world was divided and conquered by sale and confiscation, and the introduction of individual Pākehā ownership of tracts of their former lands. For good reason, the Treaty of Waitangi was concerned to portray Māori as owners in the new dispensation of British sovereignty, along with guaranteeing their rights to sell first to the Crown – underlying the fine language, however, was a potential real estate deal. For Tūhoe – who had not signed, but were nevertheless not exempt from settler land hunger – the presence of the Native Land Court on their borders and the growing incursions of surveyors were the logical extensions of Cook's journey and project: exploration leading to annexation and the privatisation of communal resources.

As the founders of the Polynesian Society were preparing the first edition of their journal in 1892, Tūhoe hapū – who would be amongst their literary subjects – were facing fresh incursions by the surveyors and mapmakers who had inherited Cook's mantle, this time within the coasts he had charted for his king and country. Land sales had continued amongst other iwi in areas surrounding the Rohe Pōtae, and some leases had occurred within it – but in general, the government had left Tūhoe almost unmolested through the 1880s. Attempts had been made at covert surveys by J. C. Blythe, in 1885, but Tūhoe at Ruatāhuna told him he must do no surveying and they would not allow roads to be made. Best writes that at the time they 'did not wish to have any dealings with the government or with any Europeans'. The feelings of bitterness seen in the 1870s after their defeat and the confiscations were still present, when a carved post had been set up on that boundary at Rūātoki – '*hai arai i te pakeha me āna mahi* – to keep off the white man and his works'.[3] The 'Children of the Mist' appeared to remain staunch while other nearby hapū lost land on their borders.

Nevertheless, cracks were appearing in Tūhoe solidarity by the early 1890s, and the incoming Seddon Liberal government was in a mood to push for the opening up of this last bastion of perceived Māori 'resistance'. Tūhoe were still determined to manage their own affairs, while the government became increasingly determined to bring them under 'the Queen's writ'. Best – when he did finally arrive in search of pre-history – would find himself part of a highly politicised present. In April 1889 the Resident Magistrate Samuel Locke had met leading chiefs – including Tutakangahau – at a hui at Rūātoki to make arrangements to open up the Urewera.[4] Reasons given for the need to do so included the ability to prospect for gold and other minerals and the milling of valuable stands of tōtara. It appears Tūhoe leaders were willing to co-operate, as long as they were in control of persons entering within their boundaries – those which they defined anew in a subsequent letter to the Native Minister.[5]

Gold mining and timber milling also meant roads would be required – a development which many Tūhoe would resist, but over time, more and more would come to welcome. The older leaders could control to some extent the political atmosphere within their boundaries – but they could not easily influence what was happening in the minds and the pockets of those young men who left Tūhoe for seasonal work on shearing

Tutakangahau, a hand-tinted photographic portrait, photographer unknown, *c.* 1900? He holds a ceremonial toki (adze).
Author photograph, courtesy of Tīpene Ohlson, Kaingaroa

gangs in Hawke's Bay and other surrounding areas. Exposure to the world of Pākehā farming technology and the purchases they could make with their earnings in the money economy – along with the less evident but nonetheless powerful contact with other ideas – meant the next generation were having a different experience of the modern world to that of their elders. Having tasted work for money beyond the Urewera, the prospect of paid employment within their home areas would become an expectation and a norm. Work on the roads was just such an opportunity – and local leaders like Tutakangahau could perceive these benefits, as well as the risks they would bring. Whereas inner sanctions could pressure those working a common garden in tribal land, 'no comparable sanctions operated in joining a public works gang'.[6]

Government leaders began to arrive: in 1891, Lord Onslow, the Governor, made the first official visit to meet Tūhoe leaders. Tutakangahau was one of those who had signed the invitation. Earlier in March, at a hui in Ruatāhuna – where Te Kooti was present, for the opening of Te Whai-a-te-motu, the meeting house dedicated to him – a policy excluding surveyors and prospectors had been passed unanimously. Onslow, however, was allowed in to the Urewera by Tūhoe to demonstrate their loyalty to the Queen (as opposed to the settler government), and 'their determination to show their authority over their lands'.[7] Around the same time, just after Onslow's visit – and despite their professed determination to exclude Pākehā – some Tūhoe in the Rūātoki area had lodged an application for what would become a controversial survey of the Rūātoki block. A surveyor named Foster said that this was 'the beginning of the breaking up of the Urewera country' – hoping somewhat naively that it might 'proceed peacefully'.[8] The resulting conflict – amongst Tūhoe themselves, and with government authorities – was a sign of things to come.

Onslow's visit was something of a feint by both parties: for the Governor, to assess the current influence of Te Kooti, if it still existed; for Tūhoe leaders, an opportunity to demonstrate their remaining authority and to put forward to the Queen's representative their grievances over earlier land confiscations. At that point, even major newspapers such as the *New Zealand Herald* and the *Auckland Star* agreed on Tūhoe's rights of ownership, and that it was better in a military sense to let sleeping dogs lie. The *Star*, however, did hint that while 'a community that has proved itself so worthy of self-governing powers ought not to be lightly interfered with', such interference was always possible where 'this *imperium in imperio*' continued.[9] It was to this large territorial power base within the nascent nation-state that the Liberals under Seddon turned their attention, after both Ballance and Te Kooti had died in 1893. The breakdown in Tūhoe solidarity signalled above was to provide the opportunity for the incoming Seddon administration to tame 'the turbulent Tuhoe' – who were patently capable of taming themselves.

For all that the chiefs were to do and say regarding their local powers and overall Tūhoe authority in the Rohe Pōtae, it remained an advantage to them to maintain the alliance of sorts that they had formed in the 1871 agreement with McLean, to manage their own affairs. Many of them (including Tutakangahau) were in receipt of government pensions dating back to that time.[10] In the case of Best's prime informant, the money was to continue being paid – albeit with certain punitive deductions, when he gave his support to Rua Kenana – right up until his death in 1907. Having important leaders on the payroll – however the Tūhoe chiefs regarded this affirmation of their mana – gave the government a significant poker chip in the game that was about to be played out. It was in the chiefs' interests to work both with their own people and the government, some being more willing than others to compromise.

When the surveys began to go ahead at Rūātoki in February 1893, amidst the protests, a few leaders were arrested – and Numia Kereru, a supporter of 'progress', advised the Native Minister to punish them severely. Tutakangahau's daughter was fined for her part in the fracas, after she went into hiding and armed police entered the area. Her father, however, was described by the surveyor Creagh as a man of great influence, 'in favour of opening up the country'. Clearly, it is too easy today to try and simplify this complex situation, when a single issue such as this is seen to be so divisive amongst Tūhoe at that time, both on an inter-hapū level and even here, within a single family.[11]

Whatever Onslow discovered of Te Kooti's ongoing influence – women could be found in Best's day, weeping over his image in a book by Major

Walter Gudgeon – there was now a power vacuum in the Urewera, which the new Premier Seddon moved to exploit.[12] When Best began his relationship with the Tūhoe chief in 1895, Tutakangahau was already cultivating one with another more powerful Pākehā. This had begun face to face when the Premier visited Rūātoki as part of a North Island tour of rural Māori centres in April 1894, to address a series of large hui over land issues. When Seddon had become Premier on the death of Ballance, he also replaced Cadman as Minister of Native Affairs, hoping to win Māori over to trusting the Liberals. He aimed especially at turning Tūhoe from pursuing separatist options, such as an alliance with Kotahitanga, the Māori parliamentary movement that was flourishing in the 1890s.[13] Seddon – in conjunction with the Māori MP James Carroll (Minister Representing the Native Race) – would pursue reforms in Māori land legislation during the 1890s and early 1900s.[14] Bringing Tūhoe under his wing, and obtaining their agreement to the divisive surveys while avoiding further military conflict, was an important part of his reformist agenda.

Seddon was a populist West Coast politician with little experience of Māori and North Island land issues. He nevertheless combined an authoritarian gusto with a natural sympathy for the underdog – while at the same time working to release more land for settlement and employment. His overall aim was to strengthen his grip on office, the results of which would first raise and finally dash all Tūhoe hopes of maintaining autonomy in the Rohe Pōtae. They were anxious to consolidate the earlier verbal agreements with McLean from the 1870s, and gain legal recognition of their status in local self-governance. Carroll was looked to as a representative of their views in Wellington – leading to an invitation to Seddon to come to the Urewera and discuss their concerns, as he had done with other iwi since becoming Native Minister.

In March of 1894, Seddon and Carroll commenced a tour of the remaining Māori landholdings in the North Island, arriving at Rūātoki late in the month. Local leaders Numia Kereru, Heteraka Whakaunua, Tutakangahau and others gathered to meet them. A robust debater unafraid of confrontation, Seddon made clear that he had come to listen and, by coming in person, he was treating them as he would any Pākehā rangatira: they 'should not be afraid to be truthful'.[15] Indeed, he was the first Premier to take the trouble to visit Tūhoe, and the record in the *Appendices to the Journals of the House of Representatives*, on which the following discussion is based, portrays him as listening, at least some of the time. His lengthy replies, however, seem to occupy a disproportionate amount of written space, compared to that accorded his hosts. It is difficult to know quite how the hui was recorded: the writer may well have edited the contributions of the Māori speakers. Whatever occurred, the results are depicted as a fascinating contest of oratory.

Seddon had come with a firm agenda: to loosen the grip of all Māori on their remaining 'under-utilised' lands, and to open them up for further sale, lease and settlement. Pressure from the Pākehā electorate, combined with his own unstoppable paternalism, ensured that his desired outcome would clash with that of most of the assembled Tūhoe. He was aware of the shortcomings of the old Native Land Court, but remained committed to surveys and the establishment of title. Seddon was overseeing the reintroduction of Crown pre-emption, its incorporation under the new Native Land Court Act of that year, and the setting up of Māori as leaseholders, whereby the proceeds of their land sales to the Crown would be invested in the Public Trust and paid out as dividends. His model was the paternalism of a benevolent despot, and however flattered Tūhoe may have been by his arrival for such an important event, they were soon to get a sobering view of his modus operandi. The fulsome welcomes would evaporate, to reveal the steel behind the fine words from Wellington.

Numia Kereru was first to stand and welcome the Premier and was not slow to lace his respect with a warning: 'Some of the remarks that have fallen from you I will eagerly devour, those that are palatable; those that are bitter, I will reject.' This guarded response set the tone – while Tutakangahau, who spoke next, gave a far more effusive greeting:

> Welcome! Welcome! Welcome to you O my parent! Your coming here is what the heart has so earnestly desired, as also that of what I might call the orphans and the poor. It is only by the law that difficulties can be removed and remedies be obtained – that is, through you, who have brought words of love to me, and who represent the law. When the law became established, the evil passed away. . . . The desires of the heart shall be fulfilled; those things that the heart does not desire shall be rejected.

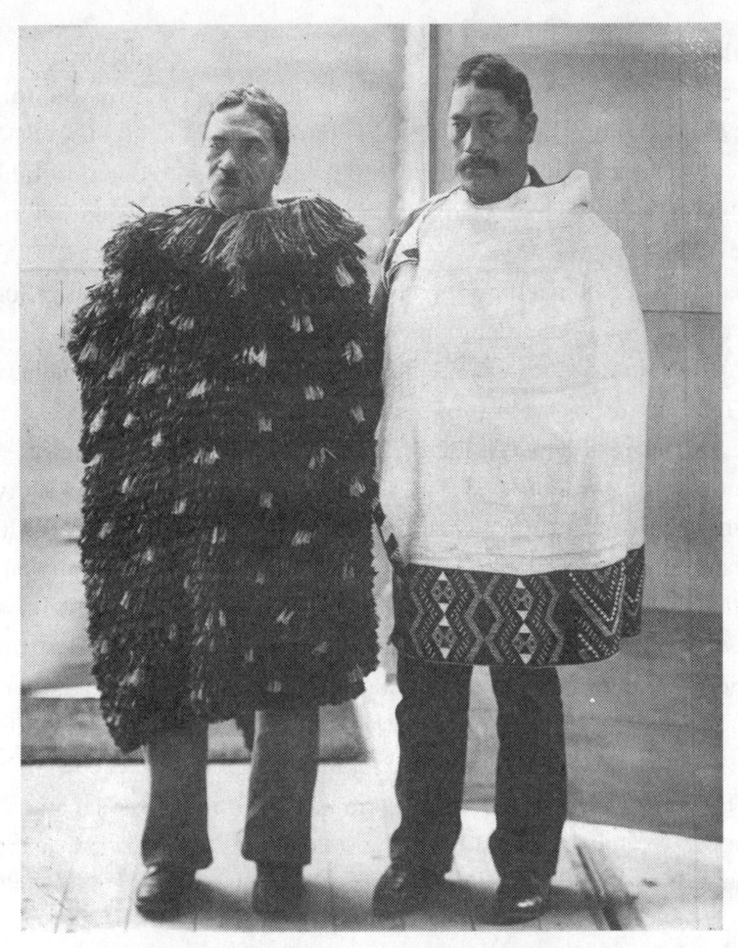

Tutakangahau and Numia Kereru, Tūhoe chiefs, *c*. 1898.
Alexander Turnbull Library, Wellington, NZ, PAColl-7273-07

How rich an item of historical testimony is this late nineteenth-century kōrero by a Māori leader in his seventh decade, one who had lived through all the significant and transformative cultural upheavals and subtle changes that had overtaken Māori since his birth in the 1830s.

He begins by addressing Seddon as his parent, styling himself as an orphan, as one of the poor, in the biblical sense, while conflating the law with the person of the Premier, telling Seddon he is in fact the law's embodiment. We have no way now of knowing just what word Tutakangahau used – translated here as 'represent' – but he certainly implies he expects far more than we today might of a visiting politician.

Tutakangahau is repeating Te Kooti's teachings: from henceforth it is only by the Pākehā's own law that the government itself may be turned back from law-breaking: 'ma te Ture ano te Ture e aki – only the Law will correct the Law'. The law, by implication, is the civil outworking of the biblical law on which Māori at first assumed the European civil codes were based.

Seddon is challenged by the old man on ethical and moral grounds, to act like an Old Testament king (a David, not a Saul) – to look after his people, as would God. Christianity – in the form it had now taken for this Tūhoe leader – was deep in his thinking, and he treats Seddon as if it were also in his. The evil he refers to here as having 'passed away' was the unrestrained killing and war, brought down upon Māori society by the introduction of muskets and rifles, making monstrous traditional warfare, and shaking social stability to its roots. Tutakangahau wanted that same law to protect Tūhoe interests – including his own – and Seddon's presence, in a traditional sense, answered the earnest desire of the heart that the old man highlights. He came from an older world, from his exposure to an era where words had active power, great deeds were done and alliances cemented kanohi ki te kanohi (face to face). Now that the very *person* of the law was present amongst Tūhoe, something authoritative and lasting could and should take place. This verbal appeal to the written law is a moment of consummation in the old man's culture – and in the new Māori world so recently born.

Even so, the old man seasoned his words with a rider resembling Numia's: what he found disagreeable he would not accept. A number of other leaders spoke and sang waiata, including Makarini, who reminded Seddon and Carroll that he had seen Donald McLean in the 1870s, reinforcing the message that Tūhoe had a verbal contract to support the Rohe Pōtae that remained outstanding with any following administration, including Seddon's Liberals. Some spoke out against the arrests of those who had obstructed the surveyors in 1893; still others stood and pledged their loyalty to the government as friends. In reply, James Carroll affirmed that McLean's words 'still live over the land of the Tuhoe people' – and then promptly accused them of straying off the right path since the days of McLean. Those Tūhoe who had fought at Ōrakau 'were swept off the face of the earth': an insult to those who had lost relatives there, and a clear message that military force waited in the wings for those who might harbour thoughts of a resort to arms. It became a kind of 'good cop, bad cop' performance: telling the chiefs that McLean's words still had a moral authority, but threatening them with the same fate as the Ōrakau fighters if they tried to defend what was theirs.

In case that message was not clear, Carroll invited them to show him what was wrong with the hated Native Land Court, when it was clear they were 'allowing the land to lie waste'. The government was looking after their interests: 'Here now is a Government you should propitiate.' As he and Seddon showed their hand, Purewa responded with this astringent mihi: 'salutations to you both, who may destroy my body and my land!'. A stronger challenge came from Numia Te Pukenui Kereru, who gave a sharp-eyed analysis of the destructive work of the Native Land Court. The expense of the surveys, passed on to Māori owners, was turning them into debtors. Seddon, backed by Carroll, replied that Tūhoe would be unable to retain their lands if they were not surveyed; the Māori MP argued that they 'were not in a position to say the land was [theirs] simply because [they] were in possession of it'. The situation so reasonably affirmed by the *New Zealand Herald* and the *Auckland Star* in 1891 – that Tūhoe were capably running their own affairs on traditional lands – no longer seemed to apply. That *imperium in imperio*, a kingdom within, was about to be overruled.

The government feared that any exceptions made for Tūhoe would undermine their overall sovereignty, and letting the people of the Urewera run their own affairs on unsurveyed land would encourage separatist sentiments amongst other disaffected Māori groups such as Kotahitanga. In the midst of the debate, Seddon found he had something of an ally when Tutakangahau spoke again, calling him 'the Premier, the light of the world'. He said that he and Hetaraka Whakaunua and their five hapū had 'already made the first application for a survey', sent to the Surveyor-General Percy Smith (soon to be Best's employer). Not all Tūhoe were opposed: 'It is not that I am objecting to the surveys,' said Tutakangahau. 'No; it is that the chiefs of Tuhoe may be able to proceed in a definite manner in respect of this business.' Even in a public arena such as this, unity was difficult to maintain: Tutakangahau was responsible to his own hapū at Maungapōhatu, as well as to the wider interests of the Mātaatua waka.

Heteraka attempted to buy time by asking Seddon to delay any surveys until after the Tūhoe leaders had been able to come to Wellington, but the Premier would not promise this. Affirming that nothing would proceed without the full knowledge of Tūhoe, he appealed to the needs of the nation and to knowledge itself: Percy Smith was having 'the colony mapped throughout' and it was for 'scientific purposes these topographical surveys are necessary . . . so that in mapping of the colony your country may appear on our plans'. The ghost of Captain James Cook appears to hover over proceedings: the Urewera was to be surveyed in the cause of science, for the advance of knowledge. When the theodolite swung over the Urewera, however, the effect would prove the same as when the carbines of the militia had cast their shadow twenty years earlier. There would be more dispossession, and the gradual loss of whatever local autonomy existed for Tutakangahau and his fellow leaders.

When Seddon left Rūātoki, he took with him Rongokaeke, Kereru's famous taiaha – an important gift cementing the peace, and intended to characterise the iwi's relationship with the government from that day on. He and Carroll proceeded next to Galatea, Te Whāiti, Ruatāhuna and Waikaremoana, taking their opportunities at these hui to play on any rivalries they found existing amongst Tūhoe and their nearest neighbours. The desire for roads and for work and trade would be wedges the government could drive between Tūhoe hapū and surrounding iwi, breaking down the solidarity that had existed up until the 1890s. Moderates like Tutakangahau were a gift to Seddon and his agents. It was no accident that Tutakangahau made contact with Best, and 'adopted' him when he arrived as quartermaster on the Waikaremoana road. A Pākehā who could speak Māori and was dedicated to gathering all the material he could from Tūhoe would have been a rarity at this time – one not to be ignored for the advantages a relationship with him could bring.

From as early as 1872, after his surrender in 1870, Tutakangahau has a history of moderation and negotiation traceable in the literature – proving willing to compromise on such issues as roads and schools. Where others saw the dangers – which were real enough – he seems more open to the opportunities presented by economic and social changes. This is hardly surprising: his had been a life of change and adjustment, since Colenso first stepped onto his father's marae to find a tiny local Bible school in operation, part of the massive social experiment that was to flower from Māori literacy. Such conclusions are not always palatable: men like Tutakangahau can be easily reimagined as freedom fighters in the cause of Māori nationalism, or guardians who reluctantly fed curious Pākehā like Best with selected portions of what constituted Māori knowledge, while taking the deep secrets of their peoples to the grave. When such positions are aligned with the record of what Tutakangahau himself wrote from 1872 to 1906, what he is consistently reported as saying, and the evidence of what he actually did – then it seems more likely that such positions say more about their proponents than they do about the old man in his time.

In these troubled years – the time of Best's residence amongst Tūhoe as a fieldworking ethnographer – Tutakangahau lobbied the Seddon government to protect Tūhoe interests; he also appears at times in the public record seeking to advance his own income, to advantage his son Tukua-i-te-rangi and his own hapū. His pension, from the days of McLean, was increased in December 1895, following his requests in two consecutive letters to Seddon as Native Minister in October and November, after the Premier's visit the previous year. The Secretary replied for Seddon concerning this matter and the request was agreed to: 'ka whakanukuhia ake te utu tau ki te rua tekau ma rima nga pauna i te tau – your pension has been raised to twenty-five pounds per annum'.[16]

Based on today's values, that amount equates to around $2,500 to $3,000 – not a fortune, but an appreciable income at the time, and one that the chief obviously was anxious to protect. Both sides valued their relationship: Tutakangahau was attempting to walk the line between progress and autonomy, while the Premier Seddon and Percy Smith – as Chief Surveyor – were looking to cultivate any local leaders who were open to assisting the surveying and roading of the Urewera. In July of that same year, the Tamakaimona chief had written to Smith to advise him that the trigonometrical station at Maungapōhatu was not yet finished, and spoke of his affection for the survey party: 'E hoa, ka nui toku pai kia Piripi ratou ko wana pakeha – friend, I like Piripi [Phillips] and the Europeans who are with him very much'. He went on: 'Otira hai pakeha tuturu maku hai ruri toku takiwa – however I would like him to be permanently here to make the surveys in my districts'.[17]

This request occurred in a situation involving ongoing disputes amongst Tūhoe about such surveys. Phillips' party had earlier been embroiled in a standoff with Ngāti Whare and others, and were turned back from passing Te Whāiti at the end of the old Galatea road and pressing on to Ruatāhuna. The Rotorua newspaper *The Hot Lakes Chronicle* of 5 June 1895 reported that some Tūhoe feared they would be taxed 'and that the land would ultimately be acquired by the government'. Earlier obstructions of such surveys at Rūātoki had been met with the dispatch of soldiers, as was the case with this incident; plainly, all was not well in the wake of Seddon's recent visit and his premature hopes of peace under the rule of law. Best would enter this tense arena and quickly become embroiled, and in Tutakangahau he would soon find a potential ally.

For Seddon and Percy Smith, the old man was already accommodating: Phillips the surveyor, writing to Smith his boss in the same year concerning the atrocious weather conditions encountered by the ill-advised winter road survey, had this to say about the chief:[18]

> I am happy to be able to report that myself and party were met at every settlement en route with much kindness . . . we luckily got native guides and got names of streams etc. On arrival at Maungapohatu were met by Tutakangahau who housed us and gave us his son as guide to the mountain. [The natives of] Maungapohatu are most loyal and I feel confident no more obstruction will occur there or elsewhere.

His relief is obvious – and the level of co-operation that existed apparent in his following remark, that he had reached agreement to 'erect the station on a good hill some 20 chains inland of the very highest point' – which was near to the site of an urupā (burial ground).

As well as co-operating to advance the surveys, Tutakangahau was active in promoting the rule of law amongst his people and reassuring the power brokers in Wellington that Tūhoe chiefs could exercise control in their areas. As Phillips was writing to Smith, Tutakangahau and a number

Tutakangahau and his son Tukua-i-te-rangi, *c.* 1896, just after Best's arrival in the Urewera. Tukua-i-te-rangi (also known as Pinohi) was his father's right-hand man. *Photographer unknown, Alexander Turnbull Library, Wellington, NZ, PAColl-7273-06*

of other leading men (including Pihopa Tamihana, Te Whatanui and Te Tuhi Pihopa) wrote to Seddon and Carroll with the following salutation: 'Kia ora korua kai arahi i nga iwi e rua i te motu nei i runga i te ture nui o te ao katoa – may you be spared to guide the two races of this land under the great law of this world'.[19] Tutakangahau advised the men in Wellington that he was 'advocating some parts of the law to my hapus and also my children – kai te whakahaere ahau i etahi kupu a te ture ki runga i oku hapu me aku tamariki'. Some of his hapū were listening to him and others were not: they were seeking 'nga matauranga o te motu nei i runga i te kotahitanga o nga tangata maori o te motu nei – information from the Kotahitanga (Native Federation Council of New Zealand)'.

This reply was in response to the Premier's attempts to influence leaders such as Tutakangahau to trust the government, and avoid alliances that would strengthen pan-Māori political movements, such as Kotahitanga and the Kingitanga. In Tutakangahau's case, the argument seemed to have some sway: he wrote here that any expectations that Kotahitanga could help them were unlikely to be fulfilled. He would do all in his power to administer the law in his district: 'ka kaha tonu au ki te whakahaere i etahi kupu o te ture ki runga i oku hapu me oku wahi whenua i roto i tenei rohe'. It is important to note his emphasis on 'the words of the law – i etahi kupu o te ture', which meant far more than implementing local ordinances.

This was indeed the 'great law of the world' he had spoken of at Rūātoki in 1894 – biblically derived standards of civilised behaviour with which Tutakangahau had aligned himself in the hope of retaining the best of both worlds. The letter also mentions his support of road making and further surveys, saying he has charged Te Tuhi Pihopa with the task of explaining these matters to the parliamentarians when he goes to Wellington, bringing back the government's reply. He concludes by writing that he intends to go to Wellington himself on 14 July 1895. These early discussions between Seddon and Tūhoe leaders, and those of a meeting in September of that year, would lead directly to the drafting and passing of the Urewera District Native Reserve Act of the following year, 1896.

While Tutakangahau was not alone in his estimation that co-operation with the government was the inevitable choice, not all who saw the underlying threats to Tūhoe independence were quite so resigned, or accommodating. In late June of 1895, the same Te Tuhi Pihopa mentioned above accompanied the surveyor Wilson from Te Whāiti to Ruatāhuna, where at a local hui the Pākehā faced a vigorous challenge from Paraki on the issue of road building.[20] Te Tuhi supported the government official at this point, saying a road of their own could be useful to Tūhoe, and as things stood, 'ki ta te kawanatanga te mutunga – the Government will have its way in the end'.[21] At a further hui at the Mātaatua meeting house in Ruatāhuna, however, Paraki, along with the chief Te Whenuanui, opposed Wilson and the government. He likened them to deaf pigs whose ears had been torn off by pig-dogs: 'I mohio ahau he waewae he kanohi to te ture kaore ia he tahorehore – I always knew that the law had feet and eyes but I did not know it was also tahorehore (deaf)'. He continued: 'This [condition] is like unto the Government in its determination to have this road made – it is deaf.' Wilson responded by saying he had his instructions and the law was certainly not deaf; Te Whenuanui then warned him that persistence in the surveys would bring further obstruction.

After this passionate standoff, Te Tuhi then records Te Whenuanui's expression of Christian hospitality to the surveyor and his party: 'when an enemy is hungry, feed him – kua karanga ki te matekai tona hoariri'.[22] This richly detailed encounter is typical of the prevailing forces at work in the world of Tutakangahau that Best would enter, with its complex weave of characters and conflicting demands on local leadership. The man who would become Best's major long-term informant was busy making strategic alliances with local Pākehā officials on the ground, and with those at the top in Wellington. Forging another such alliance with Best would have been normal and natural.

Others, such as Paraki and Te Whenuanui, offer both insults and defiance, while in the same breath citing Scripture commending biblical grace towards those they opposed. The mixture seen in this document – Tūhoe oratory freighted with pithy metaphors of bestial power, seasoned with the Apostle Paul's exhortation from the Book of Romans to feed one's enemies – is once more a powerful reminder of the *present* nature of culture, as experienced in the moment, the only place where the past can actually *exist*. This would be part of Best's challenge when he finally arrived in search of 'the old-time Māori': how to reconcile a turbulent present with his mission to find and document an elusive past.

Despite their expressed differences of opinion, some Tūhoe leaders – including Paraki – were eager to accept the invitation to visit Seddon in the capital, made by him at Rūātoki in the previous year. In September of 1895 they travelled to Wellington to meet the Premier and Carroll; due possibly to ill health, it is almost certain that Tutakangahau was not present. He did, however, maintain a close interest in the discussions, which took place over a series of meetings, culminating with a major hui on the 7th of September 1895, when Seddon, Carroll and Wi Pere met with the visiting Tūhoe chiefs.[23]

By late 1895, 'it was agreed that there would be legislative protection for the Urewera District', including the establishment of ownership through means other than the Native Land Court, cost free; hapū authority would be recognised; and the chiefs and their people would 'retain significant . . . local government [and] home rule'. This was to answer Tūhoe demands for ownership and autonomy; Seddon, both romantic and pragmatist, wanted to somehow conserve their estate while developing its potential for mining and tourism. While he acknowledged the chiefs' desire to protect their historic forms of authority, he was committed to electoral democracy for the proposed local committees. This was an implicit threat to powers retained by hereditary leaders.

Carroll dreamed that the Urewera could be reconstituted as the bastion of a remnant culture, the 'last tract of native country in its natural state', where the government might create 'a District in which the natives, the *remnants of the name Maori* could gather themselves together'.[24] Wi Pere, too, wanted 'a territory for the Maori people and the indigenous birds' – further, advising Seddon that he should not take opposition such as the obstruction of surveys too personally. Māori had been sat on for so long, it was understandable they should 'kick and bite and possibly grasp you in the tender parts' – having been 'driven to distraction' by past government actions.[25]

Both Wi Pere and Carroll were exploiting Pākehā sentiments: a wildlife sanctuary and a reserve, where the feared extinction of 'authentic, old-time Māori' and their way of life could be prevented – or at the very least, slowed – and still remain open for inspection by the curious traveller. A Pākehā commissioner was to be appointed to oversee the process of establishing ownership after completion of the surveys, and management at customary hapū level would be formalised with the creation of the local committees.[26] Here was hope for a new system which might placate both Māori and settler interests, as the Native Land Court remained poised to investigate title in the Rūātoki block.

Seddon had made clear he regarded this meeting as having a constitutional nature: it was a link to McLean's 1871 agreement with Te Urewera chiefs. He acknowledged the need in Māori society to honour the spoken word: 'The words of the Government will be kept because *it is the words of the Law itself*, the word of servants of the Queen, who is mother to us all and whose laws we must obey.' He recognised Tūhoe's fear of land losses and promised them 'your lands will not leave you'.[27] He was also taken with Carroll's earlier suggestions of a sanctuary – a kind of Jurassic Park, if you will – a living museum for Tūhoe and the tourist trade. Progress, however, ought not to be impeded: this combative West Coaster, sprung from the goldfields of Kumara, wanted to see individualised prospecting and mining rights retained in any lockup of natural resources. How such powers would devolve was not specified at this point, so the Tūhoe delegation returned home with Seddon's words in their ears: a measure of local self-government conceded in return for the recognition of the Queen's mana.[28]

A letter was composed by Seddon and sent out to the delegation members on September 25th – for them to share with their hapū, and absent leaders such as Tutakangahau. Debate and discussions began immediately, and by the close of Parliament's 1895 session a draft Bill had been circulated, and sent on to Tūhoe in the recess before the 1896 session. The final Bill would pass into law in October of that year, just twelve months after the visit of the chiefs. While Tutakangahau was not in Wellington for this hui, a letter published on 21 September 1895 in the *Auckland Star* shows him to be fully conversant with the meeting's progress.[29]

Beneath the headline 'Urewera Natives: A Friendly Letter', the newspaper reported the arrival of a letter addressed to 'the Premier and the lion, Mr Carroll. The writer is a chief called Tutakanahu [*sic*] . . .'. The political smarts here displayed by the old chief are worth considering: he is making to Seddon, Tūhoe's case (and his own) for peaceful progress, and supporting the intent of the September meeting. He wanted to stay involved in the process. It also shows the widespread Pākehā concern for the absorption of Tūhoe into the body politic, that an Auckland newspaper should see fit to selectively quote from the letter of a little-known Urewera chief, apparently 'giving evidence of the good disposition of the formerly lawless natives' in that district.

According to the *Star*, Tutakangahau expressed pleasure at news brought 'from Wellington by Te Teti'; he agreed with the proposal 'that all Tuhoe and their land should be put under the law, and that the losses that occurred outside the law in the days of foolishness should cease'. He wanted 'young Maoris' to get work on the Queen's roads, and asked

'Ministers to state how many chains are required for it'. He looked to have a post office established at Waimana; for orderlies to carry mail until a regular service was set up. He also mentions the issue of gold prospecting, a matter he had formerly placed in government hands, a 'wish that has not ceased'. This progressive stance makes an interesting contrast to the pleas made by Carroll and Wi Pere for a cultural theme park where old-time Māori might dwell undisturbed as a colonial curiosity. Tutakangahau is actively seeking the fruits of progress, rather than squatting resignedly in some form of Neolithic Bantustan that might somehow replicate the never-existent stasis of an imaginary bygone Māori culture.

Instead, here is a co-operative and ambitious elder who seeks equality: the power to run his own affairs, certainly, but the right to enjoy the good things he sees the modern world has on offer – he is living in the present, and not in the past. The newspaper's implication that Tūhoe wanted to put the land confiscations of the past behind them does not accord with the record, however: wanting losses to cease was allied to the restitution of past losses. The attitude displayed towards the road, the schools and the mail runs is pragmatic: in a modern world, they needed these services, and the economic opportunities they would bring. In Tutakangahau's view, roads were a risk worth taking, and the mail services expedited by them were necessary for him and other Tūhoe leaders to engage in national politics by travel, and prompt access to the latest information. The impression in this article of Tutakangahau as compliant and biddable is politically expedient for the proprietors of the *Star* and its intended audience. The politics of gold, however, were another matter.

While this report undoubtedly edits the contents of Tutakangahau's letter, his interest in gold prospecting in his rohe is a matter of record elsewhere. In January of 1896, Te Tuhi Pihopa and Paraikete Taumutu had written to Percy Smith, reminding him of applications made by 'Tutakangahau and Tukua Te Rangi' to Smith and Cadman 'when you came to Ruatoki' (in 1893). They write 'Te kupu ki a koe e te tumuaki honore mo nga ruri mo *nga mahi koura* i roto i taku rohe potae – the application to you, Chief Surveyor, about surveys and gold prospecting licences in my area', made by the writers, Tutakangahau and his son, to Smith and Cadman at Rūātoki.[30] Not only does Tutakangahau give aid to surveyors, he also has a mind to prospect for gold; Smith's reply for translation advises the writers to contact the Minister of Mines. Plainly, not all Tūhoe were averse to taking advantage of new technologies and income sources.

In June of the same year – not long after he had met Best in the April, and asked Smith for payment to act as his guide around Lake Waikaremoana – Tutakangahau wrote to Seddon, supporting the appointment of a commissioner – 'he tautoko i te komihana'.[31] He vowed that his 'pieces of land within the Rohe Potae' would not be put into the 'hands of the Federated party, but that they should be under the general law – kaore hoki au e pai kia hoatu ki te kotahitanga engari kai raro i te ture nui o te ao katoa'. In the same breath, he asks the Premier to see to it that Europeans with mineral expertise be sent to Maungapōhatu – 'pakeha titiro kohatu i tae nei ki maungapohatu i nga apiha o nga kawana'. This willingness to invite mineralogists – who could assess gold-bearing stone – into his area of influence was applauded by Carroll, who saw the letter and wrote in the margins that Tutakangahau should be congratulated for his desire 'to advance from the darkness of the past into the growing light of civilisation – kia puta mai koe ki te ao marama, a kua mahue atu nga mahi o te wa pouritanga o te tangata'.[32]

These lost expressions of a vanished world – 'te ture nui o te ao katoa' and 'te ao marama', as understood and used by men like Tutakangahau and Carroll – are today more valuable than the gold here in prospect. Along with the heady infatuation of a mechanised modernity, which the Māori politician here lauds, such thinking is a window on the changing culture of the times. The great law of the whole world speaks of Tutakangahau's desire to belong in the new order; to Carroll, it is part of the world of light – literacy, progress – and his hopes of belonging to a civilised prosperity. They stand in the mid-1890s as two very different power brokers for Māori, seeking on their parallel paths to find forms of equality in the new dispensation. This was not about losing one's culture but adjusting to what culture – to what life – essentially is: change and managing change, whatever its pace may be. That the changes they faced brought conflict and demanded compromise was inevitable: this was their world in the here and now.

As Best packed his bags for the Urewera, Tutakangahau and his son were at odds with their neighbours over prospecting and surveying. Tukua

Te Rangi had written to Smith in 1895, making the point that he and his father had broken ranks with Tūhoe – 'naku i wahi nga ture a Tuhoe mo tenei rohe potae, otira na maua ko taku papa Tutakangahau' – by allowing such intrusions.[33] The disagreements that arose from individual hapū taking local advantage opened gaps in solidarity in which the Liberals and Seddon were able to move. Tutakangahau was willing to act alone when it suited him, while trying to remain loyal to the overall strategy of maintaining Tūhoe autonomy. It was a difficult balancing act, as his relationship with Best would also prove to be, bringing him criticism from his own people. Just as he had his own agendas with the government – and pursued them – this 'wiseman, he ruanuku no Tuhoe' would in the next decade cultivate a chosen relationship with the eccentric and driven Pākehā ethnographer, helping to slake Best's thirst to know and record the fabled ways of old. All the while, he was aiming to achieve some significant ends of his own along the way.

CHAPTER EIGHT

Into the Mist: In Search of the 'Mythopoetic Maori'

Ethnography is actively situated *between* powerful systems of meaning.[1]

Mr Best left today for Galatea. (Percy Smith, diary entry, 28th April 1895)[2]

To imagine the departing Elsdon Best, leaving Wellington for the old fort at Galatea in April of 1895, as anything less than a man with a mission – an evangelist with the ethnographic scriptures of his day – would be to see him in a very prosaic light, as simply the new quartermaster for the Waikaremoana road project, his official task. He was far more than that: while he was certainly paid to oversee the provisioning of the road work and the payment of wages, would later serve as a secretary for the Urewera District Native Reserve commissioners, and finally, as a health officer, Best's real purpose was to undertake what Smith had sent him there to do. His task was to find and record the 'kura huna' – the concealed treasure of knowledge – by gaining the confidence of the oldest and wisest men amongst Tūhoe and persuading them to commit what they knew to paper for preservation in the historical record.[3] The kura huna – these two words – would become the touchstone for any

Elsdon Best's Field Box, where he kept his documents and other valuables while working amongst Tūhoe in the Urewera, 1895–1910.
Author photograph, by kind permission of Janet Mackey

form of esoteric or specialised traditional knowledge and practices that remained in his day. This was to be the holy grail of emergent New Zealand anthropology.

Men like Paitini Wi Tapeka, Hamiora Pio, Te Makarini Tamarau – and Tutakangahau – would become his 'faculty' of kaumātua, filling whakapapa books, their 'paipera', throughout the villages, but first he needed to get his feet firmly planted.[4] When Best arrived at Galatea, he stayed at the home of the master of the Native School, Mr Wylie, whose daughter Adelaide would come to share his life when they married some eight years later in December 1903. Initially he concentrated on getting stores for the road works at Waikotikoti packed up to the Whirinaki River.[5] There was tension amongst Tūhoe, due to the presence of members of the Armed Constabulary (with their artillery) who accompanied the party; a confrontation took place when local hapū confiscated the surveyors' instruments. Word was sent to Seddon who dispatched the Native Minister Carroll to mediate; an uneasy peace was restored, but it was clear Best's ethnographic aims, combined with his role as a government agent in the construction of the road, would cause some conflicts of interest in the time ahead.

'Camp of Writer at Heipipi Ruatahuna': image from *Tuhoe: The Children of the Mist* (1925), facing page 11.
Photographer: Elsdon Best

Best's role as Smith's eyes and ears amongst Tūhoe – and by extension, the Polynesian Society's agent – is clearly articulated in his descriptions of the developing relationship with Tutakangahau. While Paitini of Ngāti Maru was one of the first to approach him on his arrival, seeking paid work as his personal guide – a request Best could not grant – it was with the Tamakaimoana chief that he would forge the deepest bonds.[6] The arrival of a Māori-speaking Pākehā to manage the stores on the road would not have been unusual in itself – many government officials in regular contact with Māori were fluent speakers, or at least able to get by; there existed a necessary level of bilingualism on both sides – but few Pākehā officials would have been so interested in talking to Tūhoe about their history and culture.

According to Craig, however, when Tūhoe discovered Best could speak Māori, 'they flocked to see him'.[7] His linguistic abilities in themselves were not the likely attraction; rather, his obvious desire to seek out and record the knowledge of the history held by the tribal elders. That so-called 'darkness of the past – te wa pouritanga o te tangata' spoken of by Carroll was not a subject the majority of Pākehā wanted to explore. Over the previous fifty years, the pressure of shame had been gradually brought to bear on Māori, to reject and abandon their supposedly primitive past with its stereotypical 'savage' customs. Best's interest in Tūhoe, their history, customs and distinctive world-view, was an affirmative reversal of this prevalent attitude.

The evidence of the Smith–Best correspondence over these early months and years – along with the articles and books Best began to publish, full of information he could only have obtained from Tūhoe – raises the question of why would these elders so readily commit to paper for preservation by this strange Pākehā matters pertaining to their history, culture and identity? We have already seen how fragile and conflicted was Tūhoe's relationship with the settler government – the road itself was a political issue and Best was one of those employed to see it go through their territory. To that degree, he was part of the threat seen by many Tūhoe to their autonomy and territorial control. On the other hand, there were some leaders – including Tutakangahau and Numia Kereru – who wanted roads and schools, and actively assisted the process of government surveys and road making.

Part of the answer to the relationship that developed lies in how Tutakangahau – as a representative of his people – might have viewed his present culture and its relationship to the past. As a literate man with political acumen, schools and roads were now part of his world – Te Ao Mārama – as was the perceived need to commit to paper the knowledge he had, that would once have been passed on orally in the old whare takiura (houses of learning). His was a world where his teachers had been both Tūhoe elders – tohunga from a vanished world – and a new breed of missionary catechists. He now stood between what was passing away and what was to come – rapid change was an essential dynamic in his experience of new cultural forms. He knew he must continue to move with the times, and we can infer from his earlier relationship to Seddon and other power brokers that he would have seen Best as an opportunity and not as a threat.

Tutakangahau was already a beneficiary of the money economy, and could see more possibilities for himself and his hapū, with the road improving communications and offering employment – along with the Native Schools equipping the next generation to engage on more equal terms in the Pākehā world. He was well aware of his own political status, both in his role as a Tūhoe leader but also as a player in national politics – as in his references to himself as an upholder of the law, and his reluctance to support pan-Māori aspirations such as Kotahitanga. While Best would search him out to gain access to the past, Tutakangahau needed Best to secure a hold on the present and to prepare for the future. It would have been even more surprising had the older man avoided the Pākehā, and retreated to Maungapōhatu to protect his sacred knowledge from the inquisitive ethnographer.

By initiating contact with Best, and sending the government the bill, Tutakangahau asserted his power and his mana. Paitini's earlier approach makes a similar point, and this was Tutakangahau's backyard: by meeting with Best and taking him under his wing, he took charge of the relationship. What he gave over the next ten years of his life demonstrated not a compliance with what Best wanted, but rather his authority as a self-styled 'wise man of Tuhoe'. Best's dependence on Tutakangahau and other 'mohio' – men of knowledge – was clear from the beginning, and

Tūhoe group: Tutakangahau (second left), Tukua-i-te-rangi (with hat), the chief's daughter-in-law Te Kura, and Te Kokau. Photograph taken at a road camp, possibly near Te Whāiti, *c.* 1896, by Elsdon Best.
Alexander Turnbull Library, Wellington, NZ, PA1-o-1240-12-1

cultivated by him until the last of them died in 1908, two years prior to his leaving the Urewera.

Whatever is known now about developments in the Urewera before and after this period in Tūhoe history, it is clearly patronising these men to insist that they did *not* do what they plainly *did* do – committed vast amounts of knowledge to paper for transmission into literary preservation. Denying their part in the co-authorship of our first store of truly indigenous literature, through a conviction that Tūhoe elders would never have co-operated with perfidious agents of Pākehā power, flies in the face of the written evidence. Nevertheless, it remains true that relationships in colonial anthropology were seldom equal: the very fact that Tutakangahau and others turned to Best and Smith to preserve their history is proof that they did not have equal access to power and the means of literary production.

It has been observed that 'anthropology does not merely apprehend the world in which it is located, but that the colonial world also determines *how* anthropology will apprehend it'.[8] Colonial power structures made such anthropological contacts possible, but men like Best, as participant-observers, seldom examined the effects of the system that gave them access to men such as Tutakangahau, under conditions of radical inequality. The investigations he undertook were 'rooted in an unequal power encounter' that gave him and his peers 'access to cultural and historical information about societies [they] progressively dominated'. Best never became a Pākehā-Māori – 'taking the blanket' as it was characterised – whereas Māori were expected to adapt or die; this asymmetry is part of that same 'dialectic of world power'. While he indeed would share with Tutakangahau 'a sympathetic recording of indigenous forms of life that would otherwise be lost to posterity', he was a powerful agent from the world of change that was bringing about such losses.[9]

Before looking more closely at what these two important figures left on the record about their early contacts, it is important to consider such power differentials – and to avoid the temptation of acting as advocate or apologist for either man. It is our shared humanity with Tutakangahau and Best that attracts us: we know them to be as flawed as we are. It was not uncommon, for instance, for Best to pay his informants, either with cash or in kind, as he informs Smith here: 'I gave Parakiri one of the 50s flour wh. I bought with your £1'.[10] On the very same day, he removes his ethnographer's hat and writes again to Smith in his capacity as road quartermaster, that 'Tutaka Ngahau, a leading man of the Tamakaimoana and Ngai-Tawhaki hapus . . . [is] willing to accompany an exploring party in search of a route for Road'.[11]

That was Best's point of view, but the record also shows that in April, soon after this meeting, Tutakangahau wrote to Percy Smith to say that Best had received Smith's instructions to go to Ruatāhuna and Waikaremoana with a wise man of Tūhoe. He gets to the point: 'Kua ki mai a pehi kia haere au hai hoa mona – Best has asked me to go as his companion'. He goes on: 'Ko au hoki te ruanuku i roto i a Tuhoe, a kua whakae au hai hoa mona – I am the wise man amongst Tuhoe, I have agreed to be his companion'.[12] He suggests that since Smith knows it is appropriate for him to be paid for his services, he can arrange for that payment: 'Kia tika te utu mau e whakarite te utu moku'. He will arrange also for some young men to go with them as companions (as paddlers and

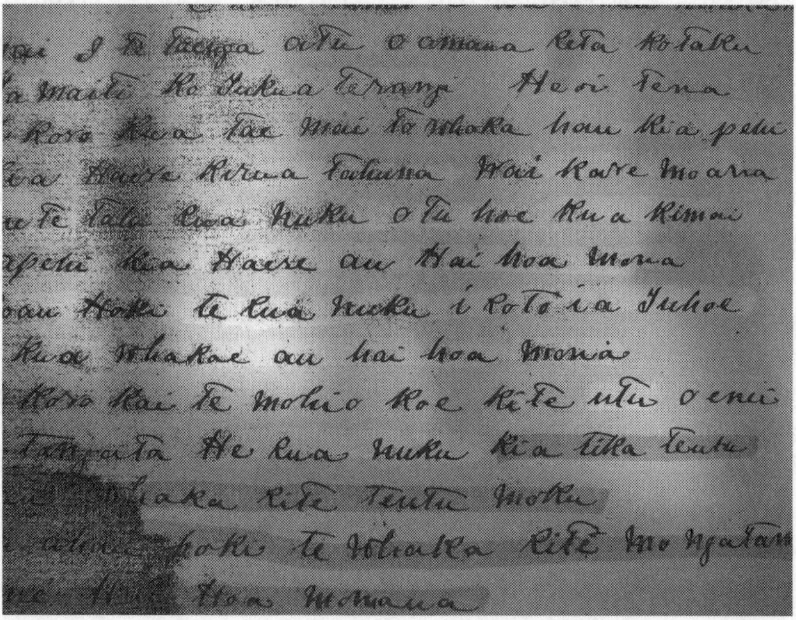
...ai I te taenga atu o a mana reta ...
a maite Ko Tuku a Te rangi Heoi Tena
Koro Kua Tae mai te whaka hau Kia pehi
Kia haere Kia Rua tahuna Wai Kare moana
Te tata Rua nuku o Tu hoe Kua Kimai
a pehi Kia Haere au Hai hoa mona
au Hoki te Rua nuku i roto i a Tuhoe
Kua whakae au hai hoa mona
Koro Kai te mohio Koe Kite utu o enei
Tangata He Rua nuku Kia tika te utu
Whaka rite Teutu moku
... hoki te whaka rite mo ngatam...
... Hoa mo ma na

Letter from Tutakangahau to Percy Smith, 10 April 1896: a Tūhoe 'wise-man' who will go as a guide with Best ('Pehi') to Waikaremoana.
LS-1, 21734, Archives New Zealand/Te Rua Mahara o te Kāwanatanga, Head Office, Wellington

porters) – all of which the government translator abridges thus: 'Asks that he may, as a "wise-man", receive some pay, if he accompanies Mr Best to Waikaremoana to write a description of it.'

This is not simply a request for payment: it is also a declaration of his status and rank. By 29 June 1896 he is writing to both Seddon and Smith, keeping them up with developments and putting in his bill for services to the Surveyor-General. To the Premier he writes at length about the Commission, the road and other matters, extending an invitation for Seddon and the Governor to come and see for themselves the situation at Maungapōhatu, and whether or not the lack of 'i tenei taonga nui i te rori – this inestimable treasure the road' is an inconvenience to his people.[13] This underlines the importance to him of the road: his place in the new world and the view he had of himself as a powerful agent of change was bound up in having access to modern communications. The fact that Seddon and previously the Governor had come to Rūātoki to speak with Tūhoe chiefs gave Tutakangahau the confidence to believe they might come, as had Colenso to this remote marae, to sit and confer as equals.

Of course, they did not accept the invitation, but this is a revealing glimpse into the old man's world at the very moment he is beginning his relationship with Best. The Pākehā writer would paint him in a very different manner in the book that would emerge in 1897 from their forthcoming journey around the lake: *Waikaremoana: The Sea of Rippling Waters*. Tutakangahau's letter to Smith dated the same day states that the orders for he and Best to leave for the lake have arrived: 'ki a maua ko Te pehi kia haere maua ki Waikaremoana'. He then asks for payment to be made to his son who is in Wellington: 'E hoa me hoatu e koe te moni. I whakaturia mai e koe e £5. Hoatu ki a Tukuaterangi hai oranga mona.'[14] The request for money at that point was for financial assistance to his son – in Wellington on his father's and Tūhoe business – to defray whatever it was costing Tukua Te Rangi to stay there, as the letter states: 'for his wellbeing'.

Best was certainly in a high state of expectation as they prepared to set out. His letters to Smith since his arrival the previous year were full of a feverish excitement, especially in the relationship he had begun to make with Tutakangahau, 'a mine of kura and very ngawari'; knowledgeable and obliging, the old man has also promised Best 'to continue writing'.

Along with other Tūhoe elders like Parakiri – who had 'a Paipera written but not yet finished as he is taking it to kaumatuas of diff. tribes to compare & correct' – Tutakangahau was committing to paper the whakapapa that Smith so earnestly desired, to devise a history that would date the arrival of Māori in New Zealand.[15] By February 1896, Best was sending to Smith copies of whakapapa lists made by Tutakangahau showing his complex descent lines. He sounds excited: 'If I get into Ruatahuna with the road I think I can get the best a/c obtainable from the most primitive people of the Maori race in N.Z.'[16]

Such a description reminds us of the anthropological thinking that Best was taking into the Urewera, in the way he frames his informants. 'Primitive' is meant to be a scientific description here, shorthand for the anthropologist Tylor's notion of primitive survivals: traditional cultures now marooned in colonial settings that provided the keen ethnographer with a window on the earliest developmental stages of the human race. Best saw himself as having the capacity to access that psychology; responding to a compliment Smith had paid him about his articles for the *Journal of the Polynesian Society*, he writes: 'E hoa! e hara i a au. But I possess the faculty of thinking as a savage! And can put myself in his place and think as he does. That is it as far as I can explain.'[17]

Best protests it is not really his own efforts, but some atavistic ability to identify with men like Tutakangahau that confers on him a kind of natural empathy – which should restrain our twenty-first-century rush to judgement, equating what are now emotive terms with an assumed ignorant racism. Tūhoe did not come to trust Best without good reason. By 1901 he was writing that 'whenever Hakopa, a withered old warlock of Tuhoe who fought at Orakau, meets me, his invariable greeting is, "Greetings to you, the *ahua* of the men of old". His meaning is that I am the semblance, or am endowed with the personality of the old time Maori, on account of my incessant search after the history, customs, &c., of bygone generations.'[18]

When Best writes that 'Tutaka has written me some grand w. [whakapapa]. He is a fine old chap to get along with . . .', it is not surprising that he concludes: 'Taihoa [wait, be patient], for verily I do believe the kura to be within my grasp. Item. when Galatea Roads are of the pathetic past I shall disappear from the world of light for 1 calendar month and camp with old Tutaka.' The old man appears as a willing partner in their project: Best wanted to get away from the mundane world of roads and stores to obtain from Tutakangahau as much as he could possibly commit to paper. From Best's description in this February letter, the Tamakaimoana chief was bringing him written information which he then copied: '[I] enter it in my Bible so that I can return his book.' He writes that he has also 'sent to Auckland for a strong Day book for [Tutakangahau] as he is much taken by the one I have here'.[19]

Best's use of the terms 'paipera' and 'Bible' to refer to the books in which he and his informants wrote and copied whakapapa and other information is not simply a literary conceit – this kura huna was holy writ to him, and for Tūhoe, written records of their ancestry containing their own spiritual power. The nature and purpose of whakapapa had already changed through literacy and conquest: to prove title to land, such genealogical lists were used by claimants in Native Land Court

19-2-96.
Old Tutaka is in from Maungapohatu
and has given me a Bible. with some
good matter therein. But more of this
anon as the mail is about to leave.
Tamatea-Kai-hauni
" -pokai whenua } one & the same
" -mai Tawhiti } man Tutaka
says. He came fr. Hawaiki in Nukutere.
Is there anything to connect Nukutere
with Horouta?

Letter from Best at Te Whāiti, to Percy Smith in Wellington, 19.2.1896, concerning the whakapapa and history Tutakangahau and other elders were writing down in the exercise books and journals he had provided.
Alexander Turnbull Library, Wellington, NZ, MS-0072-08

sittings. Nevertheless, the need to preserve them must have been a strong imperative, for many Tūhoe to give so readily such material to Best when it provided no legal or fiscal advantage in the matter of land ownership. Something was developing in the relationship between Best and Tutakangahau, which would come into sharper focus when they took their projected trip around the great lake and found themselves alone at the campfire with all of a long night to smoke their pipes and converse.

A majestic inland lake system of 54 square kilometres, 600 metres above sea level and over 250 metres at its deepest point, Lake Waikaremoana and its western arm, Wairau Moana, is an awe-inspiring natural feature that continues to attract those who seek its primeval power, and vistas such as the commanding view from the sacred mountain bluffs of Panekiri. Best and Tutakangahau set out on a journey there sometime in August 1896, ostensibly for Best to write a description of its charms, with – according to Percy Smith – the aim of 'furnishing information to tourists as to the scenes of beauty on the lake'. Smith also trusts that the writer will 'invest the different places with a human interest by preserving the old Maori history relating thereto'.[20] Best's informant will be 'principally . . . the "Kaumatua," so frequently alluded to. This old man, whose name is Tu-taka-ngahau, is the hereditary chief of the Tama-kai-moana section of the Tuhoe tribe.' He has the right by 'birth and education . . . to speak authoritatively on the history of his country'.

And so he does: but for Best, writing a travel book with this kind of brief was a long-awaited opportunity to get into print his years of self-taught anthropological knowledge, albeit through an unconscious filter of nature mysticism and colonial realpolitik. The book weaves together prospects of the sublime Nature so beloved of the Romantics with the blind nature of a deterministic social evolutionism. *Waikaremoana: The Sea of Rippling Waters* is as much a philosophical and political statement as a travelogue, dignifying the takeover of Tūhoe lands under the cloak of crude evolutionary theory. Māori had been militarily defeated and, sooner or later, the tourist road would make manifest their marginalisation and displacement. This is not your average travel book: from the very first page,

Panekiri Bluffs, Lake Waikaremoana, 2008, from the north.
Author photograph

we hear of 'the Kaumatua's' yearning for his 'beloved mountain solitudes' and 'the Pakeha' (Best) struck by 'the glamour of the wilderness'.[21]

The ideological context is from the very beginning one of struggle and dispossession. Along with his 'desire to look upon the unwrought wilderness', Best writes of the imperative to note 'the war that has been waged for untold centuries between it and primitive man – neolithic man' who has acted as a trailblazer for 'the incoming pioneers of the Age of Steel'. Whereas the men of the Stone Age could not conquer the wilderness, the men of steel pass through, 'leaving behind them peace in place of war, thriving hamlets for stockaded pas, and fields of waving grain for jungle and forest'.[22] What is clear from the outset is that 'nature' here owes everything to culture; and the kind of material transfer of lands, forests and fisheries he outlines will be echoed in the book's centrepiece. This consists of a nightlong kōrero – a conversation – between Best and Tutakangahau, where the old man informs the Pākehā interloper that he has guided him there to effect the transfer of the oral kura huna Best was seeking, into the safekeeping of the ethnographer's book. This is the way Best will set it down.

Before this occurs, the book unfolds in its first section as the kind of tourist guide Smith had promised, with local interest and colour provided by the kaumātua. Accompanied by members of the old man's hapū acting as porters, Best is guided around a majestic inland sea rich in historic connection for Tutakangahau and his people. Tramping first to the summit of Huiarau en route to Hereheretaua to connect with the boat and its crew, Best gives the first intimate glances of the old man that had appeared so far in a written form. On the summit, the midwinter snow is deep, obliterating the trail, but 'the Kaumatua . . . trudges on barefoot, with a serene indifference, through the ice-cold snow, dislodging heavy masses of the same from the sturdy bushes as he pushes his way through the thicket'.[23] Here is a picture of a man in his mid-sixties climbing barefoot in winter over ranges that would challenge a fit young tramper today.

Best makes frequent reference in his writings to the astonishing powers of endurance and sheer physical toughness possessed by the Tūhoe mountain hapū of his day. No sluggard himself at a fit forty, his admiration for the older man is plain, as they 'break out on a clear brow at Te Whaka-iringa-o-te-patu-a-Te-Uoro'. With his characteristic dry bush wit, Best explains that it was actually the length of the name that tired them out – the spot where a Tūhoe chief 'some seven generations back' had met a Ngāti Ruapani woman, Te Amohanga. After some discussions as to whose was the land on which they stood (she was from an enemy tribe), love conquered all, and as the name suggests, Te Uoro hung up his patu as a sign of their compact, and their genealogies – so to speak – were soon joined. What Best chooses to pass over here is the clear sexual reference: 'whakairinga' means to elevate (an erection). Te Uoro's patu is a somewhat metaphorical weapon.

Best proceeds in this manner throughout, connecting stories the old man tells him with the geography of the area, alerting the reader to the links between conquest, place, ritual, whakapapa and the ensuing kōrero that link lines of descent to the land. Tutakangahau is physically dramatising these Tūhoe stories in a quintessentially Māori way, by taking Best to the places that are stories *in themselves*, forever peopled by men and by spirits, the living and the dead. The Pākehā repays the honour by placing on record a tangi (lament for the dead) with which the old man breaks the silence as they emerge from the bush to see below them 'the grand panorama of the lower country . . . the voiceless forest, the rugged crags, the shimmering waters – silent, imposing and grand'. 'Standing alone on the cliff brow . . . [he] chants a long wailing lament for his old comrades who have passed on to the Reinga . . . for his ancestors who dwelt and fought here in the long ago.'[24]

Tutakangahau calls to the land and to the hunga mate: the dead whose bones still lie 'beneath dark waters, in the burial caves of old' – men, women and children whom he names: Hatiti, and Toko, 'Children of the Mist' whose villages 'are silent and deserted . . . [their] lands trodden by a strange race'. There is no longer smoke rising from camps around the silent sea and 'I alone of your generation am left . . . of the fighting men of old', though his strength to avenge them has passed away. As his mihi ends, he cries out that he may never return to climb 'this great *ika whenua* [backbone] to greet you. *E noho ra!* (farewell).'[25]

This powerful event is captured very early in the relationship between the two men, dramatising its purpose. Tutakangahau cries out to an invisible world by way of an ancient historical art that calls for prodigious emotional recall; what Best records is what we read later, through the objectifying eye of print. The old man is conscious he is passing from one world to another, and grants Best the chance to be his audience at an essentially private and historic moment. What we have enacted here is orality handing over its power to the written word – this becomes even more apparent later when Best, alone with Tutakangahau at Maahu on Wairau, learns what the kaumātua expects of him.

It was hardly a conscious decision by Tutakangahau to mihi to the dead at that point, as if Best was standing by taking shorthand – but it was still part of an unfolding process to do so in his presence. With no further ceremony, the 'old patriarch of the "People of the Mist" finished his tangi for the dead of his tribe, grasped his staff and strode forward without a word'. The anonymous porters 'take up their burdens and move on after the Kaumatua'. The ancestors have been greeted, history brought into the present, and it is time to move on; by 'cliff and fall and rugged ways', the party descended to the lakeside at Hereheretaua to meet the boat and its crew for the journey. They set out over 'Waikare-whanaunga-kore' – Waikare without relations – for Onepoto and the chance to rest. Best footnotes that the lake is 'so called because its winds and waves are no respecters of persons' – reminding his readers of the dangers for small craft when the great lake cuts up rough.[26]

As the canoe and its occupants paddle out over the lake and begin to explore its storied history, Best also reminds the reader that he is more than just a travel guide: 'We are drifting back to the remote past now, and the *ao marama* (or world of light and being) is far behind us.'[27] This is a metaphysical journey, a search for the grail of Māori knowledge and a rescue mission, for 'the lands of Waikare are in a transition stage – the Maori has gone, though the Pakeha has not yet arrived; yet a little while and it will be too late'.[28] Too late, Best implies, to learn what 'the guide and the philosopher of the party', old Tutakangahau, knows. After the descriptions of natural wonders – and the signalling of Tūhoe's imminent dispossession – the heart of the book is to be an extended meditation upon Waikaremoana's ancient history, passed from the old man to the Pākehā ethnographer.

What began as a journey into the wilderness becomes a form of ōhākī (a deathbed speech) for a passing age. Best and Tutakangahau are alone by the campfire, smoking their pipes: the younger men have taken the canoe back to Onepoto to obtain more supplies. In nature's remote heart, Europe and the Pacific are to enter into dialogue: 'alone in the great silent expanse of Wairau-moana, the time has surely come to learn what is known of those who lived and fought and died in these mountain solitudes, long before the white man dared adventure the great ocean of Kiwa'.[29] The natural setting of the lake's shore becomes a site where myth and tradition, 'the deeds of the god-like men of old', are to be recounted in a new political order in which Best will depict the transfer of oral Māori metaphysics into the custody of the paipera-bearing Pākehā power culture.

Can we trust that what Best sets down as occurring next actually happened as he tells it? Did he put words into the old man's mouth? Has the account perhaps been slanted, to make it appear that Tutakangahau was placing Best in charge of recording Tūhoe knowledge for posterity? Some answers to such troubling questions may be found if we examine more closely what 'the Kaumatua' is recorded as saying and just why he might have done so at that point. It is clear from Best's letters to Smith in the previous year that he had already formed a relationship of some trust with the older man. Whakapapa lists he gave Best before this journey and 'bibles' of written material do support the ethnographer's claim that the 'Oracle of the Rocky Mountain' disclosed to him the kind of information that follows in this account.[30]

Tutakangahau was powerful in his own right and realm, and he knew it. So was Best, and the old man knew that too: Best had power as a government agent, as a genuine seeker of what the old man possessed, and as a Pākehā literate in Māori matters, willing to record whatever he could of a changing cultural inheritance under threat. If the chief did not behave as Best records him here, and if he did not say in some form or other what Best has set down, then we are dealing with a degree of fiction, and the ethnographer cannot be trusted. The question arises: why would Best lie, or distort information? There are certainly issues of how he recorded and edited the large amount of material that follows, but the case for its overall veracity appears stronger than any alternative.

From the viewpoint of a modern anthropologist, Best's weakness would primarily be his romanticism and the difficulty the reader has in establishing quite when and where the old man is speaking, and the writer is commenting. However, this is not modern anthropology; there is certainly a clear indication of what Tutakangahau says to Best when he begins his kōrero – and why he is doing so. It is appropriate, he begins, to tell him 'the legend of the "Sea of Rippling Waters", for that is why I followed you [here] . . . it is not an idle journey, but one in which there is much to be learned and much to be seen'.[31] Best should not be alarmed 'at the monsters which inhabit this "Sea of Waikare", for I am an *ariki taniwha* [Lord of Dragons]'.

In proclaiming himself an equal of supernatural beings, Tutakangahau moves his disclosures into another realm, one of magic and danger, and great spiritual power. Best is safe with him – 'no *taniwha* will molest me'. The old man tells Best that he must be 'strenuous in retaining what I impart', as the Pākehā, while protected by him, has not taken part in the traditional ceremonies that bind oral knowledge from expert to pupil. This is to be a new form of teaching, a necessary exchange, as Tutakangahau's children 'have little love for the gallant stories of old' – the new world, Te Ao Mārama, has broken the link with the past that preserved its reality in oral traditions. 'I will tell them to you', he declares, 'and one other and no more, that you may preserve the traditions of my people and record their ancient customs, that they may be retained in the world of light.'

What this historic and inevitable declaration signifies is the end of tradition as lived, known and practised by the old man's forebears: he is bowing to the pressures of modernity by inducting Best and his pen into the whare takiura, well aware that if he does not, much of what he knows will die with him. What was his alternative? Those Māori with a level of literacy, bilingualism and the access to power and privilege required to record and publish this material were almost certainly MPs like Carroll, engaged elsewhere. Best's arrival in the Urewera must have seemed greatly providential to someone like Tutakangahau, who realised that his son's generation belonged to a new age and could not be trained as he had been. He instructs Best as if he were a pupil: 'Do you plainly write them in your *paipera**, that all who love such things may understand.' It is a moment of great poignancy; he is clearly distressed about the loss of interest in the ancient stories he knows so well: 'I would even hope that my children may yet return to the *kura*‡ of Tuhoe and of Potiki and be proud of the achievements of their ancestors. *Tena!*'[32]

There follows a thirty-page account of 'the ancient people of Waikaremoana', their legends and their wars, with accompanying whakapapa, karakia, laments, and a more recent history of wars between Ngāti Ruapani and Tūhoe. This consists of direct recordings of what Tutakangahau told Best, interspersed with commentaries by the Pākehā. At one moment, the reader hears Best, at another, the kaumātua – there is no certainty about exactly what the old man said, nor about the way Best edited what he wrote down. Nevertheless, this is the kura huna – hidden knowledge – to the degree that it was not available before, beyond the boundaries of the Urewera, and most likely would not have survived Tutakangahau's passing on.

Best notes that some of the material here is a version of similar legends elsewhere (the story Tutakangahau tells of Rakahanga resembles that of Wairaka); but he has certainly been given a Tūhoe view on the mythical origins of Waikaremoana, and kōrero concerning those he calls 'the Tauira, or aboriginal people of Waikaremoana'. The conversation continues over a long night until, with the campfire burning low, a 'chill breeze comes in from the silent waters . . . the Kaumatua ends his long speech anent the days of old'.

Best puts away 'the valued note-book containing so much of the ancient lore of Waikare', adding a fascinating footnote: that some of this lore is 'conserved in the mysterious phonographs so puzzling to the "children"' – i.e. early attempts at recording on primitive Edison cylinders. The tantalising possibility that Best had recorded Tutakangahau and others has not proved easy to confirm – except that a number of decomposing cylinders were apparently destroyed when the old Colonial Museum (after 1913, the Dominion Museum) was moved in 1936 from its original site behind Parliament Buildings. *Sic transit historia mundi*: what value could be put on these records had they survived?[33]

The remainder of *Waikaremoana* tracks the return to civilisation, with descriptions of flora and fauna, people and places, in a more conventional travelogue. As they paddle past Pa Pouaru and Te Waiwai, Tutakangahau 'breaks forth into a *tangi* for the ancient homes of his tribe', noting afterwards how warring hapū would not now have to leave their pā to fight each other, 'for a bullet will travel a hundred miles – or is it a hundred yards?'.[34] The worlds of the past and the present are both equally real to the old man – but Best is always at pains to depict Tutakangahau as a product of the former, at odds with the latter. *Waikaremoana* lays a template for what will become the ethnographer's underlying assumption about an authentic Māori being and culture – that it lies in the past. This is why it was important for Best to write the story of the journey as he did: he becomes the curator and bearer of that record, the psychology and spirituality of the 'old time Maori'.

What is also interesting here is the evidence that emerges of Best's psychology in these early years amongst Tūhoe and the Urewera wilderness – and how it shaped his thinking as it appears in his later writings. He wrote prolifically for New Zealand newspapers over the Urewera years up until 1910, especially for the *Canterbury Times*; a series of articles 'From Tuhoeland' ran there from 1897 until 1906. An unnamed 'old guide' appears in a 1902 article, pointing out the sites of 'old combats' – the anonymous Tutakangahau.[35] The same tropes of displacement and extinction that appeared in *Waikaremoana* are here: 'the booming of dynamite resounds across the sounding waters in place of the warhorns of the men of old'. This is a 'racial contest', in which the 'sacred karakia and Neolithic weapons of my friends of Tuhoe' will prove unavailing before the remorseless engines of Pākehā progress.

With these standard views, which could have been written by any city journalist, there is also a hint of the transcendental experience of the primitive that is still available if the visitor eschews the creature comforts of 'the pakeha house' and the 'fire-boat steamer', and instead, 'camps on the shores and islets' to enjoy 'the glories of the Earth Mother'. Best is advancing the Romantic's proposition that an overdose of the inevitable forces of civilisation chains and restricts human freedom. To encounter unmediated nature is an act of psychic liberation, and proximity to the last bearers of a Neolithic culture is a key to this adventure. Three months after publishing this article in the *Canterbury Times*, he follows it up with another that lays bare this psychology.

'On Solitude and the Primitive Mind' was published on 22 October 1902, five years after Best had arrived in the Urewera. He had made good use of his access to the vast and forbidding rainforest – like any good Transcendentalist, he was never one to avoid his own company. Employing the pseudonym 'Te Mohoao' – man of the woods, a barbarian – he compares his own happy state to that of his comfortable urban readers. 'Woe unto him that is never alone, and cannot bear to be alone', he quotes the English art critic Hamerton, opening a discussion on the type of man most suited to solitude – one 'who Nature has claimed'.[36] The one who responds to Nature's siren song is 'admitted to the high place of the forest gods' as a kind of priest and mediator. His work 'shall be to interpret the ways of those gods and their offspring . . . to explore and understand [Nature's] realm', as she calls to him in her own tongue.

This pseudo-biblical imagery of the prophet's call will be familiar to those who know their Emerson, and the American philosopher's prescription for the ideal Transcendentalist in his 1843 essay of the same name.[37] More than a little intoxicated with his subject, Best continues: 'The glamour of the forest is upon him' (the same expression used on the opening page of *Waikaremoana*). No longer will this individual 'list to the call of the haunts of man, but the gulf between them shall widen in the changing year'. This language and thought are highly derivative, the type of Emersonian commonplaces that were a part of the intellectual atmosphere Best had long been breathing. The American had written of the way 'many intelligent and religious persons withdrew themselves', to find 'a certain solitary and critical way of living', holding themselves aloof from 'the common labours and competitions of the market and the caucus'.[38] Or as Best puts it here, 'he will go his own way, silent and reserved, for after all, his friends are many' in the unpeopled forest.

This protoypical Man Alone image, that would re-emerge in the outsider artist stereotype of the Sargeson-Pearson critical realist school, was in itself a vintage Emersonian formula: 'They are the lonely; the spirit of their writing and conversation is lonely; they repel influences; they shun general society.' The Man of Nature (a long way from Rousseau's 'natural man') as conjured here is a stranger to human affairs. He finds a home in a spiritualised Nature, theorised with a Transcendentalism that has rejected the God of revealed religion, but not the impulse to worship – common enough in the experience of anyone who enters the profuse environment of New Zealand's native bush. The 'book of Nature' or creation had become Best's scripture, a local planting of those Transcendentalist seeds that were to flower in the counterculture of New Age philosophies with a fresh 'back-to-nature' movement that would resurface from the late 1960s onwards.

This is important for his work amongst Tūhoe, post-1897: these ideas were antithetical to the way Tutakangahau had understood the natural world in his formative years, and they could not accommodate the indigenous forms of Christianity that were now part of the old man's culture. In this populist vision, Māori do not emerge from their world on their own terms, but into Best's world – on his. The man who would become their most active champion would gradually translate the Māori experience of nature into Western cultural norms. The old nature-bound culture of traditional Māori society had lost its coherence under the pressures of colonisation and settlement; their relationship with the natural world would henceforth be reproduced by agents of Western culture. Margaret Orbell has stressed the importance of Māori kinship with nature, exemplified by the tendency to 'personify all aspects of the environment'.[39] This is characterised as a fellow feeling 'for the life forms and other entities that surrounded them', but she does not – as did Best – elaborate these observations into an overriding metaphysical system based on the primitive mentality of 'the mythopoetic Maori'.

For Best, this primitive phase was the bedrock of all human imagination: the type of Pākehā nature-lover he envisaged was a link between primitive and civilised societies. While primitives peopled the forest with 'demons, elves and fairies' – as did Māori – and lived in fear of such unseen and malevolent presences, the civilised mind could both understand this psychology and identify with it, while remaining emotionally aloof on the higher cultural plane of civilisation. His own literate, imaginative and self-chosen solitude was a far cry from what he believed Māori experienced in a teeming spiritual environment, 'surrounded by sentient beings, demons, sprites of the dead, etc . . . the strain is too much for him'.

Best's romantic solitudes with their transcendent moments were not of the same order as that of a lone Tūhoe finding himself unprotected in a spiritual war zone. The ethnographer's Pākehā self had a different set of rules to those Māori selves he was encountering; their way of being in the world was qualitatively different from his, and he was right to point this out. Where he becomes fixated on a pyramid of human cultural difference, however, and substitutes a static model of primitive psychology for the processes of ongoing change, he is clearly unwilling to see all cultures as dynamic, in states of flux, changed and changing over time by those who produce them.

If what were real beings for Māori had become creatures of the imagination for this educated, rational Pākehā bushman, there was still the exciting possibility of 'treading the mental trails of primitive man' – a kind of tourist pass to pre-history. The visit, however, came with a health warning: the trail if followed past the point of no return would end in the kinds of superstitions that had bound his English ancestors. It was always necessary to 'get back into open country for a spell. Destroy the forest or it will conquer you.' If a civilised person moderates and monitors their relationship with Nature, Best reasons, a love for her will result, as will the ability to 'probe the mind of primitive man, to see with his eyes, to think with his mind'. This caution against the perils of reversion – 'going bush' – had appeared earlier in Best, in his writings on the natives of the

Philippines and the terrors of the tropics. There is the risk of becoming a Pākehā-Māori, taking a road of no return; but if the lover of Nature can bear solitude for a safe period, they will find the power to encounter an earlier phase of their own evolutionary psychology – albeit from a safe psychological distance.

Best's philosophical foundations here rely on European Romanticism combined with American Transcendentalism: West meets East in the Urewera. In his culture wars with the missionaries, he was party to a larger, longer-lived debate that saw nature as the voice of a depersonalised world spirit, through which he attempted to interpret the Māori relationship to the natural world. His embrace of comparative religion and anthropology and the dogma of progress were the tools he used to analyse Tūhoe culture – while rationalising its imminent demise. Such theories of a Romantic Nature would frame the model of the mythopoetic Māori; while an evolutionary nature, blind and progressive, would explain their inability to assimilate into modernity. Both were seductive in explaining the inevitable extinction of an authentic Māori presence. What is obvious now is that the power culture of his day was producing these views of nature – and the place of Māori in this scheme of things.

Best's intellectual salvation during this period was his preference for fieldwork over the academic study of such matters – not that this was an option in his case. While he was dignifying the type of commonplaces outlined above with a measure of intellectual respectability, on the ground amongst Tūhoe he was fully engaged as a government official by day and as a fieldworking ethnographer in any spare time he could wangle, and over long candlelit nights in tent and whare. The interweaving of both worlds demanded a balancing act: the new world of the road, and his role as quartermaster, with his pursuit of vanishing treasures amongst the ageing but prodigious memory banks of his 'mohio' – men of knowledge. Writing to Smith in response to the older man's hunger for more whakapapa, he notes, 'You will see that Tutaka gives 23 gens. from Oho.' and that he has 'a golden kura from Tutaka just in'. He can hardly contain his excitement: 'Verily here are grand kaumatua, I never tire of them. Men whose minds were old a thousand years ago but are a thousand years behind now.'[40]

This expression of Tylor's theory of primitive survivals links with what has been seen of Best's attitude to the wilderness: these Tūhoe elders maintain unchanged an earlier level of human psychology, which at the same time had been overtaken by human progress, leaving them 'a thousand years behind'. Both through access to a primal natural world and the primitive human psychology of its inhabitants, Best could reach a vanished substratum of human evolution – while by implication, these grand kaumātua were not equipped to keep up in the present. It suited his purposes to keep them there, to ignore the political acumen and involvement we have seen demonstrated by Tutakangahau and other Tūhoe leaders. Best's mundane duties are also recounted, however: in the same letter to Smith, he writes of the 'Rotorua Office . . . looking out for an asst. for Store here as I am practically alone', in duties which included paying his Māori and Pākehā road crews.

In spite of the colonialist mentality at work here and the language in which it is couched, there is little doubt of the genuine respect and affection Best felt towards his closest mōhio – especially Tutakangahau – and there is strong evidence that the old man reciprocated, both in personal and professional relationships. Craig records that in 1896, some time after their Waikaremoana expedition, the old chief approached Best 'to look after his three grandchildren while they attended the native school at Te Whaiti'.[41] This was a signal honour: a mark of the personal respect Tutakangahau had for Best, but a sign also of his recognition of the mokopunas' need to be educated in the ways of the Pākehā. There is no better indication of the old chief's bicultural literacy than this aspect of his attempt to straddle both worlds. He had already laid claim to Best's abilities to record the past during that long night's kōrero on the shores of Wairau Moana. He was now taking out insurance that the same children for whom he had done this would be prepared to embrace a future where a bicultural education was imperative – that they would be literate like him, and able to participate fully in the new world.

In the case of his favoured granddaughter Marewa-i-te-rangi, the relationship was to be short-lived – an influenza epidemic struck the district and she was one of those who died. Best was invited by her father to 'say goodbye to your grandchild' and saw her draw her last breath as the poroporoaki (farewell) filled the house of death.[42] He was also expected to accompany her and the funeral party on the journey back to Maungapōhatu where – suffering from guilt by association with the European disease that had killed her – he was reluctant to face the grandfather who had given her into his care. Yet Craig records that the old man requested Best to take a photograph of the dead girl on her bier, and bore him no malice – in spite of giving an oration that sheeted home the cause of the girl's death to the arrival of Pākehā sicknesses amongst them, and the dire consequences for Māori mortality and survival. Best remained amongst them for the duration of the tangi on the precincts of the sacred mountain, and was farewelled at his leave-taking with the words 'Haere, haere ki a Marewa – go, go and return to Marewa'.[43]

There is little doubt that Best had attained an unprecedented level of acceptance amongst Tutakangahau's people at this time; indeed, it is not too great a stretch to claim that he was in some degree whāngai – adopted – by Tamakaimoana. For Best to have been granted the care of Tutakangahau's mokopuna tells us as much: this was not just a matter of another Pākehā administrator (a surveyor or mineralogist) welcomed by the old man to serve his interests. It was far more – and if it were not so, we would not have the account that Craig has given us both from Best's notes and from his wife Adelaide Wylie, who was herself a Native School teacher at Te Houhi near Te Whāiti when she became engaged to Best in 1902. She would have been well aware of these stories and familiar with the locals of the area.[44] It has been suggested to me only recently by a kuia from Tūhoe that in fact, 'Best is one of our tūpuna, he lived on our land'.[45] This assertion would not necessarily be welcomed by some of her iwi today, more particularly those who for reasons of political persuasion regard Te Peehi as, at best, a necessary evil in the Tūhoe colonial encounter, and, at worst, a government spy who stole the knowledge of their tūpuna. One suspects that Tutakangahau would not comprehend this attitude, nor sympathise with those who find it difficult to understand and accept his necessary actions in history.

Best's camp and house at Heipipi, near Ruatāhuna, *c.* 1902.
Source copy from Isobel Eggers' original thesis, 1934, courtesy of Kevin McFadden

By the following year, 1897, Best's literary career was beginning in earnest: *Waikaremoana* was published, his newspaper articles in the Christchurch *Press* and the *Canterbury Times* began to appear, and his first scholarly article for the Polynesian Society on Tūhoe spirituality was published in the June issue of the journal. This period of his life initiated a non-stop flow of collecting, editing, writing and publishing which would continue until his death in 1931 – and afterwards, in terms of posthumous publication. Best was on his way to becoming the great white tohunga of matters Māori. The spate of journal articles in the first ten years constitutes his most sustained period of collection, analysis and intellectual challenges, as the emerging scholar of Māori history and culture struggled to come to terms with what he saw happening around him, and to understand what he would call 'the Maori mind'.

Behind all his research was his 'faculty': Paitini, Parakiri, Hamiora Pio and Tutakangahau. He depended on them for all of the material he collected: they were the curators of the times and the psychology he sought to document. As one of the old frontier guard who spoke Māori – himself an endangered species – he was determined to make a mystique of their rapidly disappearing past. Writing in *The Press* from 'Tuhoe Land' in January 1897, he saw these survivors of the Pākehā dilution of their culture as needing protection: the Urewera was undesirable for settlement, but its geography made it a perfect 'permanent reserve for the Tuhoe tribe' where their customs might be preserved.[46] The same strategy was being pursued by Tūhoe, but for different reasons. Far from being locked up in a cultural preservation compound, Tutakangahau and his fellow chiefs wanted to preserve political power to retain their lands in the here and now, and access the benefits of the Pākehā world: schools, roads and the money economy.

Even as he sought to delineate the past, Best was clear-eyed about the way Tūhoe were living around him: their food staples were hardly endemic, with potato, maize and pumpkins supplementing the forest fare of old – along with a less benign crop, tobacco, pipes of which were even given to children, earning his disdain. Older men such as Tutakangahau continued to hunt birds and fish in traditional ways, but the young were deserting snares for the shotgun. He notes (in a second 1897 *Press* article, 'The Present Condition of the Tuhoe Tribe') that attempts in the King Country to find Māori still living in 'barbaric simplicity' had failed, and had shifted to Tūhoe. However, 'the primitive Maori is a thing of the past' – as the above evidence showed – and the mix of Māori and European clothing worn by Tūhoe should be 'too startling and repellent to those in search of the noble and poetic savage'.[47]

It is remarkable how un-Romantic Best could be when he observed others seeking something of what he aspired to find. Young Tūhoe shearers and their love affair with guns and horses were proof enough that times had changed. Yet he still believed a reservoir of traditional psychology survived untrammelled in the hearts and practices of his remaining ruānuku – who he compared at times to Solomon in their wisdom.[48] He could admit that Tūhoe had adopted such elements of Christianity as suited them; and alongside the Bible, the influence of alcohol was beginning to have effects of a different spiritual nature. However much he could see and document cultural changes and their effects, it was the fate of 'the old time Maori . . . out of place in this era of the *pakeha*', that fascinated him. The new generation he saw were not authentic, and he could cite Māori sources to prove it: 'They are not Maori, but a kind of brown paper edition of the Pakeha . . . as I heard a great Maori once express it, a *whakatupuranga purei piriote* – a billiard-playing generation.'[49]

Around the same time, he was citing Tutakangahau on the fate of the older generation, determined by the loss of the old tapu prohibitions: 'E heke ana ki te kore – we, the Maori people, are drifting down to oblivion'.[50] It is likely it was the old chief who had made the comment on those young wasters of his people who now haunted Pākehā billiard halls, as a result of working with the settlers and adopting their leisure pursuits in public works camps and rough bush taverns. To the degree that the old tradition-bound culture had been radically transformed, those who had been born in its sunset years were taking its remnants along with them. The real issue, however, was whether *Māori themselves* would disappear with the impact of the cultural dislocation they were managing – time has proved that not to be the case. For Best and for some of his informants at least, Pākehā ways did mean the death of some things essentially Māori, and if they could not be retained, they must be preserved in the historical record. It was this that Best and his mōhio proceeded to do: 'Te Rehu-o-Tainui: the evolution of a Maori atua', published in June 1897 in the *Journal of the Polynesian Society*, was the place where this partnership first bore scholarly fruit.

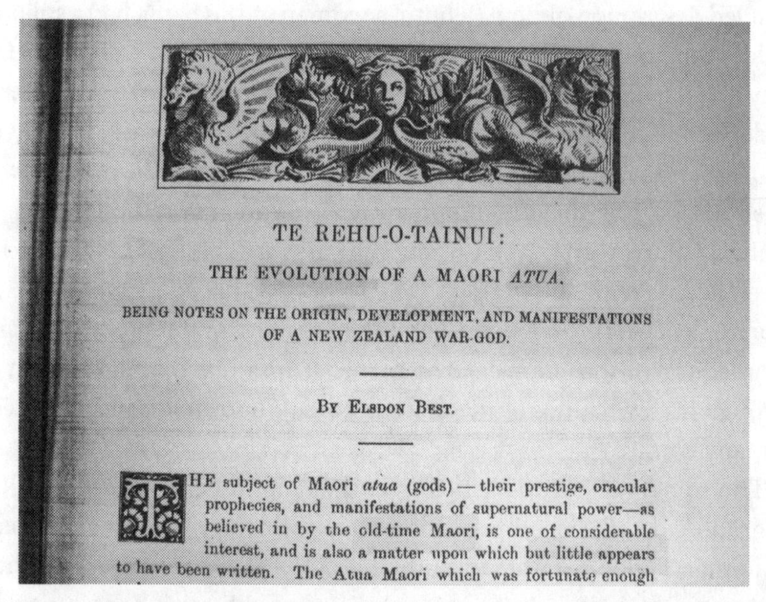
TE REHU-O-TAINUI:

THE EVOLUTION OF A MAORI *ATUA*.

BEING NOTES ON THE ORIGIN, DEVELOPMENT, AND MANIFESTATIONS OF A NEW ZEALAND WAR-GOD.

BY ELSDON BEST.

THE subject of Maori *atua* (gods) — their prestige, oracular prophecies, and manifestations of supernatural power—as believed in by the old-time Maori, is one of considerable interest, and is also a matter upon which but little appears to have been written. The Atua Maori which was fortunate enough

Title page of Best's first ethnographic article from the Urewera, from the *Journal of the Polynesian Society*, Vol. VI, 22 June 1897, page 41.
Author photograph

Best made the claim for himself in this article that it was probably 'the first case in which the origin and development of an *atua* has been traced'.[51] Best describes atua as gods manifesting supernatural power – in this case through a human medium (kauwaka) called Uhia, a now deceased member of Tutakangahau's Tamakaimoana hapū. There is little doubt then that the old man was his principal source for the detailed descriptions of the atua's manifestations and the many successful battles in which Tūhoe prevailed, as a result of heeding the matakite (oracles) of Uhia, the medium of the war god Rehu. He wrote to Smith of how 'Te Rehu o Tainui alone has brought me many grey hairs and I broke the record by walking from here to Maungapohatu in 1½ days to get Tu to straighten out that gentle atua for me'.[52]

The article is an important example of Best's early fieldwork practice – working as a modern anthropologist, living amongst Tūhoe and using his increasing fluency in Māori to have them provide the information first-hand. While there is little in the way of attribution, it is possible to source the material with a high degree of certainty, given that the atua in question made his presence felt amongst Tamakaimoana. There is a detailed description of how Rehutu, a woman of this hapū, had a stillborn child, Hope-motu. The spirits of whakatahe (stillbirths) were feared, as they were believed to develop into kahukahu (evil spirits) unless they underwent a ceremony to render them harmless. In this case, the powers of the foetus were not destroyed, and were passed on to the mother, who was possessed by the atua Hope-motu. This atua passed on again – or evolved – into an ariā, an incarnation in the form of a moko-kakariki or green lizard. With an offering to the newborn atua of a green parakeet (porete, kakariki), Uhia propitiated the atua and in the process became the medium of the god, which he named Te Rehu-o-Tainui. He went on through his divinations or matakite to guide Tūhoe to legendary success in many battles.[53]

The remainder of the article recounts a number of these conflicts in graphic detail, becoming as it does so a history of Tamakaimoana and other Tūhoe hapū up until the time of Pākehā contact, until these 'unwritten archives' merge with the recorded battles occurring with Europeans long after Uhia had died. Other tohunga took his place, but they had never acquired 'the marvellous power and prestige of the *atua's* first *waka*'. (Best claimed to have met a descendant, Uhia II, who was ten years old in 1896.)[54] The significance of 'Te Rehu-o-Tainui' lies in Best's determination to put Tūhoe culture on the record with specific local detail possessing wider application. For Tutakangahau, it represents an investment in his commitment to the literary preservation of Tūhoe lore, the purpose for which he had first recruited Best by the campfire on Waikaremoana.

There is a striking example of the same kind of language used at that earlier moment, when the narrator rejects the belief that the ariā (the green lizard) was the atua, as 'the common people' believed. 'We of the *ariki-taniwha** know', he writes, 'that the real form of a god, if it have a form, is never seen by mortal eyes.'[55] This is the precise description recorded by Best, used by the old man of himself, when he began his disclosures beside the lake, in the same year. The footnote from the asterisk has: '**Ariki*, firstborn in male line of descent; *taniwha*, here used as representing esoteric knowledge: of the high-born priestly caste'. It is doubtful that Best was passing himself off as a priest, so it is fair to assume that he is speaking for an invisible Tutakangahau within the text.

The final two paragraphs are quotes from an unnamed source: 'in my youth we possessed *tohungas*, who were mediums of Te Rehu-o-Tainui' – but these were not of the same vintage as Uhia, 'as it was we of Tuhoe who fell on those fields'. He laments the coming of the Pākehā with Bible and gun, the forsaking of the 'old customs and the old beliefs', which led to gods such as Te Rehu-o-Tainui departing the field. 'The gods of our ancestors forsook us forever. For we had trampled upon the ancient *tapu*. That was the end.'[56]

It is hard to escape the conclusion that this is the voice of his principal informant – in which case, it is only reasonable to begin viewing Tutakangahau (along with his peers) as the co-author of Best's researches. While the language, and the publication that carries the information, derive from Pākehā culture and speak back into it, the substance, the kura, the teaching contained therein is Māori – Tūhoe – in origin and significance. While Best was always liberal in his acknowledgement of his debt to Māori, it would hardly be possible to undertake such research today without attributing a fair share of the credit to the informants who were involved.

There is much that might be criticised – from a twenty-first-century perspective – about his methods, and the conditions whereby he took advantage of Māori vulnerability to gain access to their culture; but it would be short-sighted to underestimate the content and the shared ownership of this early work. Tutakangahau took his own advantage of Best's mission. In material such as Te Rehu-o-Tainui, he had achieved some of his aims as disclosed to Best at Wairau Moana. The Pākehā was recording the stories of the old man's people as a link to the past and a deposit for his children's children in the years to come, that they might have pride in their history and their ancestors (himself included). The indefatigable ethnographer also deserves credit: a man who would walk for a day and a half in pursuit of a kind of knowledge most of his fellows regarded as primitive superstitions, in his zeal was not far behind missionaries like Colenso and Taylor, nor the hardihood of Tūhoe in his Spartan physical determination to gain the prized kura huna.

Best continued to gather information from the old chief and his other mōhio. Between 1900 and 1901, the *Journal of the Polynesian Society* published an important two-part article on Māori spiritual beliefs and practices, 'Spiritual Concepts of the Maori', in which he described the major spiritual terms in common use, attempting to define and illustrate the meanings of such 'concepts' as wairua, hau and mauri.[57] His work in this area has had a profound and ongoing influence on the meanings attached to these important words, none more so than in the case of mauri. A substantial amount of Best's work in this period would find its way by 1917 into the revised fifth edition of the Williams' *Dictionary of the Maori Language*, as he gained recognition as a principal authority on the esoteric knowledge and beliefs in pre-European Māori society. The definitions given here in 1901, and in subsequent Urewera writings, have also made their way into the wider world and have been used by a variety of international anthropologists throughout the twentieth century. This aspect of his inheritance is investigated more fully in the closing chapters.

Best began Part II of 'Spiritual Concepts of the Maori' with a discussion of the meaning of mauri, 'which has been termed the "breath of life" or spirit of life'.[58] He gives examples from everyday speech, showing how mauri was also spoken of metaphorically when one was startled, as in the example given in an early 1852 edition of the Williams' *Dictionary*: '*Ka oho taku mauri i te puhanga o te pu* – my *mauri* was startled by the firing of the gun'. Mauri was felt to be the seat of the emotions: fear, love and anger, and Best distinguishes it from the manawa, or heart (a more physically based concept, the breath, the belly). The influence of F. Max Müller, the German philologist so loved by Best, is evident when he writes: 'The Greek *thymos* more nearly equals the Maori *mauri* than any other term I have met with.' He goes on: 'Like the *thymos*, the *mauri* ceases to be at the death of the body.' The missionary Taylor, Best notes, had 'translated *mauri* as "the living soul", but "the breath of life" is a better term, and *thymos* the best of all'.[59]

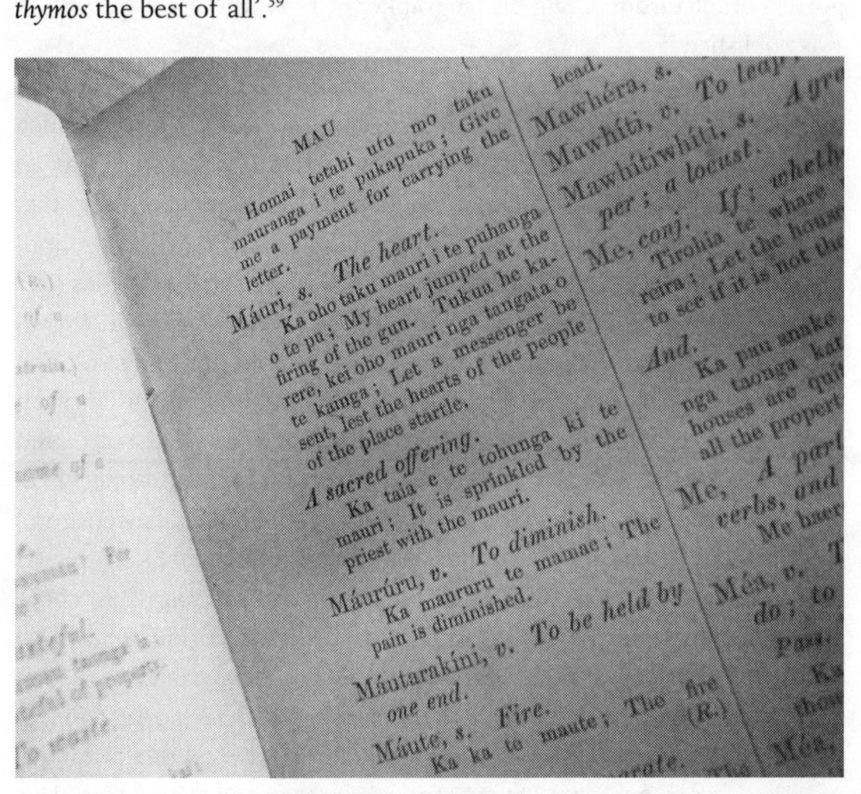
MAU

Homai tetahi utu mo taku mauranga i te pukapuka; Give me a payment for carrying the letter.

Máuri, s. *The heart.*
Ka oho taku mauri i te puhanga o te pu; My heart jumped at the firing of the gun. Tukua he karere, kei oho mauri nga tangata o te kainga; Let a messenger be sent, lest the hearts of the people of the place startle.
A sacred offering.
Ka taia e te tohunga ki te mauri; It is sprinkled by the priest with the mauri.

Máurúru, v. *To diminish.*
Ka maururu te mamae; The pain is diminished.

Máutarakíni, v. *To be held by one end.*

Máute, s. *Fire.*
Ka ka te maute; The fire (R.)

head.
Mawhéra, s.
Mawhiti, v. *To leap*
Mawhitiwhiti, s.
per; a locust.
Me, conj. *If; wheth*
Tirohia te whare
reira; Let the house
to see if it is not the
And.
Ka pau anake
nga taonga
houses are qui
all the propert
Me, *A part*
verbs, and
Me haer
Méa, v.
do; to

Definition of 'mauri' from the 1852 (2nd) edition of the Williams' *Dictionary of the New Zealand Language*.
Author photograph

This is an act of cultural translation that is symptomatic of the autodidactic methods Best employed at this early stage of New Zealand's anthropological practice. He is merging the information given him by Tutakangahau, Paitini and other Tūhoe elders with earlier definitions by Pākehā collectors and lexicographers, all of which he filters through the second-hand definition of a term from classical Greek, got by reading a German philologist who specialised in comparative religion. Best was nothing if not a very early cross-disciplinary scholar, working outside the academy. He had little or no classical Greek, and this reading of *thymos* comes from his copy of Müller's 1892 work, *Anthropological Religion: The Gifford Lectures*, in the section 'The Discovery of the Soul in Man and in Nature'.[60] It is possible to place this work in Best's hands between 1895 and when this article appeared, as his signed, annotated copy was in the possession of Elsdon Craig his biographer in 1964 when *Man of the Mist* was published.[61]

Best's *thymos* was Müller's *thymos*, and became in effect, Best's mauri – it is this Orientalist-inflected mauri that has come down to us through such literature today. While his definition of human mauri at this point was 'an activity, an immaterial element, a sacred spark' – yet he noted also that this spark 'may be represented by a material object' – the material mauri. Canoes had mauri, tribes had mauri – sacred objects and activities over which incantations were uttered by tohunga to give whatever the desired spiritual blessing: a safe journey, a good catch, victory over enemies. The sacred, the supernatural realms in traditional society were indivisible from the manifest realm – a place of spiritual warfare and danger that required those who navigated the seen and unseen world to take precautions. There was no question of mauri – physical or spiritual – finding its existence and meaning in the pages of a dictionary, or learned articles.

This goes to the heart of the kind of salvage anthropology Best chose to practise: in saving these accounts of a vanishing world, he was also hastening its disappearance – not that there was a great deal of choice. Mauri survives today outside of the dictionary in the Māori language, in formal expressions, and as a quasi-authentic survival and reminder of Māori difference. In 1984, Māori claimants in the Wai 8 Manukau Claim before the Waitangi Tribunal aired their reservations about an 18-kilometre slurry pipeline that was to carry ironsand concentrate from Maioro. The water was to be drawn from the Waikato River to the New Zealand Steel mill at Glenbrook, and after separation, to be discharged into the Manukau Harbour – and the claimants expressed both environmental and cultural concerns. Fishing and water quality would certainly be affected at the site of the discharge – something the Pākehā world could easily understand. Their second objection, however – that 'the proposal is culturally offensive. The mauri of the two water bodies is incompatible. The waters of the Waikato should not be mixed with those of the Manukau' – was the kind of explanation that gets the talkback airwaves running hot. After all, a river is a river is a river.[62]

For those Māori who still hold to the vestiges of this belief in site-specific mauri as a spiritual quality inherent in the inanimate world, there is a long thread running back to Tutakangahau's world. For many others, however, like the writer Keri Hulme when she attempted to explain mauri in an important piece of literary criticism in 1978, her first resort was to the Williams' *Dictionary* and the definition crafted by Best from his mentor, Max Müller.[63] There will be more to say later on the half-life of mauri in New Zealand lexicography, but for now it is worth noting that between the two of them, Best and the old chief contributed as much to cultural change as cultural preservation. Hulme is aware that mauri were also powerful objects, and so was Best; for Tutakangahau, mauri was still alive and active in his world. Indeed, it might be said that the old man himself was a mauri: the mauri of a disappearing world, its vital spark – and one that would cease or be greatly diminished at the death of his body.

A further step would be to make the daring claim that it was something of his own mauri – the mauri of Tutakangahau – that was being imparted to Best. We have seen an element of this process in the declaration made at the lakeside; there is further evidence in a later article published shortly after the chief died in 1907. 'Maori Forest Lore' appeared in the *Transactions and Proceedings of The Royal Society of New Zealand* of 1909, after it was read before the Auckland Institute on the 22nd of November.[64] In a section on 'The Lore of the Whare Mata – The Art of the Fowler',

Best quotes a number of authorities, Māori and Pākehā, on the bird-snaring practices amongst Tūhoe and other iwi.

As well as Paitini, Tamarau Waiari, and Tamati Ranapiri of Ngāti Raukawa, Best quotes Tutakangahau extensively on the ways birds were caught and speared. Paitini also discourses on mauri: 'the *mauri* represents and protects the land and birds of the forests', and if members of another tribe entered this birding area and could not find the mauri, they would be unable to work their magic, to drive away the birds and render their enemies' forest unproductive.[65] However, it is what Tutakangahau has to say – and what is written of him – that makes this article so vital in understanding their relationship.

It is here that Best publicly acknowledges the death of 'the most learned man among Tuhoe' – and sets down an account of their last meeting, and what it meant for him. The section of the article that dates his death at November 1907 continues with a detailed description of how mauri operated as talismans in protecting food sources and gives a long series of descriptions of the important ahi taitai purification rite, in which the first fruits of birds and fish were consecrated by tohunga in tapu ceremonies. Tutakangahau related to Best the story of a stone mauri concealed in the roots of a birding tree near Toreatai for over ten generations; and of the incomprehension of an Irish surveyor who wanted to fell the tree to clear a stock track to Tūranga (Gisborne): 'Old Tutaka went to look for his *mauri*, and tried to explain to the overseer the meaning and uses of *mauri*; but the subtle metaphysics of the Maori were too much for [the surveyor] to grasp. He was hopelessly befogged.'[66]

While Best manages a laugh at the expense of the Irish overseer, he is making a serious point: that *he* does understand, and that Tutakangahau is treating him as a fellow mōhio by letting him in on the story of the surveyor's incomprehension. This is underlined in the lengthy discussion on the ahi taitai rites that follows. The first birds taken were offered to the gods (whakaaweawe), in a ceremony known as the ahi taitai (tapu-lifting by means of fire). After the sacred fire was kindled and the tohunga with a wand in his hand repeated an invocation, the fire was rendered sacred by the karakia taitai he chanted. Once the tapu had been lifted and Tane and other gods were placated, it was safe after an ahi tukupara ceremony for the people to harvest the birds of the forest, to cook and eat them for food. This summary is the very barest description of what Best had imparted to him by the old man on the subject of the ahi taitai rites. It leads us to one of the most intriguing assessments by the Pākehā of the old chief's legacy and records a last bequest which, if true, goes some way to explaining the trajectory of Best's life thereafter.

The fulsome mihi which Best gives to Tutakangahau, a decade after their first significant kōrero throughout that long night on the shores of Wairau Moana in 1895, sums up the value of his kura (teaching), then and now. He 'possessed a vast amount of very curious knowledge . . . a storehouse of primitive lore . . . he knew the old Native names of every tree, shrub, plant, or fern in the forests of Tuhoeland'. More than all of this, 'he was thoroughly conversant with the modes of thought of the ancient Maori . . . the strange metaphorical expressions of the men of yore . . . the belief in the life principle of inanimate objects . . . a knowledge that shall not be acquired by the *pakeha*, strive he never so hard'.[67] There is a genuine poignancy here, as Best digs deep to find words appropriate to express his respect and gratitude to the man he considered the *sine qua non* of his Tūhoe informants – and a friend too, over his long and often lonely mission to recover and record what could be saved of this rich oral storehouse, for future generations.

In the next paragraph, there appears a description of their final meeting which implies there was at least one Pākehā who Tutakangahau believed could and should acquire this ancient knowledge: Elsdon Best. 'On the occasion of my last interview with the old man', he writes, 'he gave me some curious and archaic invocations of the men of yore'; these were powerful karakia as to how the priests made the sacred fires, 'and located therein the dread presence and power of the gods'.[68] This was not to be taken lightly: Best had written earlier to Smith in August 1902, to the effect that 'old Tu's son and others are slating the poor old chap for giving me his karakia etc. It appears that his divulging these caused a violent storm here just when he left my camp.'[69] Imparting such tapu lore to any outsider – let alone a Pākehā – was still held by many Tūhoe to be dangerous: Best might employ witchcraft against them, as did traditional enemies in the past. Another letter to Smith three years later – not long before the final meeting Best is writing about – speaks of 'Old Tutaka . . . [having had] a dream that he had been emasculated

. . . [which was] a warning to him to whakatika the genealogies etc of Matatua'.[70]

Tutakangahau at that late point in his life was actively engaged in setting down the whakapapa correctly ('whakatika'), as part of a series of meetings taking place throughout Tūhoe. He had written to a Māori newspaper of Best's involvement in recording Tūhoe history.[71] There is little doubt that there was pressure on the old man from within and without to leave a bequest in both worlds. It is clear too that his choice of Best as a vehicle for his disclosures had remained steadfast over the twelve years they shared in this enterprise. What comes next in the account Best gives in 'Maori Forest Lore' should be no surprise: Tutakangahau tells him he is the last man in Tūhoe who knows of these things – and Best is about to have the mantle of succession laid on him. His kōrero – as reported – is dramatic: '*E tama! Ko au anake o Tuhoe e mohio ana ki enei mea. Katahi ano au ka korero i enei mea, kore rawa nei au i korero i mua. Ko koe anake e mohio ana. Ka waiho ko koe hai tohunga mo te iwi.* (O son! I alone among Tuhoe know of these things, and now for the first time I tell them. I have never divulged them before. You alone know them, and you shall remain as a *tohunga* [priest, adept] for the tribe.)'[72]

This is not quite a deathbed ōhākī, yet if Best is to be believed, the old man was laying upon his shoulders something of the patriarchal blessing of an Old Testament prophet, Elijah to Elisha. Those who might question the veracity of this account need to answer at least two pressing questions: why would Best risk his reputation by inventing this conversation (as well as the one at Wairau Moana in 1895)? Why did the ethnographer spend the rest of his life acting as if he was indeed the last suitable candidate available to a man like Tutakangahau, long after he had 'lifted the trail of Maui of old, and entered the snare of great Hine'? It is not as if he thought he knew it all: '[The chief] has taken the bulk of his knowledge with him. Only the fragments, filched by a member of an alien race, are here offered.'[73]

There will be more to say of their relationship: the political manoeuvrings that constituted the public side of their dealings in the establishment of the Urewera District Native Reserve from 1896 onwards. But there is little doubt that their ethnographic relationship and the friendship that grew out of it was long and cordial, until the final year of the old man's life. As his mental powers faded and his energies waned, the messianic presence of Rua Kenana's community at his old Maungapōhatu home offered him a return to a semblance of the enclosed religious culture prior to Colenso's coming in the 1840s. There is a telling anecdote relayed by Best in the early 1920s, of the time in September 1898 when Tutakangahau and a Tūhoe delegation travelled to Wellington to meet the Premier Seddon to hasten the setting up of the Urewera Commission. At a public address to a WEA audience at Trentham in 1921, on the benefits of comparative anthropology, Best discusses Māori and their 'communistic usages'. He relates that as he lived amongst Tūhoe 'on friendly terms, they treated me as one of themselves'.

By way of illustration, he refers to an incident involving 'my late friend and mentor Tutakangahau . . . [who was] on his way to the Wonder City, and being desirous of cultivating European amenities, he called at my camp in order to borrow my toothbrush for a few weeks'. Best cannot resist playing to his audience: 'This may be cited as one of the pleasant little communistic usages that we have improved upon.'[74] The story is a good indication of the nature of their relationship: that Best (with his implied mock horror at the violation of European oral hygiene standards) would consent to go without his toothbrush for that length of time, as he assuredly had to, unless possessed of a spare. Was the old chief, with a lifelong respect for the extreme tapu value of the head (and a chief's head at that), so impelled to display his knowledge of Pākehā tikanga (customs) in the white man's city that he allowed another man's dental device to come within those sacred precincts? Was this perhaps another sign that such tapu were becoming drained of their former influence, along with the many other spiritual strands that had once held the power of such leaders in place?

Who knows if he used it? It was unlikely that many Pākehā would come calling on the Urewera delegation in their lodgings, at Mrs Smith's boarding house in Molesworth Street – let alone join them in the bathroom.[75] The old man knew what would matter to the Europeans in Pōneke. He was not about to look as if he didn't know how to play the part of a Tūhoe ambassador come to town. Most of all, he knew that Te Peehi – as one of the family – was able and bound to oblige him with the loan of his toothbrush.

CHAPTER NINE

'A territory for the Maori people and the indigenous birds'[1]*: Tūhoe and the Rohe Pōtae, 1896–1909*

Tutakangahau's 1898 visit to Wellington – equipped with Best's toothbrush – was a vital part of a process alluded to earlier: the demand for an expression of Tūhoe autonomy. This was to be the fulfilment of Donald McLean's commitment to them from the early 1870s, and Seddon's affirmation of the same in the 1894 hui at Rūātoki, that they would not lose control of their territory: 'your lands will not leave you'. In bearing away Numia Te Pukenui Kereru's taiaha from that meeting, the Premier had styled himself as 'a friend and father' to the tribe, one who would look after their interests as well as those of his Pākehā electors. The legislation they had travelled south to discuss that September, the Urewera District Native Reserve Act, had been passed into law in October 1896, noted in the House at the time by Seddon as 'a legal recognition of the agreement made with Donald McLean 25 years earlier'.[2]

While wanting to assure the nation that the 'turbulent Tuhoe' had come under the same law that obtained throughout the rest of the Dominion, he knew he would have to make concessions to their desire for local autonomy. Under the 1896 legislation, owners of blocks could elect local committees, but only a larger general committee would hold the power of alienation of land. Under the legislation, however, before the General Committee could be set up, surveys showing hapū boundaries must be made, and once the ownership was agreed, and partitions set, the owners of local blocks could elect one member to represent them on that umbrella committee, which could then speak for all of Tūhoe to the commissioners.

The machinery to set up the General Committee and local hapū block committees, and the appointment of the commissioners, ground on slowly. Tūhoe quickly chose their five Commission members – including Tutakangahau – but Seddon's government, distracted by the Diamond Jubilee of April 1897 and the looming Boer War, did not gazette the members until February of 1898.[3] The Pākehā commissioners were W. J. Butler (uncomfortably for Tūhoe, a Native Land Court judge) and Percy Smith, the Surveyor-General, Best's fellow Māoriphile and boss. The delays were causing frustration, and local disputes were breaking out over ownership, before the Commission had gathered for its first sitting.

Smith had ensured that Best – his man on the spot – was appointed as Commission Secretary, setting up a final twist in the relationship of the ethnographer and Tutakangahau. As they had collaborated in recording Tūhoe history and customs, so they would sit together on the troubled century's last viable experiment in the fulfilment of hopes for tribal sovereignty: te mana motuhake o Tūhoe. It began with high expectations from them – but from early on, the portents were not good. It was partly from frustration at the limited progress, that this deputation of leading men had come to meet the Premier and his Māori ministers. The official record of this hui gives us a clear picture of the old man's view of events: ten years before his death, he was pouring out his heart at the seat of Pākehā power. Were his hearers listening?

On 26 September 1898, the Tūhoe deputation – Numia Kereru, Te Whiu, Te Aoterangi, Pihopa, Tutakangahau and his son Pinohi, also known as Tukua Te Rangi (or Tukua-i-te-rangi) – met with the Premier and the Māori MPs, Wi Pere, Henare Kaihau and Henare Tomoana (the last newly elected to the Legislative Council).[4] The Urewera leaders were anxious to inform Seddon of the volatile situation amongst their people. Tutakangahau spoke first on the Tūhoe side: as their senior chief, it was he who delivered the salutations, and oiled the pleasantries, before getting down to the issues at hand. 'In the year 1896 the Urewera District Native Reserve Act was passed dealing with the land within the Tuhoe outside boundary' – but nearly two years on, there was little progress towards implementation.[5] He had been feeling 'very *pouri* at times', waiting in an increasingly troubled frame of mind at Mrs Smith's boarding house in Molesworth Street for Seddon to meet them. Now, his depression was lifting.

This was a very frank and intimate expression of the relationship the old man felt he enjoyed with the Pākehā Premier, following his equally bold assertion about why he had come to the hui: 'I have come with my young people, and we do not desire to go back *to the old order of things, because the law has now been established.*'[6] The commissioners had been empowered under the Act and they must now get on with the job – as a member of the Commission himself, he must have been more than a little frustrated at the slow progress. The statement the old chief makes about his living culture is crucial: he has internalised the rule of law and so he appeals to that law. The days of the taiaha and the rifle are gone, and Tutakangahau demonstrates his grasp of that rule as the basis for a 'Maori modernity . . . a bulwark against the rejected alternative of endless conflict'.[7]

The law he appealed to – recalling his earlier statements and those of others – was a biblically-based civil law, but an assumed *moral* code nonetheless. Seddon's words of 1894 still had force and must be enacted; there was an existing personal relationship between them that the Premier acknowledged when he shortly thereafter spoke of these men as 'old friends'. He had looked forward with pleasure to the meeting, apologised at length for the delays beyond his control, and congratulated the delegation for writing him a kind note when news of the hold-up had reached them. He still regarded the 'sceptre or *taiha* [*sic*] . . . presented to me by [Numia's] late father' as a sign that he must watch over their interests, 'because you are my children'.[8] It is tempting to dismiss this rhetoric as mere paternalism, but it is doubtful the Tūhoe chiefs saw it that

Tukua Te Rangi (Pinohi), Tutakangahau's son, taken some years after the Wellington visit in 1898. There is no known image of his father with Seddon at this meeting. This portrait hangs in the wharenui Tanenuiarangi at Maungapōhatu. *Author photograph, original photographer unknown, courtesy of Tīpene Ohlson*

way. If Seddon truly was bound to them by links greater than office and obligation, their mana and their prospects could only be strengthened.

Reading Tukua Te Rangi's response later in the meeting – when he presented Seddon with a woven mat – tends to confirm this view. As Seddon looked upon them as his children, 'including the old men', it was Tukua Te Rangi's desire 'on behalf of the old man here [his father], and also on behalf of his children, who are also your children, to present you with a mat'. In doing this, it was his hope that the Premier's 'good-will, *aroha* and affection will remain for all time'.[9] Tutakangahau and his son had brought this koha (gift) to honour Seddon, and did so with these significant words: 'on behalf of his children *who are also your children*'. This is more than an effusion of temporary goodwill brought on by the exchange of power and promises. Seddon is invited into the family, a binding compact that would leave him less able to break the expressed trust (compare this with Tutakangahau's gift of his granddaughter Marewa's educational supervision to Best, three years earlier).

Seddon in his turn had jokingly chided the visitors with the complaint that even 'though they had not been able to see him due to his business', why had they not 'been to see Mrs Seddon and [his] children?' – where a cordial welcome always awaited them. It seems a man called Tupaea had saved the Premier's life, on his last visit to the Urewera: 'it was owing to his careful guidance that I was brought safely through the Urewera country'.[10] Mrs Seddon had since then harboured very warm feelings towards Tūhoe – failing Tupaea's care and guidance, she 'would probably have been a widow'. Putting aside for a moment the political context of the meeting, there is a definite quality of feeling that emerges from this text, one that need not be diminished by the shadow of cynical hindsight regarding what failed to eventuate. For Tutakangahau and for Seddon, this was personal.

Nevertheless, there was business to address and serious problems to confront. Other chiefs present spoke of the many hui that had been held in the Urewera over the proposed changes the new legislation was meant to bring. Some hapū were becoming fractious at government delays in setting the Commission in motion. Te Wakaunua wanted 'a great committee of the Tuhoe' empowered to look after their interests by way of a clause inserted in the Act. This was vital: various meetings, he said, had required that 'the *mana* should be established from the top to the bottom' – that the structures of devolved power from the government through to Tūhoe leaders and local hapū should be made clear, so the work could begin.[11]

Numia Kereru had already pointed to serious troubles arising from the delays: some of the people 'even had recourse to guns'. He had made it plain what Tūhoe wanted from the Act: they understood their lands were to be a reserve, and so 'the Commissioners shall proceed to investigate and subdivide the land'. They should immediately be sent to their duties amongst Tūhoe, so that 'the Tuhoe people may as speedily as possible enter into the *mana* proposed to be issued under the Act'.[12] Mana, that is, which conferred the power and the dignity to run their own affairs. Behind the anxiety provoked by the delays was the ongoing fear of incremental land loss that would be suffered by their people if ownership and authority were not assured to Tūhoe. Those living within the borders of the Reserve were well aware they were surrounded by a land-hungry Pākehā settler majority whose numbers by the mid-1890s were well over half a million.

Tutakangahau touched on this in his next address to the meeting, referring to a 'Premier's Bill' that might have some application to the 40 to 50,000 acres of Tūhoe land 'not situated within the Rohepotae'.[13] He was referring to the Native Lands Settlement and Administration Bill of 1898, which entailed plans for Māori councils, marae committees and land councils, encouraging many to hope for a new dispensation involving some local self-determination.[14] He wanted to see clauses inserted in that Bill 'with reference to Tuhoe lands', in an area that had already been dealt with by the Native Land Court. He was, he said, 'desirous that this Bill should be passed', that 'effect might be given to the Queen's words when she desired that the *land shall be absolutely tied up for the benefit of the Maoris*'.[15] There could hardly be a more passionate statement of the old chief's motivations, nor expression of what was at stake if land continued to be leased, sold, or worse – confiscated – at the rate it was passing out of Māori ownership. Control of their remaining lands and resources meant for him the survival of any Tūhoe hopes for a viable future.

Seddon responded by insisting on the need to get the commissioners appointed: they would then establish a temporary committee. The blocks could then be surveyed and titles ascertained, the final form of the General Committee having 'full power for dealing with the whole'.[16] He could see no obstacle to having this system in 'full working-order in the course of a few months' – which did in fact prove true, the Commission beginning its work in February of the following year. Turning to Tutakangahau's concerns about the Native Lands Settlement and Administration Bill, he was of the opinion the new measures would not affect their country – 'unless you desire it'. In that case, they should let him know the boundaries, and 'give [him] the clauses that [they] wished inserted', for careful consideration.[17] He was also keen to see reserves set aside in each block, land 'given voluntarily by the different hapus for education, for hospitals, and for your poor'. Whether or not this proposal was workable, it shows that the Premier was aware – after his 1894 visit – of the parlous state of the Tūhoe economy since the land wars and the ruinous effects of the alliance with Te Kooti.

Tutakangahau was in full agreement with Tūhoe making their own provision for the poor and the needy: in their straitened circumstances, that would have been the majority, and they were already sharing their resources. He declared himself buoyed up by the explanations Seddon and Wi Pere had given them: he had been pouri (depressed), but now that feeling had 'given way to one of satisfaction'.[18] Whereas he had 'not been certain at all about the Tuhoe Rohepotae . . . I feel filled with joy at the replies we have got today'. This is hardly surprising: for over twenty-five years, he had been working with his fellow chiefs, wrestling with the government to maintain control of their territory and regain lost lands. It seemed they were on the verge of obtaining recognition as owners and administrators of the historic Tūhoe rohe. It was a joy that would not last – but in September of 1898, Tutakangahau was again demonstrating that 'internalised belief in modernity'; he was supporting 'the rule of law, not because he trusted Pākehā, but because it was part of his culture'.[19]

His fellow chiefs seized the opportunity to appeal to Seddon to sort out legal issues over various local land disputes, and also – on the question of the conveniences of modern life – for the siting of a telegraph office and a money order office at Rūātoki. Numia Kereru pointed out the inconvenience for 'those of us who are sheep-owners', having to travel to Whakatāne to complete their financial transactions. These mundane details depict a people in transition, somewhere between a vanished world of chiefly authority and the commercial imperatives of the money economy. The request for the latest in modern communications – little different than today's cries from farmers and those in outlying rural areas for high-speed broadband internet services – shows a forward-thinking perspective, an awareness of their need to be in touch with the wider world.

For Seddon, these requests confirmed his conviction that the rebel Tūhoe psyche of the past was disappearing. Requesting for a policeman at Rūātoki, post and telegraph and money order services, was a sign that they had 'arrived at a fair degree of civilisation'.[20] In spite of the fact that the Premier's vision of a local elected democracy would never mesh with the hereditary power of hapū structures that had formed Tutakangahau's world, there existed at that point in time a coincidence of interests. Seddon wanted to bring Tūhoe under the sway of civilisation, as he saw it; they wanted the benefits of that world, while avoiding the peril of land losses. The latter would render them not only homeless and without an economic base, but cut off from the land that gave them both their history and identity, a people formed outside of Western time in the mists of myth and kōrero that no other iwi could claim. Bereft of the Urewera, they could no longer feel themselves to be truly Tūhoe.

While this negotiation was unfolding, Best the road quartermaster had got himself embroiled in an example of the kind of inter-hapū tension the chiefs had pointed out to Seddon. His friend and informant Paitini and his wife Makurata had become involved in a land dispute with the Ngāti Whare hapū, Ngāti Te Karaha, near Te Whāiti. A revisionist critique by Richard Hill, written in 1988, says Paitini's hapū were in favour of waiting for the investigations of the new Commission to prove ownership of the land, whereas Ngāti Te Karaha, unwilling to wait, had fenced and cultivated the disputed turf.[21] According to this account, Best was accused of favouring Paitini's people; after Makurata had been charged with an assault in the affray, Best took up arms on her behalf against Lowry, the local constable. Craig, Best's biographer, has an otherwise unspecified Tūhoe hapū claiming the Ngāti Whare land and preparing to sow grass seed to establish a prior right of usage. This led to 'a full-scale battle . . . police action . . . and the arrest of the offenders'.

Craig's version has Best persuading Tūhoe to let the Commission settle the issue, then being accused of stirring up the trouble himself. At this, he threatened to leave the Urewera, abandoning his real mission as ethnographer – whereupon an agitated Percy Smith took the initiative and offered him the role of secretary to the Commission. Once he had calmed down, Best agreed, and so entered a new phase of the relationship with his fellow appointee Tutakangahau, who was about to begin work as one of the seven Māori commissioners. It was during this new period in his Urewera sojourn that the seeds of a 'magnum opus', the massive two-volume history *Tuhoe: The Children of the Mist*, began to take shape in his mind. Best had never intended to write such a work. However, the kōrero he heard on a regular basis as he sat on the Commission in the courtrooms and marae meeting houses where the hearings were held, listening to the elders reciting their whakapapa and hapū histories – heroic deeds of old, spiced with waiata and proverbs – presented him with a rich supply of

Best's 'magnum opus': *Tuhoe: The Children of the Mist*, begun in the late 1890s, a draft manuscript by 1907, and not published until 1925. *Author photograph*

material. This experience was to supply an answer to what many of the elders of the tribe now wanted from him: a written history to preserve their tribal memories in the face of Pākehā obliteration.

Best was now effectively the overseer of the Ruatāhuna road works, a government agent for the district, and the prospective Commission Secretary. His work included delivering pension vouchers to Tūhoe beneficiaries, including Tutakangahau at Maungapōhatu – which increased his opportunities to spend time talking with the ageing ruānuku, writing down all he could, in prospect of the eventual loss of his greatest mōhio.[22] As secretary, Best would literally be the old man's servant, although he was to be paid more: Smith and Butler, the Pākehā commissioners, received fifteen shillings per day expenses, Best seven shillings and sixpence, and the seven Māori commissioners a humble five shillings apiece.[23] The latter amount came from a grant of £15 to defray the considerable expenses incurred by the Tūhoe hosts at these sittings, feeding the large numbers that attended and followed the hearings from place to place. So Best – with an eye to the past condition of Tūhoe, and Tutakangahau, with an eye to their future wellbeing – sat down together with the other members of the Commission, to prove who owned the land by right of conquest, prior occupation and usage.

Deciding such matters as historic and defined hapū boundaries from an aggregation of hunter-gatherer domains would not prove easy – especially to those Pākehā politicians and the settler interests who made no secret of their contempt for Māori abilities to adjudicate their own affairs in the matter of land title. One such, the Opposition leader Captain Russell speaking in the House,[24] derided Tūhoe hopes of now having 'control of their lands'. Once the Act was operating, the 'autocratic Native Minister [Seddon] will do what he chooses . . . [and] settlement will follow on subdivision'. The wagons were circling: most settlers regarded such 'under-utilised wastelands' as too good to be left in Māori hands. Some, such as the cynical Bay of Plenty MP W. H. Herries, speaking nine years after the Act had been passed, were to prove equal prophets of Tūhoe doom, seeing landless Māori as a potential urban underclass: 'I say our legislation ought to be in the direction of enabling him to go into a factory.'[25] His experiences with Māori agricultural contractors in his electorate had obviously convinced him that a deracinated native proletariat would be excellent workers in the dark satanic mills of the bustling colonial cities.

With pressures from without and within, the Commission finally began its work in February 1899, but was soon to face the inherent conflict of aims apparent in the opposing interests of its members.[26] Tūhoe solidarity had only a recent history: there had long been inter-hapū rivalry on 'borders' within the Rohe Pōtae, and the government had already begun to exploit territorial disputes on its fringes by the use of leases with neighbouring hapū and iwi who had fought Tūhoe in the past for land, such as Ngāti Whare, Ngāti Manawa and Ngāti Ruapani. Many 'boundaries' simply overlapped, and as the sittings went on, the original 58 hapū inside the 656,000 acres of the Reserve had their territories compressed, 'down to what was considered a more manageable 34 blocks'. In practice, it was found that the 'nature of Tūhoe customary tenure meant that the neat division of the area into hapū blocks was impossible to achieve'.[27]

Separate hapū were placed together in single blocks, which led to later appeals for partition.

The composition of the Commission also proved problematic: Māori commissioners – at their own initiative – were required to abstain from voting on lands where they had an interest. By 1900, Tutakangahau was complaining about the section of the Act that said 'this land should be investigated according to Maori customs'. He was now 'afraid that this Commission is rather inclined to the Native Land Court system of procedure'.[28] As a chief with a number of interests in hapū to which he was related (including those at Rūātoki and Waimana), the senior Tamakaimoana leader's influence was increasingly neutralised; this almost certainly was a factor in his final disillusionment with the tactic of engagement with Pākehā power. Title orders published in 1903 reveal 'that many of the blocks are signed by just two or three commissioners; Tutakangahau in particular appears on very few orders'.[29]

Percy Smith, one of the Pākehā commissioners, might well bewail the problems caused by intermarriage – 'it is difficult to say to what hapu any particular individual of the tribe belongs'. In practice this meant that both he and Judge Butler (formerly of the Native Land Court) effectively marginalised the compromised Tūhoe commissioners, reducing them to the kind of role given to that of the Land Court's native assessors: second fiddle.[30] Smith resigned in 1900, replaced by another Native Land Court official, Judge Scannell. In 1899 when hearings began, in a symbolic gesture Smith had presented a flag sought three years earlier from Seddon by Tutakangahau, to be inscribed 'Te Mana Motuhake o Tuhoe' (The Separate Authority of Tūhoe). The flag the Commission received bore instead the words 'Ko Te Ture Motuhake o Tuhoe' (Separate Law) – a more specific reference to the Act, avoiding the impression that Tūhoe were an independent 'nation within'.[31] In spite of having a law made for Tūhoe, the authority that makes any law operate increasingly lay with the government and its Pākehā appointees, who took turns in chairing each sitting of the Commission. Symbol and reality rapidly moved apart.

For the commissioners to decide how to translate Tūhoe occupation and usufruct rights into ownership on the lines of English law was a challenge: take tīpuna and ahi kā roa (ownership by reason of continuous occupation), take raupatu (by conquest), and take tuku (by gifting) all had to be proved somehow.[32] This was no easy task, with hotly contested hearings of claims, most of which stretched back into times of nomadic food gathering when use was occasional, and seasonal. In the end, the commissioners chose to view those who had lived on the land for 'three or four generations . . . merely to collect food' as occupiers.[33] Conflict sometimes occurred along the way: in 1900, Tutakangahau wrote to Percy Smith about a dispute over Ngaputahi in the Te Whāiti block where fences and houses had been targeted and destroyed. The old chief asked for instructions after a hui was held at Ruatāhuna; Smith advised him to await the Commission's dealing with the block. Best was apparently doubtful much good would come of any interventions by the Tūhoe commissioners.[34]

Tūhoe hapū were not only pitted against each other: there were also recriminations against their own commissioners. At the same time as Tutakangahau was describing the troubles at Te Whāiti, in June 1900 Hurae Puketapu wrote to Smith. There were plans, he wrote, to remove himself, 'Tu[takangahau] and Te Pou. Tamaikoha told me this personally. I asked him the reason but he would not divulge it, the only reason is jealousy.'[35] There were also objections raised by some Tūhoe about the payment of the Māori commissioners: in attempting to author their own collective fate, their leaders were seen to be feathering their own nests. Jealousy and rivalry were poisoning the chalice. Numia Te Pukenui Kereru's trenchant critique of the Native Land Court's shortcomings – made to Seddon in 1894 at Rūātoki – was coming true in the Reserve. Tūhoe were pitted against each other in a process that was to transform 'customary overlapping resources into exclusive "winner-take-all" interests in land'.[36] In hastening the process, to establish the best and therefore exclusive rights to land, the Pākehā commissioners were evolving a strategy similar to that of the despised Land Court Tūhoe had been desperate to keep out of their rohe, coining the proverb: 'kaua e hoko! – don't sell'.

Once titles were individualised, the senior chiefs knew from experience that leases and sales inevitably followed as people broke ranks. They, however, were gradually relegated to supporting roles in the Commission, as the Pākehā members exploited their advantages and began to impose a Land Court-style system for proof of ownership. By 1900, in a discussion related to the Waipotiki block, Tutakangahau is recorded in agreement with them – 'yours is a wise decision' – and consenting to it, along with other Tūhoe members.[37] The Pākehā former Land Court judges increasingly took control. The amendment of the Act in that year brought the disputed Rūātoki lands into the Reserve, out of the jurisdiction of the Native Land Court. Costs associated with prior surveys were carried into the Reserve, against the spirit of Seddon's 1894 promise the government would bear them.

There was strong settler pressure to have this Rūātoki land made available for lease and sale; rents from any leases were to go towards paying the survey costs. Those Tūhoe commissioners with interests in this land (including Tutakangahau) were unable to adjudicate, so it was proposed that non-Tūhoe Māori could take part, acting on their behalf. The vision of the 1894 Rūātoki hui – and that of Te Whitu Tekau in the 1870s – was beginning to unravel. The arrival of Judge Scannell as a commissioner after the resignation of Percy Smith left that troubled body looking even less distinguishable from the Native Land Court. Its work continued: the sittings placed considerable strain on a fragile local economy beset by food shortages due to crop failures, floods and sickness.[38] By October 1902, 'title to [the] whole reserve [was] complete' and the first Commission was adjourned. More than 200 appeals were to be lodged against its decisions – these were heard by the second Commission, from 1906 to 1907. This group, however, had no Tūhoe members: Paratene Ngata of Ngāti Porou (the father of the rising star Apirana) was 'the only Maori appointed to this three-man panel of "experts"'.[39]

The experiences of Tutakangahau and his peers in trying to merge Pākehā lawmaking with Tūhoe tikanga must have soured them. In the wake of their dissatisfaction and resentment after the first Commission concluded its work, in March 1904 the government rewarded the chiefs with a viceregal visit. Governor Ranfurly met the Tūhoe rangatira and other Māori leaders in a great hui in Rūātoki, when many more fine speeches were made, prior to the great man's departure for England. There was a wider political motive for the well-travelled and adventurous Governor's visit: the second Māori Councils Conference was taking place there, and

Paitini Wi Tapeka with his pack-horse on the Huiarau trail, during the viceregal visit to Rūātoki, March 1904.
Photographer: Malcolm Ross, Elsdon Best Collection, Alexander Turnbull Library, Wellington, NZ, PA1-q-634-13

he was present to open it as the King's agent.[40] Accompanying him were Maui Pomare, Gilbert Mair, and the author of the Māori Councils Act of 1900, the progressive modernising Māori MP James Carroll.

It was to the precursor of this Act – designed to give Māori some local control of their own affairs – that Tutakangahau had referred when speaking to Seddon in 1898 about managing land interests (including some of his own) outside the Rohe Pōtae. The Act was ultimately to fail in practice (Carroll's long-term aim was to lower support for Kotahitanga), but at this stage it was still an ongoing experiment, working alongside the Reserve Act.[41] Ranfurly's visit – part of a farewell tour through the north – was something of a coup for both sides. An earlier attempt by a predecessor Lord Onslow in 1891 had been blocked at first by Tūhoe hostility, and Ranfurly's immediate predecessor Glasgow made no effort to visit. The tour was recorded by a member of the party (the journalist Malcolm Ross), who produced an historic photo album of Tūhoe life, along with newspaper accounts and a published journal.[42]

Ross wrote that 'a high Chief, Tutakanahau . . . asked us to penetrate into his country, so at last we shall be able to go and see for ourselves'. They did so, entering the storied fastness of the Urewera armed with this invitation, accompanied on the rough ride from Waikaremoana to Rūātoki by none other than Best's first close Tūhoe informant, Paitini Wi Tapeka.[43] Ross's photographs – with their graphic images of the rugged and dangerous trail – bring the journey to life, as does his partisan but colourful account of their adventures. Lord Ranfurly's aide-de-camp Dudley Alexander also left a series of diary entries that combine a tourist's enthusiasm with an occasional kerchief held to the Pākehā nose.

While it is impossible to avoid the racial overtones that make both Alexander and Ross uncomfortable to read at times, both accounts are replete with observed delights, along with the inevitable patronage – and give privileged glimpses of Tutakangahau's late-life milieu. The party passed tiny villages en route to Ruatāhuna, noting the poverty in these small kāinga as they travelled: women 'in faded non-descript clothes . . . men clad in garments that had seen better days'.[44] With his legions of Te Arawa warriors, the old bush fighter Gilbert Mair had traversed these same trails and climbed the mountains chasing Te Kooti – and fell to reminiscing as they passed the old sites of fierce battles. Paitini, who followed them with his pack-horse, recalled the time when he and Te Kooti were escaping with their wives and an 'enemy bullet cut his belt in two'.[45] Bush fighters all.

On reaching Ruatāhuna they were welcomed at the famous Ringatū meeting house, Te Whai-a-te-motu, built in the 1890s to commemorate the very pursuit of Te Kooti that Mair and Paitini were recalling as they pressed on. The fulsome welcome of an elderly chief's whaikōrero – 'Oh my parent the Governor, come hither!' – was soured for Ross when the old man 'dropped from the realms of poetry and began to whine about the securing of their land to their people', a school to be built, the pā fortified and 'the dog tax!'.[46] Were these the intrepid sons of Tūhoe, he wondered, who had braved ocean storms in the 'frail Mataatua canoe'? Distrust of the government and complaints about the dog tax: he writes that later, at Rūātoki, they would hear 'more manly speeches . . . [concluding that] those left in the ancient capital [Ruatāhuna] were but degenerate sons of famous ancestors'. The Governor, in his reply, 'wisely avoided political matters'.[47] Reading between the lines, it is not difficult to discern the conflicting agendas – matters that were to be avoided at the major hui ahead of them.

At a second meeting there the following day, with Tūhoe from near and far in attendance, Carroll, the Minister of Native Affairs (Seddon's successor in the portfolio), took up the challenge of answering to 'political matters'. He exhorted the assembled hapū to show gratitude for the Pax Britannica they now enjoyed under the Queen's mantle, and berated them for their complaints. 'Your lands are now settled upon you', he chided, so whose fault was it 'that father has been turned against son and brother against brother' – a nice New Testament twist. Their appeals to Wellington – after the work of the first Commission was completed – were their own responsibility to solve locally. This was exactly the kind of inter-hapū rivalry that surveying and individualised titles were bound to produce, but according to Carroll, it was now Tūhoe's infighting that was keeping them out of Te Ao Mārama, the new world. 'Were this beautiful land owned by another tribe the people would be living in a state of prosperity. *I tell you now that the old order must pass away, and a new one begin.*'[48] They needed to avoid the threefold worldly evils: liquor, laziness, and wastefulness.

After such an upbraiding, it would be interesting to have had access to an account by those Tūhoe present; Ross leaves the reader with the viceregal party bedding down in their tent, 'pondering over the problem of the Maori people'. No doubt his hosts lay down in their own whare, pondering the exact opposite. The viceroyal progress made the outskirts of Rūātoki on 16 March and the great welcome began – hundreds of Māori had gathered, including representatives of all the Māori Councils of New Zealand. Ross's invaluable photographs even show us Best, speaking before a great hui at Rongokarae marae. In a group photo taken before the meeting house ('Lord Ranfurly and the principal chiefs of N.Z. Ruatoki, 1904'), we can see sitting on a mat directly in front of the Governor an elderly chief, bearing a more than passing resemblance to Tutakangahau.

It was a massive gathering: 'about [a] 1000 Natives were present', wrote Ross of their arrival, all greeting the viceregal party with 'a very

Elsdon Best speaking – from notes – at Rongokarae marae, Rūātoki, during the viceregal hui there in March 1904.
Photographer: Malcolm Ross, Ranfurly Collection, Alexander Turnbull Library, Wellington, NZ, PA1-q-634-47-2

fine war dance and poi'.[49] Chiefs had assembled 'from all parts of the North Island . . . this being a very important gathering'. The locals 'made us very comfortable by putting us up in one of their small houses, and entertained us right royally'. This impressive traditional pōwhiri certainly energised the journalist's pen: 'a wild war dance . . . the warriors, most of them stripped to the buff . . . with piercing yells . . . and all the grim barbaric ardour of bygone days'. Such a passionate welcome – complete with mass poi displays and the earth a-thunder with a final haka – was a giddying display of Māori cultural authority.[50] Carroll responded with a greeting, mentioning their extreme difficulties in getting to Rūātoki, and the weary travellers retired early.

Ross was awake at 6 a.m. and proceeded to give a brief ethnography of Māori hygiene: 'The Maori is a very cleanly person, and is forever washing himself, he does not seem to object to the cold water at all.' Dudley Alexander also took an outsider's view, with a description of the evening worship sessions in 'the ill-ventilated hall . . . rank with a mixed assortment of odours'. He noted the varieties of 'Torori and Egyptian cigarettes [clashing] with Jockey Club and Violet de Parma . . . and much unwashedness'. Different conclusions were drawn by the two

Lord Ranfurly with the principal chiefs of New Zealand at Rūātoki, in front of the Rūnanga House (Rongokarae), March 1904. Tutakangahau appears fourth from the left, seated, with Numia Kereru and Ranfurly standing behind him on his right. *Photographer: Malcolm Ross, Ranfurly Collection, Alexander Turnbull Library, Wellington, NZ, PA1-q-634-44*

observers.[51] Ross also seemed surprised that the settlement was 'quite un-Europeanised', there being 'hardly a white face to be seen anywhere'. He was impressed with the 'song of kai', as those Māori present brought food to the dining shed, dancing with 'many gesticulations as they advanced with the pork and potatoes on plates and dishes in their hands'.

Religious observances held night and morning – 'a Service in the large meeting house' – were attended en masse 'by the Natives of this district [who were] Hauhaus'. This was he believed, 'a form of religion of their own, somewhat similar to Christianity. It takes the form of a man saying some prayers and then there is the singing of psalms.'[52] What he was observing was the religion that had begun as Te Kooti's karakia, witnessed by Pākehā at the first meeting of Te Whitu Tekau in 1872. These rituals were what became known in time as Ringatū, rather than any late-blooming version of Te Ua's Pai Mārire, as Ross imagined.

Alexander's account of the worship in the crowded meeting house recalled 'our first hauhau service in the fastnesses of Tuhoe Land long ago'.[53] His vivid report depicts 'impassioned orators . . . shrill women's voices . . . male barytone [*sic*] . . . [and] a deep far-away strain of phenomenal bass'. In the 'huge runanga house', lit with 'meagre flickering candles . . . the participants visible as ghosts', speakers would rise suddenly in a mood of great intensity. He begins to fear 'an hysterical outburst of religious fanaticism', but is relieved when the service ends and 'song and story from hoary-headed warriors' takes over.

Here is perhaps the last and most intimate picture of Tutakangahau's spiritual milieu before the rise of Rua Kenana and the old man's late retreat to the new messiah's community at Maungapōhatu. He was certainly on the marae that day and that night – he would have been one of those who took part in Te Kooti's karakia, reciting as he had done for over thirty-five years the Psalms of David imprinted in his memory together with the karakia of old, carrying both in his radically altered spiritual visions to the grave. Yet his religious activities were not confined to the past, recent or distant: in his active life as a frequent correspondent to Māori newspapers such as *Te Puke ki Hikurangi* (1987–1913), he wrote on many matters including Māori spirituality and whakapapa. Like Best, he had found an audience in print, an aspect of both lives seen in the next chapter of their story.

Ross, too, noted the presence of the 'Hau-Hau religion' at this meeting, 'originated by a Taranaki native named Te Ua', who he believed was later caught by 'Mair's men near Whakatane and hanged as a rebel' (he actually died in 1866, of tuberculosis – Ross is mixing him up with somebody else).[54] These solemn-faced men 'singing the psalms of David' were quite harmless, he thought, unlike those who had so recently decapitated the missionary Völkner – which remembrance sets him off on a lengthy rehearsal of the atrocity and its related history. Reminding his Pākehā audience of those old 'fearful scenes of barbarism' now displaced by the peaceful gathering before him, he makes no mention of the scorched earth policies inflicted by government forces on Tūhoe in those same valleys, shortly after Völkner's death. He notes 'it is only a few years ago – 1893 or '94 – since the Sovereign's writ would not run within their bounds'. These Māori, 'enlightened frock-coated gentlemen – for gentlemen they are – were now welcoming the King's representative' at their own request, the taste of missionary blood forgotten.[55]

Having put the past in perspective, he turns to the matter at hand: the official welcome of Lord Ranfurly. In a colourful and detailed account, Ross brings the energy and significance of the hui to life: sombre mats of rare kiwi feathers, the brilliant colours of the women's blouses giving 'an air of romance and unreality' to the occasion. Kereru the principal chief spoke first, showering the Governor with warm wishes and farewells; another speaker following referred to Ranfurly as the 'shadow of the King', he kotuku rerenga tahi, rare as the flight of the white heron. 'An old tattoed man' spoke next, recalling the Governor to the pleasure of their prior meeting in Wellington: 'you showed me great kindness. I have never ceased to love you since then.' If this man was not Tutakangahau (a strong probability), it is certainly possible that the next orator mentioned was: 'an old chief wearing the Duke's medal' began chanting a karakia, 'which, he said had been the means of bringing the Governor in safety to that meeting-place'.[56] The Tamakaimoana chief, senior enough to be high on the paepae (ranks of orators), would certainly have spoken.

Ranfurly responding spoke for a good three-quarters of an hour, expressing his regret at the passing of senior leaders such as Tamahau Mahupuku and Henare Tomoana. He pleased 'his hosts greatly by quoting one of their old proverbs – 'Tuhoe, the wasters of the world's treasures; the leaders of men down to death' (Tūhoe moumou kai, Tūhoe moumou taonga, moumou tangata ki te pō). He went on to moralise over that very issue of wasting the world's treasures – well beyond the poetry of the original – telling the assembled people how fortunate they now were to have their own lands 'by special Act of Parliament reserved to them for all time'. It would soon prove to be little more than a few years – well short of forever. The Urewera would not become the place of Ranfurly's imaginings for Tūhoe, where 'their children might grow up secure in their native possessions' in a forested bird sanctuary, attracting hordes of tourists. Rather, it would be a place where poverty and struggle became the order of the day, as more land slipped from their possession and local Tūhoe farmers were left without much-needed development capital.

Congratulating the delegates from the twenty-four Māori Councils, Ranfurly then cited an English proverb on the relationship of wealth and power, in the same breath exhorting the dignitaries to weed their fields to produce more of the 'excellent crops of maize' he had observed in the Rūātoki valley as they descended. Having thus told them off, he declared the conference open, concluding with patriotic appeals, promising to make known to the King on his return to England that 'the Maori people are true friends of the British flag'. With a final exhortation to these fine warriors to retain their old traditions, he was, according to Ross, 'heartily cheered', after making a profound impression on all present. No specious orator, 'he did not flatter the natives unduly; but where there was fault he found it; and where advice was necessary, he gave it'.[57] According to Alexander, 'Kapai! Kapai! Kia ora! Kia ora!! Kia ora!!! A perfect fusillade of gratification and pleasure [greeted] His Excellency's down sitting.' No doubt there was some relief that the lecture was over and kai time drew ever nearer.

But they first had to listen to Native Minister James Carroll, a recognised master of oratory in both tongues: 'gifted with cunning turns of phrase, graced with classic allusion, brightened by lively wit, unpalatable truths cunningly concealed in proverbial philosophy, or rendered more digestible by a coating of humour'.[58] In other words, Carroll was the tough cop to Ranfurly's somewhat more schoolmasterly paterfamilias, letting the assembled rangatira know that the assimilationist policies that drove his time in government were for the best, and not the divisiveness of the Kingitanga. As the architect of the Maori Councils Act, he was on an upward trajectory amongst rural Māori at that point in his career – but the policy was not to succeed.

Alexander, however, seemed somewhat drunk with the euphoria of the occasion: 'Friends long sundered meet with the universal hongi; mutual griefs beget a mutual tangi. What a haunting weirdness quivers through its inexpressible sadness. How minor cadences recurring and repeating cling to one's memory, piercing our pakeha reserve and appealing to our sense of loss and bereavement.'[59] Even as Tūhoe and the other Māori delegates – to the evident satisfaction of the dignitaries – were now on the way to becoming Pākehā in civility and progress, men like Dudley Alexander were somehow touched into becoming just a little Māori.

What Best made of all this is apparently not on the record – he was also a speaker on the manuhiri (visitors') side. One imagines Tutakangahau's

'Mr Elsdon Best, the historian of Tuhoe Land', photographed at Rūātoki by Malcolm Ross at the time of the 1904 meeting of chiefs with the Governor. His gaunt frame and his habitual erect, military bearing are evident.
Ranfurly Collection, Alexander Turnbull Library, Wellington, NZ, PA1-q-634-43-3

satisfaction: as a Tūhoe power broker, attracting the King's viceroy to Rūātoki was an affirmation of his mana, and the high point at that historic moment of his long political involvement with the settler government and its emissaries. As a commissioner, and as a kaitakawaenga (mediator) between his people and the Pākehā polity, his sun and the light of his generation of leaders were by now at their zenith, as another was about to begin its rise over Tūhoe: te mihaia hou, Rua Kenana, the new messiah.

As a final act, Lord Ranfurly bestowed on thirteen dignitaries present the gift of a special commemorative medal: of the twelve Māori recipients, Tutakangahau, Te Tuhi Pihopa, Te Whenuanui and Numia Kereru are prominent in a list sent to the former Governor in January 1905 by his agent Reeves in London, to an address at The Palace Hotel in Switzerland. The silver medals were on their way 'by to-day's mail via Suez and should reach the Colony about the 6th of March', he wrote.[60] Inscribed on each was the following: 'one side – Hei whakamaharatanga ki te Hui nui Na tetahi hoa pono o te Iwi Maori; other side – Ruatoki March 16, 1904 (Arms) Ranfurly Governor 1897 to 1904'. This medal – 'a remembrance

Tukua Te Rangi, also known as Pinohi Tutakangahau, photographed during the trial of Rua Kenana, Auckland, 1916. He wears the medal given to his father in 1904 by Lord Ranfurly, on behalf of the government.
Photographer unidentified, Elizabeth Murphy Collection, Alexander Turnbull Library, Wellington, NZ, PA1-o-358-24

of the Great meeting, from a true friend of the Maori People' – would have been worn with pride by the old chief and his peers, as it later was by his son Tukua Te Rangi (Pinohi), eight years after his father's death, in the year of Rua's arrest in 1916.[61]

On 10 March 1905, the Native Minister wrote an effusive letter to the former Governor, conveying the joy of the chiefs on receiving their tokens of esteem, complete with the Ranfurly crest – they 'rejoice at this mark of your special favour – they will have a place amongst the most cherished family heirlooms'.[62] This was certainly true for Pinohi: such recognition indicates again the old man's deep involvement in the Pākehā world he had worked with for so long. It was an honour due. Carroll helpfully mentions that the Governor's accompanying Māori message 'required very little alteration'. Maui Pomare also wrote to Ranfurly in May of the same year, recalling their journey 'through the fastnesses of the great Tuhoeland'. Ranfurly's medal, he writes, will remind him 'that in you my race has a "Hoa pono" tried and true'. Pomare concludes that 'the Ureweras are awakening. Over eighty buildings have been erected.' He promises to send his annual report to the retired eminence, signing off with a mention of the hapless Lord Plunkett, Ranfurly's less than dazzling successor, who Māori were to christen 'Blanket'.[63]

The medals bestowed by the departed Ranfurly may soon have lost some shine, as the shadows of compromise and bad faith fell over the work of the Tūhoe commissioners. The system that had been enacted to implement promises made by Seddon in 1894 at Rūātoki had indeed surveyed the land and given title, but brought with it destructive forces: 'expenses, prolonged litigation, internal dissension and the undermining of chiefly and hapu authority'.[64] By the time the second Commission began its work in December 1906, Tutakangahau was no longer a member, and had come to the government's notice for his involvement in Rua Kenana's messianic movement.[65] By 1908, a year after his death, the Stout-Ngata Commission was advising the government that the Urewera titles were now 'far advanced enough to allow the Native Land Court exercising jurisdiction in partition, succession and other cases'.[66]

An amendment to the original Act in 1909 extended the jurisdiction of that hated court to the Urewera, as settler attacks grew on government tardiness in making more Māori land available for lease. The control by the General Committee of land alienation was undermined by the sale of individual shares in blocks, and 'non-sellers' were gradually outflanked by 'aggressive Government purchase of individual shares in the Urewera'.[67] Between the years 1910 and 1921, the government purchased over half of the Urewera Reserve, as the powers of the General Committee leached away in doomed attempts to balance conflicting hapū and iwi interests. Government control was made complete by the Urewera Lands Act of 1920–1921, which consolidated Crown authority over Tūhoe lands: the owners would henceforth 'hold "ordinary" Native land under the jurisdiction of "ordinary" Native Land Acts'.[68]

So ended a protracted phase of Tutakangahau's dream: establishing a viable measure of Tūhoe autonomy within the settler state, ensuring the retention of the land that would make such a vision workable. The road to modernity was mined with hidden pitfalls: Tūhoe could no longer remain sequestered behind the broken barrier of tradition, nor unmolested within the natural barriers of the Urewera's geography. Nor did they wish to: access to literacy, education, the money economy, health and wellbeing were rights of citizenship in that modern world. They could not be expected to accede to a system that denied them these benefits, unless they gave in to settler pressure to lease or sell the best of their remaining lands, and opened their forest and mineral resources to uncontrolled exploitation. The negative evidence of previous Māori encounters with settler land hunger was obvious; their own entrance into the modern world needed careful management. Forces beyond their control within and without would not allow this to happen.

In 1894, when Seddon accepted the eponymous taiaha Rongokaeke from Numia Te Pukenui Kereru, it was as a sign of his obligation to protect the tribe. He failed in that duty of care: pressured by loyalty to a larger tribe – the Pākehā electors – and their intoxicating ride on the locomotive of imperial progress. His death in 1906 severed the personal connection Tutakangahau and the other chiefs had been at pains to cultivate, shown clearly in the bonded declarations between Tūhoe and the government at the Wellington hui in 1898. If the old man were not pouri enough then, as Seddon kept them waiting in Mrs Smith's boarding house at No. 5 Molesworth Street, he must have been radically depressed by the outcome of an Act that was meant to bring security to Tūhoe. The joy he was espousing by the end of that meeting, and the hope given him by the Premier's assurances, were certainly absent ten years later, as he retreated to Maungapōhatu with Rua – to live out a final year where his rich and fruitful life had begun.

CHAPTER TEN

'Wiped off the slate of life': The Last of the 'Mohios'[1]

Exercising authority and control over the land Tūhoe still held was not the only concern of Tutakangahau in the full life he led over his final years: protecting and preserving traditional knowledge – intellectual property as it might be described today – was another of the old chief's overriding concerns. Thanks to the industry of his pen, we have a written record of his work in this area, as it has come down to us today in the Māori newspapers with which he maintained a vigorous correspondence from 1900 onwards – especially *Te Puke ki Hikurangi*, the official newspaper of Te Kotahitanga, the Māori parliamentary movement.[2] His reputation as Māori scholar, ethnographer and repository of endangered knowledge is established through a search of these rich sources, and the visible parallels of his own work with that of Best's.

Along with his engagement in recording the past to enrich the future, there is also evidence of his involvement with the final messianic prophet of Tūhoe, Rua Kenana. This raises a number of questions about the relationship of the passing order of a late nineteenth-century hereditary chief to a commoner without rank, who nevertheless found a new source of authority in laying his claim to a mission of divine deliverance. Best's reaction to this latter development – hostile and dismissive – also requires scrutiny, as at the same time he struggled to conceive of and complete the great tribal history for which he is best known to this day: *Tuhoe: The Children of the Mist*.

His letters to Smith in the first decade of the new century form a tantalising account of what the book meant to him, and to Tūhoe, and of his own feelings as the last of his 'mohio' – the old men of knowledge – fell to the inevitability of death. Frustrated and alone, he would finally depart the Urewera in 1910, returning to Wellington, 'the Wonder City', where his dogged researches and writing were to make him a household name and bring 'the old mudslinger' from the frontier a good measure of global fame. What emerges from the first decade of the twentieth century for these two men is the way in which both – in their own ways – were hard at work as Tūhoe tribal historians.

Turning first to Tutakangahau's presence in these Māori newspapers, the question that arises is why whakapapa, and why at this time? Certainly, this seems to be his most pressing concern and one shared with others. In a letter to the editors of *Te Puke ki Hikurangi* dated 15 June 1902, he writes from Maungapōhatu on 10 June of that year, signing off 'Na Tutakangahau'.[3] This letter is part of a long-running discussion of whakapapa by many correspondents who appear in the issues of *Te Puke ki Hikurangi*. As well as local and national news, the newspaper contained reports of proceedings from the Māori Parliament at Pāpāwai in the Wairarapa, parliamentary news from Wellington (especially bills and laws affecting Māori), news from abroad, from local councils and marae committees, and a vigorous and prolific correspondence from numerous Māori elders, including Tutakangahau and Tuta Nihoniho, both informants of Best.[4]

The old man writes particularly on the subject of whakapapa, and his contributions are both learned and eloquent, attesting to the ongoing importance of literacy to his generation, born prior to the signing of the Treaty. The June 1902 letter consists of the usual mihimihi and salutations, then lengthy discussions of the various canoes, the navigators and their descendants (waka, tangata, iwi), right through from Maui to Tūhoe Potiki and his descendants. He concludes the kōrero (paraphrased):

> That's enough: it is simply that we are broadcasting this (knowledge) to the world, so my genealogical friends can examine it, the words of our ancestors, and disagree with them if they choose. For it is not as if (we / I) have made them up (here / now / today) for these words come from them (na ratau – from the ancestors) and their whare wananga (houses of learning).

The use of 'na ratau' here signifies *agency*, confirming that these words have authority, and they were passed on to Tutakangahau and other elders of Tūhoe. Now that they are finally written down, that authority remains with Tūhoe:

> . . . as for the other people (authorities) that have published (their whakapapa) in our precious taonga "Te Puke" and "Pipi" (the Māori newspapers), that is all good, but my thinking is that this activity (of recording and discussing whakapapa) is not an attempt to diminish the mana of anyone, nor to increase that of others.

On the contrary, he wants to place his knowledge of Tūhoe whakapapa in the public arena, where the stories of all iwi can be considered, with the understanding of these accounts – so he is 'loading up the waka' of *Te Puke* with these few words ('ena korero ruarua' – a modest self-deprecation).

Literacy enabled them to write their histories in Māori, bypassing the medium of Pākehā institutions to create a conversation and leave a record for future generations. Near the end of his life, the old chief is busily engaged as a Māori historian, a self-taught scholar, working in a similar mode (and from not dissimilar motives) running parallel to his Pākehā compatriot, Te Peehi. In another letter to *Te Puke* written three years later (to be considered), again discussing whakapapa, he may be seen to be deliberately aligning himself with Best and the Pākehā's authority in these matters.

One of the newspaper's contributors was a woman of Rangitane and Kahungunu descent, Niniwa-i-te-rangi, who with her bilingual skills translated material from English into Māori, and also become a recognised leader and expert in Māori history and custom, speaking frequently on marae – unusual in her day. From 1904 to 1906, she was instrumental in convening a number of whakapapa hui at local centres to record genealogy and history. Tutakangahau became involved in this process, initiating a correspondence on whakapapa with her in the newspaper's columns between 1905 and 1906.[5]

A combination of the ethnographic impulse observed in Pākehā culture, and the preservationist anxiety already seen in the willingness of Best's informants to record what they knew, had by this tenuous point in the survival of remnant oral traditions impelled the remaining elders of various iwi at the fin de siècle to record their own history. This was done both for its potential value to future generations and to connect Māori history to the larger historical drama they were now aware of from contact with the European world and its books – in particular, the Bible, from which their literacy had originally derived.

The founding editor, Hāmuera Tamahau Mahupuku, was also instrumental in publicising the need for Māori to record traditions, history and whakapapa. In the paper's pages, he advertised hui arranged for that purpose, encouraging knowledgeable elders like Tutakangahau to contribute, and also attend. It was these whakapapa hui that led to the establishment of the influential Tanenuiarangi Committee, whose authentication of the sage Te Matorohanga's teachings recorded by Te Whatahoro Jury in the 1860s and the 1880s was to have such a crucial bearing on Best's later writings on Māori religion.[6] This matter will receive more detailed consideration in the next chapter.

There were important links between what Best was doing with his sources, and Tutakangahau and his Māori peers with theirs; how closely allied were their projects, yet how differently supplied. Culture, timing and power were on Best's side: he was younger and had access to resources available to those Pākehā and who wrote in English for an English-speaking audience. Te Peehi, however – as Māori called him – was not the only intellectual on this frontier: the old chief and these other Māori writers and publishers stood alongside him in this endeavour.

By 10 April of the following year, Tutakangahau was writing directly to Niniwa, complimenting her and Te Whatakorari on the whakapapa hui they had been involved in at Martinborough on the Ngāti Kahungunu Takitimu marae, Kehemane (Gethsemane), on March 22nd, as reported in an earlier edition of *Te Puke ki Hikurangi*. This marae at Tablelands had been opened – making another connection to the old Tūhoe warrior – by Te Kooti in 1891, and became a strong centre for the Ringatū faith in the Wairarapa.[7] There, Niniwa and others had been involved in discussions to bring together the origins of their ancestors, and an increase of their own authority in these matters, as explained by Te Whatakorari in the newspaper. After this mihi, Tutakangahau gives some more personal details of his recent activities.

The old chief and his people had travelled from Waimana to Rūātoki for the funeral of one of his grandchildren; around that time, he writes (17 January), they were sent for by the Commission Secretary Elsdon Best, to come to his home at Rūātoki and discuss matters concerning the history of Tūhoe. Best asked them questions about their ancestors and the authority descending from ancient times to the present day. What the old man does here is link his own work in the recording of whakapapa with that of Niniwa and Te Whatakorari; moreover, he is associating his mana and authority at that time with Best's well-known work in the field of recording Māori history and tradition.

His attitude to the collection and collation is obvious as the letter concludes. He addresses Niniwa, Te Whatakorari and the newspaper's readers personally, urgently: 'E Hine, e pa, otira koutou katoa kaua hei paahitia nga whakapapa i heke mai i o tatau tipuna i puta ai ki te ao marama' – do not pass over or ignore the whakapapa that have come down to us from our ancestors into the world of light. He goes on: 'kaore he tikanga o te wehenga ki ia iwi, ki ia iwi' – there is no reason to separate one tribe from another in the gathering of whakapapa, since from the beginning there has existed a primal unity deriving from the parents, Rangi and Papa, from whom are all things. This is a very forceful statement: 'engari hoki nga take i puta ai, ina hoki kotahi tonu o tatau tipuna, ko Rangi anake raua ko Papa, na ana nga mea katoa' – a biblically cadenced declaration of their originating powers.

He enumerates their creations: the world, the waters, the sea, the heavenly bodies, the land, all of the peoples, the living and the dead, the very authority of the ancestors from the beginning until the present moment. This account so closely shadows the Genesis story he knew so well that it is hard not to believe he is appealing to biblical authority. In the same moment, he calls upon the authority of Best's ethnographic mission to support his own – the Pākehā's obsessive search for the 'kura huna' contained in those whakapapa lists Te Peehi had been so assiduous in collecting, from his arrival in the region ten years earlier.

In reply to Niniwa, the old man concludes that he too will be calling another whakapapa meeting – 'ka karangatia ano e au he hui hei whakakotahi i nga whakapapa o tatau tipuna' – to unify the ancestral genealogies, where he hopes that those who come can bring together stories, knowledgeable men and women, at a time and place to be advised. Don't forget to reply, he writes, 'loading up this our sacred mountain (*Te Puke ki Hikurangi*, the newspaper) with these words (letters, discussions)'.

The strength of this passage – the warning against separating whakapapa into mere tribal records to authenticate temporal status (such as proof of entitlement to land in the government's Native Land Court), and the call to recognise the unifying creative powers of the primal parents, Rangi and Papa – indicates something even more far-reaching than the need to preserve Māori culture and history. It is just as likely to demonstrate an unconscious drive to create a spiritual universe that both parallels and agrees with that of the Bible, an impulse where whakapapa – once orally preserved, now in print and permanent – become an authentic spiritual link for Māori to the written whakapapa of the Hebrew Scriptures.

This is the real significance of whakapapa that came from the ancestors ('i heke mai i o tatau tipuna'), delivered by word of mouth in an oral culture; whakapapa that must now make their way in the world of light ('te ao marama'), into a world that records and transmits such knowledge in writing – the culture of modernity. Here in New Zealand, Māori were employing the same Gutenberg print technology that had transformed the traditional culture of medieval Europe, and was now placing theirs on the page. Standing between these worlds as a final bridge, Tutakangahau who had *heard* the word was now determined to *write* it.

The recording and transmission of whakapapa had become his

overriding concern: in a letter that Best sent to Smith the following month, the old man had confided in him about a dream where he was emasculated.[8] This he interpreted as a warning to him that he must urgently 'whakatika nga whakapapa o Matatua': ensure that the genealogies of Tūhoe were correctly arranged and recorded, lest he lose his very manhood. Pressing matters indeed: the old world calling to him from the depths of his unconscious, in his spirit, in his wairua, to a last and lasting work in the new.

On 12 June 1905 in the same newspaper's columns, Niniwa replied to Tutakangahau and other correspondents on these grave matters. After congratulating them on their correspondence in the paper about whakapapa hui, she assures Tohungia, Tutakangahau and Petera Whakahoro that their 'treasures' have been sent to Ngāti Kahungunu for safekeeping. She then makes specific reference to concerns held by Petera Whakahoro: 'kaore oku pouri mo te rironga o tatau tipuna ki roto ki te Kooti whenua Maori' – I am not upset about our ancestors being taken to the Māori Land Court – 'ki reira korero parau ai te tangata kore rawa atu' – where people with nothing can lie.[9] Niniwa is referring here to spurious claims that were sometimes made in the Native Land Court, using suspect whakapapa to authenticate the claimants' rights to land.[10]

She is at pains to allay the fears of her contributors: the hui that she and others are running at Pāpāwai is to correct such misinformation; what they produce will go onto the record, will be obtained by Pākehā historians who will then become fully aware of Māori ancestral histories. 'He hui whakatikatika tenei', she emphasises, collating, correcting and putting right 'nga korero a o tatau tipuna' – the stories of the ancestors. We almost hear an echo of Tutakangahau's warning dream in the same year: 'whakatika nga whakapapa o Matatua'. Here is a communal project of history-making that will gain the respect of the Pākehā community as an authentic history of Māori, by Māori. This is the material that will eventually come into the hands of Percy Smith, to see the light of day in 1913 as *The Lore of the Whare-wananga*.

She is not concerned about those who write to the paper disagreeing with whakapapa hui: she has been collating this information since 1902, and it has now been sent to the Ngāti Kahungunu elders of the Tanenuiarangi Committee. Others who place notices in the paper about whakapapa do not damage the wide-ranging work of Pāpāwai: 'kaore hoki i te mea i poka noa te whatorotanga atu ki enei mahi o Papawai'. She seems to have concerns about conflicting information, yet assures Tutakangahau and the other contributors that the editors of *Te Puke* are in control, and they should not be upset at any delay in the publication of their papers, treasures indeed from their ancestors – 'he taonga ano tenei no o tatau tipuna'.

What matters is the collating – 'kia whaaiti' – of these stories of the kaumātua in the one place, so all the people can then see and understand them. Differing material can be left out (a method of reconciling stories had already been determined), and so the paper would continue to function as an open forum for 'nga kupu korero me nga whakapapa a nga kaumatua' – stories and genealogies from elders such as them. Here was a contemporary Māori wānanga – where, in today's terms, we might see Tutakangahau and his peers as contributors to an upcoming academic conference. These contributors were mōhio – learned and wise – taking part in a wide-ranging project to deliver a measure of intellectual autonomy to Māori at a time in their history when morale had ebbed to its nadir and was beginning to recover.

Niniwa's concluding remarks contain the promise of future publication – a form of today's conference proceedings where contributions emerge as a collection of learned papers in a refereed book. 'Ko taku whakaaro me mahi ki roto i te Paipera pukapuka', she writes – it is my wish that they are put into a bible, i.e. a permanent bound volume that would carry their work into the future. Over the next two years, the work of the Tanenuiarangi Committee oversaw the authentication of a number of manuscript books – including those copied by Te Whatahoro Jury, of the teachings of Te Matorohanga – and lodged this latter collection in the Dominion Museum in 1907. Percy Smith went directly to Te Whatahoro Jury and obtained other copies of these teachings, including some material bearing the official seal of the Tanenuiarangi Committee – and proceeded to publish this 'esoteric lore' in the following decade.[11]

While Tutakangahau's contributions to the collation and publication of historic kōrero and genealogies do not figure in Smith's particular enterprise, his was nevertheless a significant part of the attempt by Māori at the turn of the century to write themselves onto the pages of history:

to connect with the *writing* of history as opposed to the *telling* of it. Smith – and later Best – would come to regard Te Whatahoro Jury as a reliable source of information on the spiritual world of pre-contact Māori, and would champion his 1865 written recordings of the sage Te Matorohanga as a pristine source. At this time, however, the Tūhoe chief was a far more reliable guide to what was going on for Māori in the here and now: a better guide in fact as to why they wanted to get what they knew onto paper.[12]

His attitude to the literary record immediately prior to his death is consistent with his approach to Best ten years earlier, and his recruitment of the Pākehā as a scribe: 'ko au anake he ruānuku o Tūhoe' – I am a wise man of Tūhoe, wise enough to read the writing on the wall. Oral transmission of his knowledge was no longer tenable: the writing culture he had absorbed for the past forty years was now as natural and normal to him as speaking on the marae had been to his father when he welcomed Colenso to Toreatai in 1844. He would also have a significant hand in assisting Best with the gathering of the information that became the Pākehā's best-known legacy – the tribal history *Tuhoe*, completed in the year of Tutakangahau's death but not published until 1925. Before this phase of their collaboration was fulfilled, the relationship of both men to the prophet Rua Kenana intervened, as this charismatic figure became entangled in the latter stages of the Best–Tutakangahau relationship.

Rua Kenana Hepetipa (1869–1937) was the last of the messianic leaders of the Māori millennial movements already seen in this account.[13] Born at Maungapōhatu, he was a relative of the old chief; sent away from his family to Ngāti Kahungunu, he returned at the age of nine. He worked for some years as a labourer on Pākehā farms, and appears to have refined a psychology of rejection that resulted in him positioning himself as Te Kooti's successor – a claim not accepted by many at first, but eventually winning over large numbers of Tūhoe and Whakatōhea, disillusioned with the government's land policies. After prophetic visions in the epiphanic mists of the sacred mountain, this graduate of Ringatū was baptised as the new messiah, Te Mihaia Hou, by an elder in that faith, Eria Raukura, in the Waipaoa River near Gisborne in 1906.[14]

He gathered support amongst Tūhoe in the Rūātoki and Waimana areas with prophecies of the repatriation of the settlers to England; it was here that he first came to the notice of Elsdon Best, working as a health officer based at Rūātoki. His move to Maungapōhatu with his followers in 1907, and his subsequent establishment of a messianic community there, with aims of Tūhoe economic development, proved to be a threat to the government long-term – as well as provoking opposition from powerful Tūhoe leaders such as Numia Kereru of Rūātoki. With his many wives, his sartorial splendour, and his refusal to co-operate with government dealings with other Tūhoe leaders, Rua incited powerful elements of hostility amongst the press and public – which led in time to a predictable showdown.

Best, in the midst of writing his massive history at around the same moment Rua Kenana is emerging, in a footnote citing some discrepancies between his informants' accounts, suddenly laments: 'But alas! The last two years have wiped my old teachers off the slate of life, save one who has cleaved unto the New Messiah.'[15] The 'Messiah' is of course Rua, and the last of his old teachers Tutakangahau. It is a sobering fact that biography is so often dependent on cryptic gleanings from obscure footnotes and incidental government records: tax returns, court orders, and letters from minor bureaucrats. This is nowhere truer than in this attempt to cover the final years of the old chief's life, to obtain a clear picture of his relationship with Rua and its effect on Best. Thanks to such a detail – a letter to a pensioner from a government department – we can date with some accuracy the time when Tutakangahau's involvement with the prophet came to the notice of the authorities in Wellington.

Was it Best who informed them of this development, or the policeman Andy Grant at Te Whāiti, who would later notify the Justice Department of the old man's death?[16] A letter of 10 August 1906 from the Native Affairs Department that gives the information is unequivocal. Tutakangahau stood accused of forsaking the Ruatāhuna mail run from Te Whāiti to Maungapōhatu to follow the work of the prophet – 'kua riro koe ki te whai i nga mahi poropiti'.[17] The mail run and the contract money had therefore been passed to Te Whenuanui, and furthermore – rather spitefully – the old man's long-standing chiefly pension from the days of Donald McLean had been reduced, by order of the Minister James Carroll himself, back to £25: 'kua whakaitia e ia to penihana kia noho ki te rua tekau ma rima £ pauna i te tau'.

In view of the old chief's mana and his status as a moderate and moderniser, supportive of the government in many respects, what prompted Carroll to take such a harsh and punitive step? The pension was a mark of the respect in which men like Tutakangahau were held, and also an insurance policy towards encouraging loyalty; by following Rua, as the letter proposes, had he now made himself an enemy of the government? The possession of a mail run was also a matter of status, an income, and the certainty of controlling the reception and delivery of letters and other documents important to the chief's political involvement and his contacts with the Pākehā world in Wellington. Was this the actual point of his retreat from such involvement, disillusioned with the workings of the Urewera Commission – and as Best was to hint in his letters to Smith in the following year, old age and loss of memory causing some diminution of his powers?

From Carroll's point of view – an aggressive moderniser and apostle of progress for Māori in the arts of civilisation – the message and methods of Rua Kenana which looked to take Tūhoe backwards into isolation were anathema, and were in large part responsible for the Tohunga Suppression Act of September 1907.[18] Section 2(1) of this notorious piece of legislation prescribed fines of up to £25, or imprisonment of up to six months, for anyone who 'misleads or attempts to mislead any Maori by professing or pretending to possess supernatural powers' for the cure of diseases and foretelling the future. Specifically directed at restraining any millennialist movement, it remained on the statute books until 1962 – by which time Rua was long dead, his reputedly seditious utterances finally dealt with by military means in the 1916 raid on his community Iharaira at Maungapōhatu.[19]

Rua's millennialism, based on an eclectic familiarity with Scriptures, was a powerful challenge both to the authority of the settler government and to local Tūhoe leaders such as Numia Kereru, who still saw co-operation with the Pākehā Liberal administration as the way forward, in line with Carroll's view. Claims of the right to issue gold-prospecting licences and land leases made the prophet even more dangerous to the chiefly establishment. A man like Rua might undo all they had striven to gain and maintain from the days of Te Whitu Tekau until the Urewera Commission. Although not truly working for Tūhoe interests, the Commission was still active in the period that this self-proclaimed inheritor of Te Kooti's mantle emerged from obscurity. Rua was a farm worker, a commoner of no rank – yet another example of the way in which, since the time of Te Ua, literate and charismatic leaders were able to step outside of the old hereditary orders of rank and power. His time spent beyond the confines of the Urewera working for Pākehā farmers provided him with the important insight of the need for capital to develop land – he was to combine his spiritual ministry with the earthbound realisation that Tūhoe needed both.

It certainly seems from Best's evidence and that of the official letter above that a split had developed in the old man's loyalties and aims at this point in 1906. Up until that time, Tutakangahau and Numia Kereru had as hereditary chiefs pursued with some success very similar policies and aims: managing settler encroachment, mediating between their peoples and a settler regime anxious to bring them under its sway. When Rua emerged as Te Kooti's prophesied heir to challenge that status quo, Kereru resisted him – in fact encouraging Carroll to go after the prophet with the 1907 Act – yet Tutakangahau went with the new man and his claims to prophetic succession.[20] Here was a traditional leader who had lobbied the government for roads, schools and police in his area, yet by all accounts had now joined forces with a self-proclaimed messiah who predicted the expulsion of Pākehā from New Zealand. Rua encouraged Tūhoe children to leave the Native Schools, forgo the study of an English language soon to be redundant, persuading his followers to abandon their favourable valley marae at Waimana and Rūātoki to journey with him and his apostles to remote Maungapōhatu – and a first winter of starvation.

In many respects, Rua was the classic embodiment of the cult leader, inspiring seemingly irrational loyalty in a large number of people many of whom had seen his like before (Te Kooti) and turned away from both confrontation and retreat. Tutakangahau was older than most: he had lived through the Pai Mārire/Hauhau movement as well, and yet he joined with his younger relative – or perhaps a younger self – to move one last time into the mountain isolation of Maungapōhatu, his childhood home. Best is quite unequivocal about this development; close to the time they had shared their last intimacies, he writes to Smith: 'Old Tu of Maungapohatu is fast losing his memory and has also embraced the cult of the "New Messiah".'[21] The language is plain enough: old age has caught up with the last of Best's mōhio, and he has thrown in his lot with Rua.

The letter makes a strong connection between the two events: the old man is losing his memory, his powers are fading, and this is why he has become a follower – he has lost his grip on reality. The ethnographer's deep hostility to Rua ('I have come to the conclusion that all Messiahs is pisen')[22] appears to prevent him from considering the influence on Tutakangahau of the same factors that impelled the majority of Tūhoe to listen to the prophet, leave their homes and follow him up into the mountains. Old and growing tired he most certainly was, from seventy-five hard-lived Urewera years, and quite possibly suffering from the onset of senile dementia; but blind and insensitive to the conditions of his people, most certainly not.

As they continued to suffer over a decade of crop failure, disease and poverty, Tūhoe had become frustrated with the workings of the 1896 Act and could see that government land purchases were ongoing – that the local committees had no real power. Rua offered something else: a return of agency and power, the promise of local self-government at Maungapōhatu, with the prospect of land ownership and development through capital raised by selling off land belonging to his followers, financing the consolidation of land in his new Iharaira (Israel). Rua was eventually able to sell land in the Tauranga block, gaining with the assistance of no less a luminary than Apirana Ngata places for himself and his followers on the General Committee set up under the 1896 Act. With the funds realised, Rua began to build up and develop his New Jerusalem as a centre of economic independence for Tūhoe.[23]

Tūhoe had been outmanoeuvred by Seddon's successors, and in December an amendment to the Urewera District Native Reserve Act 1896 had been passed, section 12 of which 'confirmed the authority of the General Committee to alienate land exclusively to the government', extending the jurisdiction of the Native Land Court into the entire Reserve.[24] By now, Tūhoe were being charged for the surveys, breaking Seddon's word to the assembled chiefs at Rūātoki in 1894; further land sales were needed to clear debt, and Rua wanted money for roading to connect his economic base at Maungapōhatu with the wider world. His sale of 40,000 acres of his followers' land in mid-1910 (at government valuation of £31,535) was the Crown's first purchase inside the Urewera Reserve, opening a door for later sales, proving also to be an end to Rua's usefulness and no protection against the government coming to confront him with deadly force in 1916.[25]

Nevertheless, it was almost certainly this kind of agency and initiative that had appealed to his distinguished elder relative: Rua's father was Kenana, closely related to Tutakangahau, who had died fighting for Te Kooti at Ngā Tapa in January 1869.[26] Rua's new world, emerging from the old, was a world that promised Māori control; in the absence of further evidence, this seems the most likely reason for Tutakangahau's 'embrace' of the younger man's mission. Far from losing his mind – the onset of senility notwithstanding – he is just as likely to have been making it up, and changing it, away from the failing policy of co-operation to which Numia was still wedded, and choosing in what became his last act the comfort of a religious milieu on his home ground controlled by Tūhoe, for Tūhoe. If power and control are the issues here, then the very factors that attracted him to Rua were those that provoked a violent and caustic opposition in Best.

The emergence of the Māori Councils in the early 1900s and the creation of a Māori Health Service saw Best gain an appointment in 1904 as a health inspector for the Mātaatua district and he moved camp from Heipipi to Rūātoki, building the house near Haukapua for himself and his new wife Adelaide.[27] It was in this capacity as missionaries of Western hygiene standards that they both set about trying to change Tūhoe attitudes and behaviour with regard to community health. At the time he held this role, Best was to make his first contact with the activities of Rua and his followers. His duties – such as inspecting water supplies and improving sanitation – also included a brief to oppose the activities of native healers, Tūhoe tohunga, held by the authorities to be little more than charlatans who preyed upon superstition. Into a situation where 'typhoid, measles, whooping cough, mumps and influenza'[28] were rampant and crop failure was causing widespread malnutrition, Rua arrived in 1905 to pray for the sick, preaching renewed faith in God and prophesying a return of the confiscated lands in the Whakatāne River valley.[29]

There was no love lost between them early: ever the sceptic in regard to religious fervour, and Māori Christianity in any shape or form, Best was bound to disapprove of the zeal and confidence Rua inspired in followers such as those he met in his rounds, who took Rua's prophecies literally. Preparing the manuscript for his major work, *Tuhoe*, discussing the confiscation of Ōpouriao Valley land, he writes: 'They tried to regain it through European lawyers two years ago, and now, Rua the Keka, the latest thing in shamanistic humbugs, has promised them that all these lost lands shall be regained by them.'[30] The use of such an insulting term (mentally deranged) sets the tone for all of Best's future tirades against a man he considered an impostor and a threat to the welfare of Tūhoe. He called the gathering of Rua's people at nearby Waimana, 'Kekataone' – crazy town – and was just as disparaging about the prophet when he met him in person.

Elsdon Best sartorially resplendent in 1906, on a rare visit to the South Island, leans on his spade. He is supervising the erection of the Māori village in Hagley Park, Christchurch, for the New Zealand Exhibition.
Photographer unknown, Museum of New Zealand Te Papa Tongarewa, B.021335

In 1906, Best was told by Rua's followers that King Edward VII was to arrive in Gisborne to arrange the repatriation of all Pākehā to England – therefore they would require his stove, washboard and potato peeler on his departure. One of them had a bet with Best – £10 to his £100 – that the King would 'arrive at Gisborne before July 1st' (another was more sanguine, adopting a wait-and-see attitude).[31] In the *Canterbury Times* newspaper article of July 1906 from which this information comes – pejoratively entitled 'The Darkened Mind' – Best uses the opportunity to attack both Rua and his credulous followers, laying out his opposition to superstitious adherence to a primitive psychology whose day, in his view, was done. Noteworthy for its mocking, sarcastic tone, and the cruel character assassination he performs on Rua, it has all the worst aspects of his peppery character and none of the careful and compassionate anthropologist.

Best had gone twice with a police party to Maungapōhatu that same year; he met Rua on the second occasion, writing to Smith: 'I have been hunting the New Messiah who is to expel all Europeans from N.Z.'[32] He concluded that Rua was suffering from delusions of grandeur due to the adulation of his followers, and was not a man he could deal with. Certainly, here was a man of a different stripe to his preferred traditional chiefs, moulded by the mid-nineteenth-century culture – those who had lost in battle with government forces and learned the arts of negotiation from weakness. Rua was not amenable to Best's ethnographic project: he was of a new breed, breaking tapu and citing Scripture in ways certain to antagonise Best's prejudices. There may well have been an element of jealousy too, along with a genuine concern for the welfare of Tūhoe, who Best had seen in the Rūātoki and Waimana areas leaving their homes, selling their ploughs, and dropping out of the Pākehā wage-labour farm economy.[33] Rua was a threat to the established order, and would not fit into any of Best's models of authentic Māori psychology located in a vanished past world.

Best's role as health officer would have been difficult enough without the influence of a religious revival where predictions of catastrophic floods and the demise of the new order had stirred up his clients. He would complain bitterly in a 1907 report to Maui Pomare, chief Māori health officer in Wellington, of the apathy and obstruction of the locals, the inadequacy of his travelling allowance, and the lack of support from the Māori Council members whose interests he was ostensibly serving (this standoff would eventually lead to his dismissal in March 1909). In his attempts to improve sanitary arrangements and hygiene, he stated that the Council 'never back me up in the slightest degree'.[34] Observing the effects of what he terms '*The Messiah Craze*', he notes how Rua's followers live in large camps, having sold their portable property and moved to higher ground to avoid the impending biblical deluge. 'The influence of these madmen is also seriously affecting the Native schools, and militates against the success of any plans for the betterment of the Natives.'

Patronising as this may sound a century later, there is nevertheless genuine concern at the breakdown of Tūhoe society, his evidence here an epidemic of enteric fever due to sewage polluting water supplies. This led to milk deliveries to the local dairy factory being refused, and whatever spare finances the people had were being 'donated to Rua . . . to purchase food for his camp of loafers'. Deserted villages, disease, religious fervour, resistance to his well-intentioned ministrations: it is not surprising that Best became frustrated, turning his anger on the man he felt was exacerbating Tūhoe sufferings. The article cited in the *Canterbury Times* from the previous year had a wider target than its apparent subject, Rua. Best was a champion of 'reason and progress' over 'religion and ignorance', and his experience in the United States witnessing Native American religious revivals had convinced him that whether it was 'Dakota Sioux' or 'Doukhobors', such charlatans should expect little mercy at the hands of the 'authorities' (that is, the colonial rulers).

There is a threatening note to this section of the article: another new messiah from 'the Sioux of Pine Ridge Agency . . . did not flourish long, but died with great suddenness – of lead poisoning'. He seems grimly amused at this leader's vain attempt to expel the white man, his earthly career 'cut short by a 45.60'. The implication is clear enough: this is the way to deal with such troublemakers, including 'the newest Messiah, who is a member of the Tuhoe tribe, and a gentleman of sinister character'.[35] While Best does not state explicitly here that armed force should be used to deal with Rua – even up to the point of a fatal outcome – there is little else to deduce from this intemperate piece. Best would prove a prophet of sorts, when Maungapōhatu was attacked in 1916, and Rua's son Toko

Rua and Te Maipi Te Whiu were shot and killed.[36] Such attitudes were of their time: Best certainly contributed to the climate of fear and disdain Rua in his pomp attracted from most Pākehā, along with the hostility and prejudice surrounding his trial following the raid and the aftermath of his unsound conviction on charges of sedition.

There are significant ironies in Best's continued refusal to accept what was happening to Māori religious thought over his lifetime: while his focus was on the past, and attempting to locate Māori origins in Irihia (India), in an Indo-Aryan gene pool, Māori themselves had sailed off in another mythical waka, reinventing themselves as persecuted Polynesian Hurae – akin to the Jews.[37] Rua's Iharaira was another manifestation of the power of literacy, and the primary literature of the Scriptures, giving them the authority of a new identity with which to navigate the waters of modernity. From Te Ua Haumene to Rua Kenana, Best, Percy Smith and their peers kept missing the point: while Pākehā moderns saw themselves going forward on a rejection of revealed religion, a great many Māori moderns went in the same direction by recreating the Word in a flesh of their own making.

It would be naive of course to paint all of Rua's initial supporters as faithful to the end: over the course of many difficulties, this unique and quite amazing mountain citadel saw its share of defections (many formerly landless Whakatōhea left in 1911), and there were conflicts early and late with Rua's authoritarianism. While Rua remains to this day a hero for Tūhoe, not all of his followers were enamoured of him long-term, and in particular, Tutakangahau's daughter (Huhana) and his son (Tukua Te Rangi-Pinohi) had issues with his attempts to control their lives, especially after his return from prison in 1918. This is hardly surprising: they were already residents of the mountain valley as Tamakaimoana, and with their father had fought through the Commission's sittings to retain legitimate shares in the Maungapōhatu block.

Huhana, who became involved with the Presbyterian minister John Laughton's church after 1918, wrote in 1923 that her 'poor and ignorant people' had been subject to 'Rua's will' as he 'played on our superstitions and frightened us'. None would dare oppose him 'except my brother . . . Pinohi. Pinohi believed in the law of the pakeha' – as had his late father, until his final days. Rua, she wrote, 'has oppressed us & kept us under

Huhana Tutakangahau, the chief's daughter, Pinohi's sister, with Tahu Hirawana and Waereti Irohia, outside the Supreme Court, Auckland, during the trial of Rua Kenana.
Photographer unidentified, Elizabeth Murphy Collection, Alexander Turnbull Library, Wellington, NZ, PA1-o-357-23

his will, claimed our homes our lands our all & we knew not that there was a stronger law than his'. The prophet, she concludes, 'did whatever he wished with us, he took whatever he fancied, he said whatever he wanted to'.[38] The man who in 1924 Best ironically terms 'my very worthy friend' – while going on to describe him in the same paragraph as one who 'thought himself above the law' – would outlive his Pākehā opponent by some six years. While both men have gone from the face of the earth, their contest goes on in the literature they either wrote or inspired.[39] Neither were saints: in the link they shared with Tutakangahau in his final years, they are part now of this entangled kōrero of Tūhoe identity and their ties to the land.

While Rua was emerging on the scene, Best was steadily pursuing his studies of Tūhoe life, customs, and history. He was about to commence work on what he would describe in his letters to Percy Smith as a 'taniwha', and the 'M.O.' – his magnum opus, the great tribal history for which he remains famous to this day: *Tuhoe: The Children of the Mist*.[40] This massive 1200-page, two-volume study comprised a two-part first volume, of which Part I is a history of Tūhoe, and Part II, the traditions, myths, folklore, and religious beliefs and practices of the Mātaatua tribes; with Volume II consisting of thirty-four whakapapa tables, and accompanying maps. *Tuhoe* was completed by April 1907, but for many reasons, including the intervention of the Great War, did not see the light of day until 1925.[41] In an opening mihi to his sources, he includes Tutakangahau in a list of six 'koeke' (elders) and many others not named, who have 'laid out together the treasures desired by the Ancients, those who have opened up this finely adorned basket to the outsider'.[42]

Looking past the poetry for one moment, Best is acknowledging his complete dependence on such men: 'I give the stories as they were told to me', he writes – 'most of the information . . . I owe to the friendliness and patience of native friends'. He continues, 'it is a small enough return to make when I prepare their historical traditions for publication'. The book is now figured as a canoe: 'let Mātātua be launched' so that 'the descendants of Toroa, and Toi, and Hape, of Potiki and Tuhoe' – Tutakangahau's children – may search for the knowledge this waka contains in the days ahead. That cargo of treasure comprises 'old-time sagas imparted to the intrusive Pakeha', of those 'courageous forebears' who 'carried the *mana Maori* across the curve of the earth' to Aotearoa.[43] This bequest, from his informants and himself, was for Tūhoe generations yet unborn. In using such a metaphor – canoe for book – Best was being authentically Māori in his time: witness the number of occasions Tutakangahau and other correspondents write of 'loading up the waka' when they fill the pages of the Māori newspapers with their cargo of knowledge.

It is hard not to hear some echo of Tutakangahau's directive on the Waikaremoana journey they took together in 1895, when at the fireside camp the old man commissioned Best to this very work. These books were long revered amongst Tūhoe for this reason, and so was Best, by many – but times change. Since the 1980s, the ethnographer has attracted a share of criticism from Māori and Pākehā alike for his role in the government's handling of Tūhoe and their lands.[44] Best has been

Cover image, first edition of Best's *Tuhoe: The Children of the Mist* (1925). *Author photograph*

accused of writing primarily for a European audience, fragmenting Tūhoe history by sifting 'believable "facts" from unbelievable "fancy"', writing badly by mixing genre, of stealing whakapapa from the Native Land Court sittings, of being a government agent – that is, a spy – and as a man, of being 'whakahīhī', proud and boastful. What were his motives then – and who were his patrons – in this endeavour?

It is certainly true that Percy Smith was behind him in producing this material (he wanted to publish it serially in the Polynesian Society's journal). The placing of Māori origins, dating their arrival and the existence of a pre-Māori tangata whenua (Maruiwi), were high in his priorities, and Best was still functioning as his eyes and ears in the Urewera, gathering evidence for a colonial history that would write Māori into a European chronology. The correspondence between the two men (especially from 1905 to 1908) shows an increasing urgency to achieve these aims. Nevertheless, it remains true that Best was also doing this work for Tūhoe and their posterity, while at the same time being willing to stand corrected by others coming after him, who might be 'moved to publish more correct versions, as from their point of view . . . more power to their indignant elbows'.[45] There have been few takers: the moment had already passed, and Best was the man on the spot to seize it.

The Smith–Best correspondence of his final five years in the Urewera reveals a man increasingly concerned with the writing of his projected Tūhoe history. Smith had pursued him on this, and in August 1905 Best wrote: 'my idea of the M O is to make a sort of compendium of Tuhoean ethnography, manners, customs, myths, religion, folk lore etc etc, but not including the tribal wars which are absolutely void of interest to the genuine anthropologist'.[46] He had hoped to keep the history separate for articles in the *Journal of the Polynesian Society*, but was at a loss to see how 'the M O can appear in [the] journal' – it was simply too vast, even if it were to be published serially. He repeats the same distinction between 'petty tribal wars and matters purely ethnographical' in another letter to Smith a month later.[47]

This seemingly offhand judgement is vital in understanding the later development of Best's interests, as he continues in the same letter: 'My aim is to spend most time in hunting up matters regarding ancient rites etc which has for me a much deeper interest.' Best had grown weary of recording the endless and often conflicting accounts of local battles; what mattered locally for Tūhoe was not attractive to him. He did go on to write a more general series, 'Notes on the Art of War', for the *Journal of the Polynesian Society* between 1902 and 1906, and faithfully set down in Part One of the book the settling of Tūhoe on what became their lands, and the fighting that followed, right down to the last shot of the Te Kooti campaign in 1872 – but his heart was in the material that would become Part Two: myth, folklore and religion.[48]

By January 1906 he had relented somewhat, resolving 'to take in the whole of Tuhoe once and for all and end'. He felt it was now or never, and had been 'copying all Tuhoe historical notes under divers headings ever since'.[49] In a letter to Smith from Rūātoki in November, he declares: 'I have a taniwha [monster] before me. I began my Tuhoe history by a few remarks on the old original Toi and Potiki tribes of this district. I have finished it but have 125 f/cap pp Ms written. If you want to run it through the journal it will take seven years to do so.' He was determined 'to get more of my other matter into the Transactions or I will never get rid of it'.[50] These 'Transactions' were the *Transactions and Proceedings of the*

New Zealand Institute; 'the other matter' presumably is the non-historical material that would go to comprise Part Two of the book. By early 1907, this too would be complete in manuscript form – a change of focus from the historical origins, whakapapa and scenes of battle that make up the first half of *Tuhoe*.

There has been extensive analysis of Best's historical models in Part One of *Tuhoe*, critiques of the 'heroic model' of Māori origins and the Maruiwi theories, less so in the case of Part Two.[51] Yet it is obvious that this was where Best's primary interest lay, in Māori myths, legends, in questions of comparative religion and the vexing issue of the pre-Pākehā existence of a Māori Supreme Being, the High God Io. Consideration will be given to the former matters in the following chapter – the interest here should lie where Best's does, especially because Tutakangahau is one of the first authorities he cites on the question of Io. Fascinating tensions arise when he reports on their conversations in that regard.

Section I of Part Two concerns 'Historical Traditions', from origins in Hawaiki to the arrival of the *Mātaatua* canoe and the dispersal and settlement of its crew. We learn here in passing that Best did make some additions and alterations to the 1907 manuscript, when he speaks of a modern 'Mātaatua', a cargo steamer plying its trade 'in this year of 1909'.[52] The first three hundred pages of Section II, 'Myth and Folklore', table the familiar figures of Rangi and Papa and their rebellious children, tracing them back from Te Pō (darkness, the unknown) to Te Pū (the root, the origin).[53] From Tane, Tū and Rongo, through to heroic Maui stories and the doings of fairies and elves, Best gives a comprehensive account of major atua and minor tūrehu (fairies) – in the process, according with Tutakangahau's lists of mythical ancestors as recorded in the chief's letters to *Te Puke ki Hikurangi*.

The newspaper and the whakapapa records left on its pages would have been a venue – and an opportunity – for the old chief to have written of Io, had he considered him a vital part of traditional Māori religion. In *Tuhoe*, we do not get to read of this deity until the third and final section, 'The Spirit World: Maori Religion and Priestcraft' – a discussion introduced by a quote from one of Best's teachers in absentia, F. Max Müller. Müller had stated in his work *Anthropological Religion* (1898) a two-point creed that Best obviously aspired to in his own ethnographic practice: no one was to be quoted as an authority on 'savage races' who was not an eyewitness and proven 'free from the prejudices of race and religion'. If such objectivity was in all likelihood impossible to achieve (Best certainly had a few entrenched positions), he did more nearly approach the next qualification. Any authority quoted on customs, traditions, and especially 'the religious ideas of uncivilised races' must have 'an acquaintance with their language sufficient to enable him to converse freely on these difficult subjects'.[54]

The story of what became one of Best's principal conclusions on Māori spirituality – their capacity for abstract thought and a high level of religious development, seen in the survival of the Io cult amongst a higher level of tohunga – was the direct result of the operation of both these factors. His virulent anti-missionary attitudes, and his scepticism about debased Māori forms of Christianity, were prejudicial to his judgements; yet his linguistic skill and his life amongst Tūhoe conferred upon him the authority Müller points to, even when he got it wrong, sometimes for the right reasons. In an age when Māori culture was tokenised and discounted, Best took them seriously, and many of his arguments in this realm are a way of defending Māori against their detractors, a desire to ennoble their pre-European achievements, without the beneficial and civilising effects of a literary culture.

Something of Best's intellectual development and his exposure to mid- to late nineteenth-century views on the issue of the emergence of gods high and low in human societies over recorded history have already been seen. In the pages of *Tuhoe*, he makes public his maturing views on the question of a High God or Supreme Being in traditional Māori society. These views were at first tentative, but in his 'museum years' from 1910 onwards, under the influence of Percy Smith and Te Whatahoro Jury, they would crystallise into a form of speculative theology – as opposed to a demonstrable anthropology. In what has been described recently as 'New Zealand's greatest tribal history', Best lays out his views on the nature of Māori religion in a shape that has come down to us in the present – in the process, bequeathing an ongoing controversy.[55]

In discussing the Māori spirit world, he makes important distinctions between what early observers saw and noted on the subject, the language used to describe Māori belief and practice, and what his contemporaries may have understood. He is at pains to point out that 'mythology, superstitions and magic' were inseparable from religion in traditional society, that a God of love was unknown, as was worship in the Christian sense. Fear, rather, and awe, with rites of placation obtained in a system where breaches of tapu in the here and now demanded propitiation of vengeful spirits: 'a peculiar form of invoking termed *whakatara*, a word that means "to stimulate by entreaty"'.[56] Māori were deeply religious in the sense that such a spiritual awareness structured their lives, in a society where Western-style laws and morality were unheard of, and social stability maintained by the fear of breaching spiritual prohibitions. Tapu (sacredness) and mākutu (magic) disciplined the people: in Best's opinion, Māori were ruled from birth to death by the need to manage a malevolent and capricious spiritual universe for 'the purpose of craving some boon, or of averting some evil fortune'.[57]

He held the view that the elemental, departmental gods (such as Tane, Tū and Rongo) were not creator beings in themselves, and, as atua, were as much ancestors as gods; he argues that the adoption of the word 'atua' by early missionaries as an equivalent for 'the Supreme God of the Christian religion' was a solecism, an unhappy choice.[58] Evil acts were not in themselves an offence against some universal moral code, but against the gods themselves, as in the infringement of tapu. Punishment was not in the next life, but immediately, in this world. Following on his own observations and a careful reading of the early writers, Best was able to build up a coherent and persuasive account of the Māori spirit world and its practical effect in the life of the people. For the remainder of the book, he shapes this into a generalised ethnography of religious practice, and a more specific account of Tūhoe instances given by his informants.

Prior to making a more detailed account of Māori atua, divinatory practices and other rituals, he moves the local into the global and begins something of a digression on degeneration in native religions, 'the idea that animism supplanted a higher form of belief, the belief in a Superior Being'.[59] This debate was current at the time: it harked back in Best's experience to the belief Richard Taylor and other early missionaries held.

Primitive peoples in the colonial world were like all of humanity, subjects of the biblical Fall, who having known God through his manifest works in creation, now, in the Apostle Paul's words, 'worshipped and served the creature more than the Creator'.[60] Stated thus, such thinking was intolerable to the younger Best, but the theories of 'high gods of low races' he was about to subscribe to were little different, proposing that present-day animists may once have possessed the 'intellectual vigour' that knew a 'monotheistic system of faith'.[61]

Best is quizzical about the theory, finding it strange that a higher level of intellectual development could revert to a lower, but in the same breath asserts that 'some proof' exists and, specifically, that 'presented in a very old Maori belief'. Citing Colenso and Shortland from the camp that believed Māori had no such concept of a Supreme Being, he then gives counterarguments – based on textual evidence – from John White, a genealogy preserved by Major Mair, the Rev. T. G. Hammond's supportive opinion, and that of others of similar persuasion. Best had only ever met one Māori who knew anything about Io: 'Tutakangahau of Maungapohatu, who in the forties of the 19th century was taught much of the old ritual by his father, Tapui'.[62] What follows derives from two conversations Best had with the old chief on the subject: one where Tutakangahau gave the Pākehā a reply to his question, the second where he would say no more, 'as close as the proverbial oyster'.

To his first approach on Io, Tutakangahau replied, '"That is a very old doctrine. He was a god of very ancient times. He caused all the [other] gods to appear. He was the beginning of the gods." (*Ko Io, he reo no nehera tena. He atua no mua noa atu. Nana i whakaputa i nga atua katoa. Koia te timatanga o nga atua*).' When Best tried again later to elicit more detail, he reports he was met with silence, which he interpreted as pressure from the old man's family who had heard of 'certain information' being imparted. 'This was, however, *the only subject on which he declined to talk*'.[63] This brief paragraph is a key to the entire debate about what the old man told Best (in toto), and whether indeed there was an ancient generative High God for Māori, on the basis of such evidence.

Many Tūhoe and other Māori will today assert that Best's informants – including Tutakangahau – did not tell him everything, keeping the deepest secrets to themselves. According to Best, that only happened once, at least of those things he asked this acknowledged expert. The book *Tuhoe* itself is some kind of evidence that his informants were forthcoming – Tutakangahau in particular, whose name as a source is found everywhere in this history and in all of Best's other studies of Māori society. While he was certainly not told 'everything', it is reasonable to contend that he was told what mattered – especially given the circumstances that suggest he was recruited by the old man as a scribe for the preservation of Tūhoe knowledge for the coming generations of new Māori, born of a culture transformed by literacy.

There is another way of interpreting the sage's silence on the matter of Io, at the second time of asking: that there was no more to tell. The first utterance as it stands is without context or reference, and does not fit with the understanding Best has already given on the reality of Māori religion. If Io was so important, why did the old man not seek to include him in the whakapapa he gave in the letters to the Māori newspapers? What seems to attract Best at this point is the very thing that gives him pause: the possibility that Io was not of the lower order of belief and practice but part of a hidden, esoteric cult, 'practised by the higher order of the priesthood alone'. Here is a god with no attributes, functions, manifestations, or rituals – at least, none that the old man can or will speak of – yet what does Best conclude, in the face of what he has already communicated about Māori spirituality? That it is 'quite evident that this mystical concept of a primal god was an extremely ancient one among Maori people, and certainly not due to the teachings of the Christian missionaries in the last century'.

It seems Tutakangahau had spoken to him about 'the lower orders of *tohunga*', from which Best assumes it is 'highly probable that they would not be allowed to take part in the ritualistic functions pertaining to Io'. A reader can sense operating here a willingness to believe – on the basis of little evidence – that such a cult existed, and an indecent haste to conclude that Christian literary influences could not possibly have given rise to the equalising appearance of a Māori Supreme Being. Missionary ethnographers such as Herbert Williams and T. G. Hammond, his colleagues in the Polynesian Society, would later oppose Smith and Best on this point, as the initial Io cult theory was touted as a late discovery by Pākehā insiders, of a previously overlooked esoteric Māori belief system.[64] For Best, 'this belief in Io is the finest theistic conception we meet with in Maori tradition'.

While in 1907 he readily admits that 'whether or not the cult of Io was an ethical system we shall probably never know*', the footnote to that thought advises the reader, '*since this was written much information pertaining to the cult of Io has been collected'.[65] The note dates the revision of this section of the book to the years 1909 to 1913, when Best was made aware by Smith of the Whatahoro Jury material on Io delivered to him via Downes, material that went on to become *The Lore of the Whare-wananga* (1913).[66] A controversy was about to be born: in the next decade, Best would slowly but surely assume the mantle of the literary executor of a newly-born deity, according to the will of his mentor and champion, Percy Smith. Tutakangahau would also later be recruited in the debate, as Best's defence of the existence of a Māori High God reached the eyes of the world's anthropological audience with an article in the British periodical *MAN*, the *Journal of the Royal Anthropological Institute*, in 1913.

Ironically, for someone who believed there could have been no Christian influence on his informant, he proceeds in *Tuhoe* to discuss the presence amongst the Urewera hapū of a Ringatū religion, one 'based on the Scriptures' – of which, as we have seen, the old chief was a long-time adherent. Best gives a lengthy and detailed account – sourced from Tutakangahau – on the arrival of biblical literacy at Toreatai, and the tests to which the new faith was subject. Written notes were carried afar, their ability to transmit thought a wonder to behold, convincing the old man's people that 'the god of the white men must be much more clever and powerful than our native gods'. That the passage of time saw the chief supplicating the old gods along with the new, to save his grandchildren afflicted with mortal illnesses – to no effect – seems to have given Best some satisfaction. 'His faith wavered between the two cults, and he wanted to make sure. Neither came to his aid.'[67] For the rationalist Best, the death of the children appears to equalise and confirm the emptiness of both superstitions.

Concluding his thoughts on Io in *Tuhoe*, Best defends Māori against charges of atheism: if they had produced such a god, requiring faith and a priestly cult, they could not have been the irreligious savages some had painted. He was not able to say whether Io was a 'survival of a superior creed of times long past away [*sic*], or simply an explanation of the origin and existence of minor gods'. Personally, he found it difficult to imagine 'primitive folk' grasping monotheism; but whatever was the truth, 'the Maori Io seems to have been an uncreated god, the original deity who existed long before death was known, long before any of the deified personifications, or deified ancestors were known'.[68]

Best could not accept at that point the idea of spiritual degradation, from a higher level of religious development, and concludes instead that a religious parallelism pertained. 'Three different conditions or phases of religious beliefs and practices' existed side by side: the 'cult of Io the Supreme Being was apparently confined to the few; it was the aristocratic cultus'; then came personified departmental deities; lastly a form of 'shamanism . . . followed by the majority of the people'. This was very neat as a solution to the problem, but unfortunately he presented no proof – there was none available.

Such speculations about Māori religion in pre-Pākehā times were not based on hard evidence, which was unobtainable in the last decade of the nineteenth century. Does this matter today? Certainly – if the wheat in Best's monumental labours is to be sifted from the chaff, especially in the area of Māori spirituality. His output in this area was continuous, from the time of his arrival in the Urewera in 1895 until his death in 1931, by which point his mediation – especially in the matter of Io – had conferred upon him the deathbed authority of high priest to a vanished belief system. Whatever might be said in considering the motives and the methods of the man who wrote this landmark in our literature, it remains true as Jeffrey Sissons has written, 'this is also a work for our time because it is about things that endure – ancestors, land, identity. It is a book of names: names of people, names of places, names of things woven together in a cloak of history, a cloak of mana.'[69]

It is also true that those who dismiss the book because of its author's ethnicity and human weaknesses are in danger of missing that mana of which Sissons writes. This work, while written by Best, was dictated by Tūhoe wise men long gone; once the last of them died, Best himself soon lost heart, and was not long afterwards packing up to leave the Urewera. He had arrived as Elsdon Best, but he left as Te Peehi, mourning most especially the man who was his closest ally – Tutakangahau. On 22 October 1907, Andy Grant, the District Constable at Te Whāiti, sent a message to the Justice Department in Wellington, reporting the death of an important local chief, Tutakangahau of Maungapōhatu, on the eighteenth of that month.[70] Best himself would confirm this, although he seems to have got the month wrong: 'Tutakangahau, our most learned man since old Rakuraku passed away . . . died himself in November 1907.'[71]

It is hard to imagine that the death of such an important and long-lived Tūhoe leader would not have been the occasion for a huge and lengthy tangihanga at Maungapōhatu – yet reports of this event are hard, if not impossible, to source. For much of the biographical insight into his life, we are dependent on excerpts from Best's *Tuhoe*, where a clear trail is discernible, his growing years and public career picked out over the book's 1200-page length. The old man died in the first year of Rua's arrival in the mountain stronghold of Tamakaimoana, and certainly Iharaira, the prophet's Israelites, would have mourned him long and loud amongst his own. Best, as we know, was not present: he was not welcome amongst the messiah's disciples, and his antipathy towards Rua had caused a breach of contact and intimacy with Tutakangahau. This was a sad ending for the two men, leaving us with little more than the imagination to build a picture of the old chief's final year. Yet it is also further evidence of how much we owe to Best for what has come down to the present day.

In April of the following year, Best wrote to Smith from Rūātoki: 'I have now not a single mohio left. Tutaka, Te Piria, Tamarau, Pirihi – all have crossed the great divide and I am now tutorless.'[72] By November he is writing again of the loss – in relation to a dearth of informants on Māori star lore – and letting slip a piece of his armour. 'I want old Tu back and Tus are non est in Tuhoeland now. E taea hoki te aha' (What can be done?).[73] The truth was, little more: what was passing away was not just Best's 'academy', but the remains of the colonial frontier to which both men, and the Pākehā's other mōhio, had belonged.

The Edwardian era supplanting that of the Treaty's Queen was moving the country towards an unseen catastrophe that would undo all the confident notions of perpetual progress cherished by Best and his peers: the Great War, a mere seven years ahead. The wheels of a militarised modernity that had overrun all colonised peoples in the European imperial century just closed were about to roll over their creators – their imagined masters. New Zealand's gaze would turn outwards, and the possibility of Tūhoe independence, that motuhake the old chiefs had struggled to institute, would be swallowed up in the ongoing disenfranchisement of Māori landholders, until the taniwha of protest awoke again in the 1970s.

Psychologically speaking, Best was now ceasing to belong: he was always to some degree the mōkai of his ruānuku, dependent on the old men not just for information, but for a sense of purpose, for some measure of his own identity. He could no longer find those bearers of the golden kura he had sought for so long – 'the last two years have wiped my old teachers off the slate of life . . . And I alone am left.'[74] His mission to the Urewera was over, and the next stage of his life was about to begin: museum ethnographer in Wellington, scribe and recorder of the vanished world he had pursued. In February 1910, no longer a government servant, Best packed up his Tūhoe existence: delayed by floods until early March, he took horse, making a series of farewells, finally leaving his adopted

Best's old house, 'Heipipi of later years', photographed by Isabel Eggers in 1934, three years after the writer's death.
Courtesy of Kevin McFadden

people in echoes of the chants that followed his poroporoaki at the Maungapōhatu marae.[75] On Sunday 13 March he records in his diary somewhat cryptically, 'To Maungapohatu. Kua kahurua aku [. . . *shorthand* . . .] dim sight', crossed out.[76] 'I am too short-sighted to see anybody' – an entry that appears later in the Williams' *Dictionary*. Even in grief at his loss, Best was still at work.[77]

With no job to go to – although supporters such as Percy Smith, Walter Gudgeon, Edward Tregear and Te Rangi Hiroa (Peter Buck) were already at work in Wellington, lobbying for him to have the position of government ethnologist, that would eventuate later that year – Best's ride south must have been lonely, wistful and more than a little anxious at times. He was broke, he had a wife to care for, and if he had to return to his bushman's skills to make a living, he was at fifty-three no longer a young roustabout. What he did possess – and what he would come to honour in the next twenty years – was the commission given him by his senior Tūhoe mentor, so recently deceased: 'And you shall make a book – a large book – of these things. And that book shall remain for our descendants to gather information from, even from the days of Maui and Tapeka.'[78]

E koro, e Tutakangahau, haere, haere, haere atu rā, haere ki Te Rerenga Wairua, ki Hawaiki nui, ki Hawaiki roa, ki Hawaiki pāmamao, moe mai, moe mai, moe mai rā!

CHAPTER ELEVEN

The Māori according to Best: 'Ka tō he rā, ka ura he rā!'[1]

The final productive phase of Best's remarkable life began on 29 July 1910 when the Director of the Colonial Museum, Augustus Hamilton, engaged him as an ethnologist on a six-month contract at £180 per annum: the frontier intellectual had come back to town.[2] Best – the 'great white tohunga' he was destined to become – would spend the remainder of his life as the Museum Ethnologist, editing and publishing his works on traditional Māori society, burning the candle at both ends, bending his pen to the fiercest of wills, until his time ran out on 9 September 1931.[3] For the next twenty years, collating and refining the copious notes and journals he had gathered mostly from Tūhoe but also other Māori informants, he would publish a body of work which remains in print to this day. By any estimation, Elsdon Best and his Māori 'academy' have proved to be foundational figures in a distinctive New Zealand literature.

The mature Best at the height of his tenure as Ethnologist (the first government official employed specifically to such a task) at the Dominion Museum, Wellington, *c.* 1925. *Photographer unknown, Alexander Turnbull Library, Wellington, NZ, PAColl-4249-08*

While Best could relax a little now and enjoy his new-found status, his time at the museum was not without problems: he was poorly paid initially, as a beginner in the Public Service in his fifties, even when his salary was raised twenty pounds and his position confirmed at the end of his first six months' service. He had a testy relationship with Hamilton – a seemingly class-based conflict heightened by the chip on Best's self-taught shoulder. Best resented the irksome norms of bureaucracy – such as signing the attendance register – and the tiny room he was given to work in, shared with a chain-smoking night watchman who fumigated the study overnight, littering the floor with his butts. Best's protests – and Hamilton's response, a practical joke entailing offering him a smaller room upstairs, enraging the ethnographer – only heightened the tensions between them.[4]

Feeling undervalued and certainly underpaid, he was quick to attack his superior for a case of what he saw as outright theft of his intellectual property. When in 1912, Best was about to publish his first bulletin on Māori material society, *The Stone Implements of the Maori*, he was further enraged to discover that Hamilton, who had kindly supplied him with some illustrations, was claiming joint authorship, and there on the title page was the Director's name alongside his. This was Best's first serious independent publication – one that would be immediately acclaimed, winning the prestigious Hector Memorial Medal for ethnology in 1914, remaining in print over ninety years later – and he was not about to share the glory.[5] He threatened to expose Hamilton throughout the world's scientific community unless he removed his name from the book – and the other man buckled.

Best never forgave this slight, leaving a note discovered after his death: 'Every item was hustled and written by me . . . all the new matter . . . was paid for privately by me. When the bulletin was finished A.H. wrote on the title page, "By A. Hamilton and Elsdon Best", thus generously allowing a modicum of credit to the rouseabout who did all the work on the wages of a mud shoveller. Thus do Maori experts achieve fame!!!!!'[6] Hamilton died in October 1913, but Best was still not finished with him, and sent out a bitter and sarcastic memorandum. In January 1914, the Under Secretary of Internal Affairs, Hislop, wrote to J. Allan Thompson, the Acting Director of the museum, concerning 'certain remarks made by Mr E. Best on the late Director of the Dominion Museum'.[7] Best's apology was swift, and Thompson responded that Best had sent him a memo 'in which he unreservedly withdraws those comments and expresses regret'. Best claimed that he had drawn up the disputed report on Hamilton and the work still to be done 'while I was still smarting under a supposed injustice. Doubtless I was quite mistaken in my view of the matter, but in any case I realise now that the time to ventilate my supposed grievance had gone past.'[8]

Best was fortunate to get out of this fracas with his position intact: his stubborn streak, fierce pride and thin skin had led him to make an intemperate attack that even today leaps off the page at the reader. In his Maori Notebook No. 15, begun in 1911, he accuses Hamilton of multiple instances of plagiarism, both in the case of his own earlier volume, *Maori Art* (1901), and a paper that had appeared in the English Anthropological Institute's journal *MAN* in June 1913: 'Necessity for Accuracy in Treating of Ethnological Subjects'.[9] Best claims that he had in fact written this paper, but it appeared in the journal under Hamilton's name, where the

Director had 'altered the wording of the final paragraph to make it appear he himself had written it'.

The paper in *MAN* was 'really a damning indictment of Hamilton's own methods'; Best cites *Maori Art*, where he claims 'all descriptive matter in M.A. was copied from printed works' – that is, plagiarised from secondary sources. Worse, Hamilton purportedly had 'stolen from an American writer'; here was a man 'who has been filching my board wages out of my pocket for three years!'. He went further: 'The Dominion newspaper says that Hamilton represents "the highest type of English gentleman"! Well, well – maybe he does. But what must the lowest type be!!! E.B.' Best had every right to be annoyed with Hamilton and take him up on these issues; however, the severe ad hominem nature of the above remarks betrays a man ill at ease with his own place in the world. He appears afflicted with a strong sense of inferiority, masked by the strident assertions of his rights in the matter, and the kind of class-based colonial cringe first revealed in his earlier, sarcastic glosses to the missionary Richard Taylor's *Te Ika a Maui*, some thirty years before.

Best's need for security was to play him false early in this new domain. At home in the bush and the world of physical challenges, well able to hold his own amongst Tūhoe in an environment that would have defeated most fellow Wellingtonians, Best was about to make an alliance with another Māori informant, who to some degree would function as a replacement for his lost mōhio, Tutakangahau, and the other wise men of Tūhoe. In his Introductory Remarks to *The Stone Implements of the Maori*, in the process of citing a wide range of Pākehā experts and observers on the manufacture and use of stone tools, he makes reference to his departed Tūhoe ruānuku in the matter of a karakia used with the toki henahena adze. A tree-felling chant given by the old man and recorded by Best appears as follows: 'He ao pukapuka / He ao mahamaha / He toki henahena / He toki ta wahie / Ka pa ki tua / Ka pa ki waho / Ka pa ki a Tane'.[10]

No translation is offered: such karakia are notoriously difficult to translate precisely; in essence the chant is a propitiation for the felling

Te Whatahoro Jury (1841–1923), fully posed, in his role as Tutakangahau's successor as a repository of traditional Māori lore.
Date uncertain, photographer unknown, Alexander Turnbull Library, Wellington, NZ, F-24827-1/2

of one of Tane's children, the tree a relative of the axeman. Best had recorded the karakia where it was still efficacious, chanted at a tree felling to enact the spiritual and physical contact between a child of Tane and the forest god himself. But Best is no longer in the Urewera, Tutakangahau is dead – and a sign of this is the appearance of the name 'Te Whatahoro' in a number of places in that introduction, especially in relation to this adze. On the previous page, when Best first mentions this toki, he writes that 'on asking Te Whatahoro the meaning of this term he at once replied that this was the name of an ancient Maori agricultural implement, hafted and used as an adze or hoe'.[11]

His brother in fact 'had such a tool made of greenstone that is famous throughout the district of the Wairarapa, and is a prized heirloom in the family'. In Te Whatahoro's world, the toki had become a sacred object, too valuable to be used in the type of work Tutakangahau employed his for – it was a museum piece, symbolic of the steady exoticisation of traditional culture. Over the next ten years, this transfer of Māori knowledge into what has been called a 'textual museum'[12] would become a shared project for Best and his new Māori informant, this 'remarkably intelligent and intellectual native . . . who was taught the old-time beliefs of his people during his youth'.[13] So, who was Te Whatahoro Jury, and why does he come into prominence in the museum years of the Best–Tutakangahau story?

Hoani Te Whatahoro Jury (1841–1923), the son of an English mission carpenter and a Māori mother of Ngāti Kahungunu descent, was also something of a self-taught scholar and recorder of Māori traditions, in the Best mode.[14] Working as an interpreter, a recorder and an advocate in the Native Land Court, gradually amassing his own store of traditional lore written down into various notebooks (some 125 over his long career), he would assume some prominence in the first two decades of the twentieth century, when his material brought him first to the attention of Percy Smith, and then shortly afterwards, to Elsdon Best.[15]

Born at a mission station on Mahia Peninsula and moving in the following year to the Wairarapa where he would spend much of his life, Te Whatahoro was present at a series of wānanga (teaching schools) in the mid-1860s, which first took place at Hautawa near Masterton in 1865. It was here that he wrote down the teachings of Te Matorohanga (Moihe Torohanga) and others – copied and recopied transcripts of which would eventually find their way into the possession of Smith and Best. This man – a Ngāti Kahungunu elder – who had received training in whare wānanga and a mission education – will loom larger in the story ahead.[16]

In the late 1890s Te Whatahoro was a member of the Tanenuiarangi Committee – featured earlier in the story of Tutakangahau's efforts to record whakapapa – who were busy authenticating traditional written material collected for publication by Tamahau Mahupuku and other members of the Kotahitanga movement. Te Whatahoro was also a member of this pan-Māori political development and by this time had been baptised into the Mormon Church. He had also become a corresponding member of the Polynesian Society in 1907 – a man of two worlds indeed – and a very different kind of informant from Best's mountain-dwelling Tūhoe mōhio. Te Whatahoro Jury represented a further step away from the oral sources Best had sought to record face to face in the Urewera, and those who had written down what they knew directly into notebooks for him. Transitionally oral-to-literate informants that most Tūhoe were, Te Whatahoro's methods were in essence the same as Best's; and while he was of Māori descent, his field methods were in a sense thoroughly Pākehā.

He would be presented to Best by the Museum Director Hamilton as 'an aged and learned Maori chief' whose invaluable transcripts contained 'knowledge for which he is well qualified, having passed through the Whare-kura, the Maori College, in olden days'.[17] Te Whatahoro was used as a token of authenticity to put pressure on the authorities to retain Best's services – one of the few remaining tohunga whose knowledge must be salvaged – and pressure also on Best, to pocket his qualms about the expert's expertise and work with him. After their first meeting in 1909, and in subsequent discussions, Best became concerned at conflicting information garnered from this tohunga, along with a growing disquiet at his apparent ignorance of the Māori language. Te Whatahoro was adept at providing answers to lists of questions – something that charmed Percy Smith, but a technique Best called into question, on the basis of his own experience in the field.

In Notebook 11 (1905–1913), one of a number of important folios in which Best collated his handwritten field notes for future publication, he gives the following caution in a section entitled 'Collection and compilation of Ethnographical Lore'. It is 'a matter of great importance', he writes, 'the way in which questions are put to a native; in this respect one has to be extremely cautious, for you can get any information required . . . if you put certain leading questions in a certain way.'[18] Dated between 1912 to 1913, when Best had already known Te Whatahoro for three years, he warns in Māori, 'He taonga nui te tupato' (great caution is needed). His experience had taught him that an informant will give what 'he <u>thinks</u> was the custom, or name, or method', but asked the same question some months later answers differently. 'I have got totally different answers from

Whatahoro, Tuta [Nihoniho of Ngāti Porou] and others', he concludes, dating his private concerns well on into a relationship that publicly, at least, he had come to accept as of great value.[19]

As sources for tracing Best's relationship with Te Whatahoro – and his deepening psychological involvement with the tohunga Te Matorohanga who the scribe had recorded in the Wairarapa hui of the 1860s and 1880s – these Notebooks are priceless primary records, as a chronicle of Best's conversion to the Io doctrine. They show too, working from the earliest notes, the fading influence of Tutakangahau: from December 1905, when Best records his presence in a Native Land Court dispute where Ngā Pōtiki were looking to claim descent rights 'to Ruatoki lands' (at which point the old man left the meeting), until a few pages later when we read, 'Tutakangahau Tapui, of Maungapohatu, died in November 1907. Born about 1830 [or 28, crossed out].'[20] A few pages later, dating from 1912, the name Whatahoro appears with increasing frequency (along with some occurrences of Tuta Nihoniho), until the Ngāti Kahungunu elder has assumed the role of Best's chief source of 'traditional lore'.

It seems that even with his reservations, Best could not refrain from turning to a man he would have avoided as suspect only a few years earlier. He certainly needed to retain his position at the museum – although whether that would have been under threat had he not embraced the new expert is moot – and so he began a series of visits to Te Whatahoro's home in Castlecliff, Wanganui. Smith was by now in possession of some of Te Whatahoro's Wairarapa manuscripts and was translating and editing this material derived from the Te Matorohanga sessions, to be published as *The Lore of the Whare-wananga*, I & II, between 1913 and 1915. A public profile for the transcriptions, copied by Te Whatahoro, sealed as authentic by the Tanenuiarangi Committee in 1907, and now given the imprimatur of some of the Polynesian Society's leading lights, was creating an impetus that would be hard to reverse. This placed Best under even more pressure to work with the Wairarapa material and its bicultural amanuensis.

Between the three of them over the next decade – then by the energy and personality of Best alone in the 1920s, after first Smith (1922) and then

Te Whatahoro (1923) died – a trinity of enduring myths were to emerge, promulgated and propagated as genuine history. A pre-Māori tangata whenua, Māori mass migration in a great fleet of seven canoes, and the existence of a pre-European High God, the Supreme Being Io, whose esoteric doctrines were known only to a small number of highly secretive tohunga – all began to enter the New Zealand psyche as historical fact from this time onwards. There was not always agreement or concert between the three on each of these; there were certainly other historic matters they attended to which survived. These, however, are typical of the main areas of historical debate where Smith, Te Whatahoro and Best acted upon each other and left enduring legacies, which have proved hard to dislodge from the national consciousness ever since.

Both Best and Smith were anxious to establish that Sir George Grey and the missionaries could not possibly have set down all there was to know about pre-Pākehā Māori society. Access to Te Whatahoro's material would by 1911 inspire Best to write to Smith and sarcastically put any such ideas in their place: 'And the Pol. Soc. was started too late to get good matter. O ye of little faith. Grey is nowhere . . . '.[21] Between 1907 and 1915, a series of meetings and the transmission of a number of manuscripts brought together in one place a seminal work of literature, which would subtly change the nation's perception of its history. This work helped to provide the basis for a body of settler writing that combined displacement of Māori and the inevitability of Pākehā succession: Stephenson Percy Smith's aforementioned two-volume work, *The Lore of the Whare-wananga*.[22] The first volume, *Te Kauwae-runga, Things Celestial*, was published in 1913, and its companion, *Te Kauwae-raro, Things Terrestrial*, two years later.

Neither book was a bestseller in its time, and its audience – principally the type of gentleman scholar who supported the society that published it – was divided on their merits and accuracy. Te Whatahoro Jury had supplied Smith with his twice-copied copies of Te Matorohanga's teachings; Elsdon Best absorbed and later popularised the contents of Smith's work in his own books on Māori culture for the general reader. These seminal texts were to give generations of New Zealanders a version of Māori history and belief that cemented the settler culture's position as rightful heirs to the previous waves of Melanesian and Polynesian migrants they had supplanted.

Te Kauwae-runga, Things Celestial would provide Best with more material for his developing thoughts on Māori religion and a High God, as touched on in the *Tuhoe* manuscript some years before: was there or was there not a Supreme Being Io in the Māori pantheon before Pākehā arrived? *Te Kauwae-raro, Things Terrestrial* had as part of its earthly focus the origins of New Zealand's original inhabitants. The arrival of Kupe (Smith had dated this earlier at around AD 925), the presence of a pre-Māori tangata whenua discovered when Toi and his grandson Whatonga made landfall (AD 1150), the arrival of a legendary Great Fleet of seven canoes in AD 1350 – New Zealanders could find here all they needed to know about Māori origins.

As well as laying out a Māori arrival chronology pre-dating the seven canoes, the account of Toi and Whatonga's landfall included a 'physical description of the "tangata whenua"' based on Te Matorohanga's account. Archdeacon H. W. Williams, a fellow member of the Polynesian Society and one of the book's critics, was not impressed by its representation of this supposed pre-Polynesian wave of settlers as inferior. He could not accept, on the basis of an account attributed to Te Matorohanga, that the supposed 'ancestors of the Moriori of the Chatham Islands' had been driven there from the mainland by 'Toi's people'.[23] He did not trust the assumption that a verbatim account of such ancient traditions could survive to that present day, be taken down accurately, all the while its proponents believing that the informants had not been influenced by Western ideas and especially – in the matter of things celestial – by Christian teaching.

While he disagreed radically with much that was contained in both books, Williams waited until after both Smith and, later, Best had died, before publishing his refutation, 'The Maruiwi Myth', in the Polynesian Society's journal in 1937.[24] Others, including the rising stars of New Zealand anthropology, H. D. Skinner and Peter Buck (Te Rangi Hiroa), also harboured doubts about the credibility of Te Whatahoro and the 'Chatham Island Moriori history set out in *Te Kauwae raro*'. Buck considered that Te Matorohanga had obtained his version 'in the 1850s from Hauauru and Taki rangi in Whanganui'.[25] Nevertheless, the horse, so to speak, had long ago bolted, when these writers were active before and after the Second World War. Best had published *The Maori As He*

Was, his general history of the pre-European world, in 1924; before that, his speech at the Wellington Institute in 1915, 'Maori and Maruiwi', had appeared the following year in *The Transactions and Proceedings of the New Zealand Institute*.[26]

The adult reading audience, both lay and expert, was by these means exposed to the idea of a pre-Māori Melanesian people displaced by the finer type of Polynesian incomers, true Māori, and exiled to the Chatham Islands to await their final obliteration in 1835 with arrival from the mainland of Ngāti Tama and Ngāti Mutunga. Over the next forty years – through newspaper journalism, A. H. Reed's popular histories, *School Journal* articles from 1916 onwards (which Best may well have authored anonymously), the standard primary school text *Our Nation's Story* (1920), high school history books such as Condliffe and Airey's *Short History of New Zealand* (first published in 1938, but still in use in a revised version in this writer's high school in 1965), and even by the highly regarded historian J. C. Beaglehole, in *The Discovery of New Zealand* (1961) – the Smith–Best version of events was endlessly recycled, and persists.[27]

By the time writers such as Bruce Biggs and David Simmons began to make their close examinations of the manuscript material behind the *Lore*, resulting in Simmons' seminal work on the canoe stories, *The Great New Zealand Myth* (1976) – and later, articles in the *Journal of the Polynesian Society* on the teachings of Te Matorohanga (1994) – Māori were themselves on the streets and marching, willing and able to rewrite the nation's story. Not all of the Smith–Best version would be dislodged from its place in the public mind, nor would Māori themselves reject out of hand the 'traditional' material disseminated by these Pākehā scribes. No matter what academic research produces, convenient national myths that rest on such a foundation have proved hard to budge – even for those who appear most disadvantaged by them. Nowhere has this proved truer than in the theology of Io, now established amongst Māori theologians, academics, guardians of whakapapa, and almost every student at secondary and tertiary level who picks up a common textbook such as the Ka'ai et al. 2004 publication *Ki te Whaiao: An Introduction to Māori Culture and Society*.[28]

In this text's opening section on creation narratives, Michael Reilly freely acknowledges that 'Io, the supreme *atua*', is controversial due to nineteenth-century Christian influences on Māori thought. However, he points towards Ngā Puhi and Ngāti Kahungunu tribal narratives about Io 'that draw deeply from a Māori world view, complete with *karakia*', which suggest to him that 'this being was an *atua* for at least some *iwi* and *hapū*' before European contact and influence.[29] The Northland source he refers to is the Ngā Puhi tohunga and Anglican priest Māori Marsden, and the Kahungunu scholar Te Whatahoro. From thereon in the text, the authenticity of these narratives seems taken for granted; what is interesting is that both these informants have strong Christian influences in their backgrounds, and in Te Whatahoro's case, no mention is made of the midwifery of Smith, or Best.

Reilly adds another layer of commentary when he cites the Dominican priest Michael Shirres as an interpreter of Marsden's thoughts on Io, a Catholic brother who has 'worked for over twenty years on the inculturation of Jesus into the world of the Maori'.[30] Best might well be surprised were he to return today and find scholars, Māori divines – and contemporary missionaries – all to the fore in promoting Io as an authentic Māori Supreme Being. One suspects he would take a certain grim satisfaction from the fact that his efforts to dethrone the bloodstained Old Testament God of his understanding – while he championed the atua the missionaries had missed – had largely succeeded. Best's Io might be a somewhat ethereal and remote figure, but one who nevertheless had the significant advantage that, while he inhabited the highest heavens, he presided over no hell of fire.

Te Whatahoro and Te Matorohanga, too, might be pleased with the emergent theology they had helped to create, for Best to popularise. After all, there were only a small number of Io occurrences outside of their Wairarapa manuscripts, and Smith's own text for the *Lore* was a copy he had made from Te Whatahoro, which he had credited to Te Matorohanga.[31] Simmons and Biggs (1970) make the point that the only primary documentation for Io-matua and his pantheon of gods and messengers is found in the second chapter of *Te Kauwae-runga* – material copied by Smith from the single informant above and not found elsewhere. It does not pass any test as having traditional authority, 'that body of lore which is accepted as genuine by mature, well-informed members of the group concerned'.[32]

They also make the point that the body of the Tanenuiarangi

manuscripts delivered to the Dominion Museum in 1910 (which Best copied) does correspond with what appears in the rest of Smith's copy. The traditions from the East Coast wānanga where the Tanenuiarangi Committee approved material as authentic are now accepted as genuine, except in the case of Chapter II, which contains the Io material.[33] Te Whatahoro also compiled the material Smith used in the second volume of the *Lore*, 'a late compilation from many sources' which 'cannot be accepted as the teaching of any school of learning'.[34] As with the early Io material, much of the authority in the collection of this kura rests in our trust of Te Whatahoro and his methods.

The Io teachings begin their life as an abstraction, in thrall to the authority of the words of the Bible, which first presented a written High God to Māori. This was in part a search for equality with Pākehā: creating material that, once it found its way into his hands, allowed Best after his conversion to its authenticity to become its principal mediator. 'The Cult of Io' had its first airing in the 1913 issue of *MAN*, the *Journal of the Royal Anthropological Institute* referred to earlier, when Best took these findings to the wider world.[35] Set out in the context of issues deriving from Andrew Lang's work *The Making of Religion* (1900) – specifically the chapters 'The High Gods of Low Races' and 'More Savage Supreme Beings' – Best at first claims no position on Lang's assertions that monotheistic cultures may decline into polytheism. He claims he is simply writing to place 'original matter [collected] from neolithic man on the record'.[36]

From his earlier thoughts on the subject of Io and Supreme Beings in *Tuhoe*, it is clear he was disinclined to believe in the degradationalist stance, preferring to think of Māori as running a parallel system of religious practice concurrently. His intention here appears to demonstrate that a so-called 'inferior' and 'savage' people were well and truly capable of evolving the 'concept of a Supreme Being, a creative and eternal god, a Deity that did not punish the souls of men after the death of the body'. Best stands once more in his twin role: as defender of Māori against the missionaries and any other arrogant souls in Pākehā society, as well as a kind of Darwinian bulldog in the mould of Thomas Huxley, defending the new pieties of social science against the reactionaries of orthodoxy. Māori, he writes, were not so uncivilised prior to the European invasion that they were incapable of evolving a belief system whose god 'occupied a much higher plane that that of certain old-time Semites'.[37]

He calls two witnesses to the stand: Tutakangahau and Te Whatahoro (a nice example of the relationship these two informants had to his new manifestation as the Pākehā expert). He writes that it is about ten years since 'some information gained from an old tattoed survivor of the neolithic era . . . put us on the right track' – Tutakangahau. Since that time, he continues, 'we have obtained much more light from an intelligent and intellectual native, now seventy-three years of age, who was taught the old-time beliefs of his people during his youth' – Te Whatahoro. Neither of the two men is named here, but it is not difficult to identify them, and see Best beginning to plait their information into a single strand that accords with his own religious prejudices. This new knowledge, it seems, was 'imparted by two of the last survivors of the Maori priesthood, men who had been trained in neolithic times under the singular *tapu* system that obtained in Maoridom'; men, what is more, who 'jealously conserved that knowledge and kept aloof from European missionaries when they reached these parts' – Te Matorohanga and Nepia Pōhuhu.

Best allows himself to get a little carried away here: he was already aware by this time (according to information Te Whatahoro had supplied) of Te Matorohanga's contacts with Christian teachers. Even as Te Whatahoro was passing on his written material on Māori spirituality in 1912, Best was elsewhere exclaiming with exasperation, 'the Maori of today is no safe guide for us. He is saturated with Christian ideas, more's the pity.'[38] If he was not aware of all the details of Te Matorohanga's early life, Best can hardly have imagined that the old man had never been exposed to Christian literacy and ideas – if not when he was writing this article, certainly by the following year when he describes with much mirth the sage's theological joustings with the missionaries.[39] There is also evidence recorded by Tīpene Chrisp that Te Matorohanga attended 'Christian "native schools" in 1845', along with another who would become one of the wānanga experts, Paratene Okawhare.[40]

In many respects, the introduction to the Io material given by Te Whatahoro was one more stick in Best's hand with which to beat the missionaries. The remainder of the article is a précis of the material as it appears in Smith's *Te Kauae-runga*: there was a higher class of priests, and Io's name was never uttered except in extremis in the form of a synonym, 'The Beyond . . . or some such term'. Nothing could exist except by the will of Io; Io's emanations were such that 'all things down to the humblest weed and fragment of clay . . . were a portion of his spirit. There is but one further step to take: that fragment of clay is Io.'[41] What Best proposes here is a Māori pantheism: that the creation, nature, and God are one and the same. It is difficult to say whether this was actually Te Matorohanga's theology, when he is quoted shortly afterwards – as 'an old teacher of the sacred School of Learning' – saying, 'All things are one, and emanated from Io the Eternal'. The old teachers had now lost control of the dissemination of their teachings, and Best was free to interpret and frame them as he wished.

It is tempting to suggest that here was the fulfilment of Best's search for the kura huna: a truly indigenous form of spiritual teaching known only to a select group, denied as authentic by the missionaries. It had become available for Best to colonise and propagate, its teachings accessible only to a small band of true believers, Māoriphiles literate in the language, with access to the few repositories where it was now stored. 'A pure cult . . . of too elevated a character for the common people' in the old world was now safely in the hands of the Pākehā ethnographer.

These late-appearing teachings could be used to prove that Māori had evolved 'a very high plane of thought, one strongly tinged with monotheistic ideas, and replete with extremely fine conceptions of the attributes of a supreme Deity'. Preserved 'through many centuries to our own time', the Io cult deserved at the very least 'admission to the list of ethical religions' – and there was still more to be revealed. A religion without a priesthood, having no rituals, surviving only in these few written records – it might well have disappeared completely, had it not met Best's unique set of needs, the man who would become its champion in the literature and almost, it seems, a new high priest.

Best's transformation from a fieldworking ethnographer into a form of secular cleric presiding over the hidden knowledge of an esoteric Māori religion began to take place in these years he spent writing up the notes he had made in his Urewera years amongst Tūhoe. The material published in *MAN* – and for later iterations of the Io material in future works – had arrived in his possession from Te Whatahoro in the previous two years, and survives in his Notebooks, attributed in Notebook 11 precisely by date, 'from Te Whatahoro'. There are notes on ethnographic techniques, the meanings of spiritual terms such as wairua, mauri and hau, and the influence of missionaries on Māori thought – all in Best's distinctive italicised hand. There are also recorded a significant number of important statements by the ethnographer on his attitude to the old tohunga Te Matorohanga, along with sayings attributed to him and stories he told, all sourced from Te Whatahoro Jury.

In December 1912, Best, 'from Te Whatahoro', writes that 'in the beginning, all men invoked Io', but finding their prayers unheard, 'evolved minor gods and demons' to help them. These thoughts, he adds, were 'the teachings of Te Matorohanga, the last first class tohunga of the East Coast. Such is the Maori explanation of polytheism, of a people originally monotheistic evolving a polytheistic cult.' Relying entirely on Te Whatahoro's written word, he concludes that 'the teachings of Te Matorohanga throw more light on the inner thoughts of the old time Maori on religious matters, and the higher plane of Maori mentality than anything that has been collected from this or any other primitive folk'.[42] In three short years away from the bush and the reality of Tūhoe society, Best had allowed himself to be seduced by suspect literary sources into holding a position he had once wisely rejected, using second-hand written material he had no hope of verifying – but why?

The arrival of such material in his possession gave Best the prospect of ownership – the exercise of power and control over its interpretation and distribution – and the temptation to step into Te Matorohanga's shoes. A secret priesthood, of high status: 'Te Matorohanga was of the high rank of tohunga', writes Best, 'he knew he had the mana and the authority to repeat invocations to Io.'[43] The sage had passed on 'to Te Whatahoro and others the sacred lore of Io and other matters . . . [and] his teachings were written in a book'. By committing this material to paper, Te Matorohanga was tacitly admitting that it would pass out of his control, as indeed it did – and in Best's hands, become open not only to preservation, but to whatever changes of emphasis might suggest themselves to the Pākehā.

This occurs in the *MAN* article, where Best insists that Io is a god on a far higher plane than that of the Jews (and their Christian inheritors); additional evidence of Io's superiority to Jehovah is put forward when he writes that the Sheol of the Old Testament and the Hell of the New do not exist. 'Kia marama!' he declares (Let there be light!), 'there is no punishment in the future world.' Io, it seems, 'gave man the knowledge of good and evil that the contest between them might be fought out in this world'.[44] His frequent insistence on this issue derived not only from his hostility to an aspect of Christian doctrine but also from his desire to show how the missionaries misunderstood Māori. He cites Te Whatahoro here, that his informant had remarked to him once that if the 'early missionaries had learned and studied the cult of Io, and had not despised our religion, I think that cult would have been incorporated with Christianity, and would now be part of the Bible'.[45]

This merits a derisive snort in the Notebook: poor Whatahoro had 'evidently not grasped the utter narrowness of the average Christian missionary, his contempt for all other forms of belief than his own, and his reliance on absurd and often degrading dogma'. No doubt Best had experienced some dogmatism and prejudice from ecclesiastics in his time, but his real point here is that Māori have not learned *enough* distrust of the evangelicals and the priests: 'Whatahoro evinces, like many Maoris, a deep distrust of missionaries and persons of the orthodox church, and strongly resents their actions in the past.' Certainly there was truth in this observation, but what Best may have missed in Te Whatahoro's remark was an underlying impulse: to find equality for Māori in Pākehā eyes, to achieve inclusion.

This also seems to underlie some of the attraction of Io, a Māori High God to match the God of the Pākehā. The experience Te Whatahoro had gained in translating the book of Mormon into Māori may well have shown him something of what happens when unorthodox teaching mingles with orthodoxy. The Book of Mormon, a genuinely syncretic text, had a relationship to the Authorised Version somewhat similar to that which Te Whatahoro seems to be advocating for the Io teaching and the Bible. His contact with the Mormon missionary culture in the Wairarapa during the 1880s would also have exposed him to their history of rejection and misunderstanding at the hands of a hostile majority in the United States (part of the psychological appeal of Mormonism to 'outsiders').

Baptised into the Mormon Church in 1900 and later confirmed, Hoani Te Whatahoro Jury was a man of multiple influences and allegiances.

His comment exemplifies the psychology of syncretism, the attempt to reconcile different religious and philosophical systems, in this case to meet his own needs and those of Māori caught between two worlds. A wise missionary accepts the need to indigenise the faith they proclaim, allowing the native prospect to feel a measure of ownership – or even to see a foreshadowing of the gospel in their own tradition. Best, however, appears as prejudiced as the missionaries he despises: evermore reliant on Te Whatahoro and Te Matorohanga, forced by degrees to fit their material into his own temperamental attraction to pantheism. As much as he is hostile to the idea of any missionary influence on the secret order of tohunga who kept Io from the common herd, he slips into admissions that his scribe Whatahoro was affected by missionary teachings.

Discussing Māori spiritual terms in the Notebook, he questions his informant's definition of 'toiora' as something of a divine essence in humanity, 'the ichor of Io' in every human being. This he concedes 'may be a borrowed idea, imbibed from Christianity, perhaps unconsciously as Whatahoro has, unfortunately, *been in contact with that cult all his life*'. 'Toiora', as given by Williams' *Dictionary of the Maori Language*, meant 'sound, uninjured', and in the realm of spiritual warfare, '*secured* by occult means from *evil influence*'.[46] Best is correct to note this conflation of the traditional meaning with influences from the Io teachings – but in so doing, he damages not only Te Whatahoro's credibility as a bearer of ancient lore, but his own, for accepting such a source for the most part uncritically. If Te Whatahoro was gilding the lily here, then where else – how much of Te Matorohanga's 'ancient' teachings were as they were taken down in 1865, and what proportion of the copied material had been edited and reformulated by Te Whatahoro?

What is more significant is the way the Notebook reveals Best's psychological involvement with the dead tohunga he had never met, whose teachings had only ever come to him as literature, and that too, mediated by a self-taught Māori scholar who by Best's admissions was both consciously and unconsciously influenced by Christian and Mormon teaching. Relying on material given him by Te Whatahoro during 1913, Best gives a short biographical picture of Te Matorohanga with his 'high, broad, square forehead' confronting unnamed missionaries at an undisclosed location, as they attempted to best the tohunga in theological debates.[47] The missionaries, he writes, 'tried to get him to discard the teachings of the whare wananga and its gods, including Io, but he steadfastly refused'. Told this was a work of the devil, he replied, '"Kai te pai. Ma Io tena māna e titari."' Io will decide which is right. "He hiku to nga mea katoa."' He is the source of all created things.

Best does not record this in a context that shows the tohunga's rejection of a faith he may have known earlier – but this becomes obvious later in the course of the encounter. A missionary then said to him, 'your religion is false. It teaches that all things possess a wairua', to which Te Matorohanga replied, 'ki te kore te wairua o te atua ki roto, kaore tena mea e whiwhi i tona ahua'. That is, 'if there is no spirit of god within, that thing will not be able to possess any attributes' – the debate centring around what we might now call questions of both immanence in nature and the reality of the animate/inanimate division. Te Matorohanga instructed the missionaries that the wairua (spirit) of any being or object was implanted when the whatu (eyes, core) were formed. If a tree had no whatu, it could not pihi (sprout), he told them; so the missionary countered, 'where are the whatu [eyes] and pihi [shoots] of a stone?'.

Best is grimly amused by all this, especially the fact that 'whatu' had a double meaning that the missionaries evidently did not grasp, assuming the tohunga meant eyes and not the more metaphysical sense of a core, or centre. Being unable to debate accurately with Māori – in Māori – on spiritual matters rendered them to some degree theologically illiterate amongst their target audience; he takes great relish in recording the way the errant tohunga points out to the missionaries their biblical ignorance. This is important in the light of Best's claim here that 'M. never embraced Christianity and stuck to the teachings of the whare wananga, and its gods, until his death'. For a man who may not have 'embraced' the Christian faith, Te Matorohanga certainly knew his Bible, as befitting one who had gained his literacy in a Christian native school.

It is necessary to quote the old man at length here: 'kua mahue i a koe to pukapuka (where it says) Ko nga mea katoa, he ahua tona. He wairua to nga mea katoa, mehemea kaore i whakaae te atua e kore te rakau e whai hua, te aha ranei. *You have neglected your own book [the Bible] . . . (where it says) . . . all things have their own likeness, their own spirit. All things have their own spirit, if the god [God] did not permit this, the tree could not bear fruit, nor any other [created thing . . . be fruitful].*[48] Te Matorohanga knew how to debate from Scripture – specifically here the first chapter of Genesis – and used his knowledge to outflank the missionaries and support his own argument. To appeal to biblical authority so confidently and with such aplomb, he had to be familiar with the Scriptures – which makes it so much harder to argue that his influence on the Wairarapa versions of the Io teachings could not have been contaminated by Christian theology.

In Te Matorohanga, it seems Best had found an ally in his dismissal of Christian claims – a man 'anathema maranatha to the missionaries, but from all accounts . . . : a fine type of man and infinitely wider minded than [them], far more liberal in his views of religious matters'. He could almost be describing an ideal version of himself: the visible likeness of the invisible Best, a wished-for ancestor and ally in his power struggle with missionary Christianity over who would gain the rights to control the Māori past – especially a description of the nature of traditional spirituality – and send their version into the future as historical fact. It is ironic that Best calls on a phrase from the Apostle Paul's First Letter to the Corinthians to describe the missionary reaction to his man: 'if any man love not the Lord Jesus Christ, let him be Anathema Maranatha' (1 Corinthians 16:22). His own familiarity with the Scriptures underlines the fact that while both he and Te Matorohanga partook of shifting views that rejected Christian orthodoxy, it was nevertheless a shaping force in their very different lives.

There is more to say later on Best's entanglement with the old sage, when the tohunga's ōhākī (final words) are repeated on Best's deathbed in 1931. The question of what place Io had found in Best's psychology will never be finally settled; nor will the long-running debate on the Māori High God's indigeneity, as opposed to his emergence in nineteenth-century Māori thought, belief and practice. For those who wish to pursue the questions further, Buck (1949), Simmons and Biggs (1970), Smith (1982), Head (1995), Simpson (1997) and Thornton (2004) – along with a host of other contributors – speak for and against both sides. What matters for the present is that Io is here to stay and will likely never leave us; tracing Best's part in this process, however, may give us 'more light', as he had demanded when earlier echoing the dying Goethe's words from 1832.[49]

There is more to say, however, on the potential impact of the Smith–Best propagation of the Io story in their writings: specifically that division of heavenly and earthly matters that Smith first laid out in *The Lore of the Whare-wananga*. We might picture the effects of this division – ki runga, ki raro, heaven and earth – as somehow prophetic. While Pākehā settled into possession of a different land, Māori found themselves inhabiting a different heaven. Smith – and Best through his dissemination of Smith, Te Whatahoro and Te Matorohanga – had begun a process of legitimising Pākehā appropriation and Māori displacement, through what would become canonical literary monuments. The settlers were the evolutionary heirs of the land in the operations of the blind machinery of human progress: ki raro, the things below. Māori, on the other hand, lost the land on which they stood but inherited a new Heavenly Being: ki runga, the things above.

This version of events creates a division between heaven and earth, the physical and the spiritual. Māori have moral authority and nowhere to stand; Pākehā have the earth beneath their feet – but have lost that authority in denying Māori their rights as citizens. There is a thirst for the legitimation of settlement on the one hand, and the spiritualisation of Māori on the other. This tension would simmer – a psychic wound comprised of buried rage and uneasy guilt – beneath what became the authorised version of New Zealand colonial history, until the return of the repressed from the 1970s and onwards, when Māori began to challenge the system by denying the story.

Best had other far-reaching effects: his researches in the Urewera resulted in his earliest – and some would say his finest – articles on Tūhoe society, as he lived in close contact with his hosts and talked face to face with men such as Tutakangahau and Paitini. His research into the Māori spiritual world and the language used for describing these phenomena excited his ethnographical colleagues, such as Herbert Williams, a fellow member of the Polynesian Society and the editorial inheritor of the great

Williams family dictionary-making project that has continued into the present. To realise how long-lived and significant Best's definitions have been in our literature, shortly we follow one of the most significant – mauri – to see what happened in the life of this word, after it arrived on the pages of the fifth edition in 1917. In particular, to see Best's influence moving post-mortem through the decades of the twentieth century, to occupy an unshakeable presence in New Zealand anthropology, history and Māori studies, as well as in the wider world where thousands daily use his work, most often ignorant of the author and his sources.

Best is a world – and it is impractical to visit all of his massive output here. The overriding themes in his writing can be clearly traced: Māori origins and arrival; whether they were of Semitic or Aryan stock; their ranking in a scheme of human intellectual development, including the capacity for abstract thought, as a pre-literate people; their essential psychology, as expressed in Best's metaphor, the mythopoetic Māori; their material and spiritual culture, especially the Io question; and the transfer of oral practice into written meaning. This requires some assessment in

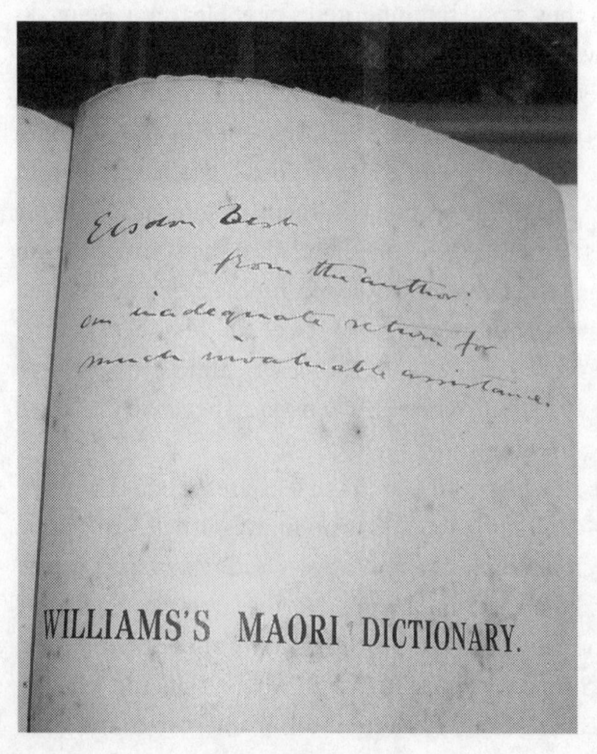

'From the author: an inadequate return for much invaluable assistance.' Herbert Williams' acknowledgement, written in Best's personal copy of the fifth edition of the Williams' *Maori Dictionary* (1917). *Author photograph, by kind permission of Warwick Jordan*

the following chapter, but it is salutary to be reminded of the vast range of Best's enquiries, whether or not the comparative historical models and the diffusionist theories he held dear have survived.

Best did endeavour in his time at the Dominion Museum to acquire new skills and keep up with developments in what has since become the academic discipline of modern anthropology – but age and temperament were against him. While he may not have been able stay abreast of new developments, given his prodigious work rate and commitment to publishing his own works on Māori society, he was unique in that he was the first and the last of the Māori-speaking, fieldworking anthropologists working on a disappearing frontier. Through his labours, the Williams' *Dictionary of the Maori Language* – one of our greatest indigenous literary treasures – fattened in 1917 to almost twice its previous size, much to the delight of Herbert Williams, the editor of the fifth edition. Since revised twice more by learned committees (1957, 1970), Best's contributions are still with us today. Anywhere one sees the source note 'J' in a dictionary entry is a reference to an original article in the *Journal of the Polynesian Society*, and some of these specifically – note, for example, 'Best in J. x, 2–7, and elsewhere', as in the mauri reference – followed now into the *Dictionary* and out into the wider world.[50]

In his Preface to the fifth edition, Herbert Williams – grandson of the legendary missionary William, Treaty translator and dictionary maker (1844) – was delighted to note that 'a large number of words, new meanings and examples collected at first hand' were now included. They were mostly from Tūhoe sources and all these were from Best: 'the most important contribution, in volume and character, is that made by Mr Elsdon Best, whose intimate acquaintance with the Maori, coupled with the scientific method of his enquiries, give to the results of his work a unique value'.[51] Best had not only supplied a large number of words, meanings and examples, he was available for Williams to make enquiries, and to give him advice, as a contributing editor. The clergyman had also made free use of Best's articles in the *Journal of the Polynesian Society*, the *Transactions and Proceedings of the New Zealand Institute* and other scientific journals, Best's 'opinion on the esoteric knowledge of the Maori being of the greatest weight'.

An earlier chapter on Best's work in the Urewera in the late nineteenth century and early in the twentieth reviewed the production of this original material, and what happened when the ethnographer passed words from Māori karakia through the filter of Western philology and his second-hand Greek, absorbed from reading F. Max Müller (see Chapter Six). Yet Best's work in defining and fixing such terms as mauri, hau and wairua became the gold standard, entering a world ignorant of any deep understanding of Māori society, and issues of orality and literacy. The dictionary's entry for 'hau' (breath, spirit, vitality) under section (iv) refers the reader to Best's *JPS* article on 'The Spiritual Concepts of the Maori Pt I', from Volume IX in 1900; the concept of manawa (heart, belly, bowels) to Pt II of the same article in the next issue, Volume X in 1901. The list goes on in matters large and small: with the assistance of Best and other Polynesian Society members, the dictionary grew from 226 pages in 1915 to nearly 600 two years later.

Today's dictionary contains virtually the same entry for mauri as it did in 1917; in 1996, an important new dictionary of contemporary Māori words, *Te Matatiki*, published by Te Taura Whiri i Te Reo Māori/The Māori Language Commission, turned to many of these Best-derived definitions of important lexical items, such as mauri, to assist them. In coining new constructions such as 'mauri moe' for 'the unconscious', the editors cite the Williams' *Dictionary* (and thus, Best) as a major source: **mauri** W.197, 'life principle, thymos of man', **moe** W.204, 'sleep, dream'.[52] On a more playful note, across on the opposite page, 'moari (noun), maypole', is sourced from page 48 of Best's *Games and Pastimes of the Maori*, as meaning swing. Best – and his Tūhoe informants – are ubiquitous in the modern Māori world.

This shows how radically Best's *transitional* work has become fixed, as if it gives *traditional* Māori meanings, when, as translations, they were subject to normal cultural bias – literary definitions of what were once purely oral formulations. This is especially true in the area of spiritual language employed in ceremonies, where the incantatory power of the karakia or chant was to have an immediate outcome in the here and now. The *effect* was what mattered – success in fishing, battle or love – not a literary meaning, which did not exist and could have no function in such a setting. Wray's psycholinguistic theory of 'needs only' analysis suggests that in any sequence of language to which we are exposed, we try to obtain maximum meaning for minimal effort. Just as children listen to adults and learn the formulas that get results, without the need to analyse the components, so adults do not break down input any further than is necessary to extract or create meaning.[53]

In oral cultures such as Māori society before the arrival of Europeans, formulaic language was the only method of remembering important information through set constructions. When it was a matter of life and death, such phrases used ceremonially had power in themselves: *meaning* was secondary. Words had power, they expressed power, and the speakers used the formulas to express and demonstrate that power. Best often complained to Smith that many of the karakia he encountered in the mid-1890s amongst Tūhoe were virtually untranslatable, so ancient were the formulations, so encoded the language structures. Hamiora Pio's five manuscript books 'contained a great deal of matter . . . [which] is beyond me especially karakia of wh. there are a great many . . . parts of them are very obscure to me'.[54] This is no surprise: lifeless on the page and of no use to Best in obtaining whatever boon or curse they were originally spoken to obtain, they were silent symbols of a vanished world, empty of more than just meaning. They were tokens in that textual museum of dictionaries Herbert Williams and his peers were bringing in with them to embalm the Māori past, while saving the language for whatever new world might await in the future.

Best was by now established as the principal Pākehā authority on traditional Māori society – that tohunga he had dreamed of being as a child in Tawa – and he set himself to his task with an unquenchable energy that seldom allowed for holidays. In the years after the publication of the 1913 *MAN* article, his prodigious output accelerated. There were eight more Dominion Museum Bulletins on aspects of traditional Māori society: storehouses, religion, canoes, games, agriculture, the pā, fishing methods, and birth customs – and six shorter monographs. With these also appeared the major two-volume work *The Maori* and the general study *The Maori As He Was* (both in 1924), *Tuhoe: The Children of the Mist*, at long last in 1925, along with a host of learned articles and newspaper pieces. In publishing these three major works, he was in large part financed by Apirana Ngata and Peter Buck, and the Board of Maori Ethnological Research, 'for the Author on behalf of the Polynesian Society'. Māori had given Best his material and Māori were fully involved in seeing it through to the public arena.

He also became an historian of the Wellington region, and a recognisable local eccentric in his daily walks to the museum to keep up his vital writing while his strength remained. His ethnographic practices and interests in the professionalisation of anthropology saw him become an important figure in the changing museum display culture, exhibiting items referred to increasingly as 'Maori artefacts'. Māori language describing display items came into prominence under Best's supervision, and his material archive of traditional Māori items and detailed explanations of their provenance would later provide resources for 'the twentieth-century cultural renaissance'.[55] He lectured to adults and children; he also found

'The house that Jack built' – Adelaide and Elsdon Best on the verandah of 'Matai-moana', 154 Barnard Street, Wadestown, *c.* 1925.
Photographer unknown, Alexander Turnbull Library, Wellington, NZ, PA1-o-1240-22

the energy to build his own home, *Matai Moana* – 'Sea Gazing' – at 154 Barnard Street, Wadestown. Along the way, he also found time to resist the tides of anarchy by joining with 'Massey's Cossacks' in 1913, cracking the heads of strikers from horseback, decked out in his leather cowboy suit. His fellow ethnologist Edward Tregear – a liberal social reformer – was mortified to see his friend so employed, 'dressed in a Texas costume, a big wide hat, a Mexican or Texas saddle, and the usual big leather stirrup foot rests'.[56]

Best kept up contact with his Tūhoe friends – such as Numia Kereru, Tutakangahau's close ally – with a correspondence on ethnographic points of clarification, as well as answering requests for money and blankets from the less prosperous members of the iwi.[57] He even made occasional visits back to his old haunts at Te Whāiti, sending instructions for his grandnephew (and future biographer) young Elsdon Craig to join him (Best and Adelaide were childless).[58] Older Māori would visit him at his post in the museum and long discussions would ensue; letters

Elsdon Best as a special constable – one of 'Massey's Cossacks' – outside Government House, Wellington, 1913.
Photographer unknown, Alexander Turnbull Library, Wellington, NZ, PA1-1204-16

addressed 'Kia Peehi, Wellington' would always reach him. His presence there increased Hamilton's circle of contacts with Māori elders 'and raised the profile of the Museum in Māori circles'.[59] The Ngāti Porou elder Tuta Nihoniho, a former fighter with Ropata Wahawaha against Te Kooti – and Tutakangahau – worked closely with Best in the museum, where he also took a vital part in getting the language used in exhibitions to be properly translated, with traditional meanings explained for the public.[60]

Best also attended important Māori gatherings such as the Hui Aroha in 1919 at Gisborne, to welcome back the Māori troops from the Great War (recordings of which do exist, where a Pākehā narrator – in all likelihood Best – introduces Ngāti Kahungunu and Ngāti Porou tribal chants).[61] He travelled on an ethnographic expedition to the Whanganui River communities in February 1923 with the British anthropologist George Pitt-Rivers, as well as similar journeys to the East Coast and Waipiro Bay in March to April of the same year, with Te Rangi Hiroa (Peter Buck) and Apirana Ngata. Seen in films made by James McDonald at this time, Best

Best and party, Dominion Museum camp, Rotorua, *c.* 1920. Best is taking notes from a Māori informant about string games (mahi whai), while Johannes Andersen watches a demonstration behind him.
Photographer: James McDonald, Museum of New Zealand Te Papa Tongarewa, B.010539

in his trademark Norfolk jacket is a striking figure: tall, with a definite military bearing, an arm placed behind his back, making his points with a raised finger. He stands upright, somewhat aloof, moving with a dignified grace in his mid-sixties. He is rangy, with no trace of spare flesh on a frame well used to a hard life in the bush: felling trees, milling, walking and riding long distances well into his fifties. At ease on a fishing expedition with Peter Buck, we have a rare picture of a man in fine physical condition, enjoying life outdoors, away from the hated urban confines of Wellington: Te Peehi in his late prime and full of life.[62]

An equally remarkable and late image of the ageing Best in his den at the Dominion Museum has been left by the British colonial historian Margery Perham (1895–1982), who visited this country in 1929 on a world tour of colonial administrations, taken to see 'the greatest living authority on Maori'.[63] A tutor in Modern History at Oxford, this courageous and far-sighted woman had much in common with Best. She was an expert on colonial governance and made numerous overseas trips in her long life – a witness to conflict in Somaliland in 1922, and Nigeria in 1968 where, at the age of seventy, she saw the horrors of the Biafran tragedy. An influence on British colonial policy, as the first Director of the Oxford Institute for Colonial Studies she had come to the Pacific on a Rhodes Travelling Fellowship. After studying the Mau rebellion in Samoa, she spent three weeks in this country, talking to as many people as she could, from all walks of life, on the subject of race relations and colonial administration – she even managed to include a trip to the Urewera, spending a few days amongst Tūhoe.

Perham – well qualified to see the wider picture – has left perhaps the last clear and unsentimental picture of the great man, two years before his death. In no way dewy-eyed or triumphalist about the fate of indigenous peoples in the Empire, she provides a rare view of the white tohunga at his desk. Best was 'so old and so valuable' she was told, that 'funds had been raised mainly by the Maoris, to keep him alive and writing until the last possible moment'. She found him engaged 'on still another work on Maori religious thought', this 'enormous man . . . eyes brilliant with intelligence and vitality'. He told her how he had fought against Māori; and of his own vanishing tribe of Pākehā hoariri (fighting friends, the enemy) – 'how men of his generation who had fought Maori loved them'.

He described his determination after these wars to live amongst Māori and how they had adopted him, in that strange blood bond of former opponents. She listened to the substance of what he had learned: not until Pākehā had fully understood '[Māori] customs and ideas . . . and [knew] their vast genealogies by heart' would they be allowed 'into the innermost secrets of their thoughts'. He spoke of 'what a tragedy the white invasion had been to the old generation of Maoris . . . the circle of their ideas . . . [broken] almost at a touch by the white man'. Māori patterns of life, 'the elaboration of tapu and mana which Best himself can hardly understand . . . were as delicate and as complex as a cobweb and were dislocated by the gun, money and Christianity'. He quoted an old chief (possibly Hamiora Pio) on the defilement of 'the sacred life principle of man' – presumably mauri. Perham says this was as close a translation as Best could manage. Pio's people were left to watch and die, to despair for themselves, and hope that their grandchildren 'might learn to become Pakehas'.

Best also recounted the story of a 'tattoed old man' – perhaps Tutakangahau at Wairau Moana – discoursing on mauri 'in Socratic fashion', picking up a stone near their campfire and questioning how 'substance could hold together unless some spiritual force existed within it'. Perham found him fascinating on the distant past, but could not draw him out on 'the Maori of today'. He is living in the past, she wrote, recreating it in his books – one of which he gave her, and sent her off to see Johannes Andersen, his understudy who would take over as editor of the Polynesian Society's journal after Best's death. He would prove more forthcoming than Best, on the present parlous state of Māori in relation to land and labour. Perham's observations are not surprising: Best was a man in his early seventies, worn out by a life of physical and mental labour; the elderly do tend to live more in what lies behind them than what remains. The ethnographer was simply dwelling where his heart had always lain – in a past populated with beings real and imaginary.

Best was 'less interesting' on New Zealand in the late 1920s: his interests and remaining energy lay elsewhere. She reveals his willingness to send money and worldly goods to old friends – 'Oh Best, I have no blanket. Give me one immediately [Tuhoe]' – but he was not so concerned with the present descendants of 'the old time Maori', except to fulfil his mission of leaving them their past on paper. The old Pākehā ruānuku appears in

Recording a Māori speaker using an Edison cylinder, Dominion Museum, Wellington, 1923. From the left: Johannes Andersen, Henare Balneavis, Best, and an unidentified informant.
Photographer: James McDonald, Museum of New Zealand Te Papa Tongarewa, B.010472

this account as preternaturally ancient, a Jungian wizard at his books – yet somehow, strangely immature.

His peculiar temperament had fitted him for the role he had fashioned and made his own: this portrait is one of a priestly figure, alone with his manuscripts, a sorcerer with his inky spells. He had become a type of that high-grade tohunga belonging to the esoteric Māori priesthood he championed, their ways unknown to the common people. His childhood days in Porirua – playing with his Māori mates from the pā, going eeling, listening intently to the old men chanting karakia to ensure a good catch – had set him on a path from which he had hardly deviated. While Māori had struggled in the coils of the modern world throughout his long life, Best the romantic in his deepest part would turn his back on that world to the end.

One of the last known photographs of Best, with the Adkin children, Nancy and Clyde, May 1931, at Pahau-hokio Lagoon, northwest of Lake Horowhenua, investigating an ancient eel-trapping channel.
G. L. Adkin Collection, Alexander Turnbull Library, Wellington, NZ, PA1-f-009-183

As Best moved into his seventy-fourth year, a world depression gathering at the beginning of the 1930s forced a halt to the planned production of a second volume of the major work *Maori Religion and Mythology*.[64] Old friends were dying: Smith was long dead, seven years since; William Baucke died in June 1930, followed a fortnight later by Sir Maui Pomare.[65] Visited by high and low, his work would feature in an MA thesis undertaken by Isabel Eggers, which emerged in 1935 – the first and last academic to attempt a sustained survey of his body of work and its impact for another sixty years.[66] With his writing at an end, he and his assistant Phillips began cataloguing the photographic negatives of his vast collection of ethnographic objects, until the beginning of 1931. Attempting to arrange items in another collection, Best suffered the first slight stroke – a sign of his approaching end. He took to his bed, never to return to the site of those Herculean labours.

Knowing his death was at hand, he packed up the tribal heirlooms given him by Tūhoe and instructed his wife to return them after he died. The manner of his death, even his final utterances, have been extensively recorded by Elsdon Craig, from discussions and interviews with family members – they bear a stark contrast to the blank slate that stares back at us when we wonder at the manner of Tutakangahau's death and his tangihanga.[67] Craig claims that Best did indeed at this late hour see himself in the roles of both pioneer ethnographer and a 'tohunga and leader' in the Māori world. It was in the latter role – imitating his oracle Te Matorohanga, the 'last high priest of the Whare-wananga' – that he prepared to die. Gathering friends to his bedside weeks before he died, he explained to them the significance of death for Māori.

What emerges close to his death is the depth of Best's identification with Māori in general and Te Matorohanga in particular (and the ghost of Tutakangahau, with whom he had also shared final secrets). Te Whatahoro Jury had passed on to him in 1912 a detailed account of the tohunga's last days, and his ōhākī (final words). Best had preserved this in the Notebooks, where Te Matorohanga is recorded as saying: '"Me he mea ko toku ra tenei, kia marama taku haere atu" (if my time has come, let there be no impediment to my journey to the spirit world). "If my dealings with atua maori (lesser gods) interferes with my going – me whakawatea e koe."'[68] Craig's account of Best's bedside instructions gives a strikingly similar recording, when the Pākehā asks his visitors to 'heed the words of the master: "if my time has come, let there be no impediments to my journey to the spirit world. If my dealings with lesser gods hinder my going – me whakawatea e koe."'[69]

'Me whakawatea – clear the way, set me free': he echoes the words of his master, and 'like Te Matorohanga, Best was prepared to slip away peacefully, knowing his teachings would remain'. He clearly had the words of the old sage close to hand: either remembered or written down. He had also written in the Notebook of the passing of Te Matorohanga's mana to Te Whatahoro, where the dying elder had instructed the younger man to touch his lips to his head: '"Me whakakaha to waha ki toku tipuaki, i.e., crown of head. Whata did so. Matoro said "Retain what I have taught. Deviate not. Believe no other version."' The authority thus went to Te Whatahoro: 'that evening he passed quietly away at about 5pm. The whakakaha act was to cause his mana to pass to Te Whatahoro.'[70]

Craig attributes the same formula to Best: 'as a tohunga he was bound to see that his mana descended to his pupils, and he could think of no better way of conferring his prized possession than by reciting the injunction of the great teacher. "Retain what I have taught. Deviate not. Believe no other version and death will find you an old man."'[71] There is no reason to think this account inaccurate – Craig would have got it from Adelaide Best. Here is a Pākehā tohunga at the point of death, reciting the words of a Māori tohunga who had died fifty to sixty years earlier.[72] What did Te Matorohanga mean to Best, that the Pākehā appears to be conferring on those present a mantle conferred on him, as if they were a group of true believers? To record and memorise the old man's death in such detail, to have his words on hand twenty years later, suggests that Best indeed saw himself as the heir apparent to Te Matorohanga's mana and knowledge – that Te Whatahoro had ceded that authority, that mana, when he passed those teachings on to him.

Who was the 'the last high priest of the Whare-wananga' – Te Matorohanga or Elsdon Best? Best had received the 'sacred teachings' – albeit through the intercession of Te Whatahoro – and he was their inheritor. In terms of *power*, in terms of *being*, Smith by 1922 was dead and Te Whatahoro also, in the following year: there were no competitors left from that generation who knew of, or cared to, preserve the hidden knowledge. Best as an advocate of the Io teachings and the concept of

Elsdon Best and his wife Adelaide in the late 1920s.
Photographer: Stanley Polkinghorne, S. P. Andrew Collection, Alexander Turnbull Library, Wellington, NZ, PAColl-8066-06-14

esoteric religious knowledge, formerly controlled by a high grade of tohunga, could now form a continuity of vision: collector, interpreter and repository of the true kura huna. Only those who had lived with Māori, spoken their language, possessing 'the faculty of thinking like a savage', having the 'ahua of the men of old', able to penetrate their mythopoetic psyche, would qualify – Best was the only candidate left standing.[73]

He lived on for a few short weeks after this ōhākī, 'left with a curious feeling of loneliness'. Adelaide tended to the ailing veteran: a butcher's bill from William Tunley, Family Butcher of Wadestown and Molesworth Street for 'Leg Mutton' at '3/3' is signed 'Paid', the meat carried home to sustain him.[74] Best spent time looking out from his verandah, over the harbour he knew as Te Whanga-nui-a-Tara, 'the bay of Tara', named for an old-time chief who tradition told of coming in the twelfth century, and deciding to stay. His last diary entry, of 28 July 1931, includes the lines, 'Here I have been lying for nearly a month, watching the world slip past me and curiously interested in watching and feeling myself die. This I may observe is quite a new experience for me. Will I miss the bus?'[75] Curious to the end, psychologist and ethnographer, Elsdon Best fell into a coma at the end of August and died some days later on the ninth day of September 1931.

E koro, e Peehi, haere, haere, haere atu rā, haere ki tō moenga roa, ki Hawaiki nui, ki Hawaiki roa, ki Hawaiki pāmamao, moe mai, moe mai, moe mai rā!

CHAPTER TWELVE

'Kia Marama – let there be light!': The Half-life of Te Peehi in Our Midst

> There is hardly an oral culture or a predominantly oral culture left in the world today that is not somehow aware of the vast complex of powers forever inaccessible without literacy. This awareness is agony for persons rooted in primary orality, who want literacy passionately but who also know very well that moving into the exciting world of literacy means leaving behind much that is exciting and deeply loved in the earlier oral world. We have to die to continue living.
>
> WALTER J. ONG (1982)[1]

The funeral of Elsdon Best took place in St Paul's Pro-Cathedral, Wellington, on the morning of 11 September 1931, conducted by the Right Rev. F. A. Bennett, the Māori Bishop of Aotearoa. Bennett, of Te Arawa and Irish descent, was the first Māori to hold such high ecclesiastical office, a minister of the church to which Best had remained resolutely opposed. The great and the good had assembled: Māori leaders such as Ngata, who was a pall-bearer; his colleague Johannes Andersen, who also lifted the old ethnographer's weight onto his shoulders for the ride to the Karori crematorium. From there, Best's ashes would begin another

Pencil portrait of Elsdon Best, 18 October 1925, by Frederick Halford Coventry. *Alexander Turnbull Library, Wellington, NZ, A-143-016*

protracted journey to their present resting place beneath a monument at Grasslees Reserve, Tawa, close by oblivious streams of Main Road traffic, near the site of his boyhood days on a Grasslees Farm long since swallowed by the advance of suburbia.

Bishop Bennett addressed the throng of dignitaries and the chief mourner, Mary Adelaide Best, in 'a last long farewell to the mortal remains of our brother'.[2] The bishop's eulogy was brief – this was not a time for many words, rather silence and contemplation – yet he felt obliged, as 'one of the children of the Maori race' to express regard, admiration and gratitude for the great work Best had accomplished. In particular, he drew attention to the way the Pākehā had brought to the world's attention 'the spiritual conceptions, the mythology, and legends of the Maori people'. So saying, he placed on the coffin the leaves of the kawakawa, a Māori custom 'when lamenting the loss of a great one'. He recalled 'three main lessons' from the leaves: bruised, its bitter, painful, pungent taste recalled the painful loss 'of the mortal side of our brother'. There was no doubt in his mind, however, that Best's 'soul and influence [would] live on . . . he has been called to a higher existence'.

Bishop Bennett summed up Te Peehi's significance to Māori in a final mihi: '"Farewell, Elsdon Best, chief and father of the Māori race! Farewell! *Haere ra! Haere ra! e koro. Haere ki te iwi! Haere ki te kainga! Haere ki te Ariki!* Depart! Depart! O father! Depart to the people! Depart to the home! Depart to thy God!"'[3] To the minds and hearts of those present, a great leader, a rangatira, was receiving his due; significantly, this poroporoaki was led by a man who descended from both sides of the Māori–Pākehā house that had come into being over the past turbulent century. The Tawa monument that today commemorates Best, unveiled by Prime Minister Walter Nash on 27 February 1960, bears inscriptions in both languages:

The memorial to Elsdon Best at Tawa, near the site of his birthplace at Grasslees Farm.
Author photograph

'1856–1931 Haere Ra Te Pehi Haere Ki Te Hono I Wairua' (Depart Best to the Meeting of the Spirits). In English, we read: 'Nearby at Grasslees Farm Elsdon Best Maori Ethnologist Was Born On 30 June 1856 His Ashes Lie Here', while above on the plinth, his raised name is slowly and remorselessly colonised by pale green stars of lichen.

The newspapers of the day were full of tributes and obituaries to the fallen tōtara, eulogies that time would pass over and the public would forget – but Bennett was right in predicting that Best's influence would surely live on. He might have added that the contribution of Te Peehi's academy of Māori elders would live on also, in the massive number of publications that had issued from their shared project. According to some instructions in the great man's will, however, many of these might never have seen the light of day, were his wife Adelaide not to receive the money he felt they were worth and should be sold for. Ornery as ever, in 1916 he had drawn up a last will and testament, which has survived in two versions: the draft, now in possession of a family member; and that from 1922, which was read to his wife after his death.[4]

As we have seen, Best's money worries and anger at underpayment had surfaced early in his museum tenure; he was also concerned to provide for his younger wife in the likelihood he would predecease her. He had written to Smith in New Plymouth in 1915, complaining about his 'board wage', making noises about destroying his papers. Smith was horrified: 'Don't again suggest that the Crematorium is the place for your papers, the Library of the Society is a far more suitable place . . .'.[5] A year later, he was of a similar mind: on 10 May 1916 he signed a will that threatened exactly that. He gave directions that if all his 'books, papers, M.S. and printed works' were not sold in three months after his death for 'five hundred pounds (£500) and no less a figure to be accepted', all were to 'be burned and utterly destroyed by [Adelaide Best], or under her eye'.

Under this will, the trials of his wife were to be extended post-mortem by the prosecution of this awful duty – destroying the sources of everything that Best, his informants and she herself had laboured to achieve. Some clue as to why is contained in the final line of this handwritten order of execution: 'These terms are the result of my being deliberately swindled by the Govt. Native [scribbled] Dept. under chief [scribbled] Carroll'. Whatever was the slight referred to here and sheeted home to James

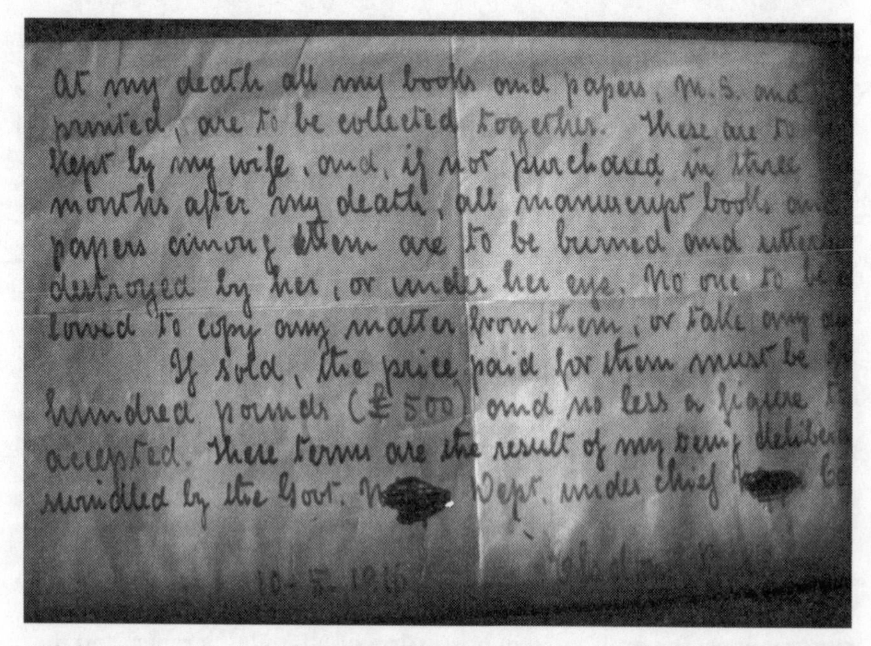

At my death all my books and papers, M.S. and
printed, are to be collected together. These are to
kept by my wife, and, if not purchased in three
months after my death, all manuscript books and
papers among them are to be burned and utterly
destroyed by her, or under her eye. No one to be
lowed to copy any matter from them, or take any
If sold, the price paid for them must be
hundred pounds (£500) and no less a figure
accepted. These terms are the result of my being delibera
swindled by the Govt. [illegible] Dept. under chief [illegible]

10-5-1916

Elsdon Best's will of 10 May 1916, with instructions to destroy his work if it did not raise enough money for his wife to benefit. Percy Smith pleaded with him not to entertain such thoughts.
Author photograph, 2008, courtesy of Janet Mackey

Carroll, it seems Best had not changed much – nor learned much either – since his written attack on the Museum Director Hamilton three years earlier. Certainly, no lawyer would have drawn up a will containing such an accusation; and the final version signed by Best on 27 October 1922, and read on 18 September 1931, bears no mention of Carroll or of any swindling.

The message is much the same, however: if within twelve months, his wife cannot obtain a sale price of 'three hundred (£300)', she is to burn 'all such written books note books and documents'. Fortunately for posterity, Best's manuscripts and notebooks were purchased by the museum and saved from the fire; certainly his published works were beyond his control, but the documentary material, his archive, had it been destroyed, would have been an incalculable loss. The curation of those materials kept by his wife and passed on to his biographer Elsdon Craig has also proved vital in piecing together this rich and complex life. Here was a man who could confidently support the immoral expedition to destroy the community at Parihaka, use his billy club on striking fellow citizens he deemed anarchists – and yet give his life to the preservation of Māori history and tradition, sending both money and clothing to anyone from any iwi who sent him a request, especially Tūhoe.

Fulsome praise of Best's contribution to the nation continued in the following year when the Polynesian Society published an 'Elsdon Best Memorial Number' of the journal. As a foundation member, a past president and editor, Best was due this tribute, from politicians (J. G. Coates and H. E. Holland), overseas anthropologists (A. C. Haddon and George Pitt-Rivers), and a host of others: Frank Acheson, Dr T. Wi Repa, Te Rangi Hiroa (Sir Peter Buck), W. H. Skinner, H. D. Skinner, Raymond Firth and Johannes Andersen. From modern academics, tribal leaders and Land Court judges, the praise resounded. Acheson – whose 1930 novel *Plume of the Arawas* spoke of Māori as 'the intellectual and spiritually-minded Brown Man of Caucasian descent and ancient lineage' – confessed his debt to Best's researches in this regard.[6]

Best he writes, had confessed to him, 'whilst exchanging strange experiences, that he had only seen the bottom of the palisades of the Hidden-Pa-of-Knowledge' guarding the secrets of Māori spirituality.[7] Dr Wi Repa, a prominent East Coast medical man and contributor to Ngata's *Nga Moteatea* (1928), wrote of Best's '*wairua*, his mind, his *mauri*, his soul, his *tawhito*' ascending into the 'twelfth heaven . . . there to join Ruatau and Rehua in the higher service of Io-matua'. Without Best's work, he believed, 'most of our systematic knowledge of ourselves as an ethnological entity would long ago have been consigned to the limbo of forgotten things'. In his day, for Māori and Pākehā, whether in literature or ethnography, Best's work was vital and indispensable. As a producer of a unique New Zealand literature in his time, he had revealed the esoteric cult of Io and 'made it exoteric', a rediscovered religion, combined for posterity in new forms. 'In his literary contributions on the subject of Io-matua to Io-taketake, his prose is like blank verse, which is a fitting subject for a poetic theme.'[8]

Dr Wi Repa's frequent insistence on Best's literary achievement is echoed by other eulogists in this edition of the journal: 'a gifted writer' claimed Te Rangi Hiroa, 'for he put into English words what Maori orators had told him'.[9] Not only that, he was a forerunner for Māori anthropology practised by Māori themselves, his 'writings and personality had been exercising a profound influence on the inarticulate students of Maori lore who had Maori blood in their veins' – himself, Ngata and Pomare. In part through his influence, they were moved to form the Board of Maori Ethnological Research in 1923, to publish Best's writings on Māori subjects. The Board 'set to work to print Mr Best's manuscripts as speedily as possible' – most importantly, the magnum opus *Tuhoe* in 1925. Here was another example of the shared project in action, which Buck is acknowledging – their debt to Best, Tutakangahau and all the other Māori contributors.

The list of eminent scribes goes on. From London, Raymond Firth, who became a major figure in twentieth-century anthropology (dying only recently, in 2002), noted how 'Best's work is monumental, hardly less as a literary feat than as a contribution to anthropology . . . whatever understanding we may have of Maori culture in its deeper esoteric aspects is largely due to Elsdon Best'.[10] In Wellington, Johannes Andersen wondered on the subject of the book *Tuhoe*, just 'how many people realize what this means to the Tuhoe folk'? In his view, 'they venerate this Pakeha who in his love and sympathy has preserved the lore so precious to them, and so lamentably lost'. Andersen was deeply aware of Best's role as our first significant scholar of things Māori: 'he indexed, not only his own notes, but all the books he had read, particularly New Zealand books, not relying on his memory or the author's index'.[11] Best may not have been to a university, but he established his own research chair in anthropology in the Dominion Museum from 1910 to 1931 – it is to this achievement that these mihi are directed.

Such a chorus of praise and respect was never going to survive the passage of time and the changing climate of academic opinion in his chosen field, nor in society in general after the Second World War. Even some of those who were heard singing his praises in public – such as Ngata and Buck – would shortly thereafter in private be confessing their reservations. Best would have expected this. In June 1928, three years before Best's death, Buck was writing to Ngata about criticisms he had heard were made of Best's diffusionist theories by the rising academically trained anthropologist H. D. Skinner. 'No reira taku kino kia te tama Te Kina e noho mai ra i Otakou . . . I rongo au ki nga tangata o konei e ahua whakahawea ana mo Peehi.'[12] Skinner is 'belittling, disrespecting' Best on this reading, one of many letters that passed between the two leaders from 1925 until Ngata's death in 1950. Skinner's tribute in the memorial number of *JPS* above was noticeably brief and prim, yet it was after all a matter of academic credibility, and it was not to be long before these two would join in the opposing chorus – of doubt.

Buck and Ngata agreed that Best was a great collector, 'a pakeha pioneer', but one whose work needed to be 'straightened up'.[13] They were encouraging each other in their respective interests and abilities in the field of anthropology: while not objectively trained like Skinner, they were, as Māori, able to approach the field 'subjectively'. Best was to be the last Pākehā linguist to enter the Māori house: 'me mutu ia Peehi nga tuhituhi Pakeha . . . mo te taha ki te reo Maori . . . kaore ratou e uru ki

Best taking notes – in his unique Māori shorthand – from discussions with Iehu Nukunuku, on the steps of Apirana Ngata's bungalow at Waiomatatini near Ruatōria, in 1923. A kōauau – a Māori flute – sits in the old man's jacket pocket. *Photographer: James McDonald, Museum of New Zealand Te Papa Tongarewa, B.002189*

roto o te whare Maori'.[14] They now considered the demise of European dominance in the field of Māori and Polynesian anthropology as well overdue: 'kua mutu haere te wa kia Peehi ma . . . the time of Best and that crowd is coming to an end'.[15] His two general works, *The Maori* and *The Maori As He Was* were singled out as particularly deficient: in 1924, the year of their publication, Ngata saw him as 'an old man who had already passed the zenith of his powers'.[16]

Best was slowly transfigured into a somewhat lesser being: Ngata wrote to Buck that the old man's museum bulletins lacked Buck's expertise 'in dissection, and analysis and arrangement'. His work 'may be full of good material, but it confuses the student'. Peehi (Best) had become 'he kupenga kaharoa tana e hao ana i nga momo ika katoa, ma nga wahine i uta e wehewehe – a drag net fishing all types of fish, for the women on shore to separate out'.[17] This came from a letter of October 1930, when Best was still alive – but it is obvious that with his greatest Māori supporters his star was on the wane even before he died. Nevertheless, Buck's work would show Best's influence early on, in his monograph *The Coming of the Maori* (1929), a precursor of his more famous work of the same name published twenty years later.

Buck was by 1949 a pre-eminent figure in Oceanic anthropology: he had cited Best's work in the earlier book (on origins, canoe traditions, material culture and language), and thirteen of the Pākehā's works appeared in the bibliography of *The Coming of the Maori*, including some of the aforementioned 'unsatisfactory' bulletins and monographs. Best was on the way to becoming that indispensable 'collector' who had the theory mostly wrong but a substance not available elsewhere. Mauri turns up here in Buck in a discussion on ritual fires (ahi taitai), based on Best's work from the 1924 volume *Maori Religion and Mythology* (Pt 1).[18] Knowledge of such a ceremony links directly to the instruction and information given to Best by Tutakangahau – as seen in their final meetings described in 'Maori Forest Lore' (1909). It is almost redundant to add that the old man and the other Tūhoe mōhio are by now appearing everywhere. Tutakangahau mā i roto i a Te Peehi, Te Peehi i roto i a Tutakangahau mā – Tutakangahau and the academy are in Best, and Best is in them.

Best, of course, gets the credit – and the criticism – yet in studying his work, any reader will see how constantly he acknowledges his sources, if not in footnotes, then in the text. In his 'Lists of Authorities' – as in *Maori Agriculture* (1925, 2005) – Tutakangahau and other Māori informants appear as expert contributors, even though the lists are predominantly from European written sources. Where it supports Buck's argument, he is willing to call upon Best's 'untiring fieldwork', and while his reliance on Best is not as obvious as in the earlier text, citations of the old man's publications pepper Te Rangi Hiroa's expanded opus. As Dr Wi Repa had observed twenty years earlier at the time of Best's death, 'ka tere te para; ka maunu te ika i tona rua – the great fish of the pool has left his hole'.[19] A great fish indeed – one that was constantly swallowed, and digested, to nourish a new generation of younger, bigger fish, in whom it was not always possible to recognise the source of the food they had fed on.

One who was willing to cite and acknowledge Best was Raymond Firth (1901–2002), the New Zealand-born ethnographer, a long-serving professor at the London School of Economics, who had been a doctoral student under Malinowski, becoming 'the Great Functionalist's undoctrinaire professorial successor'.[20] Firth published his doctoral thesis as *The Primitive Economics of the New Zealand Maori* in 1929, and went on to found a British school of economic anthropology – and become a hugely influential figure in Oceanic anthropology. This study was the first serious analysis of Māori society by a social scientist, bridging the gap between the amateur, frontier era of the Smith–Best regime – but Firth proved more than willing to pay tribute to these men, noting the 'peculiar quality of the data available', most notably 'the unrivalled research of Mr Elsdon Best'.[21]

While confessing his own limited acquaintance with the Māori language, he felt he was able to avoid 'distorted impressions which a study of purely literary sources is bound to produce'.[22] True or not, Firth was dependent to a great extent on the integrity of nineteenth-century linguists such as Best, which is apparent in his discussion of the meaning and social function of mauri. In the chapter 'Magic in Economics', he notes that 'magic permeates . . . all the economic life of the native', all crafts having their spells and incantations, magical ideas being ubiquitous.[23] He notes the presence of mauri in the magical protection of natural resources, and the 'old Maori belief' that all natural objects 'possessed a spiritual essence, a non-material life principle'. This was the mauri, and in its nature, 'this *mauri* was an intangible, imponderable presence, impersonal in character'.[24]

Firth is paraphrasing Best: in a footnote here, he cites no less than five of Best's articles and books, including 'Forest Lore' and 'Spiritual Concepts of the Maori' – both publications deeply dependent on Tutakangahau and his fellow Tūhoe mōhio. Firth is certain that 'the term "life principle", by which Best speaks of *mauri* in his valuable papers on the subject [footnote] is probably the most fitting translation that can be devised'. How someone confessedly so limited in their own grasp of Māori could assess the accuracy of Best's translations is not clear; what is clear, however, is the dependence on the old man's fieldwork, and the trust placed in him by one of his most illustrious local successors. The significance of these statements is the beginning of a reliance on Best beyond these shores for information on traditional Māori society, and his slow but certain entry into the modern academic canon.

Firth paid Best far more public respect than Ngata and Buck did privately, at the same moment. While they had the Māori language and an inside knowledge of the culture – and should therefore have been better placed than Firth to pass judgement on Best's material – they also had a more pressing need to displace the Pākehā tohunga, which Firth did not share. In the event, both Buck and Firth call upon Best's resources; and after 1931, his deep substratum of field research began its posthumous entry into the academic and popular literature. For those outside of New Zealand – such as Marcel Mauss, Marshall Sahlins and Lewis Hyde – Best, on such concepts as mauri and hau, became a standard source on matters Māori anthropological. Locally, for Māori writers – and some Pākehā – his writings, and his influence, underlie much of the essentialist quest to refashion Māori identity in the discourses on Māoritanga which arose from the 1960s onwards.

Even the most cursory search of the internet today reveals the omnipresence of Best's writings in both academic and general works – increasingly, this resource is a first stop for many, and the ethnographer's work is everywhere. A recent search of Google Scholar under 'Best Elsdon'

produced 2100 results, the first one hundred of which were all references to citations in academic writing.[25] One edition of *Maori Agriculture* (1979) had 63 citations; *Fishing Methods and Devices of the Maori* (2005) had 45; *The Maori* (1924) was cited 39 times; and *Forest Lore of the Maori* (1942), a total of 36 citations. It should also be emphasised that other editions of the same title were cited elsewhere in this list, as were other books by Best, many times over. By comparison, a noted and widely published contemporary Māori scholar and writer, Ranginui Walker, attracted 508 hits on Google Scholar, 220 of these for his best-known history text, *Ka Whawhai Tonu Mātou: Struggle Without End* (1990). This is not to compare the two as writers, simply to point up the presence of Best in the world of Māori thought and its literature. In 2005 the National Museum of New Zealand Te Papa Tongarewa republished eleven of Best's works, which continue to spread the influence of this man and his informants throughout the world.

Scholars, from historians to agricultural researchers, political scientists to archaeologists, both in New Zealand and overseas, have for decades turned to the ethnographer's work for information about traditional Māori society. Notable overseas examples are the writers mentioned above: Mauss, Sahlins and Hyde – whose work is related – have borrowed from this source over a period of forty years. A French sociologist, an American anthropologist and a US poet and essayist: all with an interest in gift cultures, the practice of reciprocity, and what is becoming known in the Wikipedia age as 'cultural commons' – that storehouse of ideas and works of art inherited from the past. The whakapapa of Best's influence runs through all three writers, linking back to Firth's earlier study of Māori economic life and its debt to the Pākehā's researches.

Marcel Mauss (1872–1950) was a nephew and pupil of Émile Durkheim, and after the great man's death became a leading figure in French sociology. Mauss's 1924 work on the anthropology of the gift, *Essai sur le don* (*The Gift*), first published in English in 1954, examined the power of the gift object and the obligation it entailed for repayment. Mauss had concluded from his readings of Best's journal article 'Maori Forest Lore' (1909) that the force of the *hau*, 'the spirit of things', compelled the recipient of a gift to make a return, and that this spirit of reciprocity was a structural force in Māori society, and in other Pacific cultures. Mauss in citing Best is dependent on a single Māori informant for this discussion of hau, Tamati Ranapiri of Ngāti Raukawa (yet there are others in the article he draws from, including Paitini Wi Tapeka and Tutakangahau).[26]

Every individual who receives something in this process comes under the power of the hau, wanting to return to its birthplace – 'the forest and clan of its owner'. His interpretation leads him to conclude – from Best's translation – that the principle of hau 'is one of the *leitmotifs* of Māori custom', where the requirement to make a return gives a donor 'authority and power over the original donor, who now becomes the latest recipient' when a return is made.[27] Mauss's notes reveal a wide reading of a number of Best's sources, including 'Spiritual Concepts of the Maori' (1901), and Williams' *Dictionary of the Maori Language* – all literary sources – but there is no fieldwork, no first-hand acquaintance with Māori, and no knowledge of the language to back up his assertions about what hau meant in Māori society. The literary life which Best and others had given to such terms – shorn of their original material and spiritual force – was releasing itself into the world of Western interpretation.

Continuing their morphological careers, words such as mauri, hau, wairua and mana travelled beyond this country, beyond Best and Tutakangahau, in space and time. Marshall Sahlins, Professor of Anthropology at the University of Chicago, a widely influential historian and ethnographer of the Polynesian world, took up the discussion on hau begun by Mauss (and Firth) in his 1979 work *Stone Age Economics*.[28] In a chapter entitled 'The Spirit of the Gift', Sahlins gives an extensive review of those who have made attacks on Mauss: Lévi-Straus, Firth and J. Pritz-Johansen. He also analyses the relationships between the priests (tohunga) and the mauri (or hau, apparently interchangeable), complete with flow charts, and a new translation by the Ngāti Maniapoto anthropologist Bruce Biggs, of Tamati Ranapiri's kōrero to Best (which differs little from Best's supposedly deficient translated offering).

Sahlins is looking to describe the social functions of material objects in forms of exchange, 'the fundamental qualities of primitive economy and polity', for the meanings behind patterns of behaviour and belief. Mauss is something of a personal hero to him, his essay *The Gift* providing 'a source of unending ponderation for the anthropologist *du métier*, compelled as if by the *hau* of the thing to come back to it again and again'.[29] In this reading, Mauss's essay has its own hau, as hau becomes a metaphor for whatever Sahlins intends by this usage – some kind of force that draws the reader back again, mystically informed in a dialogue with the text that 'renders the due of the original'. Sahlins, instructed by the general theme of the social contract reiterated in Mauss's essay, acknowledges in this chapter his debt to the French sociologist, yet admits that, in himself, he is 'unjustified by any special study of the Māori'.

It is a rather sobering confession from such an illustrious ethnographer, that without making a special study of Māori, he will nevertheless proceed to write on what certain concepts and behaviours meant to them before Europeans arrived. It is in the nature of literary transmission that words take on a reality other than that of what they represent – a life of their own. Certainly, mauri and hau post-Best grew legs and wings and left for parts unknown to their original owners: the most recent example of the widespread and popular dissemination of Best, Tutakangahau, Tamati Ranapiri, as well as Mauss and Sahlins, is in Lewis Hyde's *The Gift: Imagination and the Erotic Life of Property* (1979). First published in the shadow of the Vietnam War, Hyde's enquiry into the gift nature of creativity was a celebrated work of literary anthropology, arguing that art was not a commodity for sale. He raided a variety of sources and disciplines to support his thesis: that the arts in particular derive from the group's cultural resources and are due back to the group.

The individual has no final ownership, and commerce cannot put a price on what is essentially a creative commons. As an example of the nature of gift exchange, Hyde writes of a 'Maori sage' who explained 'to an Englishman' the way '*hau*, which translates as "spirit"' operated in the world of Māori. Here is Best once more – who would no doubt be annoyed, portrayed as English – and Tamati Ranapiri. Hyde recruits their assistance in making his point, that offerings made by tohunga in the ahi taitai ceremony make the forest abundant, 'a consequence of man's treating its wealth as a gift'.[30] Expanding on this and the increase in the power of gifts, Hyde also finds Sahlins useful in explaining that the increase comes in the power of the gift, as it moves not from the first to the second party, but from the second to the third. This is all implied, apparently, in the Māori concepts of hau and mauri, and the way they interrelate in the act of giving. This is given as evidence in his argument that, unlike the exchange of profit in a capital transaction involving a commodity, 'gifts do not *earn* profit, they *give* increase'.[31]

Hyde, as does Sahlins, claims no knowledge of Māori, but as with the American ethnographer and Mauss in his work, relies on others to make good their arguments about Māori. They expand on commonly held beliefs about what these terms meant to Māori, at a time when Māori society was closed to literary meaning, and existed on its own terms. In this wider world, mauri and hau become portmanteau words open to whatever twists and turns of meaning and emphasis such writers can find residing within the words and in themselves. Hyde's book has taken on a new lease of life, recently republished as *The Gift: How The Creative Spirit Transforms The World* (2007). A glowing review by Jay Parini in the UK newspaper the *Guardian* claims the book is 'a passionate defence of the creative gift, which issues from the wild depths of human nature, is given freely and circulates generously'.[32]

The Māori contribution was certainly generous: neither Ranapiri – nor Tutakangahau – were ever likely to see much of that capitalist commodity, money, in exchange for their collective wisdom given so freely to Best. Closer to home, since World War Two, in what has become known as the second 'Māori renaissance', Māori have also searched for meaning and identity in literary sources, as well as amongst the society of their elders – and more often than not have found themselves instructed on the life of their ancestors by Best and his academy. When stories are no longer passed from mouth to ear, and societies come to rely on what is written, oral cultures die, and the kinds of knowledge they possessed resides in the book, but it is radically changed. The subtext of this study has all along been the way in which literary cultures colonise and change societies relying on the oral transmission and retention of vital information.

We can never know now quite what mauri and hau once 'meant' in the traditional world, where to have meaning – *to matter in the spiritual realm* – was to act, to have power. Orality and literacy are qualitatively different *states of being*: like children who have learned to read, those who are literate reading this page can never return to their pre-literate, oral state of sound and rhythm as meaning. Our best literary meanings are only pointers to this vanished world. In reclaiming political power and seeking to reaffirm an identity culturally different from the dominant

The empty chair: Elsdon Best's study at Highland Park, Wadestown. The man was gone, but his writings had begun a vigorous post-mortem career in New Zealand's literary culture, and the wider society.

Photographer unknown, Alexander Turnbull Library, Wellington, NZ, PAColl-8066-01-50-1

Pākehā culture, Māori have looked both forward and back. They have looked towards the future in the present, working to gain redress and social equality from political and financial settlements that acknowledge past injustice against their ancestors and themselves. They have also looked backwards with longing, to retrieve from the past whatever that ambiguous region can provide to establish who they are in the present, and why they belong.

This reflection on the presence of Best's influence in contemporary Māori society now turns to what significant and widely read Māori writers have written in the post-war period. Beginning in the late 1960s and gathering force in the next two decades, Māori protest fractured the post-imperial status quo, shattered by the global effects of World War Two. Abroad, the old empires were crumbling, as Britain, France and Holland lost their colonies one by one. In New Zealand, an unstable social and political environment developed, created in part by Britain's entry into the EEC, the oil shocks of the 1970s, and the significant rise in unemployment occasioned by the end of the economic golden weather enjoyed since the early 1950s. In this socio-political movement and its cultural revivals, an alliance [amongst Māori] of traditional rural leaders, mature bureaucrats with battlefield credentials, activist baby-boom student radicals and women's organisations combined to shake the myth of harmonious race relations and egalitarian access to the fruits of society.

As well as making history, this movement began a new phase of rewriting history: for the first time. Māori writers broke into areas of publishing hitherto dominated by Pākehā, expressing viewpoints and perspectives in ways their forebears could hardly have imagined. In history, customs (tikanga), biography, theology, lexicography, criticism, poetry and fiction, Māori voices began to be heard in a fresh articulation of New Zealand's identity. This is obvious to us today: what may not be so obvious is that the writings of Elsdon Best – including the mauri he defined and extended – live on in this new literature. At times, his contribution is acknowledged, and at others, not; nevertheless, the Māori literary renaissance bears him in its bones, as scrutiny of some important texts bears out.

Large-scale social movements and revolutions may be sparked by ideological literature – as with Marx and Engels – and they may also produce such writing. As with the Francophone Negritude identity movement emanating from the Caribbean and French Equatorial Africa in the 1930s, and the Black Power movement of the 1960s US race wars, the social and political unrest that energised Māori protest in the 1970s produced its own ür-texts.[33] Younger urban intellectuals such as Syd Jackson and Ted Nia were influenced by overseas writers, including Frantz Fanon and Eldridge Cleaver. It was not until 1975, however, when the Pākehā journalist and historian Michael King produced the seminal collection *Te Ao Hurihuri – The World Moves On*, that a body of mature Māori voices was gathered together to articulate the new consciousness.[34]

King – a history graduate and tyro journalist on the *Waikato Times* – found himself nominated as the Māori affairs reporter; drawn into the Tainui world about which he knew almost nothing, he gradually found himself cast in a role as interlocutor of Māori views in the Pākehā press. He went on to become the biographer of significant Māori figures such as Princess Te Puea, something of a māngai (mouthpiece) for the movers and shakers of the Māori community. In some broad sense, King was a Best for his times, but the moment was brief: that old resentment by Māori – like that of Buck and Ngata – who wanted Pākehā out of 'the whare Māori', resulted in his leaving the field to Māori writers. The book in question, where leading figures of the day had their say on the subject of Māoritanga, is one of his more enduring and problematic legacies.

King presents the book as an exploration of Māoritanga (Māori culture) in its various tribal manifestations, admitting that the concept itself may possibly be 'European'. Each tribe, after all, has its own way of doing things and there remains a question mark over any global 'Māori way'. His authors, men like Ranginui Walker, Sam Karetu and John Rangihau, explore issues 'Europeans shy away from . . . identity, land, marae, processes of learning and qualities like tapu'.[35] There is a brief prefatory offering from the Ngāti Porou composer Ngoi Pewhairangi, but the eight major contributors unsurprisingly are all men. The chapter on Māori spirituality – 'God, Man and Universe: A Maori View' – written by the Rev. Māori Marsden (1924–1993), is the focus of what follows.

Marsden (Te Aupouri) was an Anglican clergyman who also had early training in Ngā Puhi tribal lore in whare wānanga. He inhabited the physical and cultural landscape of the earliest Pākehā–Māori contact, Te Tai Tokerau, the Far North, where Christianity first took root. His essay on Māori spirituality sets out to conceptualise a uniquely Māori spiritual dimension that is a subjective retort to the supposedly objectifying influences of Pākehā ethnographers like Best. He was unequivocal: 'The route to Maoritanga through abstract interpretation is a dead end'; and that above all, 'Maoritanga is a thing of the heart rather than the head'. To *experience* Māoritanga, one must *be* Māori, and enter Māori states of mind: 'only a Māori from within the culture can do this adequately'.[36] Outsiders, especially anthropologists, would only produce 'facile approaches', and with the possible exception of a man like 'James K. Baxter with the soul of a poet', Pākehā were unable to enter 'the existential dimension of Maori life'.[37]

What is Māoritanga, for this uniquely qualified insider? 'Briefly, it is the corporate view that Maoris hold about *ultimate reality and meaning.*' Already, we can hear echoes of twentieth-century questions in the way Marsden frames his definition; moreover, he appears throughout the discussion to be explaining and contextualising Māori metaphysics in biblical terms. Examples are the pure rites, with the use of 'holy water'; sacramental systems parallel to Christianity; iriiri, rumaki and uhi as baptismal analogues; the tohi rite of te whakapaa as equivalent to confirmation; and cannibalism as a form of communion. This is hardly surprising, considering that Marsden was a man of the cloth; in comparing Māori rituals with Christian practices, he is also speaking to both Pākehā and Māori audiences.[38]

Attempting to translate Māori concepts through the theological lens closest to hand – his Christian education – he was also valorising Māori metaphysics in a manner not dissimilar to that of Best's earlier strategy. He saw Māori as religious universalists in no way inferior to Pākehā, operating at their own level of cultural development: 'certain spiritual principles are universal in application', amongst which he includes 'concepts such as mauri'.[39] Marsden would seem uniquely qualified to make such assessments, but he is not necessarily in a position to assume that certain concepts, as handed down to him, have reached him in a pristine form. He needed first to consider how much influence unqualified arbiters of Māori culture – like the ethnographer Best – have had in the literary construction and transmission of what he takes to be traditional meanings. Marsden himself also proves adept at minting some new explanations of mauri – which owe more to the New Physics and process theology than to his old teachers from Te Aupouri.

In this regard, his discussion of mauri – in a section on tapu – is instructive. He writes that, traditionally, Māori differentiated between the 'essence (mauri) of a person or object and the distinct realm of the spirit which stood over the realm of the natural order and was indwelt by spiritual beings'. They further distinguished between 'the essence of inanimate and animate objects': the created order 'partook of mauri (life force, ethos)' in which all things cohered, while in humans, 'this essence was of a higher order . . . mauri ora (life principle)'.[40] This is almost identical to Best's view around 1900: mauri as the life principle, mauri ora as the spark of life, and material mauri as talismans in which the mauri of a larger entity (the sea, the forest) had been located as a protective agent.

What follows is very much Marsden's late twentieth-century interpretation: 'the essence (mauri) I am convinced, was originally regarded as elemental energy derived from the realm of Te Korekore out of which the stuff of the universe was created'. Such a mauri seems to be a quantum leap – literally – from what the missionary Williams was recording for his dictionary in 1844; it had metamorphosed even further from Best's understanding and interpretation during the 1890s. This mauri has become an evolutionary concept, *an evidential product of literacy*, having a form incomprehensible to the oral culture of power and performance from whence it came. As such, a mauri on the page, it is as Pākehā as it is Māori, a theological concept open to all interpretations; as a reader of Planck, Einstein and Heisenberg, Marsden was interpreting the traditional through the eyes of modernity, arriving inevitably far from where his ancestors stood.

Marsden's views on 'ultimate reality' and the New Physics are further elaborated in *The Woven Universe*: material collected and published ten years after his death in 1993. He had come to the conclusion that, 'like the New Physicists, the Māori perceived the universe as a "process"' that was 'more akin to mind than matter . . . [simply] pure energy'.[41] He claims that Māori created sets of symbols, like modern physicists, portraying stages in the evolutionary process: these he relates to the whakapapa of

Io, beginning with Io-taketake (creator, root, cause).[42] Marsden had been to Japan in the immediate aftermath of the Second World War and was deeply affected by what he witnessed there of the destructive power of atomic energy. He used the Māori word hihiri (brisk, energetic) to make sense of this power, to mean pure energy, as in 'Einstein's concept of a real world behind the natural world . . . comprised of "rhythmical patterns of pure energy"'.[43]

Reaching for a word to describe what happens in the rending of the universe's fabric when the atom is split, he appropriates and redefines an old usage, just as he does in applying the language of modern physics to explain traditional Māori world-views, to establish them as equal to Pākehā explanations in any field of knowledge. 'We knew all this, we just explained it differently' – that is the message here. The Io of Best's day becomes not just the Supreme Being behind all reality, but the weaver of a universe unfolded by Einstein's physics and Paul Tillich's existential theology: 'Io the Ground of Being, Root Cause, Creator . . . uttered his word into eternity and the Void . . . formed the spiritual framework in which the cosmic process could begin to operate. Thus the . . . realm of the Potential of Becoming was established.'[44]

This is a very long way from Maungapōhatu, and yet not an alien strand in the chain of reactions to literacy and modernity that Māori pioneered: in Marsden's foundation for a new Māori metaphysics, mauri appears again, as it powers 'Te Kākano, the original seed', a metaphysical shoot 'urged on by its mauri from behind in its quest for being'. Marsden, a man of his time, an intellectual who had progressed in one of the few arenas open to a man of his intelligence and generation – the church – had like Tutakangahau before him made sense out of his situation with the cultural materials at hand.

Where the old chief had combined an indigenous Māori Christianity with his knowledge of Tūhoe lore and a canny appreciation of political processes in the new world, Marsden had synthesised his earlier learning from the whare wānanga of Ngā Puhi into an amalgam of creationism, evolutionism, Freudian psychology, atomic physics and New Age spirituality. This is still a Māori world – one of many – but a world expanded and enlarged by the arrival of writing and the access literacy gives to a myriad of worlds – worlds where the objective metaphors of science may be transmuted into the subjective speculations of the mystic and the theologian. There is nothing 'traditionally' Māori left here – nor was there for Tutakangahau and Best. This is one more aspect of te ao hurihuri – the turning world – in a twentieth-century manifestation.

Best's mauri was continuing its literary migration: as may be apparent with Marsden, it has become a portmanteaux term, increasingly able – as is any word for that matter – to receive whatever loadings individuals and society choose to place within it. Meanings and functions unknown to oral usage are inevitable: conceivably the worst that can happen to a word is that it falls out of usage and dies. To change over time is to remain alive. Presentist arguments ascribe contemporary meanings to the past: an unexamined tendency to revisionism therefore risks creating anachronistic etymologies, insisting a word once meant what it never ever did. The Māori need to create a viable identity in the present may end in requiring imagined traditions to conform to contemporary demands for linguistic and cultural purity.

The attempt to fashion a resistance theology that shores up Māori identity and self-worth by appropriating an unmoored and essentially bogus 'traditional' world-view says more about who Māori are in the here and now, not who they once might have been. This literary mauri meanwhile continues to mutate into any available vessel suitable to a writer's requirements. As Ong has pointed out elsewhere, literacy has a powerful tendency to colonise oral cultures with its own agendas: 'Writing, moreover . . . is a particularly pre-emptive and imperialist activity that tends to assimilate other things to itself even without the aid of etymologies.'[45] Writing – and writers, over time – can change the meaning of the spoken word; once Māori became writers, they were transformed, themselves becoming agents of change.

Does this mean that mauri – as it was – is dead? Not at all – mauri in a lived culture is operating where it always has, in the hearts of believers in the efficacy of the practice. Just as in Best's day at Rūātoki in the late 1890s – when 'O-tangiroa was the name of an eel *mauri* in the Whakatane River', where eel fishers chanted karakia over a log in the river bed to

Roadside seatbelt safety sign near Ōhope, Whakatāne, 2009 – literally, 'take hold of your life essence', or, more prosaically, 'protect yourself'.
Photograph courtesy of Jeanette King

ensure a good catch – so mauri has a place in Māori society today. In this world, it is at work not for those seeking definitions, but rather spiritual power, to bless and protect some object, person, or enterprise.[46]

During a recent trip to attend a tangi in the Bay of Plenty, our party stopped for lunch at the White House Café near Whakatāne. Next to the marae, in what was once an old home, the owner of the business, John Hohapata-Oke, regaled us as we ate with the story of how he had discovered an old obsidian mauri nearby – and asked a local tohunga what he should do with it? 'What do you want to do with it?' was the response. So he buried it under the café, with appropriate karakia, and after a year and more the business is flourishing. Now that is a 'definition' of mauri Best and Tutakangahau could both agree on.

For the student of Māori language and culture today, however, much of their learning will be book-based, and their knowledge of such practices and their meanings will be literary. Popular studies, such as Barlow's *Tikanga Whakaaro* (1994), and more academic work, like Mead's *Tikanga Māori: Living by Māori Values* (2003), are the places learners must go to find Māori meanings, defined by Māori authors. There, once more, they find Best and his academy of experts – sometimes acknowledged, but often not. Cleve Barlow (Ngā Puhi), a lecturer in psychology, of Mormon conviction, first published his guidebook to 'key concepts in Māori culture' in 1991, claiming to rely heavily on oral sources to illustrate concepts 'important for understanding Māori culture as it is practised today'.[47] He writes that 'mauri is a special power possessed by Io which makes it possible for everything to move and live with the conditions and limits of its existence'. Everyone has a mauri, it seems, and 'no one can control their own mauri or essence'.[48]

As with Marsden, Barlow has biblical roots (in this case, Mormonism), and has been cited by many, including Shirres, as a Ngā Puhi source for the understanding of Io.[49] While he does not cite Best, it is not difficult to sense echoes of the Pākehā in this and other explanations of 'key concepts', and to note again the linking of the theology of a Supreme Being with genuinely traditional usages such as mauri, explained by a Māori interlocutor with a knowledge of Scripture. Mead, however, the other major literary source here, is open about his debt to Best.[50] Hirini Moko Mead (Ngāti Awa, Ngāti Tūwharetoa, Tuhourangi) is a leading figure in Māori academia, the foundation professor of Māori Studies at Victoria University of Wellington. Mead aims in this book to explain the nature of Māori customary usages, asserting that 'tikanga is a set of beliefs associated with practices and procedures . . . established by precedents over time . . . [and] held to be ritually correct'.[51]

In an important section, 'Te Tapu o te Tangata' (the spiritual self of each person), Mead enumerates the spiritual attributes of the Māori person, specifically tapu, mana, mauri, wairua and hau.[52] This is the same group of attributes explained at some length by Best in his seminal 1900 article 'Spiritual Concepts of the Maori', after his lengthy discussions with Tutakangahau on the subject. Mead cites Best on tapu (47); mauri (53, 54); wairua (55, 56); and hau (58), relying heavily on a number of Best's works.[53] In his entry on mauri, he acknowledges the ethnographer's writings both consciously (with appropriate references), and unconsciously (where the work has simply been absorbed into what is now a Māori kōrero).[54]

His definition of mauri comes from the Williams' *Dictionary of the Maori Language*: mauri is 'the life principle . . . the thymos of man' – pure Best. He adds the somewhat ambivalent comment that 'the Greek word "thymos" adds to the mystery of mauri and does not help us understand'.[55] Mauri, he agrees with Best, is 'the spark of life', citing the ethnographer's view that 'the Maori viewed the mauri as an activity'.[56] As for the psychology of mauri, he instances mauri tau, mauri oho, mauri rere – all discussed by Best above as instances of the activity of mauri in states of excitement – without acknowledging Best as a source. The concept of mauri as a talisman references the Williams' *Dictionary* (thus Best) and there are two further citations from *Maori Religion and Mythology*, Pt 2, concerning material mauri.[57] Overall, there are nine references to Best's work in Mead's bibliography – by far the largest of any contributor.

The point may seem laboured, but needs making: Best is ubiquitous and indispensable in modern Māori written works of cultural expertise – Best and his Māori academy, that is. As often as he is ignored, so are these great men, his silent partners. Books such as those by Barlow and Mead are hugely influential in shaping modern Māori identity: they provide a context and a source for countless students in their search for meaning in contemporary Māori society. Mead's book has been held in the library of the University of Canterbury since 2003; as at January 2007, when this snapshot was taken, the three lending copies had been borrowed 43 times. This does not take into account the in-house usage of the restricted loan copy in the Macmillan Brown Collection over the period of three years.

The Christchurch College of Education (now part of the University of Canterbury) had lent its six copies 94 times in the same period. Another year on, from numerous universities, polytechnics, wānanga, high schools, public libraries – and copies in private hands – it is not unreasonable to speculate that upwards of a thousand readers in the last five years in one large tertiary institution alone may have absorbed Best's influences through such channels. What is more significant is the fact that many of these readers have been teachers, and students, some of whom will go on to be teachers themselves, predominantly in high schools, but also in primary. This accounts for Mead's book in one New Zealand university – and a South Island institution at that, with low Māori enrolments. The influence of such a text in an institution with a high Māori student population – such as Te Wānanga o Aotearoa – would tell a different story.

As was evident from the search of Google Scholar, Best is influencing the academy at home and abroad – but his work is most pervasive right beneath our eyes. From *The Reed Dictionary of Modern Māori* to Witi

Ihimaera's *The Whale Rider*, from *The Reed Book of Māori Mythology* to *He Pātaka Kupu* (the latest Māori-only dictionary, first published in 2008), this whakapapa is alive.[58] The works of Best, Tutakangahau and the rest of such invisible ruānuku live on. These Tūhoe mōhio and men from many other iwi stand behind this research, itself a mauri buried inside the written whare of a shared culture whose history cannot be gainsaid, or undone.

Conclusion

To enter the tiny painted wharenui Tanenuiarangi at Maungapōhatu, and adjust your eyes to the temporary gloom, is to find your gaze returned by a hand-tinted image of Tutakangahau, mounted where he belongs on the poutokomanawa, the post supporting the ridgepole of the house. Hidden away high in the Urewera ranges, accessed only with permission by way of a forestry track that descends as a rutted steep suitable only for four-wheel-drive vehicles, or horses, the great man of Tamakaimoana is famous here, but little known beyond the boundaries of Tūhoe lands. This house, built by Rua's people in 1914, seven years after the old chief's death in the valley, keeps his memory warm, and his mana here is secure. Why is such a significant figure, deserving of much wider recognition and esteem, so little known?

Along with his peers – Paitini Tapeka, Hamiora Pio and many others – he provided the raw material that gave Best what he needed to write

Tutakangahau, a full-length photographic portrait that hangs on the central post of Tanenuiarangi meeting house, Maungapōhatu.
Author photograph, 2008, courtesy of Tīpene Ohlson

Tuhoe, and much of what became Te Peehi's massive output. The man Tutakangahau followed into war in the late 1860s, Te Kooti Rikirangi, and his junior in the late retreat to Maungapōhatu and death in 1907, Rua Kenana – both have become lightning rods for revisionist histories, and had their negative images in the Pākehā mind re-evaluated through the recuperative writings of the baby-boom historians from the 1970s onwards. This man – who it can easily be argued was just as significant in his time and more so beyond – has never received his due, and neither have the other Tūhoe informants.[1]

Tutakangahau and other Tūhoe chiefs like him were obviously central to the leadership strategies that took their people forward after the military reversals of the 1870s. Over four decades, eschewing unwinnable revenge crusades after the defeats suffered with Te Kooti, and avoiding the trap of circling the wagons that Rua would later fall into, Tutakangahau bargained and negotiated his way into a truce with modernity and its Pākehā benefactors. The truth seems to be that, unlike Te Kooti (who appeals to nationalists) and Rua (who portrays both martyrdom and mystique), Tutakangahau became neither exotic enough for Pākehā revisionists nor heroic enough for Māori resisters.

He had much in common with the Pākehā leadership he had to deal with: he was a modern man, having many shared values; by the 1870s, he stands out as a mediator between his people and the interwoven worlds of Māori and Pākehā. By his own estimation, Tutakangahau, as he exists in the written record, had become a moderate, a moderniser, and a loyalist. He was a new kind of literate leader who believed in the rule of law, which over the formative years of his early adult life had become part of his culture. None of this denies or subverts the old chief's birth culture

Tīpene Ohlson, a descendant of Tutakangahau, closes the door of the wharenui, Tanenuiarangi, at Mapou marae, Maungapōhatu.
Author photograph, 2008

and Tūhoe identity – whatever that might have meant to him – but there is no way to deny his biblical faith, and his support of indigenous Māori Christianity through the millennialist forms it took amongst Tūhoe from Pai Mārire/Hauhau, Te Kooti's karakia, and Rua's Iharaira. From the moment we human beings see writing, learn how to write, become both a writer and one written, we are changed; this 'fall' from whatever grace pertains to oral, traditional cultures, into the literary self, is a revolutionary transformation of our subjectivity, and our relationship to the kin group and wider society. There is no return to an unwritten innocence.

It is his knowledge, his experience of the power of literacy, which draws him to Best: the notion that Best stole Tūhoe knowledge, or received only the dregs of those who led him on, seems untenable. Of course Best could never have recorded everything: no one informant knew 'everything', but the record appears to show that he was given access to a vast store of knowledge, for the very reason that the most perceptive of its possessors saw, by the 1890s, that if not recorded, it would die with them. The inevitable colonisation of the Māori oral universe by Western literacy was not lost on Tutakangahau. While we must rely on Best for much of our evidence in assessing the old man's motives, in this case it seems less risky to take his word for it – as set down in *Waikaremoana* and 'The Forest Lore of the Maori' – than to agree with contemporary Tūhoe critics of Best, simply because they are Tūhoe. Those having a political point to prove, in the matter of genuine historical grievances, are free to choose to ignore evidence to the contrary.

Best's estimation of the old man's prodigious knowledge bears repeating: Tutakangahau was 'a storehouse of primitive lore . . . [who] knew the old Native names of every tree, shrub, plant, or fern' in the Urewera forests, and 'was thoroughly conversant with the modes of thought of the ancient Maori'.[2] Here is the evidence of Tutakangahau's co-operation; moreover, of his claim to shared authorship in the surviving literature to which he contributed. Best has had a massive influence both in founding a national literature and contributing to the field on an international stage – but without his ruānuku, he would have had little to say. Against any charges of cultural plunder or theft of intellectual property must be weighed the standards of the day and the decisions made by mature adults in control of their destiny at the given point of exchange.

Best and Tutakangahau may have embodied conflicting vantage points in the history of ideas as they developed in late nineteenth-century New Zealand, but their projects, the kaupapa that motivated their energetic relationship, led them to become allies – and friends. Best believed himself adopted by Tūhoe, and in his day, there is evidence of this in Tutakangahau's delivering his granddaughter Marewa into the Pākehā's tutelage – the feeling was mutual. An emergent Māori nationalism, combined with Tūhoe ambitions for local autonomy, articulated through the power of Christian literacy and a belief in the rule of law: Tutakangahau stood there. As a servant of European globalisation and a nascent social science, Best stood on another side of the reason versus religion divide that split the same era into warring camps. Shaped by opposing forces in this worldwide drama, these two unlikely players found a measure of concord – and in so doing, left an enduring legacy.

As for Best's search for a lost Māori way of being – 'the old-time Māori' – it is hard to avoid the conclusion that here was a holy grail too far. The hope of finding any unmediated Māori tradition in the late 1890s was forlorn: what Best found instead was a syncretic culture, mixing

Elsdon Best's portable writing desk, used in his field research in the Urewera and elsewhere.
Author photograph, 2008, courtesy of Janet Mackey

old ways with new, laying aside traditional technology for such modern accoutrements as the plough and the dray, the gun and the pen, while retaining what worked. Tūhoe may have seemed close to *what was*, but as always, they were living *what is*: culture is now, the past alive only as it partakes of the present. While Māori and Pākehā at this point certainly inhabited different worlds, what Best recorded was Tūhoe life *circa* 1895–1910, not *circa* 1795–1810. He had come a century too late to stand in the old world, even if he did believe he could still harvest its secrets.

Best's conception of Māori psychology – 'the mythopoetic Maori' – was an amalgam of observation, borrowings from overseas theorists such as Tylor and Müller, and a good deal of wishful thinking, shaped by a romantic, backward-looking gaze that sought to prove the existence of an essentialised Māori psychology. Tutakangahau came close to this ideal vision and gained approval; Rua Kenana was antithetical to it and could not. In many respects, however, these two Tūhoe relatives shared some purposes. While Smith and Best hunted for the kura huna contained in the pages of whakapapa written down for him by his 'academy', seeking to locate Māori in Western historical time, Tutakangahau and Rua used biblical traditions of genealogy and prophecy to align their past, present and future with a literate Christian modernity.

The Māori millennialists were completely disengaged from the Pākehā Orientalist project of making biblical anthropology relative, in a developing field of comparative religious studies; contrariwise, they had joined themselves to the whakapapa of Adam and the Jews. In their attempts to establish a local anthropology in the colony, and themselves as authorities, putative social scientists such as Best were at pains to discredit puerile biblical superstitions. It came to defining oneself, or being defined by others – and Tūhoe, as did other Māori in their time, took the initiative. From the very first contact with missionaries, as students and teachers, biblical co-translators, transmitters of their cosmology to missionary and official alike, Māori were early on agents of an indigenous ethnic theology. As it changed and developed over the nineteenth century, these local variations of an imported religion would lay snares for a later generation of ethnographers such as Best, seeking access to a world of pristine Māori thought.

Best in his research and subsequent writing attempted to do three things: to decipher Māori origins and locate them in history; to define their nature, and locate them in evolutionary anthropology; and to rank their spiritual achievements, situating them in a model of comparative religion. By assimilating and explaining Māori difference, he helped to establish Pākehā intellectuals in the ownership of the new frontier. The Māori according to Best is to some degree – making Māori a version of Pākehā – an effect of the self-definition attempted by the settlers, as they sought to belong in 'Maoriland'. While never truly a Pākehā-Māori, Best was, as we have seen, deeply identified with those who had retained what he saw as their essential nature, language and customs. In sensing the disappearance of authentic Māori life, Best seems to have sensed his own generation passing: the frontier intellectuals, the self-taught seekers of the kura, bilingual and bicultural, increasingly out of time.

The literary legacy left by Best and his academy – informing the Māori renaissance into this millennium and beyond – will survive. His world and Tutakangahau's may have gone, but the work they completed has survived them, and will certainly go forward, as long as that generation the old man saw coming 'return to the *kura* of Tuhoe and Potiki . . . proud of the achievements of their ancestors'.[3] Best left another little-known legacy: his bush balladry, schooled at the metrical feet of Longfellow, Bret Harte and Rudyard Kipling, and the *Bulletin* bards of the Australian bush, Paterson and Lawson.[4] A well-tried mix of nostalgia and insistent metres, in these poems Best comes closest to some kind of confession, a vision of his raw nerves on the edge of the passing frontier.

'The Men Who Break the Trail' – published in the *Otago Witness* in January 1898, while he was still in the Urewera, blows a chill wind indeed over Māori hopes of survival. On one level, it can be read as a Kipling-esque hymn to Progress: 'From the hidden Land of Tane that gave our nation birth / The mighty wave of the Western Heke is surging round the earth'.[5] The 'Western Heke' is the gathering flood of European immigrants sweeping across the globe to displace and destroy native peoples in the best tradition of species extinction. But it is not the native alone who will disappear as this wave advances: the pioneers, the trailblazers, are also

P.M. TO UNVEIL ELSDON BEST MEMORIAL

Monument Erected To Tawa's Greatest Son

A MONUMENT to Elsdon Best, Tawa's greatest son and famous New Zealand ethnologist, is to be unveiled at Grasslees Park, Tawa, on February 27 by the Prime Minister (Mr. Nash). Best was the author of many valuable books about the Maoris.

The memorial, a 5ft-high slab of roughly hewn granite, will stand on land which was part of the farm on which Elsdon Best was born. It will be on the southern side of the Kenepuru (or Porirua) Stream at the north end of Oxford Street, and near the footbridge which is now being built.

The granite, weighing a ton, will bear the words "Elsdon Best," and will be mounted on concrete steps bearing a bronze plaque with the emblem of the National Historic Places Trust and the words: "Nearby at Grasslees Farm Elsdon Best, Maori ethnologist, was born on 30 April, 1856. His ashes lie here."

The Tawa Borough Council is preparing the site, putting in the concrete base, and incorporating in it the inscription in Maori: "Haere ra, Te Pehi, Haere Ki te Hono i wairua" (Farewell Elsdon Best, fare on to the meeting place of spirits).

Elsdon Best

Name's origin

Elsdon Best's father, William Best, took over the 100-acre Crown grant from the original absentee owner in 1856, but had been living on it before that. He had previously farmed a "Grasslees" at Elsdon, near Ottoburn, Northumberland. He built a homestead on the new Grasslees near the present telephone exchange, and Elsdon Best was born there.

After the land passed from the Best family it changed hands several times and was ultimately sold to the Government for railway use. After the railway deviation had been completed the Government sold the 46 acres to the east of the motorway privately, and the 26 acres between the motorway and the railway were set aside for the post-primary school, the site for which is now being prepared. The borough council is buying the remainder for a park, and, in memory of Best, has named it Grasslees.

The Prosser Block, on the Titahi Bay Road near Mana College, newly named Elsdon, is also a memorial to Best.

The idea of a memorial in Grasslees Park was suggested to the Tawa Borough Council by councillor and author of "Tawa Flat and the Old Porirua Road," Mr. A. H. Carman. The Polynesian Society, of which Best was a foundation member and the National Historic Places Trust are helping financially. The Trust is contributing £25 plus the plaque, and the Minister of Maori Affairs (Mr. Nash) has given £50 from the Maori Purposes Fund.

The Polynesian Society had earlier explained that it had an urn containing Elsdon Best's ashes, and suggested they be scattered among the trees in the park. At the moment, however, there are no trees, so it was decided to incorporate the urn in the memorial.

The Trust was interested because it likes to mark the birthplace of famous New Zealanders, the death places usually being adequately marked by gravestones. In Elsdon Best's case, however, his ashes will lie where he was born, at Grasslees.

Newspaper clipping from February 1960, kept by Best's grandnephew and faithful biographer, Elsdon Craig.

Elsdon Craig Collection, Alexander Turnbull Library, Wellington, NZ, PA1-o-1240-59

doomed by the remorseless advance of civilisation: 'They'll pierce the realm of Further Out, to find themselves among/The tribes they left in the hidden west in the days when the world was young'.

No word of complaint is to be heard from these pioneers, but like the stoical savages of so much imperial ethnography, 'With never a wail they camp on the trail and wait for the coming end'. If Best was somewhat morbid about the future of his ilk while still safe in the surrounds of the beloved Urewera bush, his removal to Wellington after 1910 only increased his misanthropy. 'But Now! – Miramar 1200 AD 1913 AD', an unpublished poem written in a 1913 Notebook, lashes the effete citizens he must perforce share his life with, in urban exile from the heart of the bush.[6] Stanza after stanza compares their indulgences with the savage vigour of Wellington's Māori owners in the days when it was 'the land of Tara'. Trains, ocean liners, the telegraph – none of these modern

The unveiling of the memorial to Elsdon Best, ethnologist, 1856–1931, at Grasslees Park, Tawa, 27 February 1960, in the presence of the Prime Minister Walter Nash.

Photographer: Frank O'Leary, Museum of New Zealand Te Papa Tongarewa, A.003929

miracles can compare to the great days of yore, 'Where rugged Neolithic trails / Gave on their hill set pas / Now spurn the flying miles behind / Your whirring motor cars'.

The virility of the ancient warriors is in sharp contrast to the beneficiaries of Edwardian technology and its emasculating comforts. For Best, this urban Pākehā present lacks the substance of the Māori past, where the trials of survival would have done for most of the Wellington weaklings he sees crammed in the tramcars, crowding the 'soul destroying tea rooms', getting and spending to the waste of their powers. In a final irony, for one who accepted implicitly the truth of evolutionary doctrines when it came to human survival, there is a strong suggestion throughout this dyspeptic outburst that not only do the *unfit* survive in the Wonder City – they proliferate and prosper.

At this turning point in his life, like an immigrant in a state of culture shock, Best seems almost a prototype for those later Man Alone figures that came to dominate succeeding generations with their anti-female stereotypes. Filling the pages of our literature from Mulgan to Crump, there arose a parade of maladapted males, in flight from intimacy and the rapidly changing urban scene. There is a similar underlying anxiety in the late Best, which ties him ambiguously to the wheel of a Progress he had so staunchly prophesied in his first mature works. His final rejection of modernity as it manifested in consumerism and urban decadence bears within it a prophetic disdain that seems to flirt with the fascist and eugenicist notions at work in the currents of his time. Yet as he turned away from this world, and back to his calling, crouching over the pages of his notebooks and paipera like a wizard in his den, he would prove finally that a man out of time may live beyond time – and with him, the sage of Maungapōhatu, a ghostly presence moving at one with Te Peehi and his pen.

Tuhoe E! Tenei te mihi atu nei.[7]

Acknowledgements – Ngā Mihimihi

He mihi rangatira, te mihi tuatahi, ki te Runga Rawa, taku kaiwhakaora Ihu Karaiti, mauri ora! He nui āku whakamoemiti ki a koe, e Te Hēpara Pai o ngā tāngata katoa o te ao hurihuri nei.

Ki ēnei uri o ngā rangatira, Tutakangahau me Te Peehi: i te taha Māori, i te taha Pākehā, he mihi kau ana ki a Rangi tū te Maungaroa Tīpene Ohlson rāua ko Janet Elsdon Mackey, tēnā kōrua.

It goes without saying that there are a huge number of people involved in a project such as this, and I am bound to miss some helper or supporter in what follows – so please consider yourself as part of these acknowledgements if you have assisted me in any way and you are not named or recognised here.

Firstly, I need to thank Copyright Licensing Limited and their staff (Kathy, Jenny and Ann in particular) for the grant of $35,000 in 2007, one of two awards to a non-fiction project in that year (the other went,

Above Left: Rangi tū te Maungaroa Tīpene Ohlson, Maungapōhatu, 2008.
Author photograph

Above Right: Janet Elsdon Mackey, Gisborne, 2008.
Author photograph

deservedly, to Martin Edmond). Writing a researched work of non-fiction takes a considerable amount of time, and there are numerous expenses involved, especially for travel and accommodation, and rental vehicles. Without this award, pursuing writing of this kind in New Zealand would be a much more difficult proposition.

Next, I need to salute the staff and students of the University of Canterbury, both in the years since 2007, when this book was begun, and back to 2002, when the doctoral thesis upon which it rests was first embarked on. I could also return to 1997, when I re-enrolled to complete an abandoned 1970s English degree, determined to add some papers in te reo Māori me ōna tikanga along the way.

I want to pay tribute to the staff of the former Māori Department of the University of Canterbury who were my teachers, and I wish first of all to mihi to my tūpuna there, those who I never met: Bill Te Awaroa Nepia and Margaret Orbell. Between them they founded a tradition of academic rigour in the study of Māori language and culture. E ngā pou e rua, moe mai rā!

Ki te hunga ora, āku kaiako maha: Rangi Nicholson, Hariata McKean, Te Rita Papesch, Haani Huata, Matiu Ratima, Roger Maaka, Lyndsay Head, Jeanette King, and Nichole Gully, tēnā koutou katoa.

I also owe a great deal to the former English Department, especially to the former Head of Programme, Professor Patrick Evans. Professor Evans has supported my work through thick and thin. Without his intervention in the final year of my thesis, offering me shelter from a certain storm, this book may have taken far longer to see the light of day, difficult enough as was its genesis in the years 2004 to 2006. Patrick Evans is a long-time champion of the study of New Zealand writing and its bicultural nature, and I salute him.

To my former co-supervisor, Dr John Newton, he mihi kau ana hoki ki a koe, e te kaiwhakatere o tēnei waka hou. To Paul Millar, a good friend and scholar, who sent my basic proposal to Penguin Books without stopping to ask me, thank you. Thanks also to Professor Howard McNaughton, Professor David Gunby (retired), Professor Mark Williams, Associate Professor Philip Armstrong, and Jennifer Middendorf, our tireless administrator.

To my thesis examiners, Dr John Stenhouse (Otago), Associate Professor Jane Samson (Alberta, Canada), and the viva chair, Professor Mark Francis (Canterbury), my grateful acknowledgements. Among other academics and historians outside of this university, for their valuable help and support, I would like to thank especially Peter Clayworth and Mark Derby.

To other staff on campus, especially the brilliant Macintosh support people at IT, what can I say? Colin, James, Neil, Craig, Bruce – you rock! To those Māori staff on campus who supported me in the course of this research, especially my Rōpū Tautoko Viva, Dr Helen Hayward and Dr Jo Diamond, tēnā kōrua, wahine toa! He mihi anō ki a Heemi Inia me te Rōpū Tautoko, arā, ko te Māori Development Team, tēnā koutou katoa.

For the illustrations, I would like to acknowledge all the staff of the Photographic Collections of the National Library of New Zealand in Wellington, the staff of the Image Collection at the Museum of New Zealand Te Papa Tongarewa, and also the assistance offered to me by those in The New Zealand Film Archive/Ngā Kaitiaki o Ngā Taonga

Whitiāhua, who helped me to access the wonderful still image of Best and Buck fishing together, from a 1923 film by James McDonald.

To my friends and kaiāwhina amongst Tūhoe, he mihi kau ana ki a koutou katoa: to Materoa Nikora, who offered me manaakitanga on my first visit to Rūātoki in 2004, tēnā koe e te whaea. To Hemana Waaka, who used some of my research to make two excellent television documentaries on Best and Tutakangahau, and to his saxophone sidekick who starred as Tutakangahau in the second, Tīpene Ohlson, tēnā kōrua. I would also like to include Janet Mackey in this mihi to Tūhoe: recognised when a small child by a Tūhoe elder as 'te mokopuna a Te Peehi', she has a kind of honorary status here as one of Best's living relatives, the daughter of his biographer.

To Ngāi Tūhoe, all the people of the Urewera, to those I have had the privilege of meeting, especially the hapū of my friend the late Here Wilson, Ngāti Tawhaki of Ngāhina marae, Rūātoki, tēnā koutou katoa, rire rire rire hau, pai mārire. To Pareārau and Paki, tēnā kōrua. My thanks to Tamati Kruger for giving me his time, and to the late Hohepa Kereopa, he tohunga tino hūmārie. Moe mai rā, e pā.

My thanks also to Geoff Walker, Publishing Director of Penguin Books (NZ), and to all his staff, especially Jeremy Sherlock, for faith in the project, close reading and financial support. Many thanks also to Mike Wagg, the tireless and most scrupulous editor of this manuscript: through the attention to detail of such professionals, the chaff large and small is blown away. To Tracey Tawhiao of the House of Taonga, whose wonderful illustrations grace the chapter headings and appear elsewhere on the cover, e te tohunga mahi toi, tēnā koe.

To my old friend of Hokitika days, and sometime editor, Margaret Samuels, who also stood by the work and offered much wisdom, my sincere thanks. I also need to mention Warwick Jordan of Hard to Find Books, Auckland, who bought at auction in 2003 many of Best's own signed and annotated books from his personal library – and allowed me access to them; also to Kevin McFadden of Auckland for his kind help in this area, and with some of the illustrations.

Finally, to my families: to my mother who did not live to see this book, but watched and prayed through its early life as a thesis, and my own first moments on the planet – Mum, I owe it all to you. Dad, I wish you were here – sail on, sailor – you knew the power of seas the ancestors had to cross. To my brothers and sisters for their unstinting love and support, cheers. To Theresa, Timothy and Raine, thank you for being my family then and now: love is eternal, even if we are not. To my Christchurch whānau, my gratitude for everything, for surviving this far with me in the house of words we inhabit.

Nā reira, ki ngā tamariki katoa o te kohu, i ngaro i ngā ārai o tēnei ao hurihuri, i roto i te kura huna tūturu, arā, i te aroha o Te Atua Runga Rawa, tēnā koutou katoa.

Publisher acknowledgements

While every effort has been made to trace and/or contact the owners of copyright material reproduced in this book, we should be pleased to hear from any copyright holder whom we have been unable to contact. Full details of permitted sources appear in the chapter endnotes.

The quote in Chapter 6 from Tony Ballantyne's *Orientalism and Race: Aryanism in the British Empire* (2002) is reproduced with the permission of Palgrave Macmillan (UK).

Three references to Polynesian Society material, in Chapters 10 and 11, are reproduced here with their kind permission.

References to the following works in Chapters 11 and 12 are reproduced by permission of Oxford University Press, Australia: *Te Matatiki: Contemporary Māori Words*, Māori Language Commission/ Oxford University Press (1995), and *Tikanga Whakaaro: Key Concepts in Māori Culture*, by Cleve Barlow, Oxford University Press (1990).

References to J. C. Beaglehole's edition of Captain Cook's journals are reproduced by permission of the Hakluyt Society; and the quote from page 48 of *Victorian Anthropology* (1987) by George W. Stocking, Jr. by permission of The Free Press, a Division of Simon & Schuster, Inc., all rights reserved.

Note on long vowels and macrons

Long vowels in the Māori language are today signified almost exclusively with macrons. In this text, macrons are employed for contemporary usage, and where they appear in historical sources. However, where the original authors have not used them, the text of quotes in Māori is as written, or as published. Best was aware of macrons and used them idiosyncratically in certain places, as in Mātātua for Mātaatua. Every effort has been made to cite accurately and historically.

Bibliography

ABBREVIATIONS

AJHR: *Appendices to the Journal of the House of Representatives*
ANZ: Archives New Zealand
ATL: Alexander Turnbull Library, Wellington
J: Justice, Archives New Zealand
JPS: *Journal of the Polynesian Society*, University of Auckland
LS: Lands and Survey
MA: Māori Affairs, Archives New Zealand
WT: Waitangi Tribunal

THESES AND RESEARCH DOCUMENTS

ANZ: Best's final will, AAOM 6029, 49422/1931
ATL: Tutakangahau to Brabant, 11 September 1874, MS-Papers-0032-0171
ATL: Pencil note on whakapapa list sent to Smith dated '6.7.95', MS-0072-08
ATL: Best, Elsdon, letter to Percy Smith, 14.8.1895, Elsdon Craig Collection, MS-Papers-7888-063
ATL: Best, letter to Smith undated, *c*. 1895, MS-0072-08
ATL: Best to Smith, 17.9.1895, MS-0072-08
ATL: Best to Percy Smith, n/d 1895–96, MS-0072-08
ATL: Best to Smith, 29.1.96, MS-Papers-0072-08
ATL: Best, letter to Percy Smith from Te Whāiti, 20.2.1896, MS-0072-08
ATL: Best, letter to Smith, 'Camp Te Whāiti 20.2.96', MS-0072-08
ATL: Best, letter to Smith, February 1896, MS-0072-08

ATL: Best, letter to Percy Smith, Ruatāhuna, 29.8.1902 (p. 13), Best's Correspondence, MS-Papers-1187-249
ATL: Best, letter to Smith, Rūātoki, 8.9.1905, Best's Correspondence, MS-Papers-1187-249
ATL: Letter, Best to Smith, 7.10.1905, MS-Papers-7888-023
ATL: Craig, Elsdon, Notes, MS-Papers-7888-024
ATL: Craig, Elsdon, 'Notes for a biography', MS-Papers-7888-024
ATL: Craig, Elsdon, Notes for *Man of the Mist*, MS-Papers-7888-024, Craig Papers
ATL: Craig, Elsdon (1964), MS-Papers-7888-039
ATL: *Meeting between the Premier and Chiefs of the Tuhoe Tribe, at Parliament Buildings, Wellington, 26th September, 1898*, MS-Papers-0448-16, Notes of Meetings
ATL: Letter, Hurae Puketapu to Percy Smith, 25 June 1900, Polynesian Society Papers, MS-1187-297
ATL: Alexander, Dudley, 'Journey Through the Urewera Country' (1904), Ranfurly Collection, MSY-4600
ATL: Ross, Malcolm, *Through Tuhoe Land* (1 album), PA1-q-634
ATL: Alexander, Dudley, *New Zealand Journals* (1904), MSY-4600
ATL: Ranfurly Collection, Turnbull Letters 1905, MS-Papers-6357-11
ATL: Carroll, J., letter to Lord Ranfurly, 10 March 1905, MS-Papers-6357-11
ATL: Pomare, M., letter to Lord Ranfurly, 22 May 1905, MS-Papers-6357-11
ATL: Ross, M., letter to Lord Ranfurly, 22 June 1905, MS-Papers-6357-11
ATL: Best, letter to Smith, 11.6.06, MS-Papers-7888-024, Craig Papers
ATL: Best, letter to Smith, 2.1.08, MS-Papers-7888-024, Craig Papers
ATL: Best to Smith, 8.8.05, MS-Papers-7888-024, Craig Papers
ATL: Best to Smith, 8.9.05, MS-Papers-7888-024, Craig Papers
ATL: Best to Smith, 3.1.06, MS-Papers-7888-024, Craig Papers
ATL: Best to Smith, 11.6.06, MS-Papers-7888-024, Craig Papers
ATL: Best to Smith, 20 April 1908, MS-Papers-1187-249
ATL: Best to Smith, 13 November 1908, MS-Papers-7888-024, Craig Papers
ATL: Smith to Best, 12 December 1909, MS-Papers-72, Folder 5
ATL: Best's Diary, 13 March 1910, MS-0175 (173–176)
ATL: Best to Smith, April/May 1911, Polynesian Society Records, MS-Papers-1187-249
ATL: Best, Elsdon, Notebook 15 (1911), qMS 194
ATL: Best, Elsdon, Notebook 11 (1912), qMS 191, 193, 194, MS-Copy-Micro-0650-09A, Unpublished manuscript
ATL: Smith, letter to Best, 27 October 1915, MS-Papers-7888-017
ATL: Tape Copy (LC-0417) of MST7-0113, Hui Aroha, Gisborne, April 1919
ATL: Best, Maori Notebook No. 13, pp. 111–112
ATL: 28 July 1931, Best's Diary, 1928–1931, MS-0175 (MS-0173-177)

ATL: Eggers, I. M., 'Elsdon Best: man and writer', MA dissertation, University of New Zealand, 1935; Copy held in MSX-6800, Craig Papers

Best, Elsdon, 'Maori Forest Lore – Part II', Read before the Auckland Institute, 18 November 1908 (*Transactions and Proceedings of the Royal Society of New Zealand, 1868–1961*)

Best, Elsdon, 'Art. LII – Maori Forest Lore: Being some Account of Native Forest Lore and Woodcraft, as also of many Myths, Rites, Customs, and Superstitions connected with the Flora and Fauna of the Tuhoe or Urewera District. – Part III', *Transactions and Proceedings of the Royal Society of New Zealand*, Vol. 42, 1909

Best, Elsdon, 'Maori Forest Lore – Part III', Read before the Auckland Institute, 22 November 1909 (*Transactions and Proceedings of the Royal Society of New Zealand, 1868–1961*)

Best, Elsdon, 'Maori and Maruiwi', Read before the Wellington Philosophical Society, 27 October 1915 (*Transactions and Proceedings of the Royal Society of New Zealand, 1868–1961*, Vol. 48, 1915)

Binney, Judith, *Encircled Lands – Parts One & Two: A History of the Urewera from European Contact until 1878/1878–1912*, Evidence of Judith Binney, Waitangi Tribunal Report WAI 999, April 2002

Clayworth, Peter, '"An Indolent and Chilly Folk" – the development of the idea of the "Moriori Myth"', PhD thesis (History), University of Otago (Dunedin: 2001)

Colenso, William, *Transactions and Proceedings of the New Zealand Institute*, Vol. 10, 1877, 122

Colenso's Diary, December 1843–22 January 1844, 'Memoranda', MSS 67/23d, MSS 65, Hocken Library, University of Otago, Dunedin

Easthope, Jonathan, *A History of the Maungapōhatu and Tauranga Blocks*, Report for the Crown Forestry Rental Trust (2002)

——, *Urewera Overview Project, Pt II, 1878–1912*, History Department, University of Auckland (2002)

Grace, Thomas, Annual Letter to the Church Missionary Society (1877), No. Box 1, MSS 583 AIM, Auckland Institute and Museum, 285–286

Head, Lyndsay, 'Land, authority and the forgetting of being in early colonial Māori history', PhD thesis, University of Canterbury (Christchurch: 2006), http://hdl.handle.net/10092/967

Holman, Jeffrey Paparoa, 'Best of both worlds: Elsdon Best and the metamorphosis of Māori spirituality. Te painga rawa o ngā ao rua: Te Peehi me te putanga kē o te wairua Māori', PhD thesis, University of Canterbury (Christchurch: 2007), http://hdl.handle.net/10092/939

Justice: A. Foster to Native Office, 3 March 1893, J1 1893/515, Box 439, ANZ

Justice: Kereru to Native Minister, 8 March 1893, J1 1893/515, ANZ

Justice: Creagh to Cadman, telegram, 15 June 1893, J1 1893/515, ANZ

Justice: J1 1897/1389, Notes of Meeting with Urewera chiefs, Carroll and Seddon, 7 September 1895, 1–58 (5–6), ANZ
Justice: J1 1896/1802, Tutakangahau to Seddon, ANZ
Justice: Letter to Seddon, 29 June 1896, J1 1896/1082, ANZ
Justice: Note by Carroll on translation of Tutakangahau's letter of 29 June 1896, J1 1896/1082, ANZ
Justice: Tutakangahau, letter to Seddon, 29 June 1896, J1 1896/1082, ANZ
Justice: Tutakangahau, letter to Percy Smith, 29 June 1896, Urewera Surveys, LS-1, 21734, 2/2, ANZ
Justice: J1 1897/1389, Wi Pere, MP, Notes of Meeting with Urewera chiefs, Carroll and Seddon, 7 September 1895, ANZ
Justice: Letter, Tutakangahau to Percy Smith, 24 July 1900, J1 1898/1011, ANZ
Lands and Survey: Translation by government official, 23 July 1895, 21734/150, Repro. 1801 (2 of 2), LS-1, 21734, Pt 2, ANZ
Lands and Survey: LS-1, 21734/120, Pt 2, telegram to Percy Smith, Surveyor-General, from Phillips, ANZ
Lands and Survey: Translation by government official, letter to Seddon and Carroll, 7 July 1895, LS-1, 21734, Pt 2, ANZ
Lands and Survey: Letter to Percy Smith, 26 January 1896, LS-1, 21734/169, Repro. 1801, ANZ
Lands and Survey: Tukua Te Rangi to Smith, 23 December 1895, LS-1, 21734, Pt 2, ANZ
Lands and Survey: Best, letter to Percy Smith, Surveyor-General, Wellington, from Te Whāiti, 20.2.1896, Repro. 1801, LS-1, 21734/64, Pt 2, ANZ
Lands and Survey: Letter from Tutakangahau to Percy Smith, Surveyor-General, Te Whāiti, 10 April 1896, LS-1, 21734, ANZ
McDonald, James, *He Pito Whakaatu i Te Hui i Rotorua: Scenes at the Rotorua Hui* (film), F2808 (1920), Elsdon Best with Paitini Wi Tapeka of Ruatāhuna, New Zealand Film Archive/Ngā Kaitiaki O Ngā Taonga Whitiāhua, Wellington
——, *He Pito Whakaatu i te noho a te Māori i Te Tai Rāwhiti/Scenes of Māori Life on the East Coast* (film), Dominion Museum, F2815 (1923), DVD, New Zealand Film Archive/Ngā Kaitiaki O Ngā Taonga Whitiāhua, Wellington
Mair, Gilbert, Inward correspondence, 1904–1923, MS-Papers-0039-06, Cowan, James, Papers (microfilm), MS-Papers-0039, ATL
Marr, Cathy, *Urewera District Native Reserve Act 1896 and Amendments*, Waitangi Tribunal Report No. A21 (Wellington: 2002), WAI 9999, WT
Māori Affairs: Crown Law Letters, MA 4/104-417, ANZ
Māori Affairs: 14 September 1872, MA 1/1872/1162, Māori Affairs Inward Correspondence, MAICR; 24 December 1872, MA 1/1873/11, MAICR, ANZ
Māori Affairs: MA 4/103-695, Letter from Waldegrave, Secretary, to Seddon,

Native Minister, Wellington, 9 December 1895, 'to Tutakanahau, Maungapohatu, via Whakatane', Māori Affairs files, ANZ
Māori Affairs: Letter from James Carroll to Tutakangahau, 7 August 1896, MA 4/102-78, ANZ
Māori Affairs: Letter from Waldegrave, Secretary, Office of the Solicitor-General, Wellington, 31 August 1898, 'To Tutakangahau, c/- Mrs C. Smith, Molesworth St.', MA 4/102-434, ANZ
Māori Affairs: Letter from Native Affairs, Wellington, to Tutakangahau, Ruatāhuna, 10 August 1906, MA 4/104-417, ANZ
Māori Affairs: Andy Grant, letter, to Justice Department, 22 October 1907, in MA 1/1907/27, ANZ
Māori Affairs: Huhana Tutakangahau to Under Secretary, Native Department, 12 July 1923, Urewera Consolidation, MA 29/4/7, 1, ANZ
Miles, Anita, *Te Urewera*, Rangahaua Whanui District 4, March 1999, Working Paper: First Release, Waitangi Tribunal, Wellington, 245, 503, WT
O'Malley, Vincent, *The Crown's Acquisition of the Waikaremoana Block, 1921–1925*, Report for the Panekiri Tribal Trust Board (May 1996)
Ormond to Te Purewa, 20 November 1871, Agent General Government, Hawke's Bay, 4/8, Supporting Papers, 98, ANZ
——, Letter from Tutakangahau to Ormond, June 1872, AGG-HB 2, 2/1, AGG-A 1/1-4, AGG-HB 2/1-3, ANZ
——, Tutakangahau to Ormond and McLean, 1 December 1872, AGG-HB 2/1, ANZ
——, Letters to Ormond, Russell and McLean, 4 December 1873, Agent General Government, Hawke's Bay, HB 2/2, ANZ
Porter, T. W., Enclosure 26, *AJHR*, 1871, F-No 1, Friday 19 February, Maungapōhatu, T. W. Porter, Captain and Adjutant
Preece, letter from Tutekanahau [Tutakangahau], 1 December 1872, AGG-HB 2/1, ANZ
Te Kaha, Akuhata, Minute Books (5), Māori Land Court, Whakatāne, 6 May 1987, 190, microfilm
Te Papa: Series MU000148, Staff (personal) files, Best, E., Dominion Museum, Wellington, 1914–1931, Museum of New Zealand/Te Papa Tongarewa, Wellington
Urewera Minute Book 3, 26 February 1900, 137, ANZ
Urewera Minute Book 2, 19, ANZ
Urewera Minute Book 4, 18, ANZ
WT: Report of the Waitangi Tribunal, Manukau Claim, 07 Specific Claims: 7.2 Slurry Pipeline and the Mixing of Waters, WAI 8, Waitangi Tribunal, 1985–85
Waaka, Hemana et al., *Te ara pai o ngā ao rua (Best of both worlds)*, Māori TV, 2007, transcript

Waka Huia, Chapter 3, TVNZ On Demand, TV One, 28 June 2008
Wilson, triangulation surveys: LS-1, 21734, Pt 2, 3, Māori text, 5, official translation, ANZ

BOOKS

Acheson, Frank, *Plume of the Arawas*, Dent (London: 1930)
Asad, Talal (ed.), *Anthropology and the Colonial Encounter*, Humanity Books (New York: 1973, 1998)
Bagnall, A. G. & Petersen, G. C., *William Colenso, Printer, Missionary, Botanist, Explorer, Politician: His Life and Journeys*, Reed (Wellington: 1948)
Ballantyne, Tony, *Orientalism and Race: Aryanism in the British Empire*, Palgrave (Houndmills, Basingstoke, Hampshire / New York: 2002)
Ballara, Angela, *Iwi: The Dynamics of Māori Tribal Organisation from c. 1769 to c. 1945*, Victoria University Press (Wellington: 1998)
Barlow, Cleve, *Tikanga Whakaaro*, Oxford University Press (Auckland: 1991)
Belich, James, *The New Zealand Wars and the Victorian Interpretation of Racial Conflict* (Auckland: 1986)
Best, Elsdon, *Fishing Methods and Devices of the Maori*, Dominion Museum Bulletin No. 12, Te Papa Press (Wellington: 1929, 1986, 2005)
——, *Forest Lore of the Maori*, Dominion Museum Bulletin No 14, Te Papa Press (Wellington: 1942, 1977, 2005)
——, *Maori Agriculture*, Dominion Museum Bulletin No. 9, Te Papa Press (Wellington: 1925, 1976, 2005)
——, *Maori Religion and Mythology*, Pt 1, Dominion Museum Bulletin No. 10, Te Papa Press (Wellington: 1924, 2005)
——, *Maori Religion and Mythology*, Pt 2, Dominion Museum Bulletin No. 11, Te Papa Press (Wellington: 1924, 1982)
——, (Evans, Jeff, ed.), *Notes on the art of war: as conducted by the Maori of New Zealand, with accounts of various customs, rites, superstitions, &c., pertaining to war, as practised and believed in by the ancient Maori*, Reed, in association with the Polynesian Society (Auckland: 2001)
——, *The Maori As He Was*, A. R. Shearer, Government Printer (Wellington: 1974 [1924])
——, *The Maori: Pt 1*, Memoirs of the Polynesian Society, Vol. V, Board of Maori Ethnological Research (Wellington: 1924)
——, *The Maori: Volume II*, Harry H. Tombs (Wellington: 1924)
——, 'The Races of the Philippines', Parts I–II, *JPS*, Vol. 1 (1892)
——, *Tuhoe: The Children of the Mist*, The Board of Maori Ethnological Research (New Plymouth: 1925)
——, *The Stone Implements of the Maori*, Te Papa Press / A. R. Shearer, Government Printer (Wellington: 1912, 1974, 2005)
——, *Waikaremoana: The Sea of the Rippling Waters*, A. R. Shearer, Government

Printer (Wellington: 1975 [1897])
Binney, J., Chaplin, G. & Wallace, C., *Mihaia: The Prophet Rua and His Community at Maungapōhatu*, Oxford University Press (Auckland: 1979)
Binney, Judith, *Redemption Songs: A Life of Te Kooti Arikirangi Te Turuki*, Auckland University Press/Bridget Williams Books (Auckland: 1995)
——, *Untold Lives: When the Elders tell their Stories*, Hocken Lecture 2: 2007, The Hocken Collections, University of Otago (Dunedin: 2008)
Boast, Richard, *Buying the Land, Selling the Land: Governments and Maori Land in the North Island 1865–1921*, Victoria University Press (Wellington: 2008)
Bougainville, Louis-Antoine de, (Dunmore, John, ed.), *The Pacific Journals*, Hakluyt Society (London: 2002)
Buck, Peter, *The Coming of the Maori*, Maori Purposes Fund Board/Whitcombe & Tombs (Wellington: 1949)
Burdon, R. M., *King Dick*, Whitcombe & Tombs (Christchurch: 1955)
Carman, Arthur H., *Tawa Flat and the Old Porirua Road 1840–1955*, A. H. Carman (Wellington: 1956)
Carpenter, Edmund, *Oh, What a Blow That Phantom Gave Me!*, Bantam Books (New York: 1974)
Cassell Concise Dictionary, (Brown, Lesley, Consultant Editor), Cassell plc, Orion Publishing Group (London: 1989, 1997)
Cassells, K. R., *Tawa, Enterprise and Endeavour*, Tawa Borough Council (Tawa, Wellington: 1988)
Chambers, Robert, *Vestiges of the Natural History of Creation*, John Churchill (London: 1844), Chambers, W. & R. (Edinburgh: 1884), Leicester University Press, The Victorian Library (New York: 1969)
Clifford, James, *Writing Culture: The Poetics and Politics of Ethnography*, University of California Press (Berkeley: 1986)
Cook, James, (Beaglehole, J. C., ed.), *Selections: The Journals of Captain Cook*, Penguin Books (London: 1999)
——, (Beaglehole, J. C., ed.), *The Voyage of the Endeavour 1768–1771*, Cambridge University Press (Cambridge: 1955), Published for the Hakluyt Society at the University Press
Cowan, James, *The New Zealand Wars and the Pioneering Period, Vol II: The Hauhau Wars, 1864–1872*, P. D. Hasselberg, Government Printer (Wellington: 1983)
Craig, Elsdon, *Man of the Mist*, Reed (Wellington: 1964)
Curnow, J., Hopa, N. & McRae, J. (eds.), *Rere Atu, Taku Manu!: Discovering History, Language and Politics in the Māori-language Newspapers*, Auckland University Press (Auckland: 2002)
De Beer, Gavin (ed.), in Chambers, Robert, *Vestiges of the Natural History of Creation* (1844), Leicester University Press, The Victorian Library (New York: 1969)

Elder, John Rawson (ed.), *The Letters and Journals of Samuel Marsden 1765–1838*, A. H. & A. W. Reed (Dunedin: 1932)

Elsmore, Bronwyn, *Like Them That Dream*, Reed (Auckland: 1999, 2004)

——, *Mana from Heaven*, Reed (Auckland: 1989, 1999, 2004)

Emerson, Ralph Waldo, (eds.) Bode & Cowley, *The Portable Emerson*, Penguin (New York: 1981)

Figuier, Louis, *The Earth Before the Deluge*, Chapman & Hall (London: 1865)

Firth, Raymond, *The Primitive Economics of the New Zealand Maori*, Routledge (London: 1929)

Hamerton, P. G., *Thoughts About Art*, Macmillan (London: 1873)

Holy Bible, Authorised Version and New International editions

Howe, Kerry, *The Quest for Origins*, Penguin (Auckland: 2003)

Hyde, Lewis, *The Gift: Imagination and the Erotic Life of Property*, Vintage (New York: 1979)

Ihimaera, Witi, *The Whale Rider*, Reed (Auckland: 1987, 2003)

Ka'ai, T. M., Moorfield, J. C., Reilly, M. P. J. & Mosley, S. (eds.), *Ki te Whaiao: An Introduction to Māori Culture and Society*, Pearson Education (Auckland: 2004)

Kapuscinski, Ryszard, *Travels with Herodotus*, Penguin / Allen Lane (London: 2007)

King, Michael, *Te Ao Hurihuri – The World Moves On: Aspects of Maoritanga*, Hicks Smith (Wellington: 1975)

——, *The Penguin History of New Zealand*, Penguin (Auckland: 2003)

Lang, Andrew, *The Making of Religion*, 2nd edition, Longmans (London: 1900)

McCarthy, Conal, *Exhibiting Māori – A History of Colonial Cultures of Display*, Te Papa Press (Wellington: 2007)

McLuhan, Marshall, *The Gutenberg Galaxy: The Making of Typographical Man*, Routledge & Kegan Paul (London: 1962)

Māori Language Commission: *Te Matatiki: Contemporary Māori Words*, Māori Language Commission / Te Taura Whiri i Te Reo Māori, Oxford University Press (Auckland: 1996)

Marsden, Māori, *The Woven Universe: Selected Writings of Rev. Māori Marsden*, (ed.) Royal, Ahukaramū Charles, Estate of Rev. Māori Marsden (Otaki: 2003)

Mauss, Marcel, *The Gift* (*Essai sur le don*), trs. Ian Cunnison, Cohen & West (London: 1969)

Mead, Hirini Moko, *Tikanga Māori: Living by Māori Values*, Huia (Wellington: 2003)

Müller, F. Max, *Anthropological Religion: The Gifford Lectures*, Vol. III, Longman (London: 1898)

——, *Selected Essays on Language, Mythology and Religion, Vol. I*, Longman, Green & Co. (London: 1881)

Nicholas, J. L., *Narrative of a Voyage to New Zealand, Vol. 1*, James Black and Son (London: 1817).

O'Malley, Vincent, *Agents of Autonomy: Maori Committees in the Nineteenth Century*, Crown Forestry Rental Trust (Wellington: 1997)

Ong, Walter J., *Orality and Literacy: The Technologising of the Word*, Routledge (London & New York: 1982)

Orbell, Margaret & Moon, Geoff, *The Natural World of the Māori*, Collins/David Bateman (Auckland: 1985)

Owens, J. M. R., *The Mediator: A Life of Richard Taylor 1805–1873*, Victoria University Press (Wellington: 2004)

Pagden, Anthony, *The Fall of Natural Man: The American Indian and the Origins of Comparative Ethnology*, Cambridge University Press (Cambridge: 1982)

Perham, Margery, *Pacific Prelude: A Journey to Samoa and Australasia*, Peter Owen (London: 1988)

Reed, A. H. & A. W. (eds.), *Captain Cook in New Zealand*, Reed (Wellington: 1951)

He Pātaka Kupu, Te Taura Whiri i te Reo Māori/Raupo (2008)

The Reed Dictionary of Modern Māori (1997)

The Reed Dictionary of Māori Mythology, (ed.) Calman, Ross (2004)

Ross, Malcolm, *Through Tuhoe Land: Lord Ranfurly's Farewell to the Maori People*, Christchurch Press (Christchurch: 1904)

Rudwick, M. J. S., *The Meaning of Fossils*, University of Chicago Press (Chicago & London: 1985)

——, *Scenes from Deep Time*, Chicago University Press (Chicago & London: 1992)

Sahlins, Marshall, *Stone Age Economics*, Aldine-Atherton, Inc. (Chicago & New York: 1972)

Salmond, Anne, *Two Worlds: First Meetings Between Maori and Europeans, 1642–1772*, Viking (Auckland: 1993)

Scott, Dick, *Ask That Mountain*, Reed/Southern Cross (Auckland: 1975)

Secord, J. A., *Victorian Sensation: The Extraordinary Publication, Reception, and Secret Authorship of Vestiges of the Natural History of Creation*, University of Chicago Press (Chicago: 2000)

Sinclair, Keith, *A History of New Zealand – Revised Edition*, Penguin (Auckland: 2000)

Shirres, Michael P., *Te Tangata: The Human Person*, Accent Publications (Auckland: 1997)

Sissons, Jeffrey, *Te Waimana – The Spring of Mana: Tuhoe History and the Colonial Encounter*, University of Otago Press (Dunedin: 1991)

Smith, S. Percy, *The Lore of the Whare-wananga*, Vols. I & II, Memoirs of the Polynesian Society, Vols. 3–4, T. Avery & Sons (New Plymouth: 1913–1915)

——, *Hawaiki: The Original Home of the Maori, With a Sketch of Polynesian*

History, 4th edition, Whitcombe & Tombs (Auckland: 1921)
Sorrenson, M. P. K., *Maori Origins and Migrations*, Auckland University Press/ Oxford University Press (Auckland: 1979)
——, (ed.), *Nā tō Hoa Aroha, From Your Dear Friend: The Correspondence Between Sir Apirana Ngata and Sir Peter Buck, 1925–50*, Vols. I–III, Auckland University Press (Auckland: 1986–87–88)
——, *Manifest Duty: The Polynesian Society Over 100 Years*, The Polynesian Society (Auckland: 1992)
Stocking, George W., Jr., *Victorian Anthropology*, The Free Press (New York: 1987)
Sullivan, Robert, *Captain Cook in the Underworld*, Auckland University Press (Auckland: 2002)
Taylor, Richard, *Te Ika a Maui, or New Zealand and its inhabitants*, 2nd edition, William McIntosh/London; H. Ireson Jones/Wanganui (1870)
Tylor, E. B., *Primitive Culture*, Murray (London: 1873)
Ward, A., *A Show of Justice: Racial 'Amalgamation' in Nineteenth Century New Zealand*, Auckland University Press (Auckland: 1995)
Walker, Ranginui, *Ka Whawhai Tonu Mātou: Struggle Without End*, Penguin (Auckland: 1990, 2004)
Wards, Ian, *The Shadow of the Land*, Historical Publications Branch, Department of Internal Affairs (Wellington: 1968)
Webster, Peter, *Rua and the Maori Millennium*, Price Milburn/Victoria University Press (Wellington: 1979)
White, John, *Ancient History of the Maori*, Vol. V, 1888
Williams' *Dictionary of the Maori Language*, 7th edition, Government Publications (Wellington: 1971)
Williams, William and Jane, *The Turanga Journals 1840–1850*, (ed.) Porter, Frances, Price Milburn/Victoria University Press (Wellington: 1974)

NEWSPAPERS

Auckland Star, 23 March 1891; Saturday, 21 September 1895
Best, Elsdon, 'In Tuhoe Land', *The Press* (Christchurch), 18 January 1897
——, 'The Present Condition of the Tuhoe Tribe', *The Press* (Christchurch), 22 March 1897
——, *Canterbury Times* (Christchurch), 16 September 1897; 6 January 1898
——, 'From Tuhoeland', *Canterbury Times* (Christchurch), 9 July 1902
——, 'On Solitude and the Primitive Mind', *Canterbury Times* (Christchurch), 22 October 1902
——, 'The Darkened Mind', *Canterbury Times* (Christchurch), 4 July 1906
Evening Post (Wellington), 9 September 1931, obituary for Best, cited in Howe, Kerry, *Singer in a Songless Land: A Life of Edward Tregear 1846–1931*, Auckland University Press (Auckland: 1991)

'New Orleans Happy with its World Fair', *New York Times*, 16 December 1884
Price, Robert, *Through the Uriwera Country*, Napier Daily Telegraph (Napier: 1891)
Tamakihikurangi, *New Zealand Spectator* (Wellington: 1861), 13–14L
Otago Witness, issue 2289, 13 January 1898, http://paperspast.natlib.govt.nz
Te Puke ki Hikurangi, 27 September 1904; 10 April 1905, Vol. 6, No. 8; 12 June 1905, Vol. 6, No. 13; 18 May 1906, Vol. 32
Te Wananga, 29 October 1874, Vol. 1, No. 6, 25
University of Waikato: Māori Newspapers Online, Digital Library: http://nzdl.sadl.uleth.ca/cgi-bin/library, ATL
Williams, W. L., *East Coast (N.Z.) Historical Records*, Gisborne (1932), Reprinted from the *Poverty Bay Herald*

ARTICLES

AJHR, 1895, G-1, 1–89; 1907, H-31, 58; 1908, G-1A, 1
Andrews, C. Lesley, 'Aspects of Development, 1870–1890', in *Conflict and Compromise: Essays on the Maori Since Colonisation*, (ed.) Kawharu, Sir Hugh, Reed (Auckland: 1975, 2003)
Ballance, John, *AHJR*, 1885, G-1, 11
Best, Elsdon, *Christian and Maori Mythology: notes on the clash of cultures*, published address given before the Free Discussions Club, Victoria University College, 1924
——, *Comparative anthropology – its scope and advantages* (1920), Notes of lecture given to the WEA, Wellington MS-Papers-0072-33, ATL
——, 'Food Products of Tuhoeland', *Transactions and Proceedings of the New Zealand Institute*, 1902, Vol. XXXV (v)
——, 'Maori Forest Lore', *Transactions and Proceedings of the Royal Society of New Zealand, 1868–1961*, Vol. 42, 1909, 433–81
——, 'Te Rehu-o-Tainui: the evolution of a Maori atua', *JPS*, Vol. VI: 22 (June 1897)
——, 'Spiritual Concepts of the Maori', *JPS*, Pts I & II (Pt I, Vol. IX: 36, December 1900, 173–199; Pt II, Vol. X: 37, March 1901, 1–19)
——, 'The Races of the Philippines/Prehistoric Civilisations of the Philippines', Pts I–II, *JPS*, Vol. 1 (1892)
——, 'The Cult of Io, the Concept of a Supreme Deity as evolved by the Ancestors of the Polynesians', in *MAN*, the *Journal of the Royal Anthropological Institute*, Vol. 13, Nos. 56–57 (London: 1913)
'Elsdon Best Memorial Number', *JPS*, Vol. 41, No. 1 (March 1932)
Biggs, Bruce & Simmons, David, 'The Sources of the *Lore of the Whare-wananga*', *JPS*, Vol. 79, No. 1 (1970)
Binney, Judith, 'Rua Kenana Hepetipa 1868/1869? – 1937', Dictionary of New Zealand Biography, updated 22 June 2007, http://www.dnzb.govt.nz/

Brabant, Herbert, to the Minister of Native Affairs, *AJHR*, 1874, G2, 7

Brooking, T., '"Busting Up" the Greatest Estate of All: Liberal Maori Land Policy, 1891–1911', *New Zealand Journal of History*, 26:1 (Auckland: 1992)

Brown, C. Hunter, *Appendices to the Journals of the House of Representatives*, 1862, E-9-Sect. IV

University of Chicago: History of New Orleans, http://tinyurl.com/nr4rjo

Craig, Elsdon, 'Elsdon Best of Tuhoe', *Te Ao Hou*, No. 20, November 1957, ATL

——, 'Elsdon Best – a Colonial Image', *Historical Review*, Vol. 14, No. 3, address delivered to the 100th Meeting of the Whakatāne District Historical Society, 16 June 1966

Head, Lyndsay, 'The Pursuit of Modernity in Māori Society: The Conceptual Bases of Citizenship in the Early Colonial Period', in *Histories, Power and Loss*, (ed.) Sharp & McHugh, Bridget Williams Books (Wellington: 2001)

——, 'Te Ua Haumene? – 1866', Dictionary of New Zealand Biography, updated 22 June 2007, http://www.dnzb.govt.nz/

Hill, Richard, 'Elsdon Best and Tuhoe: A Cautionary Tale', *Historical Review, Bay of Plenty*, Vol. 36, No. 2, November 1988 (Whakatāne and District Historical Society)

Hilliard, Chris, 'Textual Museums: Collection and Writing in History and Ethnology, 1900–1950', in Dalley, B. & Labrum, B. (eds.), *Fragments: New Zealand Social and Cultural History*, Auckland University Press (Auckland: 2000)

Holman, Jeffrey Paparoa, 'Elsdon Best: Elegist in Search of a Poetic', Part II, Best and his poetry in the 'Māori Twilight', *Ka Mate, Ka Ora*, http://www.nzepc.auckland.ac.nz/kmko/02/ka_mate02_holman.asp

Hulme, Keri, 'Mauri: An Introduction to Bicultural Poetry in New Zealand', in *Only Connect: Literary Perspectives East and West*, Amirthanayagam, Guy & Harrex, S. C. (eds.), Centre for Research in the New Literatures in English & East-West Centre (Adelaide & Honolulu: 1981)

Kessler, C., Obituary for Raymond Firth, *Australian Journal of Anthropology*, August 2002

'Mr S Locke's Trip to the Urewera Country', *AJHR*, 1889, G-6, 1

Maclean, Chris, 'Wellington places', Te Ara – The Encyclopedia of New Zealand, updated 25 September 2007, http://www.TeAra.govt.nz/Places/Wellington/WellingtonPlaces/en

Native Lands Settlement and Administration Bill (proposed), *AJHR*, 1898, I-3A & 1899, I-3A

Native Minister: Letter of nine chiefs to the Honourable Native Minister (translation), 17 April 1889, *AJHR*, 1889, G-6, 2

'Notes of Speeches made at the Native Meeting, Ruatahuna, March 23–24, 1874', *AJHR*, 1874, G-1A, 4–5

New Zealand Parliamentary Debates, 24 September 1896, Vol. 96, 160; October 1905, Vol. 135, 963

Parsons, M. J., 'Jury, Hoani Te Whatahoro 1841–1923', Dictionary of New Zealand Biography, updated 22 June 2007, http://www.dnzb.govt.nz/

Simmons, D. R., 'The Words of Te Matorohanga', *Journal of the Polynesian Society*, Vol. 103, No. 2 (June 1994)

——, 'Te Matorohanga, Moihi fl. 1836–1865', Dictionary of New Zealand Biography, updated 22 June 2007, http://www.dnzb.govt.nz/

Sissons, Jeffrey, Preface to the 4th edition of *Tuhoe*, Reed (Auckland: 1995 [1925])

——, Best biography, 'Best, Elsdon 1856–1931', Dictionary of New Zealand Biography, updated 22 June 2007, http://www.dnzb.govt.nz/

Smith, Stephenson Percy, *JPS*, Vol. 9, No. 35 (September 1900)

——, in 'Annual Report on Department of Lands and Survey', *AJHR*, 1899, C-1

Stocking, George, 'Matthew Arnold, E. B. Tylor, and the Uses of Invention', *American Anthropologist*, Vol. 65 (August 1963), 783–799

Te Ao Hou, No. 21 (December 1957)

Te Popo, Hira, to Wepiha Apanui, 22 February 1869, *AJHR*, 1869, A-10, 14–15

Tregear, Edward, 'The Maori in Asia', *Transactions and Proceedings of the Royal Society of New Zealand, 1868–1961*, Vol. 18, 1885

Williams, H. W., 'The Maruiwi Myth', *JPS*, Vol. 46, No. 3 (1937)

Wray, Alison, '"Needs only" Analysis in Linguistic Ontogeny and Phylogeny', in Lyon, C., Nehaniv, C. L. & Cangelosi, A. (eds.), *Emergence of Communication and Language*, Springer (London: 2007), 53–70

Endnotes

INTRODUCTION

1 Edmund Carpenter, *Oh, What a Blow That Phantom Gave Me!*, Bantam Books (New York: 1974), 41, 102. My emphasis.

2 Literally, 'I am remaining in response to Best's request to take him and others to Waikaremoana'. Letter to Seddon, 29 June 1896, J1 1896/1082, Archives New Zealand/ Te Rua Mahara o te Kāwanatanga, Head Office, Wellington.

3 The author is of course aware that he is continuing that tradition; in mitigation, Māori voices are given their place in the text.

4 As, for example, with Best and the production of *Tuhoe: The Children of the Mist*, Board of Maori Ethnological Research (New Plymouth: 1925).

5 See, for example, the numerous letters to Māori newspapers such as *Te Wananga*, where writers begin letters with mihi (greetings) derived from oratory – e.g. 'Ae, tenei au ka karanga, haere mai e Te Wananga kia mihia mai nga mate, nga he, nga raru o iwi e pae nei – Here I call! Come to the Wananga and lament the dead, the wrong, and difficulties of different tribes . . .' (etc.); *Te Wananga*, Vol. 1:6, 29 October 1874, 25.

CHAPTER ONE: 'WHITE NOISE': THE HISTORY OF IDEAS AND THE UREWERA

1 See *Te Puke ki Hikurangi*, 10 April 1905, Vol. 6. No. 8, 3–4. Māori-language newspaper, see www.nzdl.org/cgi-bin/niupepalibrary/, Alexander Turnbull Library, Wellington.

2 'Building set apart for instruction in esoteric lore' – see Williams' *Dictionary of the Maori Language*, 7th edition, Government Publications (Wellington: 1971), 373, 3a.

3 In 1909, existing shearers' unions combined to form the N.Z. Shearers' and Woolshed Employees' Union. In 1910 in the Poverty Bay area, the Gisborne and East Coast Shearers' and Woolshed Employees' Union was set up. The union comprised mainly Māori shearers. Its president was Raihania Rimitiriu, its secretary James K. Morgan, a Māori, of Muritai. Membership of the Gisborne union at first fluctuated between 200 and 300 but jumped to 699 in 1914. In that year the total membership of the New Zealand union was 4093, of whom 1000 were Māori shearers. See letter from H. Roth, *Te Ao Hou*, No. 21 (December

1957), 51; http://teaohou.natlib.govt.nz/journals/teaohou/index.html, ATL.

4 Tūhoe did not sign the Treaty.

5 See Judith Binney, *Redemption Songs: A Life of Te Kooti Arikirangi Te Turuki*, Auckland University Press/Bridget Williams Books (Auckland: 1995), 490. 'Ko te waka hei hoehoenga mo koutou i muri i ahau, ko te Ture, ma te Ture ano te Ture e aki – The canoe for you to paddle after me is the Law. Only the Law will correct the Law'. The 'Law' here referred to is the Old Testament – namely, the Ten Commandments – as it relates to civil law.

CHAPTER TWO: THE END OF TRADITION AND THE FLEETS OF PRINT

1 *The Cassell Concise Dictionary*, Lesley Brown, Consultant Editor, Cassell plc, Orion Publishing Group (London: 1989, 1997), 495.

2 See Anthony Pagden, *The Fall of Natural Man: The American Indian and the Origins of Comparative Ethnology*, Cambridge University Press (Cambridge: 1982), 16.

3 See Ryszard Kapuscinski, *Travels with Herodotus*, Penguin/Allen Lane (London: 2007). See also James Clifford, *Writing Culture*, University of California Press (Berkeley: 1986), 2. 'Ethnography's tradition is that of Herodotus and Montesquieu's Persian. It looks obliquely at all collective arrangements, distant or nearby. It makes the familiar strange, the exotic quotidian.'

4 Louis-Antoine de Bougainville, *The Pacific Journals*, (ed.) John Dunmore, Hakluyt Society (London: 2002).

5 James Cook, (ed.) J. C. Beaglehole, *Selections: The Journals of Captain Cook*, Penguin Books (London: 1999).

6 See, for example, Robert Sullivan, *Captain Cook in the Underworld*, Auckland University Press (Auckland: 2002).

7 James Cook, (ed.) J. C. Beaglehole, *The Voyage of the Endeavour 1768–1771*, Cambridge University Press (Cambridge: 1955), Published for the Hakluyt Society at the University Press.

8 See, for example, Anne Salmond, *Two Worlds: First Meetings Between Maori and Europeans, 1642–1772*, Viking (Auckland: 1993), 87–89, where she describes and analyses Cook's arrival at Whitianga, in November 1769, based on the testimony of Horeta te Taniwha, sourced from John White's *Ancient History of the Maori*, Vol. V (1888), 121–24.

9 These encounters were recalled seventy-four years later (8 December 1843), when the missionary William Colenso visited Waimarama south of Cape Kidnappers: Cook's ship 'and its terrifying *pu* (guns) were still remembered by an old man' from the village (A. G. Bagnall & G. C. Petersen, *William Colenso, Printer, Missionary, Botanist, Explorer, Politician: His Life and Journeys*, Reed (Wellington: 1948), 164; A. H. & A. W. Reed (eds.), *Captain Cook in New Zealand*, Reed (Wellington: 1951), 42; William Colenso *Transactions and Proceedings of the New Zealand Institute*, Vol. 10, 122).

10 For a sound general coverage of ethnographic ideas and imagery in the Pacific in the periods 1760–1860 and 1860–1940, see Kerry Howe, *The Quest for Origins*, Penguin (Auckland: 2003), 27–41, 42–59. For a fuller account of the period, see George Stocking, *Victorian Anthropology*, The Free Press (New York: 1987).

11 See J. L. Nicholas, *Narrative of a Voyage to New Zealand, Vol. 1*, James Black and Son (London: 1817), 86.

12 John Rawson Elder (ed.), *The Letters and Journals of Samuel Marsden 1765–1838*, A. H. & A. W. Reed (Dunedin: 1932), 219–20.

CHAPTER THREE: TE AO HURIHURI: THE WORLD OF CHANGE FOR TŪHOE

1 See Elsdon Best, *Tuhoe: The Children of the Mist*, The Board of Maori Ethnological Research (New Plymouth: 1925), 476. 'He [Tutakangahau] was about 12 years of age when Colenso made his first visit to Rua-tahuna on January 1, 1842 . . . '.

2 See Bronwyn Elsmore, *Like Them That Dream*, Reed (Auckland: 1999, 2004), 3–6. Also S. Percy Smith, *Journal of the Polynesian Society*, Vol. 9, No. 35, 165–66; Best, *Tuhoe*, 533–34, 1045.
3 For this conception of traditional societies, I am indebted to Dr Lyndsay Head of the Māori Department, University of Canterbury, Christchurch, and her teaching in regard to pre-contact and nineteenth-century Māori thought. This new tradition of literate Māori scholarship goes back to the Department's late founder, Bill Te Awaroa Nepia of Ngāti Porou and the late Dr Margaret Orbell.
4 Best, *Tuhoe*, 363.
5 According to Professor Pou Temara, University of Waikato: he made the following remarks in a documentary on Elsdon Best, *Te ara pai o ngā ao rua* (*Best of both worlds*), Hemana Waaka et al. (Māori TV, 2007). 'Tutakangahau was named after a wind that blows in Maungapōhatu. There are three winds in Tūhoe: in Waikare and Maungapōhatu, there is Tutakangahau; in Ruatāhuna there is Uru Kāraerae; in Rūātoki there is Okiwa' (translation by producer).
6 Peter Webster, *Rua and the Māori Millennium*, Price Milburn/Victoria University Press (Wellington: 1979), 84–85.
7 Best, *Tuhoe*, 13. Tamakaimoana were also called Ngāti Huri in Best's day. See also Judith Binney, *Encircled Lands – Part One: A History of the Urewera from European Contact until 1878*, Evidence of Judith Binney, Waitangi Tribunal Report, WAI 999, April 2002, 11–12.
8 Binney, *ibid.*, Chapter 3, note 21, 293.
9 Best, *Tuhoe*, 1026–27.
10 Elsdon Best, 'Maori Forest Lore – Part III', Read before the Auckland Institute, 22 November 1909, *Transactions and Proceedings of the Royal Society of New Zealand, 1868–1961*, Vol. 42, 1909, 433–81, 433.
11 Elsdon Best, 'Maori Forest Lore – Part II', Read before the Auckland Institute, 18 November 1908, *Transactions and Proceedings of the Royal Society of New Zealand, 1868–1961*, Vol. 41, 1908, Art. XXXII, 246; http://rsnz.natlib.govt.nz/volume/rsnz_41/rsnz_41_00_003410.html, Alexander Turnbull Library, Wellington.
12 William and Jane Williams, *The Turanga Journals 1840–1850*, (ed.) Frances Porter, Price Milburn, for Victoria University Press (Wellington: 1974), 137–39. See also Binney, *Encircled Lands: Part One*, 2.2, 38–60.
13 A. G. Bagnall & G. C. Petersen, *William Colenso, Printer, Missionary, Botanist, Explorer, Politician: His Life and Journeys*, A. H. & A. W. Reed (Wellington: 1948), 173. Italics mine. See also Colenso's Diary, December 1843–22 January 1844, 'Memoranda', MSS 67/23d, MSS 65, Hocken Library, University of Otago, Dunedin. These are parts of Colenso's census of Tūhoe: the entry for Te Toreatai mentions an 'old chief, Tapui' and three (native) 'teachers, Tumoana, Hawiki and Tarati'. Of the 20 to 25 present, '9 could read and 3 [had] gone to Opotiki for baptism'.
14 See Webster, *Rua and the Māori Millennium*, 87–89, and Best, *Tuhoe*, 531.
15 Best, *ibid.*, facing 566.
16 Professor Pou Temera, 'Te Kohanga o Tūhoe', speaking on *Waka Huia*, Chapter 3, TV One, 28 June 2008. Available as http://tvnzondemand.co.nz/content/waka_huia_2007/ondemand_video_skin?tab=&sb=date-descending&e=waka_huia_2008_ep16#ep_waka_huia_2008_ep16.
17 Elsdon Best, (ed.) Jeff Evans, *Notes on the art of war: as conducted by the Maori of New Zealand, with accounts of various customs, rites, superstitions, &c., pertaining to war, as practised and believed in by the ancient Maori*, Reed, in association with the Polynesian Society (Auckland: 2001), 10.
18 *Ibid.*, 10–11.
19 See Best, *Tuhoe*, 605 ff.
20 *Ibid.*, 355–56.
21 *Ibid.*, 358.

22 *Ibid.*, 363.
23 *Ibid.*, 474–78.
24 Elsdon Craig, 'Elsdon Best of Tuhoe', *Te Ao Hou*, No. 20, November 1957, 9, ATL.
25 Best, *Tuhoe*, 563.
26 *Ibid.* See also Elsdon Best, *Christian and Maori Mythology: notes on the clash of cultures*, published address given before the Free Discussions Club, Victoria University College, 1924, 5.
27 Elsdon Best, Notebook 11 (1912), qMS 191, 193, 194, Unpublished manuscript, ATL, 34.
28 Marshall McLuhan, *The Gutenberg Galaxy: The Making of Typographical Man*, Routledge & Kegan Paul (London: 1962).

CHAPTER FOUR: WHITE TOHUNGA: BEST ON THE FRONTIER, 1856–1874

1 See *He Pito Whakaatu i te noho a te Māori i Te Tai Rāwhiti/Scenes of Māori Life on the East Coast*, a film by James McDonald, Dominion Museum, F2815 (1923), DVD, Section 1414 ft LS, 27:18 mins, The New Zealand Film Archive/Ngā Kaitiaki O Ngā Taonga Whitiāhua, Wellington.
2 The Māori village of Takapūwāhia is near the head of Porirua Harbour. In the 1840s, the provincial government laid out a number of new inland villages to entice Māori from dilapidated coastal settlements. A survey in 1850 recorded 252 residents at Takapūwāhia. Chris Maclean, 'Wellington places', Te Ara – The Encyclopedia of New Zealand, updated 25 September 2007, URL: http://www.TeAra.govt.nz/Places/Wellington/WellingtonPlaces/en.
3 Ian Wards, *The Shadow of the Land*, Historical Publications Branch, Department of Internal Affairs (Wellington: 1968), 288–89.
4 Arthur H. Carman, *Tawa Flat and the Old Porirua Road 1840–1955*, A. H. Carman (Wellington: 1956), 47, 50.
5 'And ye shall hear of wars and rumours of wars: see that ye be not troubled: for all these things must come to pass, but the end is not yet.' Matthew 24:6, Authorised Version. See also Elsdon Craig, *Man of the Mist*, Reed (Wellington: 1964), 14–17. Information about Best's early life is sourced here from his grandnephew Craig (1917–1980), who wrote the biography as a labour of love in his spare time and during holidays from his work as a journalist on the *New Zealand Herald*. Craig also published an earlier article in *Te Ao Hou* (No. 20, November 1957), 'Elsdon Best of Tuhoe'. He later discusses the making of the biography and gives additional information and opinion on Best in a September 1966 article for *Historical Review* (Vol. 14, No. 3), 'Elsdon Best – a Colonial Image' (Address delivered to the 100th Meeting of the Whakatāne District Historical Society, 16 June 1966). NB: In the 1957 piece from *Te Ao Hou*, he writes: 'I recollect him as a tall rugged individual with a piercing blue eye, who once delighted my boyish interest with a frightening exposition of the haka' (7). Best died when Craig was twelve. However, he writes in the 1966 article for *Historical Review* that he '*never met him personally*, as far as I can remember, I can visualise him as a rather dominating figure, intolerant of those who did not take an interest in the Maori and rather critical of those who did' (italics mine). I am unable to resolve this somewhat glaring contradiction, over a gap of nine years – especially as his daughter Janet Mackey has told me he went as a child with Best, back to the Urewera.
6 K. R. Cassells, *Tawa, Enterprise and Endeavour*, Tawa Borough Council (Tawa, Wellington: 1988), 14–15.
7 Craig, *Man of the Mist*, 18.
8 *Ibid.*
9 Craig, *Te Ao Hou*, 8.
10 Craig, *Man of the Mist*, 19.
11 Carman, *Tawa Flat and the Old Porirua Road*, 34. Letter, Susan Wall, 'Parrurua Road, Dec. 18th, 1842'.
12 Craig, *Man of the Mist*, 12–13.

13 Craig, *Te Ao Hou*, 8.
14 See Carman, *Tawa Flat and the Old Porirua Road*, 113–14. He gives details of their births and deaths, and the end of that particular line of the Best name, the males having no sons. 'I am the last of the Bests left', wrote Miss Madeleine Best on 27 November 1939, five years before she died in 1944.
15 Craig, *Man of the Mist*, 18–22.
16 Craig, 'Elsdon Best – a Colonial Image', 88.
17 Keith Sinclair, *A History of New Zealand – Revised Edition*, Penguin (Auckland: 2000), 42. The author does not, however, share Sinclair's paradigm, where in the quote cited, he begins to construct a progressive teleology of the rise of secular New Zealand and the demise of Christian influence in the nineteenth century. Certainly, Māori adapted the literate new faith to their politics and warfare, and numerous Māori syncretic Christian forms survive and, in the case of Ratana, continue to thrive in the twenty-first century.
18 Craig, *Man of the Mist*, 20–21.
19 See, M. J. S. Rudwick, *Scenes from Deep Time*, University of Chicago Press (Chicago & London: 1992), 173 ff.
20 Conversion estimate supplied by Graham Howard, Reserve Bank of New Zealand, email to author, 5.11.2003: 'This works out to be [very] approximately $92.00 using official CPI data between 1871 and 1920.'
21 Louis Figuier, *The Earth Before the Deluge*, Chapman & Hall (London: 1865), 409.
22 Robert Chambers, *Vestiges of the Natural History of Creation*, John Churchill (London: 1844), W. & R. Chambers (Edinburgh: 1884), Leicester University Press, The Victorian Library (New York: 1969). J. A. Secord, *Victorian Sensation: The Extraordinary Publication, Reception, and Secret Authorship of Vestiges of the Natural History of Creation*, University of Chicago Press (Chicago: 2000).
23 M. J. S. Rudwick, *The Meaning of Fossils*, University of Chicago Press (Chicago & London: 1985), 205–7.
24 Gavin de Beer (ed.), in Chambers, *Vestiges of the Natural History of Creation* (1969), Introduction, 32–36.
25 For a fuller discussion on Best's intellectual roots and development, see Jeffrey Paparoa Holman, 'Best of both worlds: Elsdon Best and the metamorphosis of Māori spirituality. Te painga rawa o ngā ao rua: Te Peehi me te putanga kē o te wairua Māori', PhD thesis, University of Canterbury (Christchurch, New Zealand: 2007), Chapter Two, 86–122, http://hdl.handle.net/10092/939.
26 Rudwick, *The Meaning of Fossils*, 205–7.
27 Chambers, *Vestiges of the Natural History of Creation* (1969), 294–95.
28 *Ibid.*, 306–7.
29 *Ibid.*, 310.
30 *Ibid.*, 322.
31 See Lyndsay Head, 'The Pursuit of Modernity in Māori Society: The Conceptual Bases of Citizenship in the Early Colonial Period', in *Histories, Power and Loss*, (ed.) Sharp & McHugh, Bridget Williams Books (Wellington: 2001), 97–121. Head quotes the Ngāti Kahungunu leader Renata Kawepo (1808?–1888), where he invokes the image of the Māori atua Uenuku the man-eater, in order to confront Superintendent Fitzgerald over the Taranaki land conflict in 1860 – pointing out that the Pākehā's behaviour is unchristian, cannibalistic, and potentially genocidal.

CHAPTER FIVE: TE RIRI ME TE TURE: WAR AND THE LAW, 1864–1893

1 Elsdon Best, *Tuhoe: The Children of the Mist*, The Board of Maori Ethnological Research (New Plymouth: 1925), 567.
2 Bronwyn Elsmore, *Mana from Heaven*, Reed (Auckland: 1989, 1999, 2004), 147.
3 C. Hunter Brown, *Appendices to the Journals of the House of Representatives*, 1862, E-9-Sect. IV, 23–34.

4 Tamakihikurangi, *New Zealand Spectator* (Wellington: 1861), 13–14L.
5 Brown, *AJHR*, 1862, 30.
6 Best, *Tuhoe*, 565–78.
7 *Ibid*.
8 *Ibid*., 567.
9 *Ibid*., 566.
10 *Ibid*., 567.
11 *Ibid*., 576.
12 See Lyndsay Head, 'Te Ua Haumene? – 1866', Dictionary of New Zealand Biography, updated 22 June 2007, URL: http://www.dnzb.govt.nz/. This complete section on the background to Pai Mārire/Hauhau relies on Head's extensive research as seen in the above article. All quotes are from the article in the link above.
13 See Acts, Chapter 2.
14 Best, *Tuhoe*, 578 & 579–81.
15 *Ibid*., 578.
16 'Te Rehu-o-Tainui: the evolution of a Māori atua', *Journal of the Polynesian Society*, Vol. VI (22 June 1897), 41–66.
17 See Elsdon Best, *The Maori: Volume II*, Harry H. Tombs (Wellington: 1924), 289.
18 Best, *Tuhoe*, 579.
19 See Head, 'Te Ua Haumene? – 1866', DNZB, 2007.
20 Best, *Tuhoe*, 581.
21 James Cowan, *The New Zealand Wars and the Pioneering Period, Vol. II: The Hauhau Wars, 1864–1872*, P. D. Hasselberg, Government Printer (Wellington: 1983), 133–34.
22 See Lyndsay Head, 'Land, authority and the forgetting of being in early colonial Māori history', PhD thesis, University of Canterbury (Christchurch: 2006), 229–59. Head provides considerable detail and analysis in depth on issues of Māori citizenship and the place of land in the new dispensation, based on a study of Ngāti Kahungunu documents from the 1840s until the 1860s.
23 Judith Binney, *Encircled Lands – Part One: A History of the Urewera from European Contact until 1878*, Evidence of Judith Binney, Waitangi Tribunal Report, WAI 999, April 2002, 115–16. James Fulloon (1840–1865) was a government interpreter, of Anglo-French and Māori parentage, killed by Pai Mārire at Whakatāne, 22 July 1865.
24 *Ibid*., 98.
25 *Ibid*., 177. Emphasis in source.
26 For further reading on Te Kooti's career, see Cowan, *The New Zealand Wars and the Pioneering Period, Vol. II*, 223–467; James Belich, *The New Zealand Wars and the Victorian Interpretation of Racial Conflict* (Auckland: 1986), 217–88; and Judith Binney, *Redemption Songs: A Life of Te Kooti Arikirangi Te Turuki*, Auckland University Press/Bridget Williams Books (Auckland: 1995).
27 Best, *Tuhoe*, 605–6.
28 Cowan, *The New Zealand Wars and the Pioneering Period, Vol. II*, 269.
29 Binney, *Redemption Songs*, 134.
30 Best, *Tuhoe*, 637.
31 Hira Te Popo to Wepiha Apanui, 22 February 1869, *AJHR*, 1869, A-10, 14–15. Te Popo writes that Te Kooti has gone to Maungapōhatu.
32 Akuhata Te Kaha, Minute Books (5), Māori Land Court, Whakatāne, 6 May 1987, 190, microfilm (cited in Binney, *Encircled Lands – Part One*, 193).
33 From Biddle, private manuscript, cited in Binney, *Redemption Songs*, 154 & *Encircled Lands – Part One*, 193. From a text dated 20 March 1869.
34 Inward correspondence – Gilbert Mair, 1904–1923, MS-Papers-0039–06, James Cowan, Papers (microfilm), MS-Papers-0039, Alexander Turnbull Library, Wellington; cited in Binney, *Encircled Lands – Part One*, 207.
35 Binney, *ibid*., 212–13.

36 Best, *Tuhoe*, 653.
37 *Ibid.*, 655.
38 Cowan, *The New Zealand Wars and the Pioneering Period, Vol. II*, 283–84. He cites 'Colonel Porter' as a source for this account of life in Te Kooti's Urewera camps, given by a prisoner. Best gives his rank as captain at this time.
39 Enclosure 26, *AJHR*, 1871, F-No 1, Friday 19 February, Maungapōhatu, T. W. Porter, Captain and Adjutant, True Extract.
40 *Ibid.*
41 Cowan, *The New Zealand Wars and the Pioneering Period, Vol. II*, 453, 454.
42 Best, *Tuhoe*, 662.
43 Ormond to Te Purewa, 20 November 1871, Agent General Government, Hawke's Bay, 4/8, Supporting Papers, 98. Cited in Binney, *Encircled Lands – Part One*, 259–60.
44 Binney, *ibid.*, 262.
45 See Crown Law Letters, MA 4/104–417, Archives New Zealand/Te Rua Mahara o te Kāwanatanga, Head Office, Wellington. I have not been able to establish when Tutakangahau first became involved in the mail contracts.
46 He opened the Ringatū meeting house of Tūhoe, Eripitana, at Te Whāiti, on 1 January 1883. See Binney, *Redemption Songs*, 268–311.
47 Letters to Ormond, Russell and McLean, 4 December 1873, Agent General Government, Hawke's Bay, HB 2/2, ANZ. Cited in Binney, *Encircled Lands – Part One*, 294. My translation.
48 Thomas Grace, Annual Letter to the Church Missionary Society (1877), No. Box 1, MSS 583 AIM, Auckland Institute and Museum, 285–86.
49 W. L. Williams, *East Coast (N.Z.) Historical Records*, Gisborne (1932), 79–80. Reprinted from the *Poverty Bay Herald*.
50 Herbert W. Brabant to the Minister of Native Affairs, *AJHR*, 1874, G2, 7.
51 *Ibid.*, 8.
52 *AHJR*, 1885, G-1, 11. John Ballance MP was Native Minister, Bryce the former office-holder.
53 See Binney, *Redemption Songs*, 448, 471–72.
54 A. Ward, *A Show of Justice: Racial 'Amalgamation' in Nineteenth Century New Zealand*, Auckland University Press (Auckland: 1995), 271–72.
55 Letter from Tutakangahau to Ormond, June 1872, AGG-HB 2, 2/1, AGG-A 1/1–4, AGG-HB 2/1–3, ANZ. Note: I have not been able to source the Māori original for this particular letter – this is a translation by a government official at the time. Despite some recent criticism of official translations, those translators employed were capable and, for the most part, made correct translations; where both Māori originals and government translations exist side by side, they are only on very rare occasions found to be inaccurate.
56 In this instance, there is most likely a reference to Moses and the seventy elders of Israel, chosen so that he might not bear the burden of leadership alone. See Exodus 24:1, 9–11 and Numbers 11:16, 24–25.
57 14 September 1872, MA 1/1872/1162, Māori Affairs Inward Correspondence, MAICR; 24 December 1872, MA 1/1873/11, MAICR, ANZ.
58 Tutakangahau to Ormond and McLean, 1 December 1872, AGG-HB 2/1, ANZ.
59 Binney, *Encircled Lands – Part One*, 281.
60 Tutekanahau [Tutakangahau] to Preece, 1 December 1872, AGG-HB 2/1, ANZ.
61 See Binney, *Encircled Lands – Part One*, 290.
62 'Notes of Speeches made at the Native Meeting, Ruatahuna, March 23–24, 1874', *AJHR*, 1874, G-1A, 4–5.
63 Robert Price, *Through the Uriwera Country*, Napier Daily Telegraph (Napier: 1891), 44–45.
64 Binney, *Encircled Lands – Part One*, 324–25.

65 *Ibid.*, 325. Tutakangahau to Brabant, 11 September 1874, MS-Papers-0032–0171, ATL. Contemporary translation.
66 Binney, *ibid.*, 364, 266.

CHAPTER SIX: BEST MATURES: FROM PARIHAKA TO THE POLYNESIAN SOCIETY, 1874–1892

1 The general biographical timeline here and incidental details are sourced from Craig's biography, *Man of the Mist*, Reed (Wellington: 1964), 23–51.
2 *Ibid.*, 24.
3 Dick Scott, *Ask That Mountain*, Reed/Southern Cross (Auckland 1975), 130. Bryce was the Native Minister in charge of the ethnic cleansing operation.
4 George Stocking, 'Matthew Arnold, E. B. Tylor, and the Uses of Invention', *American Anthropologist*, Vol. 65 (August 1963), 783–99, 784.
5 *Ibid.*
6 Elsdon Best, *Comparative anthropology – its scope and advantages* (1920), MS-Papers-0072–33, Alexander Turnbull Library, Wellington, Notes of lecture given to WEA, Wellington.
7 George Stocking, *Victorian Anthropology*, The Free Press (New York: 1987), 48.
8 Stocking, 'Matthew Arnold, E. B. Tylor, and the Uses of Invention', 785.
9 *Ibid.*
10 *Ibid.*, 788.
11 Elsdon Craig notes in an appendix to his biography *Man of the Mist* (1964: 239) that he had consulted an 1870 edition of Taylor's *Te Ika a Maui* 'annotated by Best'. This book and many others had come to Craig from Best's widow Adelaide, and was sold at auction in Auckland, November 2003, after the death of Craig's widow, Zita. The book passed into the hands of a private collector, who allowed the author of this study to go through it and record Best's annotations. These can be found in an addenda to the chapter appendices in the author's thesis, 'Best of both worlds: Elsdon Best and the metamorphosis of Māori spirituality. Te painga rawa o ngā ao rua: Te Peehi me te putanga kē o te wairua Māori', PhD thesis, University of Canterbury (Christchurch: 2007), 397 ff.
12 For a full account of Taylor's life, see J. M. R. Owens, *The Mediator: A Life of Richard Taylor 1805–1873*, Victoria University Press (Wellington: 2004).
13 Richard Taylor, *Te Ika a Maui, or New Zealand and its inhabitants*, 2nd edition, William McIntosh/London; H. Ireson Jones/Wanganui (1870), 62.
14 *Ibid.*, 67 ff. John Crawfurd (1783–1868) was a Scottish Orientalist and colonial administrator employed by the East India Company. He became President of the British Ethnological Society in 1861 and was an ardent polygenist. Best was later to become familiar with his writings on Malay peoples.
15 *Ibid.*, 79.
16 *Ibid.*, 87. See Genesis 9:18–29.
17 *Ibid.*, 88. Taylor wrote of three stages of colonisation in New Zealand's history: '. . . the black race . . . by Maori . . . and lastly, by the Anglo-Saxon'. Best has crossed out 'the black race'. See 711.
18 *Ibid.*, 90.
19 *Ibid.*, 99.
20 *Ibid.*, 330–31.
21 See Elsdon Best, *The Maori As He Was*, A. R. Shearer, Government Printer (Wellington: 1974 [1924]), 24–25. This is a facsimile of the 1924 edition.
22 The following outline of Best's American sojourn and those details and quotes are all taken from Craig's *Man of the Mist* (1964), unless otherwise acknowledged. This is to avoid repetition of footnotes.
23 Katherine Best is buried with her parents William and Hannah, and her grandfather, in a family plot on the upper level of the Bolton Street cemetery, Wellington, at the top of Powles Path.

24 Elsdon Best, 'The Races of the Philippines', Parts I–II, *Journal of the Polynesian Society*, Vol. 1 (1892), 7–19, 119–201. This was reprinted in 1925 in a collection entitled *Spanish Philippine History and the Beginnings of Philippine Nationalism*, National Book Company (Manila: 1925). Thirty years on, his work on Philippines ethnography was still regarded with some respect – a sign of his recognition in the international anthropological community.

25 Report of the Exhibition opening, 'New Orleans Happy with its World Fair', *New York Times*, 16 December 1884. The other information was obtained from a public domain website: http://tinyurl.com/nr4rjo.

26 Holman, 'Best of both worlds: Elsdon Best and the metamorphosis of Māori spirituality', 186. See also Elsdon Best, 'The Darkened Mind', *Canterbury Times*, 4 July 1906, 62.

27 M. P. K. Sorrenson, *Maori Origins and Migrations*, Auckland University Press/Oxford University Press (Auckland: 1979), 75–76.

28 Elsdon Best, 'The Races of the Philippines', Pts I–II, *JPS*, Vol. 1 (Wellington: 1892), 7–19, 118–125, 195–201.

29 *Ibid.*, 5. To avoid repetitive endnotes, the remaining references to this article will not be noted, but simply appear in quotes until the discussion based on it ends.

30 E. B. Tylor, *Primitive Culture*, Murray (London: 1873), Pt I, 1, Pt II, 410.

31 Best, 'The Races of the Philippines', 13.

32 Tony Ballantyne, *Orientalism and Race: Aryanism in the British Empire*, Palgrave (Houndmills, Basingstoke, Hampshire/New York: 2002), 16.

33 Kerry Howe, *The Quest for Origins*, Penguin (Auckland: 2003), 43.

34 Edward Tregear, 'The Maori in Asia', *Transactions and Proceedings of the Royal Society of New Zealand, 1868–1961*, Vol. 18 (1885), 3. Read before the Philosophical Society, Wellington, 12 August 1885.

35 F. Max Müller, *Selected Essays on Language, Mythology and Religion, Vol. I*, Longman, Green & Co. (London: 1881), 299–451, especially 320, 355–57, 362–65. All references in this discussion are there.

36 Elsdon Best, *The Maori: Pt 1*, Memoirs of the Polynesian Society, Vol. V, Board of Maori Ethnological Research (Wellington: 1924), 125; *Maori Religion and Mythology*, Pt 2, Dominion Museum Bulletin No. 11, Te Papa Press (Wellington: 1924, 1982), 626.

37 See Craig, *Man of the Mist*, Appendix II, 239. Best's copy of Müller was sold at auction in May 1969 by B. A. Sturt & Co. of Auckland on behalf of Elsdon Craig, 'inscribed E.B. 1895, with bookplate, brief annotations, $4.00'. Craig Collection, MS-Papers-7888–039, ATL.

CHAPTER SEVEN: 'KI TĀ TE KĀWANATANGA TE MUTUNGA – THE GOVERNMENT WILL HAVE ITS WAY IN THE END'

1 Surveyor Wilson's report on triangulation surveys in the Urewera, June 1895, Lands and Survey records, LS-1, 21734, Pt 2, 3, Māori text, 5, official translation, Archives New Zealand/Te Rua Mahara o te Kāwanatanga, Head Office, Wellington.

2 Ryszard Kapuscinski, *Travels with Herodotus*, Allen Lane/Penguin (London: 2007), 83.

3 Elsdon Best, *Tuhoe: The Children of the Mist*, The Board of Maori and Ethnological Research (New Plymouth: 1925), 667, 665. The recent hostile and choreographed response to the arrival of the Waitangi Tribunal as they crossed the confiscation line for sittings on marae in the Rūātoki area was a reminder of the strength of feeling that remained from this era (16 January 2005). The October 2007 police raids in the same district have only inflamed distrust and accentuated the sense of grievance.

4 'Mr S Locke's Trip to the Urewera Country', *Appendices to the Journal of the House of Representatives*, 1889, G-6, 1.

5 Letter of nine chiefs to the Honourable Native Minister (translation), 17 April 1889, *AJHR*, 1889, G-6, 2.

6 C. Lesley Andrews, 'Aspects of Development, 1870–1890', in *Conflict and Compromise: Essays on the Maori Since Colonisation*, (ed.) Sir Hugh Kawharu, Reed (Auckland: 1975, 2003), 84.

7 Judith Binney, *Redemption Songs: A Life of Te Kooti Arikirangi Te Turuki*, Auckland University Press / Bridget Williams Books (Auckland: 1995), 445–47.
8 'A. Foster to Native Office', 3 March 1893, J1 1893/515, Box 439, ANZ. Cited in Anita Miles, *Te Urewera*, Rangahau Whanui District 4, March 1999, Working Paper: First Release, Waitangi Tribunal, Wellington, 245.
9 *Auckland Star*, 23 March 1891, cited in Judith Binney, *Encircled Lands – Part Two: A History of the Urewera, 1878–1912*, Evidence of Judith Binney, Waitangi Tribunal Report, WAI 999, June 2002, 28.
10 Binney, *Encircled Lands – Part Two*, 20.
11 See Miles, *Te Urewera*, 247–48, citing Kereru to Native Minister, 8 March 1893, J1 1893/515, and Creagh to Cadman, telegram, 15 June 1893, J1 1893/515, ANZ. The fine and sentences arising were remitted in June 1895, after Seddon and Carroll had visited the Urewera in 1894.
12 Best, *Tuhoe*, 663. Best also notes here the magico-religious way in which Te Kooti is reputed by a follower to have destroyed his enemies, using powers derived 'from the Psalms of David'.
13 Cathy Marr, *Urewera District Native Reserve Act 1896 and Amendments*, Waitangi Tribunal Report No. A21, WAI 999 (Wellington: 2002), 24.
14 See Alan Ward, *A Show of Justice*, Auckland University Press (Auckland: 1975, 1995), 294–315; T. Brooking, '"Busting Up" the Greatest Estate of All: Liberal Maori Land Policy, 1891–1911', *New Zealand Journal of History*, 26:1 (Auckland: 1992), 78–98; Marr, *Urewera District Native Reserve Act 1896 and Amendments*, 21–22.
15 See *AJHR*, 1895, G-1, 1–89. All remaining quotes relating to this particular meeting come from this source, and will not be separately endnoted.
16 MA 4/103–695, Letter from Waldegrave, Secretary, to Seddon, Native Minister, Wellington, 9 December 1895, to 'Tutakanahau, Maungapohatu, via Whakatane', Māori Affairs files, ANZ.
17 Translation by government official, 23 July 1895, 21734/150, Repro. 1801 (2 of 2), LS-1, 21734, Pt 2, ANZ.
18 LS-1, 21734/120, Pt 2, telegram to Percy Smith, Surveyor-General, from Phillips, ANZ.
19 Translation by government official, letter to Seddon and Carroll, 7 July 1895, LS-1, 21734, Pt 2, ANZ.
20 See LS-1, 21734, Pt 2, ANZ.
21 *Ibid.*, 3 in Māori text, 6 in translation. Paraki's remark at Ruatāhuna (cited next) appears on 6 in the Māori/11 in translation.
22 *Ibid.*, 6/11. The Māori section is partially obscured by fire damage, but is legible. See Proverbs 25:21, Romans 12:20.
23 Marr, *Urewera District Native Reserve Act 1896 and Amendments*, 66–70.
24 J1 1897/1389, Notes of Meeting with Urewera chiefs, Carroll and Seddon, 7 September 1895, 1–58 (5–6), ANZ. My emphasis.
25 *Ibid.*, 50–51, 52, 55.
26 Marr, *Urewera District Native Reserve Act 1896 and Amendments*, 48.
27 J1 1897/1389, Notes of Meeting with Urewera chiefs, 50, 48, 51. My emphasis.
28 Marr, *Urewera District Native Reserve Act 1896 and Amendments*, 55.
29 *Auckland Star*, Saturday, 21 September 1895. Document Bank, Waitangi Tribunal, Cathy Marr, WAI 894, #21, 266.
30 Letter to Percy Smith, 26 January 1896, LS-1, 21734/169, Repro. 1801, ANZ. My emphasis.
31 J1 1896/1802, Tutakangahau to Seddon, ANZ.
32 Letter from James Carroll to Tutakangahau, 7 August 1896, MA 4/102–78, ANZ. See also original note by Carroll on translation of Tutakangahau's letter of 29 June 1896, J1 96/1082, ANZ.
33 Tukua Te Rangi to Smith, 23 December 1895, LS-1, 21734, Pt 2, ANZ. He also asks Smith to hurry up and pay him for his services – 'kia tere ta utu mai'.

CHAPTER EIGHT: INTO THE MIST: IN SEARCH OF THE 'MYTHOPOETIC MAORI'

1 James Clifford, *Writing Culture: The Poetics and Politics of Ethnography*, University of California Press (Berkeley: 1986), 2.
2 Percy Smith, cited in Elsdon Craig, *Man of the Mist*, Reed (Wellington: 1964), 55.
3 Best defines this as 'the *kura huna* – the "concealed treasure" (of knowledge)' in *Waikaremoana: The Sea of the Rippling Waters*, A. R. Shearer, Government Printer (Wellington: 1975 [1897]), 9. Literally, 'teaching – hidden'. This becomes his shorthand for esoteric Māori knowledge.
4 'I have really done no whakapapa-ing for the past 3 weeks. Yet the faculty are working for me and I receive messages from Te Whaiti telling me of the treasures that await me.' Best, letter to Percy Smith, 14.8.1895, Elsdon Craig Collection, MS-Papers-7888–063, Alexander Turnbull Library, Wellington.
5 See Craig, *Man of the Mist*, 56.
6 See Craig, *ibid.*, 56–57. Best's relationship with Paitini lasted into the 1920s; he is seen appearing with him in James MacDonald's ethnographic film. See *He Pito Whakaatu i Te Hui i Rotorua: Scenes at the Rotorua Hui*, a film by James McDonald, F2808 (1920), 10:03 mins, Elsdon Best with Paitini Wi Tapeka of Ruatāhuna, New Zealand Film Archive / Ngā Kaitiaki O Ngā Taonga Whitiāhua, Wellington.
7 Elsdon Craig, Notes for *Man of the Mist*, MS-Papers-7888–024, Craig Papers, ATL, 77. This folder contains the hand-copied notes made by Best's biographer from sources in the Turnbull Library and elsewhere. As a trained journalist, Craig transcribed entire letters to take away, in an era prior to photocopying. While the source for this particular quote is illegible, his copies can reasonably be relied upon – those where he has typed up copies of Best's letters match the available originals.
8 Talal Asad (ed.), *Anthropology and the Colonial Encounter*, Humanity Books (New York: 1973, 1998), 12.
9 *Ibid.*, 16–17.
10 Best, letter to Percy Smith from Te Whāiti, 20.2.1896, MS-0072–08, ATL.
11 Best, letter to Percy Smith, Surveyor-General, Wellington, from Te Whāiti, 20.2.1896, Repro. 1801, LS-1, 21734/64, Pt 2, Archives New Zealand/Te Rua Mahara o te Kāwanatanga, Head Office, Wellington.
12 Letter from Tutakangahau to Percy Smith, Surveyor-General, Te Whāiti, 10 April 1896, LS-1, 21734, ANZ.
13 Tutakangahau, letter to Seddon, 29 June 1896, J1 1896/1082, ANZ. Translation by government official.
14 Tutakangahau, letter to Percy Smith, 29 June 1896, Urewera Surveys, LS-1, 21734, 2/2, ANZ.
15 Best, letter to Smith undated, *c.* 1895, MS-0072–08, ATL. This dating is possible by the context of other early letters in this folder.
16 Pencil note on whakapapa list sent to Smith dated '6.7.95', MS-0072–08, ATL.
17 Letter to Smith, February 1896, MS-0072–08, ATL.
18 Elsdon Best, 'Spiritual Concepts of the Maori', Pt II, *Journal of the Polynesian Society*, Vol. X: 37 (Wellington: 1901), 14.
19 Letter to Smith, 'Camp Te Whaiti 20.2.96', MS-0072–08, ATL.
20 Best, *Waikaremoana: The Sea of Rippling Waters*, Preface, 6–7.
21 *Ibid.*, 9.
22 *Ibid.*
23 *Ibid.*, 26.
24 *Ibid.*, 27–28.
25 *Ibid.*, 28–29.
26 *Ibid.*, 29–30.
27 *Ibid.*, 41.

28 *Ibid.*, 46.
29 *Ibid.*, 48.
30 *Ibid.*
31 *Ibid.*
32 *Ibid.*, 49. Best's notes are as follows: '* Bible; any large book used for recording is so called by the Maoris. ‡ Knowledge, valuable possession'.
33 *Ibid.*, 83. The ethnomusicologist Mervyn McLean has indicated that this was the fate of a number of these old cylinders. They may well have been unplayable, as they did wear out, and there is no way now of knowing if they had been deposited there by Best. Personal correspondence, email, 2004.
34 *Ibid.*, 91–92.
35 'From Tuhoeland', *Canterbury Times* (Christchurch), 9 July 1902, 55.
36 'On Solitude and the Primitive Mind', *Canterbury Times* (Christchurch), 22 October 1902, 53. P. G. Hamerton, *Thoughts about Art*, Macmillan (London: 1873), 234.
37 R. W. Emerson, (eds.) Bode & Cowley, *The Portable Emerson*, Penguin (New York: 1981), 99.
38 *Ibid.*
39 Margaret Orbell & Geoff Moon, *The Natural World of the Māori*, Collins/David Bateman (Auckland: 1985), 216–17.
40 Letter to Percy Smith, n/d 1895–96, MS-0072–08, ATL.
41 See Craig, *Man of the Mist*, 75, and 76–81 for the account of Marewa's short relationship with Best and her early death.
42 *Ibid.*, 77.
43 *Ibid.*, 78–81.
44 *Ibid.*, 56.
45 Personal conversation with author, 2007. Name withheld.
46 Elsdon Best, 'In Tuhoe Land', *The Press* (Christchurch), 18 January 1897.
47 Elsdon Best, 'The Present Condition of the Tuhoe Tribe', *The Press* (Christchurch), 22 March 1897, 5–6.
48 In Craig, Notes, MS-Papers-7888–024, ATL. This is Craig's copy of a quote from Best – no reference. '. . . Such minds as Solomon and coy who ruled his hapu as a wild old patriarch . . . E hoa! his name is Tutakangahau . . .'.
49 Elsdon Best, *Canterbury Times* (Christchurch), 16 September 1897.
50 Elsdon Best, *Canterbury Times* (Christchurch), 6 January 1898, 49.
51 Elsdon Best, 'Te Rehu-o-Tainui: the evolution of a Maori atua', *JPS*, Vol. VI: 22 (June 1897), 41–66, 42.
52 See Elsdon Craig, 'Notes for a biography', MS-Papers-7888–024, ATL, 71.
53 Best, 'Te Rehu-o-Tainui: the evolution of a Maori atua', 42–43.
54 *Ibid.*, 42, 65.
55 *Ibid.*, 44. See also *Waikaremoana*, 48.
56 *Ibid.*, 65–66.
57 Best, 'Spiritual Concepts of the Maori', *JPS*, Pts I & II (Pt I, Vol. IX: 36, December 1900, 173–199; Pt II, Vol. X: 37, March 1901, 1–19).
58 *Ibid.*, Pt II, 2–7.
59 *Ibid.*, 3–4.
60 F. Max Müller, *Anthropological Religion: The Gifford Lectures*, Vol. III, Longman (London: 1898).
61 See Craig, *Man of the Mist*, 239.
62 Report of the Waitangi Tribunal, Manukau Claim, 07 Specific Claims: 7.2 Slurry Pipeline and the Mixing of Waters, WAI 8, Waitangi Tribunal, 1985–85.
63 Keri Hulme, 'Mauri: An Introduction to Bicultural Poetry in New Zealand', in *Only Connect: Literary Perspectives East and West*, (eds.) Amirthanayagam & Harrex, Centre for Research in the New Literatures in English & East-West Centre (Adelaide & Honolulu:

1981), 290–310, 290.

64 Elsdon Best, 'Art. LII. – Maori Forest Lore: Being some Account of Native Forest Lore and Woodcraft, as also of many Myths, Rites, Customs, and Superstitions connected with the Flora and Fauna of the Tuhoe or Ure-wera District. – Part III', *Transactions and Proceedings of the Royal Society of New Zealand*, Vol. 42, 1909, 433–81.

65 *Ibid.*, 437.

66 *Ibid.*, 442.

67 *Ibid.*, 452.

68 *Ibid.*

69 Letter to Percy Smith, Ruatāhuna, 29.8.1902 (p. 13), Best's Correspondence, MS Papers-1187–249, ATL.

70 *Ibid.*, letter to Smith, Rūātoki, 8.9.1905.

71 See *Te Puke ki Hikurangi*, 10 April 1905, Vol. 6, No. 8, 3–4. Māori-language newspaper. (See www.nzdl.org/cgi-bin/niupepalibrary/, ATL.)

72 Best, 'Art. LII. – Maori Forest Lore', 452–53. His translation.

73 *Ibid.*, 453.

74 Elsdon Best, *Comparative Anthropology – its scope and advantages*, Unpublished manuscript of public address to the Workers' Educational Association (WEA), Trentham, Wellington, September 1920, MS Papers-0072–33, ATL.

75 Letter from Waldegrave, Secretary, Office of the Solicitor-General, Wellington, 31 August 1898, 'To Tutakangahau, c/- Mrs C. Smith, Molesworth St.', MA4/102–434, ANZ.

CHAPTER NINE: 'A TERRITORY FOR THE MAORI PEOPLE AND THE INDIGENOUS BIRDS': TŪHOE AND THE ROHE PŌTAE, 1896–1909

1 J1 1897/1389, Wi Pere, MP, Notes of Meeting with Urewera chiefs, Carroll and Seddon, 7 September 1895, Archives New Zealand/Te Rua Mahara o te Kāwanatanga, Head Office, Wellington, 1–58, 50–51, 52, 55.

2 Anita Miles, *Te Urewera*, Rangahaua Whanui District 4, March 1999, Working Paper: First Release, Waitangi Tribunal, Wellington, 503. See also Richard Boast, *Buying the Land, Selling the Land: Governments and Maori Land in the North Island 1865–1921*, Victoria University Press (Wellington: 2008), 202–12.

3 R. M. Burdon, *King Dick*, Whitcombe & Tombs (Christchurch: 1955), 194–98, 204.

4 *Meeting between the Premier and Chiefs of the Tuhoe Tribe, at Parliament Buildings, Wellington, 26th September, 1898*, MS-Papers-0448–16, Notes of Meetings, Alexander Turnbull Library, Wellington. All notes in this section on the meeting refer to this document, unless otherwise noted.

5 *Ibid.*, 60–61.

6 *Ibid.*, 61.

7 Lyndsay Head, 'The Pursuit of Modernity in Māori Society: The Conceptual Bases of Citizenship in the Early Colonial Period', in *Histories, Power and Loss*, (eds.) Sharp & McHugh, Bridget Williams Books (Wellington: 2001), 119. These remarks were made in relation to Renata Kawepo's stand on the Taranaki wars in the 1860s, but apply equally here thirty years on.

8 *Meeting between the Premier and Chiefs of the Tuhoe Tribe*, 62.

9 *Ibid.*, 66.

10 *Ibid.*, 63.

11 *Ibid.*, 62, 61.

12 *Ibid.*, 61.

13 *Ibid.*, 63.

14 Angela Ballara, *Iwi: The Dynamics of Māori Tribal Organisation from c. 1769 to c. 1945*, Victoria University Press (Wellington: 1998), 310. See also Native Lands Settlement and Administration Bill (proposed), *AJHR*, 1898, I-3A and 1899, I-3A.

15 *Meeting between the Premier and Chiefs of the Tuhoe Tribe*, 63. My emphasis.

16 *Ibid.*, 64.
17 *Ibid.* Seddon responds to 'the remarks of our young friend Tukuaterangi' when addressing the matter of this Bill – when it is obvious his father was recorded as having made them, just prior. There is the possibility that the son echoed his father's words: he was present, but little is recorded here of any comment he made, save for some salutations towards the end of the report.
18 *Ibid.*, 65.
19 Head, 'The Pursuit of Modernity in Māori Society', 121.
20 *Meeting between the Premier and Chiefs of the Tuhoe Tribe*, 65.
21 See Richard Hill, 'Elsdon Best and Tuhoe: A Cautionary Tale', *Historical Review, Bay of Plenty*, Vol. 36, No. 2, November 1988 (Whakatāne and District Historical Society), 127–30. Also, Elsdon Craig, *Man of the Mist*, Reed (Wellington: 1964), 91–92.
22 Craig, *ibid.*, 91–94.
23 Cathy Marr, *Urewera District Native Reserve Act 1896 and Amendments*, Waitangi Tribunal Report No. A21, WAI 9999 (Wellington: 2002), 137–38.
24 *New Zealand Parliamentary Debates*, 24 September 1896, Vol. 96, 160.
25 *New Zealand Parliamentary Debates*, October 1905, Vol. 135, 963.
26 See Miles, *Te Urewera*; Binney, *Encircled Lands*; and Marr, *Urewera District Native Reserve Act*: Waitangi Tribunal reports on the Urewera claims.
27 Miles, *Te Urewera*, 288.
28 *Urewera Minute Book 3*, 26 February 1900, 137, ANZ.
29 Miles, *Te Urewera, op. cit.*
30 S. Percy Smith, in 'Annual Report on Department of Lands and Survey', *AJHR*, 1899, C-1, xi.
31 Judith Binney, *Untold Lives: When the Elders tell their Stories*, Hocken Lecture 2: 2007, University of Otago (Dunedin: 2008), 16–17.
32 Miles, *Te Urewera*, 291.
33 *Urewera Minute Book 2*, 19, ANZ.
34 Letter, Tutakangahau to Percy Smith, 24 July 1900, J1 1898/1011, ANZ.
35 Letter, Hurae Puketapu to Percy Smith, 25 June 1900, Polynesian Society Papers, MS-1187–297, ATL.
36 Marr, *Urewera District Native Reserve Act*, 136.
37 *Urewera Minute Book 4*, 18, ANZ. Cited in Marr, *Urewera District Native Reserve Act*, 143.
38 Miles, *Te Urewera*, 293.
39 Vincent O'Malley, *Agents of Autonomy: Maori Committees in the Nineteenth Century*, Crown Forestry Rental Trust (Wellington: 1997), 179.
40 See Dudley Alexander, 'Journey Through the Urewera Country' (1904), diary entries and photographs. Alexander was Ranfurly's chief aide-de-camp. Ranfurly Collection, MSY-4600, 25–27, ATL.
41 See Michael King, *The Penguin History of New Zealand*, Penguin (Auckland: 2003), 326–27.
42 Malcolm Ross, *Through Tuhoe Land* (1 album), PA1-q-634, ATL. See also *Through Tuhoe Land: Lord Ranfurly's Farewell to the Maori People*, Christchurch Press (Christchurch: 1904).
43 Otherwise referred to in the text as 'Poison', an assumed transliteration.
44 Ross, *Through Tuhoe Land: Lord Ranfurly's Farewell to the Maori People*, 35.
45 *Ibid.*, 37.
46 *Ibid.*, 39.
47 *Ibid.*, 40.
48 *Ibid.*, 46–47. Emphasis added.
49 Ross, *Through Tuhoe Land*, 18 (132, alternative numbering), ATL.
50 Ross, *Through Tuhoe Land: Lord Ranfurly's Farewell to the Maori People*, 60–61. It resembled the somewhat warmer greeting that would a century later be given to members of the

Waitangi Tribunal, arriving for a sitting at the same marae, in January 2005.
51 Alexander, 'Journey Through the Urewera Country', 26.
52 Ross, *Through Tuhoe Land*, 20 (134).
53 Alexander, 'Journey Through the Urewera Country', *op. cit.*
54 Ross, *Through Tuhoe Land: Lord Ranfurly's Farewell to the Maori People*, 65.
55 *Ibid.*, 66–67.
56 *Ibid.*, 69–70.
57 *Ibid.*, 73–74.
58 Alexander, 'Journey Through the Urewera Country', 4.
59 *Ibid.*
60 Ranfurly Collection, Turnbull Letters 1905, MS-Papers-6357–11, ATL.
61 See Mrs E. Murphy Album, PA1-o-357, ATL.
62 James Carroll, letter to Lord Ranfurly, 10 March 1905, MS-Papers-6357–11, ATL.
63 Maui Pomare, letter to Lord Ranfurly, 22 May 1905, *ibid.* See also Malcolm Ross, letter to Lord Ranfurly, 22 June 1905, *ibid.*
64 Marr, *Urewera District Native Reserve Act*, 163.
65 See: Letter from Native Affairs, Wellington, to Tutakangahau, Ruatāhuna, 10 August 1906, MA 4/104–417, ANZ. This letter and the circumstances surrounding it will be discussed in the next chapter.
66 *AJHR*, 1908, G-1A, 1.
67 Marr, *Urewera District Native Reserve Act*, 508–10.
68 *Ibid.*, 514.

CHAPTER TEN: 'WIPED OFF THE SLATE OF LIFE': THE LAST OF THE 'MOHIOS'

1 Elsdon Best, *Tuhoe: The Children of the Mist*, The Board of Maori and Ethnological Research (New Plymouth: 1925), 351. 'The last two years have wiped my old teachers off the slate of life, save one who has cleaved to the New Messiah. And I alone am left.'
2 For a full account of this phenomenon, see Curnow & McRae (eds.), *Rere Atu, Taku Manu!: Discovering History, Language and Politics in the Māori-language Newspapers*, (eds.) Curnow & McRae, Auckland University Press (Auckland: 2002).
3 This letter and the others referred to may be found on the University of Waikato's Digital Library on the following URL: http://nzdl.sadl.uleth.ca/cgi-bin/library, Alexander Turnbull Library, Wellington.
4 See Steven Chrisp, 'The Tribal Society of the Wairarapa Newspapers', in Curnow & McRae (eds.), *Rere Atu, Taku Manu!*, 193–210.
5 *Ibid.*, 194, 196–97.
6 *Ibid.*, 193–97. See also D. R. Simmons, 'The Words of Te Matorohanga', *Journal of the Polynesian Society*, Vol. 103, No. 2, June 1994, 115–70 for further background on the work of the Tanenuiarangi Committee in preserving whakapapa and kōrero, and the relationship between Te Whatahoro Jury, Percy Smith and Best.
7 See Judith Binney, *Redemption Songs: A Life of Te Kooti Arikirangi Te Turuki*, Auckland University Press/Bridget Williams Books (Auckland: 1995), 298.
8 Letter, Best to Smith, 7.10.1905, MS-Papers-7888–023, ATL.
9 *Te Puke ki Hikurangi*, 12 June 1905, Vol. 6, No. 13, 2.
10 See Best, *Tuhoe*, where he refers to 'false genealogies' sometimes given by claimants in the Native Land Court 'in support of a claim for certain lands', 20–21.
11 See D. R. Simmons, 'The Words of Te Matorohanga', 121.
12 Tutakangahau was aware of the work of Te Whatahoro in the collection and collation of whakapapa; see his letter of May 1906 to Kiingi Whatuiapiti where he discusses an upcoming whakapapa hui at Tamakinuiarua (Dannevirke), and the work of Niniwa and Whatahoro, where the knowledge of Rangi and Papa will again be made manifest. *Te Puke ki Hikurangi*, 18 May 1906, Vol. 32, 4.

13 See Judith Binney, 'Rua Kenana Hepetipa 1868/1869? – 1937', Dictionary of New Zealand Biography, updated 22 June 2007, http://www.dnzb.govt.nz/; also Binney et al., *Mihaia: The Prophet Rua and His Community at Maungapōhatu*, Oxford University Press (Auckland: 1979); and Peter Webster, *Rua and the Maori Millennium*, Price Milburn/Victoria University Press (Wellington: 1979).
14 Binney et al., *ibid*., 30–31.
15 Best, *Tuhoe*, 351.
16 See: Letter, 22 October 1907, in MA 1/1907/27, Archives New Zealand/Te Rua Mahara o te Kāwanatanga, Head Office, Wellington.
17 Letter to Tutakangahau from the Secretary, Native Department, 10 August 1906, MA 4/104–417, ANZ.
18 For a background to this Act, see Webster, *Rua and the Maori Millennium*, 221–23; and Binney et al., *Mihaia*, 35–36.
19 Webster, *ibid*., 223.
20 Binney et al., *Mihaia*, 36.
21 Letter to Smith, 2.1.08, MS-Papers-7888–024, Craig Papers, ATL.
22 Letter to Smith, 11.6.06, *ibid.*
23 Webster, *Rua and the Maori Millennium*, 230–35.
24 Jonathan Easthope, *A History of the Maungapohatu and Tauranga Blocks*, Report for The Crown Forestry Rental Trust (2002), 160, citing Vincent O'Malley, *The Crown's Acquisition of the Waikaremoana Block, 1921–1925*, Report for the Panekiri Tribal Trust Board (May 1996).
25 Judith Binney, cited in Jonathan Easthope, *Urewera Overview Project, Pt II, 1878–1912*, History Department, University of Auckland (June 2002).
26 Best, *Tuhoe*, 605–6. In this brief whakapapa, the relationship descends from Mokonui of Ngāti Rakei and his wife Hau-ki-waho of Ngāti Ruapani. Two of their children were Tutakangahau's father, Tapui and his sister Hineko, Rua's great-grandmother. It appears from the evidence of this whakapapa that Tutakangahau and Kopae, Rua's grandfather on his father Kenana's side, were cousins. Judith Binney has a different reading, based on Rua's evidence at his trial for sedition in 1916, that his famous flag had been first obtained by his '"grandfather" – that is Tutakangahau (his grandfather's elder brother)'. That Rua classed his elder relative as a 'grandfather' is not necessarily meant to be taken literally: 'tūpuna', 'koroua' or 'kaumātua' can simply be a general term for a related elder. See Binney, *Untold Lives: When the Elders Tell Their Stories*, Hocken Lecture 2: 2007, The Hocken Collections, University of Otago (Dunedin: 2007), 17.
27 See Elsdon Craig, *Man of the Mist*, Reed (Wellington: 1964), 116–22.
28 Jeffrey Sissons, *Te Waimana – The Spring of Mana: Tuhoe History and the Colonial Encounter*, University of Otago Press (Dunedin: 1991), 5.
29 Best, *Tuhoe*, 595.
30 *Ibid.*
31 Elsdon Best, 'The Darkened Mind', *Canterbury Times* (Christchurch), 4 July 1906, 62.
32 Letter to Smith, 11.6.06, MS-Papers-7888–024, Elsdon Craig Papers, ATL; Craig, *Man of the Mist*, 121.
33 *AJHR*, 1907, H-31, 58. This report of Best as the local health officer contains the aforementioned appellation, 'Kekataone – crazy town'.
34 *Ibid.*
35 Best, 'The Darkened Mind', 62.
36 Binney et al., *Mihaia*, 109–10.
37 See S. Percy Smith, *Hawaiki: The Original Home of the Maori, With a Sketch of Polynesian History*, 4th edition, Whitcombe & Tombs (Auckland: 1921), 59; Best, *The Maori*, Vol. I, Harry H. Tombs (Wellington: 1924), 21–22.
38 Huhana Tutakangahau to Under Secretary, Native Department, 12 July 1923, Urewera Consolidation, MA 29/4/7, 1, ANZ, cited in Binney et al., *Mihaia*, 186–88.

39 Best, *The Maori*, Vol. I, 127.
40 Letters to Smith, 11.6.06, 8.8.05, MS-Papers-7888–024, Craig Papers, ATL.
41 Best, *Tuhoe*, Preface, v.
42 'Me etahi atu tangata nana i ropine nga taonga i koroutia e Nehe ma, a nana hoki i whakatuwhera i te putea whakanakonako ki te tangata rawaho.' *Ibid*., mihi, iv. Author's translation.
43 *Ibid*., vi–vii.
44 See Sissons, *Te Waimana*; Chris Hilliard, 'Textual Museums: Collection and Writing in History and Ethnology, 1900–1950', in Dalley & Labrum (eds.), *Fragments: New Zealand Social and Cultural History*, Auckland University Press (Auckland: 2000); and Hemana Waaka et al., *Te ara pai o ngā ao rua (Best of both worlds)*, Māori TV, 2007, transcript.
45 Best, *Tuhoe*, vi.
46 Best to Smith, 8.8.05, MS-Papers-7888–024, Craig Papers, ATL.
47 Best to Smith, 8.9.05, *ibid*.
48 See Elsdon Best, (ed.) Jeff Evans, *Notes on the art of war: as conducted by the Maori of New Zealand, with accounts of various customs, rites, superstitions, &c., pertaining to war, as practised and believed in by the ancient Maori*, Reed, in association with the Polynesian Society (Auckland: 2001).
49 Best to Smith, 3.1.06, MS-Papers-7888–024, Craig Papers, ATL.
50 Best to Smith, 11.6.06, *ibid*.
51 Sissons, *Te Waimana*, 1–53; Kerry Howe, *The Quest for Origins*, Penguin (Auckland: 2003), 159–76; Peter Clayworth, '"An Indolent and Chilly Folk" – the development of the idea of the "Moriori Myth"', PhD thesis (History), University of Otago (Dunedin: 2001), 258–79.
52 Best, *Tuhoe*, 741.
53 *Ibid*., 743.
54 Müller in Best, *ibid*., 1017.
55 Jeffrey Sissons, Preface to the 4th edition of *Tuhoe*, Reed (Auckland: 1995 [1925]), vii.
56 Best, *Tuhoe*, 1017–19.
57 *Ibid*., 1022.
58 *Ibid*., 1023.
59 *Ibid*., 1025.
60 Romans, Chapter 2:18–25.
61 Best, *Tuhoe*, 1025. See Andrew Lang, *The Making of Religion*, 2nd edition, Longmans (London: 1900). Best would refer to this book in a famous article on the cult of Io in *MAN*, the *Journal of the Royal Anthropological Institute*, Vol. 13, Nos. 56–57, in 1913.
62 Best, *Tuhoe*, 1026, 1027–31.
63 *Ibid*., 1027. My emphasis.
64 See M. P. K. Sorrenson, *Manifest Duty: The Polynesian Society Over 100 Years*, The Polynesian Society (Auckland: 1992), 36–39.
65 Best, *Tuhoe*, 1028.
66 Letter, Smith to Best, 12 December 1909, MS-Papers-72, Folder 5, ATL.
67 Best, *Tuhoe*, 1030–31.
68 *Ibid*., 1040–41.
69 Sissons, Preface to the 4th edition of *Tuhoe* (1995), vii.
70 Letter to Justice Department, Wellington, from District Constable, Te Whāiti, MA 1/1907/27, ANZ.
71 Elsdon Best, 'Art. LII. – Maori Forest Lore: Being some Account of Native Forest Lore and Woodcraft, as also of many Myths, Rites, Customs, and Superstitions connected with the Flora and Fauna of the Tuhoe or Ure-wera District. – Part III', *Transactions and Proceedings of the Royal Society of New Zealand*, Vol. 42, 1909, 442. He also writes to Smith in January 1908 that 'Old Tu is fast losing his memory', but the above citation indicates he knew of the old man's death at the time it occurred. Had the tangi not taken place in the midst

of what was now Rua's stronghold, it is hard to believe Best would not have been one of the chief mourners. Letter to Smith, 2.1.08, MS-Papers-7888–024, Craig Papers, ATL.

72 Letter to Smith, 20 April 1908, MS-Papers-1187–249, ATL.

73 Letter to Smith, 13 November 1908, MS-Papers-7888–024, Craig Papers, ATL.

74 Best, *Tuhoe*, 351. Tutakangahau was still alive when this footnote was added to Best's text, but the tone and the feeling is just as applicable to the time after his death a few months later.

75 Craig, *Man of the Mist*, 131–32.

76 Best's Diary, 13 March 1910, MS-0175 (173–176), ATL.

77 Williams' *Dictionary of the Maori Language*, 7th edition, GP Publications (Wellington: 1971, 1997), 85.

78 Craig, *Man of the Mist*, 133.

CHAPTER ELEVEN: THE MĀORI ACCORDING TO BEST: 'KA TŌ HE RĀ, KA URA HE RĀ!'

1 A sun sets, a sun rises!' This pepeha (saying) appears as the final line in Best's famous short history of traditional Māori society, *The Maori As He Was*, A. R. Shearer, Government Printer (Wellington: 1974 [1924]). It stands for his view of their trajectory in the evolutionary workings of human progress.

2 See Elsdon Craig, *Man of the Mist*, Reed (Wellington: 1964), 136–37, 138–39.

3 For a fuller discussion of the issues addressed in this chapter, the reader is referred to the doctoral thesis on which sections of this book are based: 'Best of both worlds: Elsdon Best and the metamorphosis of Māori spirituality. Te painga rawa on ngā ao rua: Te Peehi me te putanga kē o te wairua Māori', PhD thesis, University of Canterbury (Christchurch: 2007); an electronic version is available to download from the library: http://library.canterbury.ac.nz/?s=home.

4 Craig, *Man of the Mist*, 159–61.

5 *Ibid.*, 162.

6 *Ibid.*, 160.

7 See: Series MU000148, Staff (personal) files, Best, E., Dominion Museum, Wellington, 1914–1931, Museum of New Zealand/Te Papa Tongarewa, Wellington. This file contains a full account of Best's employment records and his salary increments.

8 *Ibid.*, Best, Memo to the Director, Colonial Museum, Wellington, 16 January 1914.

9 Best, Notebook 15 (1911), qMs [194], Alexander Turnbull Library, Wellington.

10 Elsdon Best, *The Stone Implements of the Maori*, Te Papa Press/A. R. Shearer, Government Printer (Wellington: 1912, 1974, 2005), 28.

11 *Ibid.*, 27.

12 See Chris Hilliard, 'Textual Museums: Collection and Writing in History and Ethnology, 1900–1950', in Dalley & Labrum (eds.), *Fragments: New Zealand Social and Cultural History*, Auckland University Press (Auckland: 2000), 133.

13 Best, on Te Whatahoro Jury, in 'The Cult of Io, the Concept of a Supreme Deity as evolved by the Ancestors of the Polynesians' (1913), *MAN*, Vol. 13, Nos. 56–57, 98–103.

14 M. J. Parsons, 'Jury, Hoani Te Whatahoro 1841–1923', Dictionary of New Zealand Biography, updated 22 June 2007, URL: http://www.dnzb.govt.nz/.

15 For an extensive account of Te Whatahoro's manuscript collections and their authenticity, see D. R. Simmons, 'The Words of Te Matorohanga', *Journal of the Polynesian Society*, Vol. 103, No. 2, June 1994, 115–70.

16 See D. R. Simmons, 'Te Matorohanga, Moihi fl. 1836–1865', Dictionary of New Zealand Biography, updated 22 June 2007, URL: http://www.dnzb.govt.nz/. It is not known exactly when he was born, or when he died.

17 Craig, *Man of the Mist*, 146–47.

18 Best, Notebook 11, qMS 191, qMS 193–194, MS-Copy-Micro-0650–09A, ATL, 264–65.

19 *Ibid.*, 265.

20 *Ibid.*, 5–12, 28.
21 Best to Smith, April/May 1911, Polynesian Society Records, MS-Papers-1187–249, ATL. I am indebted to Dr Peter Clayworth for this reference and observation.
22 S. Percy Smith, *The Lore of the Whare-wananga*, Vols. I & II, Memoirs of the Polynesian Society, Vols. 3–4, T. Avery & Sons (New Plymouth: 1913–1915).
23 See Peter Clayworth, '"An Indolent and Chilly Folk" – the development of the idea of the "Moriori Myth"', PhD thesis (History), University of Otago (Dunedin: 2001), 228–29.
24 H. W. Williams, 'The Maruiwi Myth' (1937), *JPS*, Vol. 46, No. 3, 105–6.
25 Clayworth, '"An Indolent and Chilly Folk"', 232, 235–36; Peter Buck, *The Coming of the Maori*, Maori Purposes Fund Board/Whitcombe & Tombs (Wellington: 1949), 5–8.
26 Clayworth, *ibid.*, 237.
27 I am indebted in all of this material concerning Smith and Best, and the dissemination of the Te Matorohanga–Te Whatahoro material, to Dr Peter Clayworth in his previously cited thesis.
28 Ka'ai, Moorfield, Reilly & Mosley (eds.), *Ki te Whaiao*, Pearson Education (Auckland: 2004).
29 Michael P. J. Reilly, 'Te tīmatanga mai o ngā atua – creation narratives', in Ka'ai et al., *ibid.*, 1 ff.
30 See: http://homepages.ihug.co.nz/~dominic/mylife.html. Shirres has published a number of works on Māori theology, including *Tapu, Te Mana o Nga Atua, 'The Mana of the Spiritual Powers'*, Te Runanga o Te Hahi Katorika ki Aotearoa (Auckland: 1994).
31 Bruce Biggs & David Simmons, 'The Sources of the *Lore of the Whare-wananga*' (1970), *JPS*, Vol. 79, No. 1, 22–42, 36.
32 *Ibid.*, 41.
33 *Ibid.*, 36. The Io material in *Te Kauwae-runga* runs from 110 ff.
34 *Ibid.*, 41.
35 Best, 'The Cult of Io, the Concept of a Supreme Deity as evolved by the Ancestors of the Polynesians' (1913), *MAN*, Vol. 13, Nos. 56–57, 98–103.
36 *Ibid.*, 98.
37 *Ibid.*, 99.
38 Best, Notebook 11, qMS 191, MS-Copy-Micro-0650–09A, ATL, 286.
39 *Ibid.*, 388–89.
40 See School Attendance records, qMS-1408–1413a, ATL, cited in Clayworth, '"An Indolent and Chilly Folk"', 227.
41 Best, 'The Cult of Io', 102.
42 Best, Notebook 11, 182–83.
43 *Ibid.*, 188.
44 *Ibid.*, 187.
45 *Ibid.*, 186.
46 Williams' *Dictionary of the Maori Language*, 7th edition, GP Publications (Wellington: 1971), 432. The italics in the quote from Best are his.
47 Best, Notebook 11, 388–89.
48 *Ibid.*, 389, author's translation.
49 See Elsdon Best, 'The Races of the Philippines' (1892), Pt II, *JPS*, Vol. 1.
50 Williams' *Dictionary*, 197.
51 *Ibid.*, xxv–xxvi.
52 *Te Matatiki: Contemporary Māori Words*, Māori Language Commission/Te Taura Whiri i Te Reo Māori, Oxford University Press (Auckland: 1996), 194.
53 I am indebted to Professor Alison Wray; see A. Wray, '"Needs only" Analysis in Linguistic Ontogeny and Phylogeny', in Lyon, Nehaniv & Cangelosi (eds.), *Emergence of Communication and Language*, Springer (London: 2007), 53–70.
54 Best to Smith, 17.9.1895, MS-0072–08, ATL.
55 Jeffrey Sissons, Best biography, 'Best, Elsdon 1856–1931', Dictionary of New Zealand

Biography, updated 22 June 2007, URL: http://www.dnzb.govt.nz/; cited in Conal McCarthy, *Exhibiting Māori – A History of Colonial Cultures of Display*, Te Papa Press (Wellington: 2007), 67–68.

56 *Evening Post*, 9 September 1931, obituary for Best (Wellington), cited in Kerry Howe, *Singer in a Songless Land: A Life of Edward Tregear 1846–1931*, Auckland University Press (Auckland: 1991), 192–93.

57 See Best, *The Stone Implements of the Maori*, 155–59 on the toki titaha or true stone axes. Letter to Best in Māori from Numia Kereru to 'Te Peehi' dated 'Ruatoki, Hanuere 6, 1911'; also, Margery Perham, *Pacific Prelude: A Journey to Samoa and Australasia*, Peter Owen (London: 1988), 173–74.

58 From a discussion with Janet Elsdon Mackey, Elsdon Craig's daughter, Gisborne, 19 May 2008. She is descended from Best's sister, Edith, who married the soldier and historian – and one of Best's early mentors – Walter Gudgeon.

59 McCarthy, *Exhibiting Māori*, 55–56.

60 *Ibid.*, 56.

61 Tape Copy (LC-0417) of MST7–0113, Hui Aroha, Gisborne, April 1919, ATL.

62 See Film Number: East Coast, 1923, F2815, National Film Archive/Ngā Kaitiaki o Ngā Taonga Whitiāhua, Wellington.

63 Perham, *Pacific Prelude*, 173–74.

64 This book finally emerged in 1982, reprinting in 1995, and in 2005 with eleven other Best titles (Te Papa Press).

65 The outline of Best's final year and these details can be found in Craig, *Man of the Mist*, 220–29.

66 I. M. Eggers, 'Elsdon Best: man and writer', MA dissertation, University of New Zealand, 1935. Copy held in MSX-6800, Craig Papers, ATL.

67 Craig, *Man of the Mist*, 227–29.

68 Best, Notebook 11, 394–95.

69 Craig, *Man of the Mist*, 228.

70 Best, Notebook 11, 395.

71 Craig, *Man of the Mist*, 228.

72 Henry Christie, a friend of Best's, was one of those at his bedside, and confirms Craig's picture of this occurrence in his tribute to Best, published with many others in a special commemorative issue of the *JPS*, Vol. 41, No. 161, March 1932, 31.

73 Best to Smith, reply, 29.1.96, MS-Papers-0072–08, ATL; Hakopa to Best, Urewera, in 'Spiritual Concepts of the Maori', Pt II, *JPS*, Vol. X: 37 (Wellington: 1901), 14.

74 MU000148, Best's Personal Files, Archives Section, Te Papa Tongarewa/Museum of New Zealand.

75 Craig, *Man of the Mist*, 227; 28 July 1931, Best's Diary, 1928–1931, MS-0175 (MS-0173–177), ATL.

CHAPTER TWELVE: 'KIA MARAMA – LET THERE BE LIGHT!': THE HALF-LIFE OF TE PEEHI IN OUR MIDST

1 Walter J. Ong, *Orality and Literacy: The Technologising of the Word*, Routledge (London & New York: 1982), 15.

2 'Elsdon Best Memorial Number', *Journal of the Polynesian Society*, Vol. 41, No. 1 (March 1932), 1–49. The remaining comments from this eulogy and the tributes to Best are found here.

3 *Ibid.*, 3.

4 Picture of the 1916 draft will was taken by the author with the kind permission of Janet Elsdon Mackey; Best's final will, AAOM 6029, 49422/1931, Archives New Zealand/Te Rua Mahara o te Kāwanatanga, Head Office, Wellington.

5 Smith, letter to Best, 27 October 1915, MS-Papers-7888–017, Alexander Turnbull Library, Wellington.

6 Frank Acheson, *Plume of the Arawas*, Dent (London: 1930), Foreword.
7 Acheson, *JPS* (1932), *op. cit.*, 11.
8 Wi Repa, *ibid.*, 12–15.
9 Buck, *ibid.*, 20.
10 Firth, *ibid.*, 23–25.
11 Andersen, *ibid.*, 34–35.
12 Buck to Ngata, 5 June 1928, from *Nā tō Hoa Aroha, From Your Dear Friend: The Correspondence Between Sir Apirana Ngata and Sir Peter Buck, 1925–50*, Vols. I–III, M. P. K. Sorrenson (ed.), Auckland University Press (Auckland: 1986–87–88), Vol. I, 101.
13 *Ibid.*, Vol. II, 115.
14 *Ibid.*, Vol. II, 229.
15 *Ibid.*, Vol. II, 115.
16 *Ibid.*, Vol. III, 234.
17 *Ibid.*, Vol. II, 63.
18 Elsdon Best, *Maori Religion and Mythology*, Pt 1, Dominion Museum Bulletin No. 10, Te Papa Press (Wellington: 1924, 2005), 321–22.
19 Wi Repa, *JPS* (1932), *op. cit.*, 15.
20 C. Kessler, Obituary for Raymond Firth, *Australian Journal of Anthropology*, August 2002.
21 Raymond Firth, *The Primitive Economics of the New Zealand Maori*, Routledge (London: 1929), xx.
22 *Ibid.*, xxi.
23 *Ibid.*, 234.
24 *Ibid.*, 243–44.
25 See: http://scholar.google.co.nz/scholar?hl=en&lr=&q=Best+Elsdon&btnG=Search.
26 See Marcel Mauss, *The Gift* (*Essai sur le don*), trs. Ian Cunnison, Cohen & West (London: 1969), 8–10. Best's 1909 article on 'Maori Forest Lore' appeared in the *Transactions and Proceedings of the Royal Society of New Zealand, 1868–1961*, Vol. 42, 433–81, and formed the basis of the posthumous work *Forest Lore of the Maori*, Dominion Museum Bulletin No. 14, published by the Polynesian Society in collaboration with the Dominion Museum in 1942, supervised by his heir apparent, Johannes Andersen.
27 *Ibid.*, 10.
28 Marshall Sahlins, *Stone Age Economics*, Aldine-Atherton, Inc. (Chicago & New York: 1972), 149–83.
29 Sahlins, *ibid.*, 149.
30 Lewis Hyde, *The Gift: Imagination and the Erotic Life of Property*, Vintage (New York: 1979), 18–19.
31 *Ibid.*, 37.
32 See: http://www.guardian.co.uk/books/2007/jan/20/featuresreviews.guardianreview32.
33 See, for example, Césaire, 1956; Fanon, 1952, 1967; Cleaver, 1967.
34 Michael King, *Te Ao Hurihuri – The World Moves On: Aspects of Maoritanga*, Hicks Smith (Wellington: 1975).
35 King, *ibid.*, 18–19.
36 Marsden in King, *ibid.*, 191, 218.
37 *Ibid.*, 218–19.
38 *Ibid.*, 218, 198, 201, 202, 205, 207. Italics mine.
39 *Ibid.*, 209.
40 *Ibid.*, 196–97.
41 Māori Marsden, *The Woven Universe: Selected Writings of Rev. Māori Marsden*, (ed.) Ahukaramū Charles Royal, Estate of Rev. Māori Marsden (Otaki: 2003), 30–31.
42 *Ibid.*, 31–32.
43 *Ibid.*, xiii.
44 *Ibid.*, 32.
45 Ong, *Orality and Literacy*, 12.

46 See Elsdon Best, 'Food Products of Tuhoeland', *Transactions and Proceedings of the New Zealand Institute*, Vol. XXXV (v), 1902, 45–111, 69.
47 Cleve Barlow, *Tikanga Whakaaro*, Oxford University Press (Auckland: 1991), xvii.
48 Ibid., 83.
49 Michael P. Shirres, *Te Tangata: The Human Person*, Accent Publications (Auckland: 1997), 113.
50 Hirini Moko Mead, *Tikanga Māori: Living by Māori Values*, Huia (Wellington: 2003), 53–54.
51 *Ibid.*, 12.
52 *Ibid.*, 42–61.
53 *Forest Lore of the Maori* (1942), *The Maori*, Vols. I–II (1924), and *Maori Religion and Mythology*, Pt. 2 (1924, 1982).
54 *Ibid.*, 53–54.
55 *Ibid.*, 53.
56 Elsdon Best, *The Maori: Pt 1*, Memoirs of the Polynesian Society, Vol. V, Board of Maori Ethnological Research (Wellington: 1924), 304.
57 Mead, *Tikanga Māori*, 53, 54.
58 *The Reed Dictionary of Modern Māori* (1997); Witi Ihimaera, *The Whale Rider*, Reed (Auckland: 1987, 2003); *The Reed Dictionary of Māori Mythology*, (ed.) Ross Calman (2004); *He Pātaka Kupu*, Te Taura Whiri i te Reo Māori/Raupo (2008).

CONCLUSION

1 This is about to change: in 2007, Judith Binney, one of the historians who has done major work on Tūhoe, Te Kooti and Rua since the 1970s, began work on what will become a full account of at least four of these men: Erueti Tamaikoha, Te Whenuanui I, Te Makarini Tamarau, and Tutakangahau. See Binney, *Untold Lives: When the Elders Tell Their Stories*, Hocken Lecture 2: 2007, The Hocken Collections, University of Otago (Dunedin: 2008).
2 Elsdon Best, 'Art. LII – Maori Forest Lore: Being some Account of Native Forest Lore and Woodcraft, as also of many Myths, Rites, Customs, and Superstitions connected with the Flora and Fauna of the Tuhoe or Ure-wera District. – Part III', *Transactions and Proceedings of the Royal Society of New Zealand*, Vol. 42, 1909, 452.
3 Elsdon Best, *Waikaremoana: The Sea of the Rippling Waters*, A. R. Shearer, Government Printer (Wellington: 1975 [1897]), 49.
4 For a discussion of Best's poetry, see J. P. Holman, 'Elsdon Best: Elegist in Search of a Poetic', Part II, Best and his poetry in the 'Māori Twilight', in *Ka Mate, Ka Ora*, http://www.nzepc.auckland.ac.nz/kmko/02/ka_mate02_holman.asp.
5 *Otago Witness*, issue 2289, 13 January 1898, 49, http://paperspast.natlib.govt.nz, ATL.
6 Best, Maori Notebook No. 13, 111–12, Alexander Turnbull Library, Wellington.
7 Best, final mihi, *Tuhoe: The Children of the Mist*, The Board of Maori Ethnological Research (New Plymouth: 1925), 1143.

Index

Page numbers in *italics* refer to photographs and illustrations.

A
Acheson, Frank 259
Adkin, Clyde *41*, *250*
Adkin, Leslie 41
Adkin, Nancy *250*
agriculture 31–2, 39, 243, 263
ahi taitai (ritual fires) 158–9, 262, 267
Ahikereru 74
Akuhata 5, 34, 62
alcohol 40, 150, 177
Alexander, Dudley 176, 178, 180, 182
American Indians 92, 203
ancestors 26, 34, *78*, 138, 189, 191–4
Andersen, Johannes *246*, 248, *249*, 254, 259, 260
animism 99, 211–12
Anthropological Religion (F. Max Müller) 89, 102, 156, 210
Anthropology (Edward Tylor) 89
anthropology 83–90
  biblical anthropology 24, 44, 85–90
  colonial 99, 130
  comparative 97, 146, 161
  economic 263–4
  evangelical 87–8
  fieldworking versus academic 241
  Māori anthropologists 260–4
  'salvage' 14–15, 24–5, 29, 94, 103, 156, 225
  theoretical 24
Apanui, Wepiha 76
Appendices to the Journals of the House of Representatives 110
ariā 152, 153
Arikirangi Te Turuki, Te Kooti *see* Te Kooti Rikirangi
armed constabulary 74, 80–2, *81*, *82*, 85, 126, *245*
Aryan stock 87, 101, 204, 240
Ask That Mountain (Dick Scott) 82
atheism 214–5
atua (gods) 15, 22, 26–7, 57, 151–3, 209–15, 229–33, 237–8, 251
  supreme atua *see* Io

B
Ballance, John 70–1
Balneavis, Henare *249*
Banks, Joseph 10
Barlow, Cleve 276–7, 278
Baucke, William 250
Baxter, James K. 272
Beaglehole, J. C. 229
Bennett, F. A. 254–6

Bennett (Doctor) 43
Best, Adelaide (née Wylie) 126, 148, *244*, *252–3*, *252*, 255, 257–8
Best, Edith 42, 80, 90
Best, Elsdon (Te Peehi) *23*, *43*, *82*, *95*, *178*, *183*, *201*, *220*, *245*, *246*, 246–7, *249*, *250*, *252*, *255*, *261*, *287*
as government ethnologist 93–4, 142, 219–26
as health officer 14, 125, 196, 200, 202–3
as road quartermaster 125–8, 133, 169
as secretary to Urewera Commission 125, 163, 169–71
as scribe to Tutakangahau 195, 213, 217–18, 229
as Te Peehi 216, 247
as white tohunga 41–2, 149, 219, 243, 247, 249, 251–3, 264
at Waikaremoana with Tutakangahau 135–42, 206
autodidacticism 24, 43, 80, 90, 156
awarded Hector Memorial Medal 221
bush balladry 286–9
bushman skills 42, 80–2, 94, 137, 222, 247, 288–9
cited in academic literature 259–70
co-authorship of Tutakangahau 77, 129–30, 153, 283
criticism and praise of 206–7, 259–64
dependence on mohio (men of knowledge) *see* mohio
early life, education and employment 37–48, 79–82, 90–4
decline and death 250–9
identification with Te Matorohanga 251–3
influence 270–9
marriage 148, 200, 218, 245, *252*
memorial at Grasslees Park, Tawa 256–7, *256*, *288*
overriding themes 227–9, 240, 286
passion for ethnology 24–5, 42–5, 79–80, 83
philosophical foundations 142–6
rejection of modernity 289
relationship with Tutakangahau 17–18, 114, 128–32, 140, 144, 147–8, 159, 160–1, 284
search for hidden knowledge *see* kura huna
search for 'old-time Maori' 36, 77, 92, 119, 122, 142, 150, 206, 224, 232, 284–5
significance for Māori 255–7
temperament 241, 249, 257–9
views on Christianity 46, 83–5, 87, 92, 201, 204, 210, 212, 235, 285
will *257–9*, *258*
works discussed
'But Now! Miramar 1200 AD 1913 AD' 288–9
'Collection and compilation of Ethnographical Lore' 225–6
'Cult of Io' 231
'Darkened Mind, The' 202, 203
Dominion Museum Bulletins 243–4
Fishing Methods and Devices of the Maori 265
Forest Lore of the Maori 265
'From Tuhoeland' newspaper articles 142–3, 149–50
Games and pastimes of the Māori 242
Maori, The 102, 244, 262
Maori Agriculture 263, 265
Maori Art 221–2
Maori As He Was, The 228–9, 244, 262
'Maori Forest Lore' 157, 160, 262, 264, 265
'Maori and Maruiwi' 229
Maori Religion and Mythology 102, 250, 262, 278
'Men Who Break the Trail' 286–9
'Necessity for Accuracy in Treating of Ethnological Subjects' 221–2
Notebook 11 36, 225, 234
Notebook 15 221
'Notes on the Art of War' 208
'On Solitude and the Primitive Mind' 143
'Present Condition of the Tuhoe Tribe, The' 150
'Races of the Philippines, The' 90, 93–9
'Spiritual Concepts of the Maori, The' 154–6, 242, 264, 266, 277
Stone Implements of the Maori, The 220–1
'Te Rehu-o-Tainui: the evolution of a Maori atua' 151
Tuhoe: The Children of the Mist see Tuhoe: The Children of the Mist
Waikaremoana: The Sea of Rippling Waters 132, 135

Best, Frederic 42
Best, Hannah and William 38
Best, Isabel 42, 79, 90–1, 92
Best, Katherine 42, 90, 317n
Best, Madeleine 42, 314n
Best, Walter 42, 92
Bible *78*
  Adam and Eve 85, 88, 285
  Apostle Paul 119, 212, 238
  Fall, The 51–2, 84–8, 212
  Genesis 87, 192, 238
  Israelites 24, 51, 62, 65, 197, 199, 204, 216, 283, 316n
  Jehovah 57, 63, 235
  Jesus Christ 68, 88, 230, 238
  Jews of the Old Testament 51, 57, 86–7, 204, 235, 285
  New Testament 50, 54, 58, 177
  Noah's descendants 45, 86–8
  Old Testament genealogy 192, 285
  Old Testament prophecy 18, 51, 57, 61–2, 63, 65, 68–9, 112, 160, 192, 230, 235, 285, 311n
  Psalms of David 65, 70, 179, 180
  Sheol, Hell 230, 235
  Te Kawenata Hou *50, 58*
  see also Christian literacy
bicultural literacy 14, 147
Biggs, Bruce 229, 230, 238, 266
bilingualism 40, 127, 141, 190, 286
birds *17*, 29–30, 32, 120, 150, 157–9, 181
Blythe, J. C. 105
Board of Maori Ethnological Research 244
Bopp, Franz 46
Bougainville, Louis de 21
Brabant, Herbert 69–70, 75–6
Brown, C. Hunter 51–2
Bryce, John 70, 71, 81, 317n
Buck, Peter *see* Te Rangi Hiroa
bush ballads 286–9
Butler, W. J. 163, 170, 172

C
Cadman, Alfred 109
cannibalism 22, 33
Carpenter, Edmund 9
Carroll, James
  and Rua Kenana 196–8
  Maori Councils Conference 175, 177–8, 182–4
  mediation 126
  reserve/sanctuary idea 119–23
  tour with Seddon 109, 112–14, 117
  Young Māori Party 94
Castlecliff 226
Chaldea 87
Chambers, Robert 45–8, 88–9
Chatham Islands 57–8, 60, 228–9
Chrisp, Tīpene 232
Christchurch *201*
Christianity
  Best's anti-Christian polemic 46, 83–5, 87, 92, 201, 204, 210, 212, 235, 285
  Bible *see* Bible
  Christian literacy of Māori 15, 18, 25, 30–1, 36, 89, 204, 214, 232, 237–8, 272, 284
  Māori Christianity 36, 54–5, 65, 68–9, 150, 201, 204, 210, 274, 283
  missionaries *see* missionaries
Church Missionary Society 30
Coates, J. G. 259
Colenso, William 14, 26, 30, 35, 51, 61, 86, 115, 132, 154, 195, 212
Colonial Museum 93–4, 142, 219–26
colonial power structures 130
colonisation 15, 20–5, 47, 68, 87–9, 96–7, 144–5, 217, 233, 268, 275, 283
Coming of the Maori, The (Peter Buck) 262
commerce 22, 30, 40, 168, 267
confiscation of land *see* land
Cook, James 10, 15, 21–2, 104–5, 114, 311n
Coventry, Frederick Halford 255
Cowan, James 59, 66
Craig, Elsdon 35, 40, 42, 44, 148, 156, 169, 245, 250–2, 258, 287
Crawfurd, John 86, 96, 317n
Creagh (surveyor) 108
creation stories 88, 191–2, 209, 233
creationism 45–7, 83–8, 274–5
'cultural commons' 265–8

D
Darwin, Charles 45–6, 83–4, 86
Descent of Man, The (Charles Darwin) 83
Dictionary of the Maori Language 154–7, 236, 241, 266, 277–8
Dictionary of the New Zealand Language 155, 240
diffusionism 44, 46–7, 88–9, 96–8, 240–1, 261
Discovery of New Zealand, The (J. C. Beaglehole) 229
diseases *see* sickness and disease
dog tax 176
Dominion Museum 37, 142, 194, 220, 221,

231, 241, 243–6, 247, *249*
dreams and visions 18, 54, 61–2, 120, 65, 159–60, 193, 195
Durkheim, Émile 265

E
East Coast 26, *38*, 57, 71, 231, 234, 246, 259
economic theories on Māori life *263–4*, 265–7
education *see* literacy; schools; whare wānanga
Edward VII, King 182, 202, 216–7
eeling *14*, 41, *41*, *250*, 275–6
Eggers, Isabel 149, 217, 250
Einstein, Albert 273, 274
Emerson, R. W. 143
employment of Māori 16, 106–7, 128–9, 150
Endeavour 22
English language 10–12, 15–16, 40
Essai sur le don (The Gift) (Émile Durkheim) 265–7
ethnography, defined 21
ethnographers 21–4
European globalisation 20–2, 103, 284, 286–8
evil 110–12, 152, 177, 211, 235, 236, 237
evolutionary concepts 273–5
evolutionary theory 24, 44–47, 83–4, 86, 88, 98, 101–2, 103, 135, 145–6, 147, 231, 273–5

F
fieldwork 13–14, 42, 94, 146, 152, 233, 241, 264
Figuier, Louis 44–5
firearms 16, 28, 35, 104, 150, 153, 166, 258, 285
Firth, Raymond 259, 260, 263–6
fishing 29, 37, 157, 265
Fitzgerald (Superintendent) 51, 62, 314n
flags and banners 56, 57, 61, 66, 172
food and food shortages 29–30, 31–2, 33, 39, 40, 41, 150, 158–9, 174, 182, 199, 200–1
Fort Manaia 85
French Enlightenment 24
frontier intellectualism 24, 219, 286
Fulloon, James 59

G
Galatea 55, 64, 74, 114, 116, 125–6, 133
genealogy *see* whakapapa
genocidal behaviour 47–8, 98, 314n
gift economy theories 263–8
Gift, The (Essai sur le don) (Émile Durkheim) 265–7
Gift, The: How the Creative Spirit Transforms the World (Lewis Hyde) 268
Gift, The: Imagination and the Erotic Life of Property (Lewis Hyde) 267
Gill, William Wyatt 101, 102
Gisborne (Turanga) 57, 70, 72, 158, 202, 246
God *see* Io; religion
gold mining 106, 121, 120–4, 197
government incursions into land *see* land
Government House *245*
Grace, Thomas 68
Grant, Andy 196, 216
Grasslees Farm 80, 255–7
Grasslees Park 255–7, *288*
Great Fleet 227, 228
Great New Zealand Myth, The (Simmons, David) 229
Great War, The 206, 216–17, 246
Greek 21, 102, 155–6, 242, 277
Greer, Elizabeth 39
Grey, George 23, 24, 38, 51–2, 53, 86, 227
Gudgeon, Walter 80–1, 90, 109, 218
guns 16, 35, 104, 150, 153, 166, 248, 258, 285
Gutenbuerg 36

H
Haddon, A. C. 259
Haerini 52
Hagley Park *201*
haka 22, 64, 178, 313n
Hamerton, P. G. 143
Hamilton, Augustus 219–22, 225, 246
Hammond, T. G. 93–4, 212, 213
Hape 206
Hatiti 138
hau (breath, spirit) 54, 154, 234, 242, 265–70, 277
see also mauri
Hauauru 228
Hauhau movement 53, 55–62, 68, 179–80, 283
Haumene, Te Ua 39, 51, 54–60, 81, 180, 204
Hautawa 224
Hawaiki 209
'He Ko Koti' *34*

He Pātaka Kupu 279
Head, Lyndsay 238
health 186, 200, 202–3
  see also sickness and disease
'Heathenism' 69
heaven and earth 239
Heipipi *127*, *149*, 200, *217*
Hepetipa, Rua Kenana *see* Rua Kenana
hereditary chiefly system 14, 62, 78, 119–20, 135, 168–9, 187–8, 198
Hereheretaua 138
Herodotus 21, 104
Herries, W. H. 171
High God *see* Io
Highland Park, Wadestown 269
Hill, Richard 169
Hine Pūkohurangi (mist maiden) 28
Hirawana, Tahu *205*
historical writing 20
Hohapata-Oke, John 276
Hokio Stream 41
Holland, H. E. 259
Hope-motu 152
Hui Aroha, Gisborne 246
Huiarau 137, *175*
Hulme, Keri 157
hunga mate (the dead) 138
Hurae 204
hunter-gathering 29–30, 39, 150, 171, 173
Hyde, Lewis 264, 265, 267–8
hygiene standards 161, 178–9, 200, 203

I
ideological literature 271
Iharaira (Israel) 24, 51, 62, 65, 197, 199, 204, 216, 283, 316n
Ihimaera, Witi 279
industrial modernity 16, 22, 91, 92–3, 107
intellectual climate 83, 99–103, 144, 271
intellectual property 187, 220–1, 283
Io (Supreme Being) 89, 98, 209–15, 227–39, 259, 273–4, 277–8
Io-taketake (creator, root, cause) 274
Irihia (India) 46, 88, 101, 204

J
Jackson, Syd 271
Journal of the Polynesian Society 90, 95, *100*, 33, 105, 151, *151*, 154, 208, 229, 241, 248, 259
Journal of the Royal Anthropological Institute (MAN) 214, 221–2, 231, 234–5, 243

K
Ka Whawhai Tonu Mātou: Struggle Without End (Ranginui Walker) 265
Kaihau, Henare 163–4
Kakahi, Tohu 81
kanohi ki te kanohi (face to face) 73–4, 112, 225, 239
karakia 33, 41–2, 56, 141, 143, 158, 159, 222–3, 230, 242–3, 249, 275–6
  Te Kooti's karakia 65, 68, 69, 70, 179, 180, 283
Karetu, Sam 271
Kawepo (Tamakihikurangi), Renata 48, 51, 62, 314n
Kereru, Numia Te Pukenui *111*, 173, *179*
  and Best 245
  at hui with Seddon 109–14
  meeting with Seddon in Wellington 163–9
  opposition to Rua Kenana 196, 198
  supporter of 'progress' and co-operation 108, 128, 197, 200
  taiaha 114, 162, 186
  viceregal visit 181, 183
Kereru, Te Pukenui 75
ki raro (heaven) 239
ki runga (earth) 239
Ki te Whaiao: An Introduction to Māori Culture and Society 229
Kihikihi 70
King, Jeanette 276, 293
King, Michael 271
King Country 67, 150
Kingitanga 118, 182
kiore Māori 29–30
Kipling, Rudyard 286
Kohimarama redoubt 66, 73
Kohitau redoubt 66
Kotahitanga movement 109, 113, 117–18, 129, 175, 187, 224–5
Kupe 228
kura huna (hidden knowledge) 10, 15, 94, 125–6, 133–6, 140–1, 154, 192, 217, 233, 252–3, 285
Kura-wha (wife of Tutakangahau) 63

L
Lake Waikaremoana 10, 28, 30, 58, 135–42, *136*, 139
land
  alienation 25, 73, 163, 185, 199
  annexation 105
  aukati (confiscation line) 60, 63, 75

cultural reserve 150
government purchases inside reserve 199–200
inter-hapū issues 75, 113–14, 124, 142, 163, 168–74, 177, 185–6
leases 75–6, 105, 110, 171, 173–4, 185–6
legislation *see* Urewera District Native Reserve Act 1896
mining 120–4
ownership 105, 107–8, 120–1, 134–5, 162–74, 185–6, 199–200
papa tipu (hereditary land) 70
raupatu (confiscation, conquest) 59–60, 63, 68, 70, 72–5, 79, 105, 107–8, 122, 167, 172, 201, 318n
resistance to government acquisition 49–78, 80–1, 104–24, 162–86
'sanctuary' 120, 121, 181
sale 15, 59, 67, 72, 75, 104–5, 110, 173–4, 185–6, 199–201
scorched earth policy 64, 180
surveys 60, 73, 104–24, 116–28, 166–7, 174, 177, 185, 199–200
take tīpuna, ahi kā roa (ownership by continuous occupation) 172
tuku (gifting) 172–3
see also Native Land Court
Lang, Andrew 231
Laughton, John 204
law 51–2, 68, 72, 75–6, 77, 112, 116–19, 164, 172, 311n
legends *see* myths and legends
Liberal government *see* Seddon
linguistics 101
literacy 12, 25, 31, 35–6, 44, 61, 72, 73–4, 77, 115, 123, 134, 147, 186, 189, 254, 268–9, 273–4, 275, 283
literary colonisation 268, 275, 283
literary mauri 275–9
literary versus oral transmission 138, 241–3, 266–70
literate modernity 12, 16, 77
Lloyd (Captain) 56
Locke, Samuel 75, 76, 106
logging *93*
London School of Economics 263
Lowry (Constable) 169

M
McDonald, James 246, 249
Mcdougall, Robert 79, 90
McLean, Donald 74, 75, 77, 108, 109, 112–13, 120, 162
Mackey, Janet Elsdon *292*
Mahupuku, Hāmuera Tamahau 181, 190, 224
mail service 67, 72, 122, 196, 197
Maioro 157
Mair, Gilbert 64, 175, 176, 180, 212
Making of Religion, The (Andrew Lang) 231
mākutu (magic) 140, 158, 211, 263–4, 319n
Malinowski, Bronislaw 263
'Man Alone' figures 143–6, 289
Man of the Mist (Elsdon Craig) 156
mana (power and prestige) 15, 59, 78, 129, 166, 189, 206, 215, 248, 251–2, 266, 277
mana motuhake (local autonomy) 70, 73, 163, 172, 217
manaakitanga (hospitality) 69, 294
manawa (heart, belly, bowels) 155, 242
Mangatawhiri Stream 39
Maniapoto 53, 67
Manukau Harbour 157
'Māori Christianity' 36, 54–5, 65, 68–9, 150, 201, 204, 210, 274, 283
Maori Councils 175, 182, 200, 203
Māori Councils Conference 174–5, 177–84
Māori Health Service 200–1
Māori language 10–12, 241–3, 246
Best's fluency 4, 40, 80, 94, 127–8, 152, 210, 241
colonisation of words 241–3, 266–78
dictionaries 154–7, 236, 241, 242, 266, 277–8
Māori Language Commission (Te Taura Whiri i Te Reo Māori) 242
Māori nationalism 44, 115, 284
Māori newspapers 187–95
Māori Parliament 188
Maori spirituality
described by Best 209–15
described by Māori Marsden 272–5
see also spirit world; tohunga
'Māori renaissance' 94–5, 268, 270, 286
Māori Studies 240, 277
Māori writers 12, 264, 270–9
Māori writing in Māori 49–50
Māoriphiles 24, 80, 90, 93–4, 233
'Māoritanga' 264, 271–2
Mapou marae 165, 281, *282*
maps and mapping 104–5, 114, 206
Marewa-i-te-rangi 147, 165, 284

Mariposa *92*
Marsden (Te Aupouri), Māori 230, 271–5
Marsden, Samuel 24
maruiwi (pre-Māori tangata whenua) 97, 207, 209, 227–9
'Maruiwi Myth, The' (H. W. Williams) 228
'Massey's Cossacks' 245
Mātaatua tribes 70, 118, 206
Mātaatua canoe 28, 52–3, 70, 114, 209
'Matai Moana' ('Sea Gazing'), Wadestown *244*, 245
matakite (oracles) 56, 61, 152
Maui 88, 160, 189, 209, 218
Maungapōhatu 25, 28, *31*, 58, 62–9, 312n
 Rua Kenana's community 161, 180, 186, 195–205
 Tanenuiarangi meeting house 165, 280, *281*, *282*
Maunsell, Robert 50
mauri (breath of life) 155–7, 234, 242, 263–4, 266–70, 272–8
mauri (material talismans) 42, 156–7, 158, 273, 275–6, 278
mauri ora (life principle) 273
Mauss, Marcel 264–8
Mead, Hirini Moko 276, 277–8
Melanesian migrants 87, 89, 227–9
messianic leaders *see* Te Ua Haumene; Rua Kenana; Te Kooti Rikirangi
metaphysics 12, 139, 184, 237, 272, 274
military 20, 52, 56, 62–6, 75, 77, 104–5
 see also armed constabulary
millennial movements 51, 55, 58, 62, 68, 103, 195, 197, 285, 286
mission-based literacy *see* Christian literacy
missionaries 17, 20–1, 22–5, 47, 51, 55, 68–9, 83–4, 87–8, 210, 227, 232–3, 235–8, 285
modernity 12, 13, 16–18, 123
 embraced by Tutakangahau *see* Tutakangahau
 industrial 16, 22, 91, 92–3, 107
 rejected by Best 289
 see also Te Ao Marama
Mohaka 63
mohio (men of knowledge) 129–30, 146–7, 149–50, 151–2, 154, 158, 160, 188, 194, 206, 216, 222–3, 262, 279
 payment 127–32
mōkai (pets) 17, 217
money economy 15–16, 29, 107, 128–32, 150, 168, 186, 202, 248
Moriori 87, 89, 97, 228
Mormon Church 225, 235–6, 277
Müller, Max F. 24, 47, 89, 101–2, 155–7, 210, 242, 285
museum exhibits 244
muru (plunder and reciprocity) 15
myths and legends 24, 102, 138–42, 206–9, 211, 227–9, 255
'Mythopoeic Age' 101–2
'mythopoetic Māori' 102, 144–6, 240, 253, 285
Myths and Songs from the South Pacific (William Wyatt Gill) 101, 102
myths promulgated by Best 227–9

N
names 215
Nash, Walter *256*, *288*
National Museum of New Zealand Te Papa Tongarewa 265
national myths 227–9
Native Councils Bill 75
Native Federation Council of New Zealand *see* Kotahitanga
Native Land Court 72, 76, 105, 110, 120, 167, 185
 and use of whakapapa 134–5, 192, 193
 criticism of 113, 172–4
 extension of jurisdiction into Reserve 199
Native Land Court Act 1894 110
Native Lands Settlement and Administration Bill 167
Native Schools 25, 40, 128, 147, 198, 203, 232, 237
natural world 44–5, 84–5, 104–5, 143–6, 147, 274
naturalism 45–8, 83–90
Neolithic references 136, 143, 231–2, 289
New Jerusalem 195–205
New Orleans 91–2
New Physics 273–4
New Zealand Exhibition 201
New Zealand Settlements Act 1863 59
Nga Moteatea (Apirana Ngata) 259
Ngā Pōtiki 28, 226
Ngā Puhi 35, 230, 272, 274, 277
Ngā Tapa 34, 62, 63, 200
Ngahau, Tutaka 132
Ngai Tawhaki 131
Ngaputahi 172
Ngata, Apirana 94–5, 199, 244, 246, 254, 260–4, 271

Ngata, Paratene 174
Ngāti Awa 28, 33, 34, 35, 37
Ngāti Huri 64, 68, 69–70, 74
Ngāti Kahungunu 28, 57, 58–9, 191, 193, 195, 224, 230, 246
Ngāti Manawa 55, 76, 171
Ngāti Maniapoto 266
Ngāti Maru 35, 127
Ngāti Mutunga 229
Ngāti Porou 37, 55, 57, 58, 63, 66, 73, 174, 226, 246, 271
Ngāti Pukeko 60
Ngāti Raukawa 158
Ngāti Ruanui 80
Ngāti Ruapani 59, 137, 141, 171, 325n
Ngāti Tama 229
Ngāti Te Karaha 169
Ngāti Toa 24, 37, 39
Ngāti Tūwharetoa 277
Ngāti Whare 55, 64, 76, 116, 169, 171
Nia, Ted 271
Nicholas, John 24
Nihoniho, Tuta 188, 226, 246
Niniwa-i-te-rangi 190–4
niu rituals 55, 56, 57, 61
Nukunuku, Iehu *261*

O
oceanic anthropology 262–4
ōhākī (deathbed speech) 139, 160, 238, 251, 253
Ohlson, Rangi tū te Maungaroa Tīpene 106, *282*
Okawhare, Paratene 232
'Old Shebang Club (The)' 95
On the Origin of Species (Charles Darwin) 45–6, 83, 86
Onepoto 30, 138–9
Ong, Walter J. 254, 275
Onslow, Lord 77, 107–8, 175
Ōpōtiki 26, 30, 55, 59, 68–70
Ōpouriao Valley 201
Oputao 52
Ōrakau battle 52, 53, 112–13
oral traditions 12, 65, 77, 103, 136, 254, 273, 277
  colonisation of oral culture 275, 283
  oral becoming written 103, 138, 190–5, 225
  oral versus literary culture 138, 240–3, 266–70
  oral versus literary meanings 273, 275
  transformation of oral meanings through literary processes 266–78
  Tutakangahau 139–42, 159–60
Orbell, Margaret 144–5, 292
Orientalists 46, 101, 156, 285
origins of Māori 80, 83, 87, 101, 102, 204, 207, 209, 228, 240, 286
Origins of Species (Charles Darwin) 45, 83
Ormond, John 64, 67, 68, 73, 74
O-tangiroa 275–6
Our Nation's Story 229
Oxford Institute for Colonial Studies 247

P
Paerau (chief) 63, 64, 74, 75
Pahau-hokio Lagoon *250*
Pai Mārire 31, 51, 54–8, 81, 179, 283
Pākehā–Māori 130, 146, 286
Pākehā settlers 19, 22–5, 39–40, 51–68
palaeontology 45
pan-Māori 61, 117–18, 129, 224
Panekiri Bluffs 135, *136*
pantheism 233, 236
Pāpāwai 188, 193–4
Paraki 118, 119
Parakiri 130, 133, 149
Parapara, Kopu 58
Paremata 40
Parihaka 81–2, 92, 258–9
Parini, Jay 268
Paumata 69
Pax Britannica 177
'Pax Pākehā' 75
Pax Romana 75, 88
peace 18, 35, 50, 64, 65–6, 114, 116, 136, 180
Percy Smith, Stephenson 15, 24–5, 77, 80, 83
  and Best 207–9, 229, 239, 263
  and Polynesian Society 90, 93–5
  and Te Whatahoro 225–6
  and Urewera Commission 163, 172, 174
  Surveryor-General 113–16
  The Lore of the Whare-wananga 193, 214, 226, 227, 239
  Te Kauwae-raro, Things Terrestrial 227–8
  Te Kauwae-runga, Things Celestial 227–8, 230, 232–3
Perham, Margery 247–8
Pewhairangi, Ngoi 271
Philippines 90, 96–9

Phillips (surveyor) 116, 250
philology 46, 95, 101, 242
physics and Māori spirituality 273–4
Pihopa, Te Tuhi 117, 118, 122, 183
Pinohi *see* Tukua-i-te-rangi
Pio, Hamiora 33, 126, 149, 243, 248, 280
Pirihi 216
Pitt-Rivers, George 246, 259
Plume of the Arawas (Frank Acheson) 259
Plunkett, Lord 185
Pōhuhu, Nepia 232
Polkinghorne, Stanley 252
Polynesian anthropology 262–4, 266
Polynesian migrants to New Zealand 87, 95, 204, 227–9
Polynesian Mythology (George Grey) 86
Polynesian Society 10, 24, 90, 93–9, 207, 149, 225, 226
  see also Journal of the Polynesian Society
Pomare, Maui 94, 175, 184, 202, 250, 260
Porirua 13, 24, 37–42, 249
Porter, T. W. 65
Pōtiki 206, 208, 286
poverty 167–8, 174, 176, 181, 199
Poverty Bay 21, 30, 43, 79
power relationships 129–32, 144–6
pōwhiri 178
Preece (Captain) 74–5
Preece (Reverend) 35
Primitive Culture (Edward Tylor) 84, 89
Primitive Economics of the New Zealand Maori, The (Raymond Firth) 263
primitives *see* savages and primitives
print technology 192
prophets 26, 39, 55, 56, 60–8, 177–8, 195–205
psychology of Maori according to Best 285
Puketapu 63
Puketapu, Hurae 173
Pungarehu 80
Putere 64

R
race and race identity 86, 96–8, 271
racism 47, 82, 133
Rakahanga 141
Rakuraku 60, 76, 77, 216
Ranapiri, Tamati 158, 266, 267–8
Ranfurly, Lord 174–85
Rangi, Taki 228
Rangi and Papa 191–2, 209
Rangiaohia 52
Rangihau, John 271
Raukatauri, Patara 55
Raukura, Eria 195
Raungaehe 76
raupatu (confiscation of land) *see* land
Reed, A. H. 229
Reed Book of Māori Mythology 279
Reed Dictionary of Modern Māori 278
Rehu (war god) 152
Rehua 259
Rehutu 152
Reilly, Michael 229–30
Reine, Fr. 36
religion
  and evolutionary theory 45
  comparative 101, 146, 156, 209, 285–6
  God 51–2, 54, 57, 84, 144, 211–12, 230, 233, 235
  monotheistic 46, 83–4, 99, 212, 215, 231, 233, 234
  pantheistic 233, 236
  polytheistic 231, 234
  psychology of 98–9
  revealed 39, 45, 54, 83–5, 144, 204
  syncretic 18, 21, 54, 56, 69, 235, 284–5, 314n
  universalist 272
  see also Christianity; Io; Māori spirituality
Rifleman 60
Rikirangi, Te Kooti *see* Te Kooti Rikirangi
Ringatū 51, 57, 65, 67–8, 70–2, 77–8, 176, 179, 191, 195, 214
Riou, Édouard 45
roads 16, 17, 67, 70, 74–6, 81, 104–24, 125–6, 128, 132
Rohe Pōtae (Tūhoe lands) 74–8, 104–24, 162–86
romanticism 77, 120, 135, 140, 143, 145–6, 249, 285
Rongo (god) 209, 211
Rongokaeke (taiaha) 114, 162, 186
Rongokarae marae 177, *178*, *179*
Rongopai 78
Rongowhakaata 59, 61, 65, 70
Ross, Malcolm 175–83
Rotorua *246*
Rousseau, Jean-Jacques 24, 144
Rua Kenana (Te Mihaia Hou, new messiah) 183, 185, 281, 285, 325n
  and Tutakangahau 108, 161, 180, 187–8, 196–200

at Maungapōhatu 195–205
Best's views of 92, 200–4, 205, 216
Ruatāhuna 26–36, 63, 66, 73, 75, 114, 176
road 67, 105, 116, 118, 133, 170
Te Whai-a-te-motu meeting house 71, *71*, 107, 176, 180
Ruatau 259
Rūātoki (hapū) 52
Rūātoki 105, 106, 107, 118, 162, 174, 178, *179*, *183*, 191
1894 hui with Seddon 109–14, 162, 164, 167, 173, 174, 185, 186
1904 viceregal visit 174–85
Russell (Captain) 68, 171

S
Sahlins, Marshall 264–8
savages and primitives 46–7, 60, 83–9, 92, 96–102, 127–8, 133, 136, 143–6, 147, 150, 214–15, 231–2, 253
'Sea of Rippling Waters' legend 140
Scannell (Judge) 172, 174
schools 17, 72, 75, 76, 122, 176, 186
mission 30, 35–6, 115
Native schools 25, 40, 128, 147, 198, 203, 232, 237
whare wanaga 189, 224, 231, 232, 233, 237
School Journal 229
science 21, 44–5, 83, 93, 97, 99, 103, 114, 241, 273–5
Scott, Dick 82
Scriptures *see* Bible; Christian literacy
Seddon, Richard 11, 109
land agenda 105, 108–32, 171
land developments under successors 199–200
Rūātoki hui 1894 109–14, 162, 164, 167, 173, 174, 185, 186
Wellington meeting with Tūhoe leaders 1898 161, 162–9, 175
settler government
incursions into Tūhoe land *see* land
seven canoe tradition 227, 228, 229
shearing 16, 106–7, 150
Shirres, Michael 230, 277
Short History of New Zealand (Condliffe and Airey) 229
sickness and disease 90, 96, 147–8, 174, 197, 199, 200–1, 203, 214
Simmons, David 229, 230, 238
Sinclair, Keith 44, 48
Sissons, Jeffrey 215
Skinner, H. D. 228, 259, 261
Skinner, W. H. 259
slavery 87, 92
social sciences, emergence 103, 231, 284
Sorrenson, M. P. K. 94
spirit world 15, 22, 26–7, 57, 145, 151–3, 209–15, 229–33, 237–8, 251
see also tohunga
Stocking, George 83
Stone Age 136
Stone Age Economics (Marshall Sahlins) 266–7
Supreme Being *see* Io
surveys *see* land
syncreticism 18, 21, 54, 56, 69, 235, 284–5, 314n

T
Tainui 271
Takapūwāhia Pā 24, 37, 40
Takitimu marae (Kehemane) 191
Tamaikoha, Erueti 173
Tamakaimoana hapū 28–30
Tamakihikurangi (Kawepo), Renata 48, 51, 62
Tamarau, Te Makarini 67, 74, 112, 126, 216
Tamihana, Pihopa 117
Tane (god) 158, 209, 211, 222–3, 286
Tanenuiarangi Committee 190, 193–4, 224, 226, 230–1
Tanenuiarangi meeting house 165, 280, *281*, *282*
tangi (lament for the dead) 137–8, 142, 148, 182
taniwha (monster) 140, 153, 206, 208, 217
Tapeka 218
tapu (sacred) 15, 29, 33, 56, 86, 151, 153, 158–9, 161, 232, 248, 273, 277
breaches 202, 211
Tapui (Tapuihina) 28, 29, 30, 35, 212, 312n
Tara 253, 288
Taranaki 54, 62, 80–2
Tarawera 68, 70, 92
Taumutu, Paraikete 122
Taupō 62, 64
Tauranga 199
Taurua 35
Tawa 37–42, *288*
Tāwhana 63, 64, 69
Taylor, Richard 34, 46, 80, 83–90, 102, 155, 211–12, 222
Te Ahoaho 53

Te Amohanga 137
te ao hurihuri 275
Te Ao Hurihuri – The World Moves On: Aspects of Maoritanga (Michael King) 271
Te Ao Mārama (modern world) 15, 59, 72, 77, 123, 128, 139, 140–1, 177, 191–2
Te Ao o Neherā 15, 212
Te Aoterangi 163
Te Arawa 64, 176
Te Hapū Oneone 28
Te Heuheu, Piripu 53
Te Houhi 148
Te Ika a Maui (New Zealand and its inhabitants) (Richard Taylor) 34, 80, 83–90, 102, 222
Te Kaha, Akuhata 63
Te Karetu 56, 62–3
Te Kauna/Kaunga 33, 35
Te Kauwae-raro, Things Terrestrial (Stephen Percy Smith) 227–8
Te Kauwae-runga, Things Celestial (Stephen Percy Smith) 227–8, 230, 232–3
Te Keepa 64
Te Kokau 129
Te Kooti Rikirangi (Te Turuki) 14, 18, 39, 57–72, 176
 covenant with Tūhoe 63–4
 'Te Kooti's karakia' 65, 68, 69–70, 179, 180, 283
Te Korekore 273
Te Kuiti 67
Te Kura 129
Te Matatiki (dictionary) 242
Te Matorohanga (Moihe Torohanga) 190, 194, 195, 226–39, 251–3
Te Maunga 28
Te Mihaia Hou (new messiah) 195
'Te Mohoao' (man of the woods) 143
Te Patutoro (chief) 64
Te Piria 216
Te Pō 209
Te Pou 173
Te Pū 209
Te Puea, Princess 271
Te Puehu 66
Te Puke ki Hikurangi 180, 187–95, 209
Te Purewa 66–7, 113
Te Rangi Hiroa (Peter Buck) 37, *38*, 94, 218, 228, 238, 244, 246–7, 259–64, 271
Te Rangihaeata 38
Te Rangihiroa 70
Te Rau, Kereopa 55, 57, 60, 66–7
Te Rauparaha 38
Te Rehu-o-Tainui 151–4
Te Reinga 15, 94, 138
Te Tai Tokerau 272
Te Takatanga 35
Te Taura Whiri i Te Reo Māori (Māori Language Commission) 242
Te Toroa 26–7
Te Tini o Toi 28
Te Ture (the law of God) 51–2, 62, 112, 311n
te ture (the law) *see* law
te ture nui o te ao katoa 117, 123
Te Uoro 137
Te Wakaunua/Whakauna, Hetaraka 68, 74, 109, 113–14, 166
Te Waimana 33, 76, 172
Te Wainui 63, 72
Te Whai-a-te-motu meeting house 71, *71*, 107, 176, 180
Te Whāiti 8, 10, 52, 62, 67, 68, 114, 147, 173, 196, 245
Te Whakairinga-o-te-patu-a-Te-Uoro 137
Te Whanga-nui-a-Tara 253
Te Whatahoro Jury, Hoani 190, 194–5, 210, 214, 223–36, *223*, 251–3
Te Whatakorari 191
Te Whatanui 117
Te Whenuanui (chief) 53, 63, 64, 118–19, 183, 196
Te Whiti-o-Rongomai 81
Te Whitu Tekau (The Seventy) 69, 72–3, 76, 78, 79, 174, 179, 198
Te Whiu 163
Te Whiu, Te Maipi 204
technology 15–16, 31–2, 104–5, 107, 123, 168, 192, 285, 289
Temera, Pou 33
theology 25, 51, 55, 210, 229–33, 272–5
 of Supreme Being *see* Io
Thompson, J. Allan 221
tikanga 270, 277
Tikanga Māori: Living by Maori Values (Hirini Moko Mead) 276, 277–8
Tikanga Whakaaro (Cleve Barlow) 276–7, 278
Tillich, Paul 274
timber milling *93*, 106
Tinipia 40
Titahi Bay 40
tohunga 15, 41–2, 56, 152–3, 156, 158–60, 200–1, 213, 225–6, 266
 Best as 'white tohunga' 243, 247, 249, 251–3, 264
 Te Matorohanga 234–8

Tohunga Suppression Act 1907 197
Tohungia 193
Toi 28, 206, 208, 228
Toi-kai-rakau 28
'toiora' 236
Toko 138
Toko Rua 204
Tomoana, Henare 163–4, 181
tools 220–1, 222–4
Toreatai 28, 30, 35, 51, 64, 158, 195, 214
Toroa 206
tourism 120, 121, 135–7, 139, 145, 176, 181
trade 20–3, 30, 40
tradition 28
Transactions and Proceedings of the New Zealand Institute 208–9, 229, 241
Transactions and Proceedings of the Royal Society of New Zealand 157
transcendentalism 89–90, 143–6
Treaty of Waitangi 16–17, 24, 59, 68–9, 104–5, 216–17
tree-felling ritual 222–3
Tregear, Edward 10, 24, 46, 80, 83, 87, 90, 93–4, 101, 218, 245
Tū (god) 56, 209, 211
tū-ora ceremony 33–4
Tūhoe 25, 26–36
  acceptance of Best 161, 248, 284
  autonomy within settlor state 162–86
  'Children/People of the Mist' 138
  Rohe Pōtae 74–8, 104–124, 162–86
  separate law 172
  stories 137–42
  war, religion and land 49–78
    see also land
Tuhoe: The Children of the Mist (Elsdon Best) 32, 88, 105, 127, 138, 169–70, *170*, 188, 195, 205–15, *207*, 244
Tūhoe Potiki 28, 189
Tuhourangi 277
Tukua-i-te-rangi (Pinohi) 10, 115, 116, *117*, 122–4, *129*, 132, 163–5, *165*, 184, *184*, 204, 323n
Tupaea 166
Tupaia 22
Tūranga (Gisborne) 57, 70, 72, 158, 202, 246
Turanganui River 79
Tutakangahau 14–18, *27*, *106*, *111*, *117*, *129*, *179*, *281*
  agent of change 123, 132
  alliances 103, 108, 112, 117–19, 154, 183
  and Colenso 35–6, 61
  and Hauhau movement 53–7, 61
  and Rua Kenana 187–8, 196–200
  and Seddon 110–14, 164–6, 186
  and settlor government 52–78, 115–24, 164–6, 183, 186
  and Te Kooti 14, 18, 35, 44, 51, 57–72
  and war 33–5, 49–50, 52–63
  as co-author with Best 77, 129–30, 153, 283
  as mediator 16, 74, 76–8, 183, 282
  as moderate 76–7, 114–15, 282
  at Rūātoki hui with Seddon 110–14
  Christian literacy 103, 115, 119, 214, 284
  death 216
  earlier life 26–36
  Lake Waikaremoana trip with Best 131–2, 135–42, 206
  leadership roles 69–78, 128–9, 183, 282
  letters 73–4
  literacy 35–6, 72–4, 77, 187–95, 282–3
  openness to Te Ao Mārama (modern world) 15, 77, 115–16, 121–4, 128–9, 140–1, 164, 281–2
  payment for services 128–32, 268
  pension 115, 196–7
  political status 72–8, 128–9, 183
  prodigious knowledge 159, 283
  relationship with Best 17–18, 114, 128–32, 140, 144, 147–8, 159, 160–1, 284
  Ruatāhuna mail run 196–7
  whakapapa 28
  whakapapa compilation 133–5, 188–95
  writings 180, 187–95
Tutakangahau, Huhana 204–5, *205*
Tylor, Edward 24, 84, 89, 96, 97, 100, 102, 133, 147, 285

U
'Ua Rongo Pai' 54, 58
Uhia 152–3
Uhia II 153
'Union of Mataatua' 70
United States trip by Best 90–3
universe 15, 28, 84, 103, 211, 271, 273–5
Urewera Commission 14, 78, 120, 123, 125, 132, 161–74, 177, 185, 197–8

Urewera District Native Reserve Act 1896 118, 121, 160, 162–86, 199
amendments 185, 199
General Committee 163, 167, 185, 199
Urewera Lands Act 1920–21 185
utu (revenge) 15, 26, 35, 57, 61, 62, 281

V
Vestiges of the Natural History of Creation (Robert Chambers) 45–7
Victoria, Queen 24, 51, 57, 60, 107, 120, 216
Victorian culture and thought 13, 45–6, 84, 89
Völkner, Julius 55, 57, 59, 180

W
Waerenga-a-Hika 57–8, 80
Wahawaha, Ropata 58, 63–7, 73, 246
wai taua rite 56
Waiapu River 37
Waikare-whanaunga-kore 138
Waikaremoana 10, 28, 30, 58, 135–42, *136*
Waikaremoana: The Sea of Rippling Waters (Elsdon Best) 132, 135
Waikato 26, 52, 53, 61
Waikato River 157
Walker, Ranginui 265, 271
Waimana 122, 196, 198, 201, 202
Waimana Valley 64
Waimate Plains 80
Waiomatatini 261
Waipaoa River 195
Waipiro Bay 246
Waipotiki 173–4
Wairaka 141
Wairarapa 188, 191, 224, 226, 230, 235, 238
Wairau Moana 135, 139
Wairoa 10, 26, 60, 67
wairua 154, 193, 234, 237–8, 242, 259, 266, 277
Waitangi Tribunal, Wai 8 Manukau claim 156–7
Waitara 50, 51, 59
Waituhi meeting house 78
waka imagery 189, 204, 206
Wall, Susan 40
wānanga 189, 194, 224, 231, 232–3, 237
Wanganui 14, 38, 81, 86, 226
war 33–5, 39, 49–68, 112, 141, 208, 274
warriors 55, 56, 57, 62, 65, 68, 178, 182, 288–9
Wellington ('the Wonder City') 161, 188, 289
'Western Heke' 286–9
Whakahoro, Petera 193
Whakatāne 59
Whakatāne River 275
whakạtea (reproachful song) 53
Whakatōhea 28, 70, 195, 204
whakapapa (genealogy) 126, 133–5, 160, 188–95, 206
whakatara (rites of placation) 211
Whakaunua, Heteraka 109, 113
Whanga, Ihaka 58
Whanganui 228
Whanganui River 246
whare kura 225
whare maire 29
whare mata 29, 157–8
whare puri 29
whare takiura 15, 29, 128, 141
whare wānanga 189, 224, 231, 232, 233, 237
Whately (Bishop) 84, 86
Whatonga 228
White, John 23, 212
'white noise' 10, 13–18
Wi Pere 119–20, 122, 163–4, 168
Wi Repa, T. 259–60, 263
Wi Tapeka, Makurata 169
Wi Tapeka, Paitini 32, *32*, 33, 52–3, 56–7, 126–7, 129, 149, 158, 169, *175*, 176, 266, 320n
Williams, Herbert W. 213, 228, 239–43
Williams, Leonard 69
Williams, William 30, 50, 93, 241
Wilson, John 30
Wilson (surveyor) 118–19
women 53, 63, 64, 192, 270
World's Deluge, The (Louis Figuier) 44–5
World Fair (The World's Industrial and Cotton Centennial Exposition), New Orleans 91
Woven Universe, The (Māori Marsden) 273–4
Wyatt, Tom 95
Wylie, Adelaide *see* Best, Adelaide
Wylie family 126

Y
Young Māori Party 94